BIG BUSINESS IN AMERICA

BIG BUSINESS IN AMERICA

The Corporate Century, 1900–2000

Thomas J. Dorich

LEXINGTON BOOKS
Lanham • Boulder • New York • London

Published by Lexington Books
An imprint of The Rowman & Littlefield Publishing Group, Inc.
4501 Forbes Boulevard, Suite 200, Lanham, Maryland 20706
www.rowman.com

6 Tinworth Street, London SE11 5AL, United Kingdom

British Library Cataloguing in Publication Information Available

Library of Congress Cataloging-in-Publication Data

ISBN: 978-1-4985-9597-1 (cloth)
ISBN: 978-1-4985-9598-8 (electronic)

This book is dedicated to the students, faculty, and staff at my beloved Eastern Illinois University, 1970–1973. They were there when I was young, and when it all began for me, and they will always be my first love.

Contents

Preface

CHICAGO, DALLAS, PHOENIX METRO, Huntington Beach, rural Illinois, Indiana, and Iowa; Gettysburg, Bandolier National Monument, the Oregon coast, Eugene, Twenty Nine Palms. These were the places this liberal arts gypsy lived while attempting to eke out a living with three liberal arts college degrees and lots of white-collar and public-service (albeit low-paying) work experience.

Ironically, the above life course is the root cause of how this project occurred: my education and then my circuitous career path.

Most people who were fortunate enough to have a career in academia might not have been able to write this book. In contrast, I've spent almost all my working life outside of campuses and away from the ivory tower ethos. Instead, holding several jobs in the private sector, I was an eyewitness to what I eventually wrote about in this book.

When I was in my twenties, with my teaching and master's degrees, I had to join the urban, corporate rat race, holding down eight-to-five jobs, and fit into post-consensus America (which then, during the Vietnam era, was being ripped away from its American Century moorings for the first time).

There, in the large corporations I worked in, I learned corporate culture, industrial discipline—to be beholden to the man (in this case, a steady white-collar, clerical job) and to get along to go along. Then I didn't get anywhere in corporate life, becoming a wheel spinner in my first corporate job because I didn't go out to lunch with the right people or stay after five p.m. to work a little more, talk a lot, and go to happy hours. Rather, I kept my work life and private life separate, which wasn't the way it was done by good organization men, company men (which I never was and haven't been since).

Even though I rarely missed a day of work, mastered my job role, and attempted to be a good coworker and wingman—a good employee—it wasn't enough.

There I was, a liberal arts major, wannabe teacher (who couldn't get a job teaching high school social studies and history because I didn't coach sports), exiled in corporate Babylon, a Spartan in the camp of the Persians. My time spent in that work and cultural environment, coupled with my education at Illinois-Chicago Circle and continuing at Eastern Illinois University, enabled me to do what follows here.

I researched and wrote this book from 2000 to 2007. When I researched and wrote the paper in 1997, I was unemployed most of that year. Through the duration of this corporate century project, I was either unemployed or underemployed, including substitute teaching, temp services, motel night auditing, selling food from a coffee truck, working for the U.S. Census Bureau and the National Parks Service, and proofreading a newspaper. While typing the second half of the book, I was unemployed for three years, living off of my savings. Thus, I understand the world of work more thoroughly than the typical academic or journalist—hence my odd perspective.

When I went to college the first time, all I wanted to do was to teach school. I have failed to find a full-time teaching ever since. Instead, I spent the days of my youth working mostly in the private sector as one of those later-generation white-collar clerical workers I mention in this book.

Because of that dichotomy of failed aspirations and necessary employment, I was able to do this project. Perhaps something bad turned out be good after all. That path, indeed circuitous, unknown to me then, eventually resulted in this book.

Acknowledgments

I DO NOT HAVE ANY professional affiliations or a personal network of peers whom I can thank for their help with this project. Instead, I researched and wrote this book on my own time, utilizing my own resources for support. I relied on several libraries for sources: the Chicago Public Library, including its interlibrary loan department for obtaining the few books that weren't in its voluminous, university-quality, business collection; the Central College library, Pella, Iowa, where I probably began the research with one of Roland Marchand's books; the most excellent interlibrary loan service available at the Adams County Library in Gettysburg, Pennsylvania; the Gettysburg College library for almost all the books used to construct part II of the project. My thanks to all of these library staff and to those who built those collections.

Prior to submitting this manuscript, its editing, typing, and proofreading were mine alone. I typed part II of the book on the public-access computers in the Eugene Public Library, Oregon. (I don't have a home computer.) To those who work there, my thanks for the service, the beautiful building/library, and being in such a neat little big city/big little city. I did the final editing while mostly unemployed in Oregon and then the final typing on the public terminals at Copper Mountain Community College, Joshua Tree, California.

And a huge measure of gratitude and thank you to Eric Kuntzman and Alexandra Rallo of Lexington Books for giving me the opportunity to be published for the first time.

Part I

1

Corporate Century

Overview and Paradigm

A GRAND SYNTHESIS ATTEMPTS TO explain the direction of a series of events under a single theme or force. Part causation and part ethos, such a factor, or "vital force," causes, enables, and directs change over time.

Individual human behavior and collective social behavior are influenced by specific and common psychological and social forces. As individuals, we are our past. That is, each person is the sum total of their upbringing, education, neighborhood, and work environment. In the same sense, a social group or even a nation, is the sum of its social and cultural factors.

When examining a nation's history a single factor or force may emerge as an ever-present influence, or symbolically, as a guiding hand. (Granted, no single force is the sole determinant of change because human behavior is too complex to be explained by single causation.) However, among the various psychological, economic, social, and cultural factors interacting over time, a fundamental force can be the catalyst for change. Frederick Jackson Turner called this a vital force.[1]

Near the end of the nineteenth century, Turner unveiled his frontier thesis. His hypothesis created controversy among historians and fueled further inquiry into the nature of the American Character. Since then, historians looked for other vital forces that may have been the prime movers of American life.

During the Progressive Era, Charles Beard offered an economic interpretation of history. He assumed that economic factors were at the root of historical change and the basis for grand political events. Later, Arthur Schlesinger Jr. interpreted American history as a series of reform cycles, eras that swing between liberalism and conservativism. In the 1950s, David Potter offered an alternative interpretation to the Progressive School. Consensus History is in part based on a common notion of abundance in American society. In *People of Plenty*, Mr. Potter said:

> this state of relative abundance, of material plenty, has been a basic condition of American life and that it has had a persuasive, if undefined, influence upon the American people. . . . For certainly it is an influence that impinges upon all American social conditions and contributes in the most fundamental way to the shaping of the American culture and the American character.[2]

More specific to the twentieth century, an intriguing school of thought developed from the work of Robert Wiebe and Alfred Chandler Jr.[3] Wiebe suggested that America changed at the beginning of the century from a rural, small-scale, agriculture-based society to one that was large in scale, urban-industrial, and institutional. Building on this, Alfred Chandler Jr. suggested that the organization and management of big business was a significant factor in causing and directing this economic and social change.

In the same school, Louis Galambos contributed the idea that organization was a significant factor in modern American history. He postulated that:

> The primary process of change involved organization building, both public and private, and the creation of new and elaborate networks of formal hierarchical structures of authority that gradually came to dominate our economy, polity, and culture.[4]

This is called the organizational synthesis.

However, none of these fine efforts stand alone to offer a sweeping generalization that may, like the frontier line, energize debate, or drive American historiography further. Surely, there must be a vital force, a social institution that was the prime mover of American civilization during the twentieth century.

Big business in the United States evolved and grew to increasing levels of power and influence throughout the twentieth century. The ascendant corporation directly and indirectly influenced public culture and private lives. This relationship includes the structure and function of the firm; the evolution and development of big business in the economy; the rise of its elites to positions of power and influence, and the manifestation of power the corporate sector exerts in the modern American economy, on government, and in American communities. Thus, the big business corporation may be the vital force in the twentieth century similar to the nineteenth-century frontier line.

The prime factor that affected the evolution of American society during the twentieth century was the ascendance in power and influence of the American big business corporation. The rise of big business, the evolution of its structural form and organizational ideology, created a vital force. This institutional force became the dominant socioeconomic and cultural engine that drove the course of American civilization during the twentieth century.

Corporatism rises ascendant out of the Organizational Synthesis of Wiebe, Galambos, Chandler, and Zunz. Their synthesis was designed to explain change involving modernization and the national response to it. According to their theory, the Progressive Era was marked by dramatic and significant technological, economic, organizational, and social change. This trend persisted and set the tone for the rest of the century.

Standing alone, the Organizational Synthesis presents a significant interpretation of how modern America began and how the transition was made from the old order of the nineteenth century to the new order of the twentieth. If coupled to big business, the Organizational Synthesis comes closest to offering a synthesis for the history of the entire century. Combine elements of the two paradigms, and the result is a grand synthesis. Furthermore, from my perspective, their organizational revolution was really a corporate revolution.

The Ascendant Corporation

The modern America began to form during the Gilded Age. Vernon Parrington declared what "fashioned the America we know today with its standardized life, its machine culture, and its mass psychology—an America to which Jefferson and Jackson and Lincoln, would be strangers." occurred before the turn of the twentieth century.[5] It was also the time when the modern corporate form began to take shape.[6] During the decades after the Civil War American business began to fundamentally change from small, entrepreneurial, locally oriented firms, to large, compartmentalized, nationally oriented businesses.

The availability and application of new technology enabled this change. Mechanized production and electrification, telephone communication, and expanded railroad networks provided a new infrastructure which in turn, opened up national markets. As a result, businesses expanded through vertical and horizontal integration to meet these new market conditions.

Alfred Chandler correctly argued in *The Visible Hand* that the structural, functional, and market changes made by big business caused corporations to become powerful economic institutions. According to Chandler, this corporate rise occurred, in some sectors of the economy, before World War I. By the 1950s, big business was paramount of all American economic institutions. This change was visible and obvious. Also, as the corporation evolved as a business institution it simultaneously influenced the larger culture. As a result, the American big business corporation became the dominant social institution in twentieth-century America as well.

This structural change began with the departmentalization of company administration, production, and distribution. Such an innovative division of labor gave rise to both a new managerial class and to new white-collar occupations. Over time, a managerial hierarchy evolved. Eventually, this administrative structure acquired an institutional prominence and social institutional power. Simultaneously, white-collar workers assumed their own permanent position of importance within the organization.

The personnel that implemented these changes became a new middle class of middle management, line management, and office support staff. While they executed various administrative tasks (later, we called it paper shuffling), they created a new work culture that included a work ethic of coordination, order, genteelness, good manners, discipline, loyalty, and ultimately conformity.

Also, this class and corporate culture eventually dominated American life outside the office. Just as corporate size dominated the national market, corporate culture began to alter the very nature of American society. Eventually, business values fostered social values. This emphasized a standardization of life similar to the standardization of production, distribution, and marketing. Thus, what began as an attempt to rationally control the market and administer large organizations, evolved to become an institutional social force that transformed American society. It was this transformation that eventually created the other-directed man of David Riesman, the organization man of William H. Whyte Jr., the white-collar culture of C. Wright Mills, and the people of plenty of David Potter.

The contributing factors that pushed American corporations to the forefront of American society coalesced during the 1920s. The routinization of production, distribution, and administrative support was institutionalized. Mass marketing increased the availability of standard brands resulting in the creation of a new culture of consumption.

The American marketplace and corporation evolved simultaneously, each feeding and nurturing each other. Both grew to a position of economic and social dominance prior to 1932. However, even before the Great Depression, corporations entered the lives of ordinary people through marketing. This trend began with print advertising. Mail order and mass distribution pushed the concept into America's hinter and heartland. Mass communications delivered brand names and the corporate message into almost everyone's living rooms. Once the brand name was a household word, so were the companies.

This process began in earnest during the 1920s when distribution of products became the focus of corporate attention.[7] Consequently, chain stores, salesmanship, and advertising assumed positions of importance in corporate strategy.

Chain stores became common and the principal deliverer of products in the national marketplace. Salesmen became the agents of corporations and their products in the hinterland. Customer service became an important adjunct to selling the product.

More significantly, creating demand made advertising the chief and eventually, the most advanced method of selling products and the American corporate way of doing things to the American public. Visual advertising dates back to the mid-1880s. National ad campaigns were first used at the turn of the century. At the same time, posters, signboards, billboards, and electrical images became parts of urban and rural landscapes.

By the Progressive era, product managers believed print advertising to be a significant influence on the public. Between the wars advertising expanded in volume and changed in style and tone. New modern products were introduced with the suggestion that consumption spending enhanced lifestyle. The objective was to create desire for products and instill brand-name loyalty. Indirectly, the desire for goods, created by ad agencies, simultaneously, manufactured the affiliation or identification with the company that sold the products.

Radio advertising, which also began during the 1920s, brought consumer goods and their makers directly into people's homes. As radio became more popular, programs and their advertising and the companies they represented became part of everyday life.

Together, advertising and mass-distribution strategies introduced the idea of consumerism to American society by the end of the 1920s. The resulting increased demand for goods fueled prosperity and delivered big business into the hearts and minds of American households. Corporations were product providers, employers, and displayers of wealth and power. These perceptions coalesced to iconize American big business just in time for the great crash of 1929.

Big Business weathered the storms of the Great Depression because of several interrelated factors. First, and foremost, large corporations had the financial resources to survive.[8] Second, the corporation had already developed institutionally to a point where it was able to adjust itself to traumatic change.[9] Third, the New Deal programs designed to stabilize prices and control production offered some protection. Fourth, a consumption ethic was already inculcated into the masses. This meant that as providers of goods and services, corporations did not share culpability for the crisis with the financial sector of the economy. Finally, advertising had effectively promoted brand loyalty, and latently, a sense of affiliation to the company that produced desired products. Consequently, consumer culture was too established to be destroyed, and popular enthusiasm for a consumption society persisted.

Radio sustained the popularity of this consumption-spending culture despite the economic conditions. As Stephen P. Fox argued in *The Mirror Makers:*

> In this apparent paradox, perhaps, lay radio's ultimate appeal. Real life in the 1930s was hard enough to bear. When people clicked their radios on, they were seeking not reality but escape. Radio brought relief, with a message from our sponsor.[10]

Big Business survived the economic downturn with their reputation sorely tarnished but intact. When the sleeping giant awoke on December 7, 1941, its secret weapon turned out to be industrial might. Indeed, technological innovation, organizational methods, and increased production capacity pioneered by big business now turned into a war machine. As Emily Rosenberg pointed out in *Spreading the American Dream:*

> Large businesses commanded the financial and the engineering skills to undertake technologically difficult projects; similarly, they possessed the facilities quickly to produce and deliver massive war orders. Government also came to rely on American-based international companies to procure the overseas raw materials needed for war.[11]

War mobilization ended the Great Depression, and war production launched government-contracting, big business corporations to the forefront of wartime society. It was the beginning of a new, positive, economic surge that would last for twenty years.

After the triumph of victory in 1945, America became a "people of plenty," and corporations provided their bounty. Big business produced goods and services and employed people; at the same time it exerted cultural control over its workers and customers. As Olivier Zunz suggested in *Making America Corporate:*

> By the middle of the twentieth century, the corporate reorganization of American society was a fait accomplii . . . corporations had become part of the daily life of ordinary Americans, and Americans had grown used to them.[12]

The resulting age of consensus was a product of a culture of conformity promoted by Big Business through traditional industrial discipline in the workplace and by marketing a common consumption ethic to America's households. Just like in the 1920s, American corporations became icons of American life; their images pervaded society.

During these decades, the corporation also forged an organizational relationship with its workers. Specifically, the big corporation absorbed the identities of its employees, as William H. Whyte Jr. suggested in *The Organization Man:*

> They are the ones of our middle class who have left home, spiritually as well as physically, to take the vows of organization life, and it is they who are the mind and soul of our great self-perpetuating institutions.[13]

Whyte further argued that both administrative staff and managers were the dominant shapers of American society. It was their values that set the tone for the rest of the century.

At the root of these businessmen's values and social dynamism was their all-encompassing devotion to work and the affiliation they expressed to their company. This intensity, conformity, and personal relationship to the organization was according to Whyte a major change in American ideology.

This change involved more than company affiliation. To be part of the group now meant to surrender one's individuality and creativity for the greater good of the organization. Team play and conformity to institutional norms was so important in corporate culture that it became inculcated into the company man's personality.

These values then spread to other American social institutions. American social character—the common belief structure of a society—was in part a function of this relationship.[14] That is, the corporation shaped its employees on the job and they took those values home with them. In both places, the new corporate/organizational ethos was accepted as culturally valuable.

That the corporation was tied to society's socioeconomic structure made it all the more easy for big business to become an accepted entity and ideological institution. As Eric Fromm argued, the economic environment is a strong determinant of social roles and character formation, both individually and collectively.[15]

Thus, by the end of the 1950s, the American socioeconomic system was defined by the individual's relationship to the size, complexity, and power of the corporation as an employee and customer. This was the essence of the corporate organizational revolution.

At the community level this relationship surfaced in suburbia, the "packaged villages" that became the dormitories of the organization man. As evolving social institutions, subdivisions reflected corporate values of routinization, interchangeability, order, and conformity. Here, it was easy to introduce corporate work values to the family. Thus, the corporate message to spend and acquire came from the media, while a corporate work ethic that included sociability, order, community/group importance, and conformity was delivered routinely by the head of the household.

In response to this dual corporate barrage, suburbia became the ultimate company town, or as Stuart Ewen argued in *All Consuming Images:* "the embodiment of what corporate modernism had been calling for."[16] In other words, was not the suburban way really the corporate way?

Advertising once again played a crucial role in forming this relationship. Specifically, the usage and expansion of television cemented society's affiliation with big business. It took less than fifteen years for television to become a dominant force in American society, according to Eric Barnouw in *Tube of Plenty*:

> The glistening mosaic, replacing the hearth has become the focal point of the home. In living color more real than life, the swirling dots represent the world; they tell us the good, great, beautiful, and desirable—and their opposites. They have become the environment and context of our lives.[17]

This devotion to television seriously enmeshed Americans in the marketplace. As television became more and more important in the daily routine of American households, advertising again entered their homes. Through the constant bombardment of commercials, advertisers indirectly delivered the corporation as another equitable product. Just as advertisers intended to get their client's products into the minds of consumers, identification with the corporation was a secondary effect.

Thus, television advertising finalized the manipulation of consumer demand in America. By the end of the 1960s, mass-media promotion of goods and services became a common part of household routine. Television commercial jingles and phrases were repeated enough to the public that it was an everyday occurrence to hear people singing the jingles and imitating the catchphrases, and portions of the commercials' plots. In *Global Dreams*, Barnet and Cavanagh point out that

> At the beginning of the 1980s the average consumer in the United States was exposed to something like 1,600 advertising messages from the instant the clock radio went on in the morning until the television set was turned off at bedtime.[18]

As a result, the corporate sponsors and providers subtly slipped into the households and minds of American television viewers. By the dawn of the Vietnam era, what was construed as typically American was apple pie, Blue Ribbon beer, and Chevrolet, and of course, all brought to you by corporate America.

The Corporation as Plenipotentiary Institution

Big Business as a Political Institution

During the two decades after World War II, the American corporate sector also immersed itself into American foreign and domestic policy. Big business established and maintained informal and formal relationships with the federal government throughout the twentieth century. This arrangement, which evolved into the military-industrial complex, can be traced back to its formative stage at the turn of the century when the federal government began to build an all-steel navy.

At first, this was simply procurement and manufacturing transactions. Later, during World War I, business and government forged formal organizational ties in order to successfully mobilize.[19] This arrangement continued throughout the interwar years and intensified when the "arsenal of democracy" went into full production during World War II.

After hostilities ended, Cold War tensions sustained defense production. As a result, contractual arrangements between the federal government and big business continued through the Vietnam era and beyond.[20] Instead of just doing business together, these two institutional behemoths collaborated in setting policy in both domestic economic matters and in foreign affairs. At the same time, the military-industrial complex that President Eisenhower warned us about, with all its alleged power and influence, coalesced out of this wartime relationship.

Coincidental to the meld of big business to a monolithically powerful federal government and its mighty military establishment, American corporations were also exercising their rights of citizenship in the American body politic. They did this through lobbying and influence peddling, which is probably as old as the republic, for after all, colonial agents were our first lobbyists. Political lobbying has long been a part of the American political process at all levels of government. The private sector has influenced lawmaking, policy formulation, political candidacy, and election campaigns throughout the twentieth century. It has been a common practice for businessmen to run town governments, and control boards and commissions.

Lobbying in Washington dates back to before the Civil War, and it increased with the rise of nineteenth-century industrialism. By the turn of the century, significant formal and informal business relationships existed between government officials and corporate representatives. From this partnership, large-organization lobbying became a well-established trend during the twentieth century, and corporations became the trendsetters. Since then, and despite reform efforts, the method and profession of lobbying has evolved and grown in power and influence, because the federal government has been receptive to corporate interests, and unwilling to consistently legislate contrary to what is generally good for big business.

This means that promoting candidates running for office, their platforms, and the writing of law and regulations, are all influenced by the corporation. Some contemporary critics fear that the power of money and influence promotion by big business transcends the power of government: The authors of *Toxic Sludge* comment:

> The business class dominated government through its ability to fund political campaigns, purchase high priced lobbyists, and reward former officials with lucrative jobs.[21]

Thus, this corporate institutionalization of lobbying is now an established estate in our political process. For instance, in 1990 there were 3,000 trade associations in D.C. and 80,000 lobbyists living there.[22] It is as Jeffrey Birnbaum asserts in *The Lobbyists:*

> Washington has become a club in which the line between those inside and those outside the government is not clearly drawn. Corporate lobbyists have so suffused the culture of the city that at times they seem to be part of the government itself.[23]

Perhaps the most important lobbying relationship occurs between private interests and the electoral process. Big business interest in electoral politics has reached new heights because of campaign finance. Supporting a candidate is a most effective method of influencing the legislative process, policy making, and regulation enforcement. Today, campaign finance has been added to an already effective influence peddling arsenal of lobbyists, public relations people, and lawyers. It is as Barnet and Cavanagh argue in *Global Dreams*: "Both political parties in the United States are so dependent on corporate money that neither is willing to take the issue of corporate power head on."[24] The net result has caused government to become beholden to big business to an extent that government is evolving to a point where corporate interests are of first importance. Corporate citizenship is now first-class citizenship. In *Who Will Tell the People*, William Greider asserts that we have evolved to a client democracy where our votes as citizens have less meaning. Instead lawyers now negotiate deals with legislators and influence policy for the benefit of big business and large associations.

In addition, Washington lobbying has set precedents and generated an entire subculture of influence peddling among other groups and associations. Now, it seems, that in order to draw attention to a cause, other groups must also lobby. Thus, today, college teacher unions, religious activists, and political-issues organizations use lobbyists in the same way as big business. Colleges send lobbyists to promote funding. At the local level, teachers' unions lobby about issues ranging from uniform curriculum to credentials standards. Religious groups try to meld politics and religion. Other groups promote single issues like abortion and gun control. Thus, big business' power of example and influence pervades our political economy.

Big Business as a Global Institution

As American big business expanded domestically, it began to advance globally. Before the turn of the century, American-made durable goods such as sewing machines, typewriters, harvesters, and electrical appliances were sold abroad. Prior to World War I, the largest American corporations in the various industrial sectors were involved in foreign markets. Singer Sewing Machines Company was a pioneer in establishing branch plants overseas. Other corporate trailblazers included: ITT, Monsanto, A&P, Safeway, Woolworths and Montgomery Ward.

By the 1920s, American big businesses successfully introduced products, capital, technology, and management methods to parts of Latin America, Europe, and to a lesser extent in Asia.[25] Prior to World War II, American companies increased their overseas market share, and established business arrangements with other companies, host governments, and financial institutions.

After Pearl Harbor, America's industrial might won the war and American big business reached a level of power and influence never before attained. Bolstered by its successful efforts to provision the American military, corporate America was now poised to dominate world markets and spread its influence globally.

However, postwar reconstruction and the global division into competing spheres of influence hindered the resumption of world trade. As a result, American multinationals resumed foreign-trade relations slowly and with difficulty. While the United States fostered the rebuilding of Europe, foreign trade became linked to our containment policy. Consequently, American multinational expansion finally accelerated significantly after 1955 and once the postwar political order was determined in Europe.

During the 1960s, multinational corporations began to assert a new form of market power. Big business expanded into foreign markets, selling products and services, and relocating manufacturing and distribution facilities, in earnest. Consequently, individual corporations now had physical ties to foreign soil. By providing jobs and selling goods, the American corporate ethos came into direct contact with foreign law, custom, and culture.

At the same time, American commercial culture continued to be an important export. By selling American consumer products, and disseminating technology, and administrative practices, big business gained market share, accumulated social and economic power abroad, and sold American society and culture in one huge integrated package.

Especially since 1975, the global integration of advertising and distribution created regions of consumers buying a similar lifestyle even though they are separated by great distances and still differentiated by local laws, customs, and language. Regardless of these differences, multinationals have successfully forged a consumption ethic that is subtly, globally common. Thus, today, people all over the world drink Coke, eat at McDonalds, wear Levi's and hum American tunes. In short, as Barnet and Cavanagh exclaimed: "Marlboro Country is everywhere."[26]

This globalization of corporate America has political ramifications as well. The weight of big businesses' economic power begat political influence. Over the long run, multinational corporate power and influence began to affect their host countries' formulation and execution of diplomatic, domestic, and trade policies. Consequently, corporate power enabled American multinationals to become more and more independent of foreign laws and customs. As a result, it appeared as if American multinationals were beginning to acquire a sense of nation-state sovereignty.

As the twentieth century ended, American big business continued to assert itself globally. American corporate power and influence pervade the world and have been absorbed by all but the most intense anti-Western, religiously dominated societies. During the 1990s, a previously impenetrable economic wilderness has been entered in eastern Europe.

Thus it is likely that American corporate multi-nationalism will continue to achieve greater levels of economic power and influence in other lands. Call it a corporate manifest destiny.

Just as the frontier line moved across the American continent during the nineteenth century, the American corporate frontier will probably expand and conquer the global market wilderness sometime during the twenty-first century.

Corporate Baroque

Much of this rise to globalism occurred unfettered in the 1980s. During the Reagan-Bush era, American big business enjoyed a position of popularity similar to previous ascendant eras of the 1920s and 1950s. Since the 1980s, American corporatism transcended their positions of influence, dominance, and sovereignty, and rose upward to "High Corporate Baroque."[27]

As the twentieth century ended, corporations became our society's dominant institution, and it is, as essayist Thomas Frank lamented in a 1996 issue of *The Nation*. He said that today there is a common "conviction that we have arrived at some sort of corporate utopia, that business has somehow supplanted civil society."[28] Push Mr. Frank's concept forward in time and add Neil Postman's technology paradigm and by the end of the next century we will have a world that is a mixture of *Max Headroom*, *Blade Runner*, *Brave New World*, and *Player Piano*.[29]

In conclusion then, over the past one hundred years, as big business grew in economic power and prestige, it became a social institution and a vital force to integrate social, economic, and cultural aspects of American society. Throughout the twentieth century, the corporation was the prime mover and subtle social force that influenced the evolution of public culture, and in the process, the image of society. Thus, the social reconstruction or modernization of America during the twentieth century is a derivative of the evolution of corporate power and influence. Just as the frontier altered the individual in the nineteenth century, shaping the American character, in the process, so too has the corporation affected the makeup of individual Americans and their collective character.

Chapter 1 started out as conference paper. It is a narrative presenting an overall summary of the book. Chapter 2 analyzes the emergence of the concept of corporation and its effect on society generally and on individuals as workers. Chapter 3 investigates the relationships between big business and the individual as consumer. Chapter 4, set approximately in the 1950s, melds the previous two. It coalesces the evolving corporate culture with mass consumption, thus, the corporate-organized, people of plenty; living their consensus-based lives; enjoying a sense of prosperity, not previously available.

The synthesis of the two concepts creates the 1950s archetype: the organization man, in the lonely crowd; his life within the corporate culture, the man in the grey flannel suit; his life in his neighborhood that is the view from the crabgrass frontier, behind the crack in the picture window. This chapter attempts to tie together the social factors that the corporation vectored from 1890–1960.

The second part of the book portrays the corporation as a sovereign, plenipotentiary institution that is, as something operating on the higher levels of economies, political economies, and nation-state sovereignties. (Included in that section's introduction part II, is my organizational paradigm that attempts to extend Wiebe's model into the twentieth century.)

There's one chapter for each topic: business/government relations; lobbying, interest groups, and campaign finance; globalization. Chapter 5 is a very lengthy survey of business-government relations, from approximately 1888 to 1990. Here the emphasis is on origins, with more content regarding development than current events. Chapter 6 is an examination of lobbying, interest groups, and campaign finance, from their origins to about 1990. The last chapter is on the American multinational corporation, and includes a brief commentary on globalization. Since this is a history book and not contemporary, each of these chapters fades out during the decades 1980–2000. The hypothesis I present is a synthesis of different interpretations of twentieth-century modernity. I have acted on those models and tried to meld them together on a continuum.

Notes

1. Frederick Jackson Turner, "The Significance of the Frontier in American History," in *The Frontier in American History* (Tucson: The University of Arizona Press, 1986) 2.
2. David Potter, *People of Plenty: Economic Abundance and the American Character* (Chicago: University of Chicago Press, 1954), 67, 84.
3. See Robert Wiebe, *The Search for Order* and *The Segmented Society*; Alfred Chandler Jr., *The Visible Hand, Scale and Scope,* and *Strategy and Structure.*
4. Louis Galambos, "Technology, Political Economy, and Professionalization: The Central Themes of the Organizational Synthesis" *Business History Review* 57 (Winter 1983): 471.
5. Vernon L. Parrington, *Main Currents in American Thought* Vol. III, *The Beginnings of Critical Realism in America, 1860–1920* (New York: Harcourt, Brace and Company, 1930), 26.
6. Alan Trachtenberg, *The Incorporation of America: Culture and Society in the Gilded Age* (New York: Hill & Wang, 1982)4, 82.
7. William E. Leuchtenburg, *The Perils of Prosperity, 1914–1922* (Chicago: The University of Chicago Press, 1958), 198.
8. Louis Galambos, *America at Middle Age: A New History of The United States in the Twentieth Century* (New York: McGraw-Hill Book Company, 1983), 36–37.
9. Kim McQuaid, *Big Business and Presidential Power, from FDR to Reagan* (New York: William Morrow and Company, Inc., 1982), 20.
10. Stephen P. Fox, *The Mirror Makers: History of American Advertising and Its Creators* (New York: Vintage Books, 1985), 150–151.
11. Emily S. Rosenberg, *Spreading the American Dream: American Economic and Cultural Expansion, 1890–1945* (New York: Hill & Wang, 1982), 188.
12. Zunz, *Making America Corporate 1870–1920* (Chicago: University of Chicago Press, 1990), 1.
13. William H. Whyte, Jr., *The Organization Man* (Garden City, New York: Doubleday Anchor Books, 1957), 3,
14. Eric Fromm, *The Sane Society* (New York: Henry Holt and Company, 1955), 78.
15. Fromm, *Sane Society*, 78–81, 142.

16. Stuart Ewen, *All Consuming Images: The Politics of Style in Contemporary Culture* (New York: Basic Books, Inc., Publishers, 1988), 225.

17. Eric Barnouw, *Tube of Plenty: The Evolution of American TV* (New York: Oxford University Press), v.

18. Richard J. Barnet and John Cavanagh, *Global Dreams: Imperial Corporations and the New World Order* (New York: Simon & Schuster, 1994), 172.

19. Cooling, Benjamin F. *Gray Steel and Blue Water Navy: The Formative Years of America's Military-Industrial Complex, 1881–1917* (Hambden, CT: Archon Books, 1979), 218. Pursell, Carroll W. *The Military-Industrial Complex* (New York: Harper & Row, 1972), 3-6.

20. McQuaid, *Big Business*, 149–151, 165–167, 176.

21. John Stauber and Sheldon Rampton, *Toxic Sludge is Good for You: Lies, Damn Lies and the Public Relations Industry* (Monroe, Maine: Common Courage Press, 1995), 78.

22. Birnbaum, Jeffrey H. *The Lobbyists: How Influence Peddlers Get Their Way in Washington* (New York: Random House, 1992), 7.

23. Ibid., 3.

24. Barnet and Cavanagh, *Global Dreams*, 344.

25. Wilkins, Mira. *The Emergence of Multinationals Enterprise: American Business Abroad from the Colonial Era to 1914* (Cambridge: Harvard University Press, 1970), 66, 98, 107–108, 202–203, 214.

26. Barnet and Cavanagh, *Global Dreams*, 164.

27. Thomas Frank, "High Corporate Baroque," *The Nation* (December 30, 1996), 9.

28. Ibid., 9.

29. See Neil Postman's *Amusing Ourselves to Death: Public Discourse in the Age of Show Business*. New York: Penguin Books, 1985.

2

The Monolith Emerges

The Rise of Big Business

IN 1901, THE UNITED STATES IS no longer an economic or social backwater. Instead, it is is an emerging economic, diplomatic, and imperial power. The root of its ascendance is its economic diversity. Every region seems to have an agricultural specialty, and corporations are ubiquitous in its cities. In fact, the United States is now the world's leading industrial power, the grandest of material-producing civilizations. It manufactures about one-third of global output, and its production capacity is greater than Great Britain, France, and Germany combined. About one-fourth of Americans work in manufacturing, and another one-fourth are office workers.

American industry produced a variety of goods. In contrast, the leading industries in 1860 were cotton cloth, lumber, boots/shoes, and milling. Forty years later, machinery, lumber, printing, publishing, and soon, steel, were leading industries.

Americans were becoming a nation of factory workers and clericals and soon spenders on a relative cornucopia of material things that were made by someone else, often far away. This change from subsistence and localism was fostered by the rise of big business. As a result, we became a nation of, by, and for large corporations. In September 1910, *McClure's Magazine* observed:

> Fifty years ago we were a nation of independent farmers and small merchants. To-day we are a nation of corporation employees; directly or indirectly, the corporation controls our living. And, as the corporations grow greater and greater, fewer and fewer men control them, and our individual lives with them.[1]

The paradigm shift began in the last two decades of the nineteenth century and was institutionalized by the start of World War II.

It all started with the industrial revolution in nineteenth-century America, before the age of big business. Eventually, technology became a prime mover that drove the course of industrialization forward and toward its ultimate triumph, large enterprise.

Then, technology varied. There was a transportation revolution that occurred in several waves. Roads and almost-roads penetrated the Trans-Appalachian West. Rafts and keelboats initially connected the interior of the expanding nation to the Mississippi River and then to New Orleans. In time, steamboats expanded our nascent domestic market from Tidewater to the Great Lakes and the Mississippi River Valley. Later, railroads and telegraph eventually linked regions and consolidated the national economy and infrastructure as the twentieth century began. These factors all coalesced to foster the rise of big business, which in turn, exploited then controlled the development of these very factors that enabled their advance.

Our railroad system began piecemeal as links between waterways. Eventually, railroads expanded in size and distance, and directly connected regions. In 1840, there was about 3,000 miles of track; by 1860, 30,000. The next fifty years saw 254,000 miles of track constructed, much of it during the 1880s.

This new transportation system shrunk time and distance, and offered new opportunity. People moved widely, towns sprang up or changed their purpose. Travel times from the east coast to the Midwest decreased, from weeks to days. Consequently, shipping expense decreased resulting in lower prices for manufactured goods. Communications advanced with the railroads via telegraph, invented in 1837, connecting Baltimore and Washington, D.C. By 1846, much of the east coast was linked. A telegraph line went out, even to California, by 1861. Since lines were often strung up along railroad rights-of-way, telegraphy expanded in parallel with railroads. In fact, railroad companies were the first to use the telegraph in their communications systems. Other businesses followed their example. Thus, like shipping, communications channels also expanded, connecting all regions.

Power transmission was also a contributing factor to the rise of big business. Steam power freed manufactories from riverbank locations. More and more factories went up in cities where they rendezvoused with railroads, raw materials sources, and a burgeoning immigrant labor supply.

Along with the infrastructure, the business form also evolved, modernizing.

The nineteenth-century firm was typically staffed by owners/partners, and their support staff. Their clerks made copies, kept the books, delivered messages, and ran errands. They were not specialists; they did a bit of everything. The workday was informal; everyone pitched in to complete tasks. Nearby, the shop floor, where things were made by craftsmen and their helpers, was similar.

The earliest manufacturing firms were storefront establishments or mechanic's shops where shoes, clothing, leather goods, livery supplies, and mostly wooden products were made and then sold locally. Civil War era factories were usually staffed by a manager or owner, some foremen, and their employees. They all worked together typically at a single location. They produced specific products such as farm equipment, cooking utensils, weapons, clocks, sewing machines, etc. These firms employed locally and at best sold regionally. Their size was small and so was their scope and reach into the market. That system was relatively simple. The producer marketed his product through middlemen merchants to consumers.

After 1850, the manufacturing system started to change. Larger factories replaced the small shop and putting-out system. Expansion was rapid. By the turn of the century, the new factory was typically huge. A manufacturing plant was now a series of buildings of all sizes, many of them large enough to accommodate steel-processing equipment or locomotive assembly. Each building had a purpose and, ideally, the production process from raw materials acquisition to product completion now had to be preplanned at the start, and then coordinated throughout the site until the tasks were finished.

The dramatic expansion of the American industrial sector caused change within company structures. An army of talented, lucky, and determined individuals joined forces seemingly at once to create the new form of corporation. Some of them were famous, like the du Ponts, Rockefeller, and Morgan. Most of them were comparatively anonymous, inventive engineers and innovative technicians. They grasped what was emerging around them, wrestled with it, and eventually tamed and shaped the forces of technological change, time and distance compaction, and structural complexity. They became architects and constructed a new monolith.

Businesses were growing as the nineteenth century closed. Companies became expensive to create and maintain. Machine-driven production made great quantities of a diverse collection of standardized goods. They were then advertised and sold nationwide. Thus, in about fifty years, the structure, method, and range of business changed completely. Compared to the old proprietorship system, the new corporate monolith was revolutionary.

The newly emerging corporation was different. Large amounts of capital were necessary to fund the construction of the physical plant and the procurement of equipment and raw materials and to acquire labor. Bigness necessitated public financing, so ownership was removed from the control by the few. Large manufacturing firms thus were not owned and operated by an individual or small syndicate. Now, ownership became nebulous. Controlling and administering the firm was organized and systemized through a structure of functional divisions, with specific lines of authority and responsibility, using formal methods of communication.

This upgrading in the structure and function of a company was necessary to manage the increase in size, shape, and now scope. Expanding businesses were not limited to local markets and regional distribution factors alone. The railroads and telegraph provided an improved and relatively unparallel transportation and communications infrastructure that allowed for national expansion.

Psychologically, the railroads and telegraph condensed travel time, and linked larger areas effectively. As a result, an ethos emerged where the possibility of creating a business to compete in a national market became realistic. In addition, a company could combine with others and control dispersed operations to produce a variety of products that could be sold just about everywhere. Cheaper shipping costs made marketing products more economical even over longer distances. For example, between 1870 and 1890, eastern producers could effectively sell and distribute goods to the Midwest. As a result, a region's economic insularity and local monopoly began to fade away. In turn, this new potential of an expanding domestic market fostered more corporate development and growth.

At the same time, the industrial economy expanded in response to the infrastructure advance. Demand for goods increased. National markets were enticing, and contemporary industrial leaders turned to mass production and mass distribution in response. Prior to 1900, producers of oil, sugar, alcohol, matches, soap, and grain milling made this move. By 1904, large corporations produced 75 percent of American industrial production.

Much of this emerged out of the Gilded Age, a forerunner of the era of corporate capitalism. Then, the empire builders began to construct large enterprises that had to be financed, organized, and managed on a large scale. Bigness and complexity became the new standards for corporation-building, which extended into the twentieth century. The rise of the big businesses that they created actually meant the emergence of the large corporation.

Their concept of corporation was also a product of change in the American political and legal systems. In a series of Supreme Court cases from 1886 to 1897, corporations gained the status of citizenship regarding the Fifth and Fourteenth Amendments.[2] From there, federal and state legislatures and their courts gave corporations due process and contractual rights similar to people. Also, from 1886–1898, New Jersey, Delaware, and New York passed general incorporation laws; other states soon followed. In 1889, New Jersey permitted manufacturing companies to buy stock of companies located elsewhere. At the same time, enforcement of restraint of trade varied prior to the Sherman Act of 1890. Despite its enactment, corporate mergers raged during the 1890s and into the new century. Then, about 1,800 companies merged. Oligopoly soon followed, a product of vertical and horizontal integration.

Controlling resources was one idea that led to vertical integration. It was necessary to maintain a reliable and constant supply of material to feed the new mass-production flow-process, factories. The solution was to integrate backward, combining with suppliers and raw materials producers. Electrical suppliers could absorb copper producers. Steel companies could acquire iron mines. Oil refineries could combine with oil well firms. Of the latter, Standard Oil is one such example.

In 1860, John D. Rockefeller made a living in Cleveland as a merchant. Associates of Rockefeller commissioned him to scout any moneymaking ventures in nearby Pennsylvania oil fields during their first boom. After investigating the price and supply anarchy of the fledgling oil industry, Rockefeller urged his compatriots to stay out of that business. In 1863, Rockefeller again investigated it. This time he narrowed his focus to petroleum refining because then, a small investment garnered a comparatively large return. He was approached for backing by Samuel Andrews, who knew chemistry. They formed a partnership, and Rockefeller agreed to keep the books and purchase oil.

In 1865, Rockefeller bought out one of the other partners who also had an interest in the Andrews venture. Next, Henry Flagler joined in, and the new arrangement became Rockefeller and Andrews. Now, after the Civil War, Rockefeller immersed himself into this very competitive industry. At the time there were about thirty refineries operating in Cleveland and some right in the oil fields.

Rockefeller started a second refinery and soon dominated production in Cleveland. He accomplished this by cutting a deal with their local railroaders for cheap shipping rates, a rebate as we know it today. This meant a publicized fee was paid up front, and later a portion of it was returned by the railroad. This arrangement fostered the refining company's rapid expansion by reducing its variable costs.

In January 1870 Rockefeller, Flagler, and Andrews incorporated as a joint stock company, calling themselves Standard Oil of Ohio. Now they were the largest of all oil refineries, employing over 1,000. By 1872, Standard Oil controlled 80 percent of oil refining, and by 1879 they controlled most of the industry's pipelines. Soon thereafter, they looked to vertically integrate retail distribution to production. Rockefeller's goal was to create one system that controlled the purchase of crude oil, its refining into product (mostly kerosene then), and its sale at the retail level. At all stages of the process Rockefeller wanted to eliminate both competitors and middlemen. He accomplished vertical integration early in the 1890s when he purchased crude oil, more pipelines, and eventually retail outlets. In the process of building his oil empire, Rockefeller's company became the model for creating a large-scale corporate combination.

They too combined, horizontally, vertically, and both ways simultaneously. Firms that horizontally integrated often followed a common pattern. During that era, many producers entered the market and succeeded at first. Competitive price-cutting inevitably followed when the market sector flooded. To control prices, competitors often formed cartels or made pricing arrangements through trade associations. These attempts were usually effective in the short term. Some companies did not participate; others eventually stopped cooperating. For example, Rockefeller's refinery briefly participated in a local cartel in 1872. It was an ephemeral relationship, and he switched his tactics to absorbing his competitors.

Horizontal integration eventually replaced informal collusion. A number of large firms began to combine, often absorbing their smaller competitors. Through this process, industrialists learned that larger, heavily capitalized, mass-producing plants made stuff relatively cheaper than small firms did. As a result, the wholesale price index dropped from 174 in 1866 to 82 in 1890.

This system worked similarly for distribution. Manufacturers found it more economical to sell directly to the public or to retailers instead of through middlemen wholesalers. After 1880, it was no longer standard procedure to distribute through the wholesale-merchant system. Instead, manufacturers took on directly the selling responsibility. This meant advertising, putting up warehouses, arranging shipping, and creating a sales force. They quickly learned that controlling distribution also improved market position.

Integrating vertically, horizontally, and in various combinations became a remedy to survive the market anarchy of the new industrial era. Thus, a merger movement became the trend, flourishing from about 1895 to 1905 (depending who you read). As many as three hundred companies per year combined. As a result concentration of industry and oligopoly increded. By 1910, many of what later became Fortune 500 companies had been created: Standard Oil, Texaco, Uniroyal, Goodyear, US Steel, Bethlehem Steel, Jones & Laughlin, Anaconda Copper, Phelps Dodge, General Electric, Westinghouse, Nabisco, United Fruit, Swift, Armour, Kellogg's, International Harvester, Kodak, and the like.

In that era, successful conglomerations usually maintained a position of strength in capital management, technological expertise, advertising influence, brand-name affiliation; administering prices, and market position. In the short run, they supplanted their smaller competitors. In the long run, large enterprise made the modern American economy.

Then, the empire builders and captains of industry were at the forefront of public attention. They were derided for their ruthlessness and excesses, while simultaneously admired for their fortitude and luck. Many of them became icons, and they often perceived themselves as good for the country. Once they accrued economic power they became politically and socially influential. They were church and community leaders, politically active, and subtle influencers of economic, social, and political policy. From these positions of strength they too, as a class, fostered their own interests, policies, and philosophies.

In their rise to the top of the new industrial order, the captains of corporation began to affect the whole culture. These new economic elites dominated the economy and eventually institutionalized order and efficiency in business and in the process extrapolated these business practices into society. It was done through the structure and organization of the big business corporation and the ethos it created.

The origins, of this, the American urban-industrial order, go back prior to the Gilded Age, when the first corporate empires were spawned as railroads. Once up and running, railroad operations incurred high fixed and variable costs. In order to remain profitable, it was necessary to operate efficiently. This meant creating a system to coordinate and administrate activity that was stretched out over long distances. They tried new methods of management and administration. These attempts to systemize resulted in the creation of the first large private-sector bureaucracies that were eventually run by a new class of managers.

Thus, railroads were the first prototype big-business corporations. They were the first firms to create methods to communicate within and supervise large operations. At first, railroad companies were usually managed by members of their boards of directors. Often these finance-oriented capitalists were merchants, not necessarily administrators. Their interests were not entirely dedicated to railroading, so new personnel were brought in to manage daily operations. Expansion, more tracks, necessitates specialists. Management became functionalized by skill and task: road construction and maintenance, rolling stock, run-scheduling, station operations, and yard operations. Moving freight, railcars, and passengers safely and efficiently required quicker, accurate, decision making over time and distance.

Many of these managers were formally schooled and worked as mechanical engineers. The railroad companies they worked for, such as the Baltimore & Ohio, the Erie and New York, and the Pennsylvania Railroad, became the first large, complex businesses in the nineteenth century. (Their size exceeded that of textile-manufacturing firms, which had been comparatively large enterprises.) These first professional managers, the industrial engineers, conceptualized the corporate concept, created its bureaucratic structure, and introduced professional business administration.

To address these new logistical problems, the first trunk lines became pioneer corporation builders. In 1849, at the B&O, chief engineer Benjamin

Latrobe developed a bureaucratic structure that included a division of labor into finance and operations. In the latter, expenditures and costs were monitored by a controller's office. They worked with the treasurer's office, which was in charge of incoming capital. The vice president of finance supervised the whole division. This entire division was separate from operations, a first.

The operations division was divided into regions and each had its own manager who supervised different tasks: roadbed construction and repair and machinery maintenance. These functional managers reported to their functional supervisors at the home office.

The B&O codified their new system in procedural manuals. They explained who was responsible for which tasks. Explicit lines of authority and communications were written down. After some refining, the organizational plan they molded became the first formally structured model of what became the modern business corporation.

Throughout the system, railroad management emphasized the importance of control and coordination by adhering to consistent and defined lines of authority. Specific people were in charge of certain tasks, and successful implementation depended on everyone obeying and conforming to the methods and procedures the system and organization dictated. In the private sector, such a system was the new thing.

The structures railroaders created became administrative bureaucracies, the first of their kind in the private sector. These nineteenth-century railroad engineers built an organization the way they constructed bridges and other pieces of a train line. Based on analysis and science their results allowed for flexibility of control at the top of the corporation and local decision making at the track level, far away from the home office.

Within those bureaucracies the new managerial systems developed and evolved and ultimately changed with circumstances. Over the long haul, their system provided three guiding principles for future business management.[3] They separated strategic policy making from operations. That is, strategy came from on high at the home office, authored by top management. Tactics were executed in the field by regional personnel, the middle managers.

They also developed an organizing framework, organically, a bureaucratic structure that was staffed by middle managers. They ultimately became the life force of the organization. Their talent and task-making was responsible for the success of daily operations and the ultimate persistence of the company in a competitive marketplace.

Lastly, they created a system of financial accounting that was used to monitor operations systematically, using standardized formulas to compare regional performance. Part of those standards later became depreciation. Then, in the 1870s, they started comparing the costs of repair and replacement to their receivables. Thus, along with capital accounting, they formulated a system of cost accounting.

Accountants specified costs as either fixed or variable. The former included roadbed and tracks while the latter included labor, for example. With a system formulated and applied uniformly, transportation prices were administered by analysis and managerial decision instead of just what the market proffered. The short-run ramifications of this new system enhanced competitiveness. The long-run result became revolutionary. Railroads were the first domestic businesses where proactive management decision making replaced ad hoc reactions to situations after they occurred. Or, from another perspective, management became more important to success than circumstances or purely market-based determinants. Successful management of responsibility and information would turn out to be critical developmental factors to the sustained growth and institutional expansion of large businesses.

The railroads addressed the problems of coordination, control, and costs by creating new corporate structural designs and strategies. Coordinating daily operations of the line and delegating work responsibilities over great distances within a planned strategy involving capital financing and competition necessitated the evolution of new management techniques. These first attempts eventually became contemporary systematic management, later adapted by other industries. At that point in time, this pioneering new managerial paradigm became an organizational revolution. As Blackford asserted:

> The managerial revolution that began in the railroad industry after 1841 changed forever the way business was conducted in America and began, the process known as the rise of big business.[4]

As manufacturing firms grew in size, they adopted the railroader's pioneering business administration practices. Enlarging industrial businesses had to separate ownership and management, allowing professional managers to do the supervising. In theory, managers administered along clearly defined lines of authority and through explicit communications channels. This meant a company's structure had to be subdivided by some combination of geography and function or product line. Within that structure, the field managers ran daily operations. From the top of the pyramid, at the central office, the organization was piloted. They were responsible for strategy and planning.

A good example of this is the DuPont Corporation, which went into business in 1802 producing gunpowder. The company was located near Wilmington, Delaware, on the Brandywine River.

Pierre du Pont took the company reins and eventually diversified product. He brought in Hamilton Barksdale, a civil engineer, from the B&O railroad and recently employed in their family-owned affiliate Rampauno Chemical Company. He recruited managers and introduced elements of scientific management via monthly meetings where papers were presented addressing logistical problems, central office disorganization, lack of strategy, and work duplication.

Management attacked these problems scientifically, drawing up scenarios and contingencies designed to identify difficulties and derive solutions. It was an academic approach. Statistics were used to evaluate manufacturing procedures. Production efficiencies and costs were recorded, tabulated, and used to make reports. Plant performance was thus computed, as was adherence to production standards based on specific goals.

DuPont's structural organization began in 1903. Plants were consolidated to minimize duplication. They tried a new management hierarchy. A vice president and director supervised functional departments. The former was responsible for strategy, and the latter managed operations. A committee system of vice presidents, with the company president, created general policy and monitored operations. Top management was assisted and advised by specialists in quality control, physical plant maintenance, purchasing, planning, and process/chemical engineering. Together, central office personnel consolidated statistics from the field, and formulated strategy. Eventually, they put up a building, separate from the factories, in downtown Wilmington to house these white-collar workers. Out in the field, operational plans were executed down through a hierarchy (originally adapted from the B&O plan), of plant managers, line supervisors, and foremen.

DuPont's corporate structure remained centralized until 1919. The company was still functionally divided into four departments: production, sales, development, and finance. When the company diversified, so too did its structure. At first, DuPont's growth resulted from wartime production. Then, their workforce grew to 85,000. Diversification occurred at the same time, and by the end of the war, they were producing chemicals, dyes, paint, and the man-made fibers rayon and nylon.

Overall, product diversification became a common corporate strategy to enhance competitiveness. For most large companies, this resulted in structural change, chiefly in decentralization. Within the old system, firms like DuPont that produced one basic product were able to manage and administrate centrally. Once a company expanded their product line and market or their holdings, centralization was inadequate.

Strategy and operations grew to be too large and complicated for committee management, The 1920 postwar recession emphasized this point. A lack of planning caused many firms to be unprepared. At DuPont, despite their strategic effort and initial success, their management structure did not bear the load of company expansion, diversification, and then recession. Corporate executives failed to devise general policies that satisfied the logistical demands of a diversified company. At the same time, they further complicated the problem by not effectively coordinating organizational communication. Simultaneously, those managing at the manufacturing level were eventually overwhelmed by the workload from having to market a suddenly diverse product line. Selling explosives was different from marketing consumer goods.

The slow economy after World War I compounded their structural problems. When losses occurred in 1921, DuPont changed its tactics. In September, they revamped their corporate structure, decentralizing by creating a divisional framework. This redesign included corporate-level executives working with specialized staff experts to plan strategy, make policy, and coordinate operations. The divisions took this information and ran the company out in the field. Product lines defined the divisions, and each one was responsible for their own manufacturing and distribution success. Thus, just like the railroads separated tasks at the central office and field levels, so too, did industrial enterprise. Home office managers and staff planned and coordinated. Divisional general managers executed daily operations.

Thus, between 1919 and 1921, DuPont contributed a precise theoretical model of what became the modern multidivisional corporation. Generally, to sustain themselves, large firms began to further separate planning and operations. Corporate headquarters took care of the larger planning tasks. Operations management was split away into the field, delineated into divisions based either on geography or product line.

Corporate decentralization became a trend after World War I, led by duPont, Standard Oil, Sears, and General Motors. B. F. Goodrich, Union Carbide, and Westinghouse decentralized their operations by the Great Depression. Product diversification was the common strategy that caused structural change. Over the next decades the trend evolved at first slowly then accelerated after World War II.

A managerial revolution paralleled the corporate structural revolution. Under the new models, company ownership internally disconnected from management. Over time, company founders like Carnegie, Rockefeller, and du Pont either exited or retired. In their place rose up a new class of specialists who managed the enterprise but did not own it. They carried the corporate revolution forward, effecting change to the foundation of the corporate structural pyramid, the shop floor.

The new corporate management put an end to the old ways of doing things while on the job. The shop-floor traditions ended and a new kind of worker assumed control of the production process, the daily scheme of things, and the totality of the work environment, its social reality.

Until the era of big business, the production process was controlled at the shop-floor level by the foremen. They knew how things worked, who could work, who would work, and how to work. Generally, the foreman was the technical knowledge bank of the factory. Anecdotally, he had the practical experience about how the machinery and production processes worked. His knowledge, kept to himself, memorized from experience, was not usually written down and available to others without similar experience. Thus, the foreman was generally in control of production management, personnel, costs, piece rates and quality control. He usually executed these tasks within his own daily routine, and generally without the aid of shop manuals or company rules of procedure.

He controlled people like he did machinery. Line supervisors and foreman held the power to recruit, train, divvy up the work, and terminate employment. In a way they held sway over the work environment like a padrone controlled the neighborhood and the bully the street corner. Nepotism and cronyism were normal.

As an enforcer, the foreman used the driving method to wield discipline and instigate production. Work habits were often instilled by compulsion, threats, and verbal abuse. Shop rules were the foreman's.

In today's terms, the foreman multitasked and his methods became inadequate to successfully manage large enterprise. The era of the small shop was ending, and the foreman's grip on his fiefdom was slipping away. The burly, surly, man who knew every sound and nuance of the shop was now positioned to lose his control "of the house" to an expert armed with a pencil, paper, and rule book.

The new corporate manager became first the architect and then the pilot of the new system. It was a combined effort with men from all kinds of technical and mathematical backgrounds contributing. Engineers at first dominated this new class of administrators; as a contemporary observed:

> The work of the industrial engineer not only covers technical counsel and superintendence of the technical elements of large enterprise, but extends also over the management of men and the definition and direction of policies in fields that the financial or commercial man has always considered his own.[5]

Eventually, just like the diversified structure they created, they too apportioned their labor accordingly. Thus, industrial engineering spawned functional prodigies: accountants, department managers, statisticians, administrative and financial specialists, to name a few.

One of the pioneers in systematizing shop-floor management was Frederick W. Taylor. He was one of the first efficiency experts, an original time-and-motion-studies man. His supporters viewed him as a visionary while detractors feared him as a destroyer of the workingman.

Taylor was well-born on March 20, 1856. He grew up in Germantown, Pennsylvania, near Philadelphia. His father was a lawyer and landowner; his mother hailed from well-off New England whalers. As a child, Taylor attended prep school, and he spent time in Europe from 1868 to 1871. Most of his youth was greased by wealth and family connections. He was a world away from the shop floor he eventually mastered.

His class status pointed him toward Harvard in 1874. Instead, he went to work as an apprentice at the Enterprise Hydraulic company, a Philadelphia pump manufacturer. There, at eighteen, he left the parlor-world of his class and went to work in factories that were skylight-lit, dirty, and polluted.

He mixed with piece-rate employees who worked six days per week; long hours for little pay. They could afford little. Most things were not available or were too expensive to buy. Things could not yet be cheaply made. Mass production, distribution, and the consumer society it created, was still a few decades away. The world of work, for most, was still essentially antebellum in structure, shape, and form.

At Enterprise, in a work culture still controlled by skilled tradesmen, Taylor apprenticed as a pattern maker for casting iron molds. Soon after starting, he was also trained as a machinist, that is, an operator of machine tools that cut and formed metal: lathes, planers, drill presses, and milling machines, among others.

Taylor learned these trades, and in 1878 he moved to Midvale Steel Company where he worked as a laborer, clerk, and then machinist. About one year later he became a gang boss. As a supervisor, he tried to increase productivity by getting his crew to work above the informal daily quotas they set tacitly among themselves. (Factory workers often did this to keep the owner from manipulating the piece rates.) Taylor fought this protocol, hiring and firing, for two years, attempting to increase shop-floor productivity. He was successful to a degree, to an extant that he became foreman in 1880.

That fall, he began experimenting to improve the manufacturing process. It was experimentation in machine use, not people. At the same time, Taylor enrolled at the Stevens Institute of Technology in Hoboken, New Jersey. He eventually received a mechanical engineering degree in 1883. During those years he received more responsibility at Midvale. While tending to operational and administrative tasks, he gradually formulated his principles of scientific management.

He started his experiments by keeping track of how long his crew took to complete routine tasks. (Basically, he wanted to measure how long a task would take if done efficiently, working normally, without stalling or speeding up.) He saved these records when he was gang boss and reexamined them later. Soon after he started time studies in 1883. He analyzed the physical components of tasks and timed them too. Then he determined composite times and used them as a production standard, or quota. From these observations he initiated an instruction card system for each machine that included written setup specifications. These specs became the permanent guide to execute the daily routine and the core of systematization: written instructions and standardized shop routine.

Taylor's original intent was to dismantle the work procedure, analyze it, and put it back together so it would work more efficiently. His experiments revealed flaws in the whole production process: machines, procedures, and people. For example, he discovered work stoppage, because of no material flow, machine breakdowns, and men not doing there assigned tasks.

He eventually did the same experimentation with people. As Daniel Rogers wrote:

> Taylor plunged deeper and deeper into an attack on the stubborn randomness and variety with which workers habitually went about their jobs and deeper and deeper into measures to standardize work.[6]

He created a differential piece-rate wage system that rewarded those who produced above a mathematically derived standard. Theoretically, these calculated estimates of productivity ended the prevailing, arbitrary production standards. Now these standards were imposed from the planning department, physically and eventually psychologically removed from the shop floor.

Even the foreman's role was analyzed. When Taylor looked at the amount of work the foreman did, he broke down those responsibilities into five areas: mechanical procedures, timekeeping, inspecting, and shop disciplining. Taylor believed that these tasks could be permanently moved off the shop floor, away from the machines, and put on someone's desk to execute. That is, "the control of work must be taken from the men who do it and placed in the hands of a new breed of planners and thinkers."[7] Written instructions and procedures freed the workplace of the foreman's ad hoc methods and arbitrary dictates. Creating system wound up eliminating the foreman's monopoly on how the workday was supervised. The management of the shop floor now began its slow migration from the foreman's knowledge base to the manager's. At Midvale, Taylor's system was in place in 1884, managed by a new "piece rate department." Perhaps here is where the revolutionary seed was planted. From the office, the system now flowed, resulting in a shop-floor revolution. This transition in the control of work marked the emergence of scientific management. Taylor was one of its progenitors.

Taylor was not alone in advocating a formalized system. At a convention of the American Society of Mechanical Engineers on May 16, 1886, Henry Towne delivered a paper called "The Engineer as Economist." In it, he suggested expanding the role of engineers to several matters that were usually the domain of ownership. Towne also suggested that shop-floor management should be formalized. Another presenter, Henry Metcalfe, suggested a system for monitoring production tasks and materials use. Cards and routing slips were suggested. (Taylor was in the audience.)

It is significant that here for the first time, nontechnical business administration problems were formally addressed by professionals who eventually became the first corporate managers. Here, for the first time in the industrial sector, professionals considered the importance of organization, the application of system, and routinized accountability. Here too, were brothers in arms for Frederick W. Taylor. From this time on, Taylor began to participate in the association's forum and used it as his first vehicle to disseminate his beliefs. From that podium, Taylor branched out and de facto became an efficiency and management consultant.

That itinerancy lasted from 1893 to 1898. During those years Taylor tested his ideas in a variety of situations, proselytized his cause, defended it, and honed his skills in management systems, adding contemporary accounting to his repertoire in 1893.

By then that expertise included: time study, piece rates, mechanical engineering, manufacturing processes, and standardization methodology. His consulting sojourn ended at Bethlehem Steel company where he worked from 1898–1901. Shortly thereafter he formally retired.

He left behind a legacy of sorts. He integrated his own work with that of his contemporaries. Overall, Taylor was successful in his system design. Management and operations were broken down into specifics. Thus, he applied structural divisions of labor to the daily operations, to task completion. He added to the production process, administrative control through standardized procedures, record keeping, and cost accounting. What corporate reorganizers were doing to the company structure, Taylor applied the same principles to the workings within.

In retirement, Taylor preached his philosophy from Philadelphia. Carl Barth, Henry Gantt, and the Gilbreths propagated his system with their own refinements. In its entirety, Taylor's management package was too large to be completely integrated by most firms. However, scientific management and its derivatives, often implemented in pieces, evolved to foster a new, corporate managerial system. Taylor's predecessors were its vanguard and the efficiency movement of the Progressive Era its first national showcase.

Underlying this process of system were Taylor's seminal beliefs. He attempted to develop a science of shop-floor management. Next, he wanted to scientifically select workers and then teach them their parts in the process. Overall, system was a synthesis of related ideas already in American culture. Taylor's melding resulted in a new, controversial, yet compelling package.

In hindsight, scientific management became a method in the Wiebian search for order. Efficiency and accountability provided a new methodology to solve the problems of industrialization: its complicated work environment, its multicultural workforce, its large complex corporate structure, and the labor problems the new order was causing.

These engineering and management professionals may have caught the public fancy and institutions' attention because they were the first to directly confront the disorder the new era was causing. They did their work in the center of the maelstrom. As the new era marched on, the emerging management class of experts in both the private and public sectors, moved right along with the changing times, attempting to succeed and survive. They were armed with the tenets of scientific management.

Scientific management and its derivatives formed an institutional cottage industry within the emerging management profession. Although Taylor's system was originally designed to address shop-floor production issues, his system evolved while businesses were changing, enlarging, and restructuring. At the same time, and perhaps serendipitously, scientific management became a modern, readily available, convenient, and everyday method to marshal the forces necessary to successfully function within these new large organizations. Scientific management was a message and state of mind that was proselytized by word of mouth, in trade journals, and at engineering conventions.

The application of science to create a system became the sought-after method to solve the logistical problems the new industrial age caused. At the same time, indirectly, the efficiency movement fostered a change in mindset from informal, anecdotal, ad hoc problem solving, to fact-based and formalized administrative management. For example, at General Motors, Alfred Sloan preferred to use science and system instead of intuition and hunch. In the early 1920s, GM started to use forecasting to attempt to control overproduction. Sales figures were combined with cyclic trends, economic growth, seasonal adjustment, and consumer-demand statistics. Their operational goal was to better match production to actual demand. Strategically, they then attempted to create car models for specific family-income brackets. Their system was based on four-month forecasting. That is, production schedules were created four months prior to implementing. Materials supply had to conform, and the production run had to go on a schedule.

By the mid-1920s, executives at Standard Oil realized that systematic statistical analysis was necessary to coordinate the petroleum batch runs at refineries according to crude oil supply. The source of supply and amount of oil in the pipelines had to be monitored so that planning, processing, and distribution could be smoothly accomplished. A forecasting scheme was developed based on short- and long-run demand expectations relative to available supply on hand. Refinery production pace was thus, predetermined based in part on these comparisons.

Statistical data was also used to determine costs: comparative crude oil value at different refineries and profit comparisons per refinery, and overall profit and loss per barrel, were some of the measures their accountants used. They believed that the use of statistics by the coordinating department enhanced efficiency and strategic operational planning.

Budgeting was implemented that same year, 1925. Using a standardized form, all departments had to submit an annual budget that considered estimated income versus fixed and variable costs. One year later, a budget committee and department were formed. Their responsibilities included monitoring departmental expenditures regularly, and comparing figures to the original budget estimates.

System was used even at Ford Motor Company although they did not like calling it that. For example, an assembler put together rods and pistons at the Highland Park, Michigan, plant. When timed, the foreman discovered that moving around for materials took up half the workday. In total, twenty-eight men assembled 175 piston assemblies during a nine-hour shift. A new system took the six tasks involved and distributed them among three workers, two tasks per. No one moved around. As a result, six workers and one inspector put together 2,600 rod-and-piston assemblies in an eight-hour shift.

At the Western Electric Hawthorne works in Cicero, Illinois, the most contemporary, comprehensive series of systematic measurements of production occurred from 1927 to 1932. Academics were brought in to do time studies and survey employees. It was part of a continuing effort to analyze working conditions, worker attitudes and morale, and behavior in large organizations. In the long run, the Hawthorne experiments as they were then called, were pioneering efforts that led to the creation of the human relations movement in personnel management.

Thus, in many instances Taylor-fostered derivatives were implemented by businesses. Their organizational values spread from the private sector to society in general. Efficiency became both a trend and a foundational creed for the development of industrial society. Accompanying efficiency and system were a group of derived values: discipline, deference to managerial authority, and organization. Besides these examples of the immediate value of systematization, there were subtle sociological ramifications for general social reality. Judith Merckle suggested:

> Taylorism offered a way to make the factory worker, via the work process itself into a neat, industrious, individualistic, thrifty, and sober Anglo-Saxon ideal.[8]

Fostering this mindset and implementing its specifics, the new managerial white-collar middle-class ascended.

This social ideal and management strategy may have started as a way to control the meld of men and mechanical technology on the shop floor. Indeed, their immediate goal was to make the factory worker behave: be punctual, stay on the job, work efficiently, and stay sober.

From there, the resulting culture became entrenched through larger, institutional practices like the Americanization movement, corporate benevolence programs, and an emerging body of knowledge that added industrial relations to professional management science. With Taylorism as the wellspring, the process of system was in widespread use in large industry by the end of the 1920s.

The ideas of this movement, that is of efficiency, method, and industrial discipline created a new workplace ethos from which our modern corporate culture evolved. This culture came to be based on top-down authorities' control, manifested in order, deference, conformity to system and discipline, and the groupthink way of decision making. These practices flowed together from Taylorism and combined to form a new corporatism.

A new work environment resulted, often occurring near the shop floor, but ultimately a world away. Large enterprise was controlled in the factory office, removed from the manufacturing area. Here, information combined with specialists' expertise. The direct results were the creation of management science and the field of accounting, and the creation of what would become corporate culture.

Systematizing the workplace caused the use of large numbers of clerical workers. They eventually became a new, white-collar middle class. Increasing paperwork created new jobs, and an army of clerical workers complemented the blue-collar workforce. Personnel on the shop floor became operatives of a larger, machine-driven production process, and so too their clerical counterparts.

The office, also systematized, usually by function: file clerks, billing clerks, shipping clerks; stenographers and typists replaced copyists. Like their blue-collar coworkers, the office staff too worked specific tasks that were part of a larger flow, conceptualized for them by management.

Thus, the office changed from the simple world of Bartleby to a modern environment filled with mechanical wonders introduced to these companies by other corporations: electric lighting, typewriters, Dictaphones, filing appliances, duplicating machines, telegraph, and then telephones.

The confluence of corporate growth, systemized business practices, and labor-saving office equipment created a brand-new organizational world where large numbers of people gathered in a workplace that was totally different from the manufacturing ethos.

Like shop workers, the office staff was regimented and subject to structured work discipline. Required work shifts, appropriate clothing, working without casual breaks, adhering to written procedures, behaving properly, and staying motivated while doing the same basic tasks everyday, were some of the procedural items management addressed. Efficiency, punctuality, orderly workflow, were sought-after results. In some firms, Tayloresque studies and task analysis were tried. Trade journals such as *System* and *World's Work* covered these problems.

Workplace control included arranging desks to minimize distractions, gossiping, casual visiting, flirting, clannishness, and cliquishness. Supervisors were placed at the back of the room so employees could not see when they were being watched. Overall, job anxiety, a competitive urge for self-improvement, and aspirations for work mobility subtly, stifled idleness at the desk. Ideally, a good office worker became compliant to company demands, and conformed personal attitudes to the organization's rules and mores. In this manner, a white-collar world of work emerged by 1930, another new reality spawned by corporate giants.

The white-collar middle class managed and administrated the large firm, which precipitated a corporate revolution. They, also created an organizational revolution, one that would eventually affect all of society. They, the urban-industrial middle class, started out as professionals such as doctors and lawyers and specialists such as engineers. Their corporate ascendance began when engineers assumed management roles. They in turn recruited office workers: accountants, other managers, staff specialists, and legions of office-support workers, the clericals.

TABLE 2.1
Percent of Total Workforce by Occupational Type.

Occupation	*1910*	*1920*	*1930*	*1940*
Clerk	10.2	13.8	16.3	17.2
Skilled	11.7	13.5	12.9	11.7
Semiskilled	16.1	16.4	21.0	14.7
Unskilled	14.7	14.6	12.9	10.7

Source: Dewey Anderson and Percy E. Davidson, *Recent Occupational Trends in American Labor*, p. 133.

TABLE 2.2
Total Clerical Occupations by Decade.

1870	311,889
1880	531,083
1890	830,311
1900	1,135,204
1910	1,631,926
1920	2,950,769
1930	3,829,217

Source: H. Dewey Anderson and Percy E. Davidson, *Occupational Trends in the United States*, p. 584.

Management began their organizational ascent orchestrating system and rationality on the shop floor, and within the new administrative bureaucracies. In time, they steered and helped power enterprise with their expertise and skills. They became the cement that held the corporate structure together because white-collar workers occupied most of its levels. Those working at the top of the pyramid supplied the information necessary to formulate strategy and create policy. Those within the bureaucracy at the line management level interpreted and executed those directives. Once rolling, their support staff, a corporate army of clerical workers, kept the whole thing going. Their work, in turn, kept the assembly lines humming since by now paperwork moved just about everything. The meld of business machines, manufacturing technology, better-educated people, and system, created a process of information flow and control. Ultimately, they managed the firm from behind a desk, rather than on the shop floor.

At the same time the management class became progenitors of corporatism as their roles evolved from engineers to managers of the structure and system they helped to create. Within the corporation they managed administration and hence production, and there, a new corporate culture was created. In Wiebeian terms, this new ethos became the bridge from the old nineteenth-century paradigm to the new.

In contemporary terms, management set the standards for a new urban-industrial social order. Their delivery mechanism became the workaday world of the office and shop floor they managed. It was there that they subtlety transferred their values by controlling the social and psychological environment in the course of supervising daily operations. The work site fostered friendships and even romance. Companies sponsored activities and propagandized familial camaraderie. Consequently, the work culture became a sophisticated social-interaction arena where shaping of habit and behavior took place. As a result, a person's life-course could be influenced. Management accomplished this because their knowledge, expertise, and authority made them arbiters of both corporate culture and social reality. As they steered the new bureaucratic orientation they created, they attached that reality to it.

From 1870 to 1930, the industrial, urban, corporate, and organizational revolutions ran almost in tandem. Ultimately the corporate steed pulled ahead. It was triumphant because its institutional goals were attained due to the performance of the white-collar middle class. They industrialized the economy and simultaneously incorporated society. By shaping the economy and reengineering the marketplace, middle-class managers pushed the concept of corporation to the forefront. They structured and administered the monolith. At the same, time they socialized it into their own cultural image. In turn, the social institution they created reshaped them.

It all happened initially within the confines of the workplace where corporate employment took on a human face, up close, it was personal. Middle managers, through their formal and informal daily contact with their employees, set the tone. Here, during the workday, social values mixed, and all of them were potentially the subject of individual and group acculturation. The office and the shop floor became social-engineering mixing bowls. Especially in large corporations, mid-level managers asserted their organizational authority and simultaneously promoted their class values as part of the daily work obligation.

White-collar work offered comparatively steady income, relatively clean working conditions, and the belief that self-betterment was possible. These opportunities were available with office work especially in large corporations. There, men and women mixed; there they became subject to subtle social engineering. Social values accrued from business values through the power of aspiring for personal improvement, job security, and organizational conformity. All were expected. To get along, one must go along. In the process, the work environment both enveloped the individual and shaped attitudes even beyond what was expected merely on the job.

As an employee, an individual was expected to submit to organizational authority, routinized activities, and procedural guidelines, and cooperate with others. The industrial, organizational rules that management enforced at work, spun off as a series of object lessons, prescriptions for how to do things, adages, examples, and propaganda that, taken together, became a packaged plan of social discipline. Just like going to school all over again, the public place of work, away from home, became an effective and ubiquitous learning and socialization mechanism. Derivatives of these corporate organizational expectations left the work site, morphing into generalized social expectations that were carried back to the neighborhoods and homes where the package was again internalized and proselytized some more.

Olivier Zunz asserted: "Twentieth-century Americans derived a distinct middle-class culture from their increasing participation in the corporate and governmental bureaucratic institutions of modern mass society."[9] If so, then the organizational ideology of the large private-sector corporation was the prime engine. From the Zunz perspective, the corporate iconology, through consumption spending (next chapter), and the large corporate bureaucracy through on-the-job socialization and institutional propaganda fostered middle-class conformity, commonality, and later consensus. At the core of this transition was big business: economically, psychologically, and sociologically.

Notes

1. "The New McClure Serial," *McClure's Magazine*, September 1910, 592.
2. See *Santa Clara County v. Southern Pacific Railroad*, 1886; *Pemberton Mining Co. v. Pennsylvania*, 1888; *Minneapolis and St. Louis Railroad v. Beckwith*, 1889; *Charlotte, Columbia & Augusta Railroad v. Gibbs*, 1892; *Gulf, Colorado & San Francisco Railroad v. Ellis*, 1897. Cited in Martin J. Sklar, *The Corporate Reconstruction of American Capitalism, 1890–1916, the Market, the Law and Politics* (New York: Cambridge University Press, 1988): 48–50.

In this regard, note David C. Korten, in *The Post-Corporate World:*

> Far more remarkable, however, is that the doctrine of corporate personhood which subsequently became a cornerstone of corporate law, was introduced in this 1886 decision without argument. According to the official case record, Supreme Court Justice Morrison Remick Waite simply pronounced before beginning of argument in the case of *Santa Clara County v Southern Pacific Railroad* that
>
> "The court does not wish to hear argument on the question of whether the provision in the Fourteenth Amendment to the Constitution, which forbids a State to deny to any person within its jurisdiction the equal protection of the laws, applies to these corporations. We are all of the opinion that it does."

The court reporter duly entered into the summary record of the Court's findings that

> "The defendant Corporations are persons within the intent of the clause in section 1 of the Fourteent[h] Amendment to the Constitution of the United States, which forbids a State to deny to any person within its jurisdiction the equal protection of the laws."

Thus it was that a two-sentence assertion by a single judge elevated corporations to the status of persons under the law, prepared the way for the rise of global corporate rule, and thereby changed the course of history. (Korten, *The Post-Corporate World*, 185)

3. Blackford and Kerr, *Business Enterprise*, 159–161.
4. Blackford, *Business Enterprise*, 153.
5. Charles Going, Principles of Industrial Engineer*ing* (New York: McGraw-Hill Book Company, 1911): 3.
6. Rogers, *Work Ethic*, 54.
7. Kanigel, *Best Way*, 37.
8. Merckle, *Management* 94.
9. Zunz, *American Century*, 75.

3

Good Stuff

Creating a Consumer Society

CORPORATIONS CREATED THE American Consumer Society by institutionalizing mass production and mass distribution. They attained the latter by creating the mail-order industry, department stores, and chain stores. The long-term result was a cultural transformation. American society became a consuming society.

Mass-production technology in the United States evolved from its nineteenth-century antecedent, the so-called American System. Starting with handicraft by the mechanically inclined, Americans developed a method of small-shop production that combined custom craftwork with standardization of procedure and components. This method became the American System early in the nineteenth century. Cyrus McCormick, Samuel Colt, Isaac Singer, and the United States Army Ordnance Department were among its pioneers.

Machine tool manufacture was the foundation. Once refined, this innovation was applied to making things such as sewing machines and agricultural implements. A systematic method of production slowly evolved and diffused through the American manufacturing sector. Near the end of the nineteenth century this method combined with an explosion of new technology. The resulting synthesis became mass production, and by 1930, it became the dominant method of American manufacture.

For example, knowledge about interchangeability, standardization, and continuous-flow manufacturing were applied at the Ford Motor company. In 1913, they began assembly line production. The process was designed and applied to making the Model T. It began with the coordinated manufacture of the car's components in a sequentially laid-out building. From

1906, the production design evolved to integrate component manufacture, material flow, and car assembly. The process seemed to grow outward. The machining of components was integrated with material flow and the manufacture of components sequenced. The development process morphed into the assembly line in April 1913, at the three-year-old Highland Park, Michigan, factory. New Model Ts rolled off the assembly line every forty seconds. American industry took note of the process, its efficiencies, and costs. Imitation soon followed, and the concept of mass production became the dominant form of American manufacture. It revolutionized industry and society.[1] Other corporations that adopted continuous-process production methods included: Quaker Oats, Pillsbury, Campbell Soup, Borden, Carnation, Lilly, Proctor & Gamble, and Kodak.[2]

Mass-produced goods eventually were mass distributed. During much of the nineteenth century, producers did not sell directly to retailers. Instead, middlemen bought from the manufacturer and then distributed the products into the market. They resold goods to a hodge-podge of local accounts. The scope of this system was small and uncoordinated. The products were usually generic, bulk items bought by retailers in small amounts.[3]

After 1870, this distribution system began to change. Producers started to by-pass distributors and sell directly to retailers. Two new market innovations fostered this trend. At the manufacturing level, corporations began to produce packaged, brand-name, trademarked, products and then advertised them nationally. They then sold their wares directly, often in large volume to department and chain store companies. The scope became high volume, and national. Localism started to diminish.[4]

Swift & Company, for example, was one of the first to distribute its own product. They built cooled storage facilities in several cities. Their goal was to process the meat in the Midwest and then ship it cold back East. Swift's strategy worked and Armour, Cudahy, and other meatpackers imitated. Consequently, the middleman was almost completely eliminated. Other manufacturers in different sectors soon followed: Pabst, Kodak, General Electric, Westinghouse, Nabisco, U.S. Steel, Du Pont, Texaco, General Motors, and Ford etc. Thus, over several decades, a new, national, distribution network evolved and eventually dominated the American economy. By 1930, most manufactured products were distributed and marketed by their producers. The traditional middleman, wholesaler, accounted for about one-third of total distributed volume.[5]

Transportation and communication advances, specifically the railroads and telegraph, and later the telephone were used to dilute the middleman's importance. Under the old model, the wholesaler usually knew which producer could provide products within a certain time. The middleman thus bought goods in volume and stored them in local warehouses for later distribution. In turn, the retailer depended on local supply entirely removed from the producer. At the other end of the distribution pipeline, the manufacturer, after selling to the middleman, had no control of how his product got to the consumer. Sales depended entirely on local market conditions and wholesaler distribution strategy.[6]

Telegraph, and later telephone, linked the manufacturer for the first time directly to his market. These communications advances enabled large corporations to maintain actual and constant contact with their representatives in the field, shippers, and branch facilities. Most importantly, the telegraph and telephone allowed direct communications between producer and the seller via buyers, be it a department store in Los Angeles or the J.C. Penney chain store in Jerome, Arizona. Direct communications fostered direct control of distribution and marketing.

Ultimately, the railroads made it all possible by providing an efficient, reliable, regular, and less-expensive method of distribution. As a result, large corporations could manufacture from a location and then ship their products by rail. Mass-producing industries now had access to a national market.

Using the telegraph, railroad, and telephone and integrating the production and distribution process resulted in a new system that today we refer to as a national mass market. It evolved after 1880, and its foundation was in place by 1940. Even before that, during the 1920s this system was effectively operating in urban areas and regionally in the North, east of the Mississippi River.

How did manufacturers and retailers get the message out about their goods and motivate people to try these new things? Salesmen were the first direct links between producers and retailers. A company's sales force was responsible for convincing the shopkeeper to stock a brand-name product and push it on the public. The company representative also promoted the ad campaign. He had to introduce the concept and provide material: posters, giveaways, premiums/coupons, and free samples. The salesman also became a trainer on display and product promotion. He helped and encouraged retailers to add system to their merchandise arrangement and provided background information about product production and maintenance, and about the producer. He also provided retailers with trade cards to give to customers. The cards became a collecting fad prior to 1900 and the first ads promoting brand-name goods.

Overall, the beginnings of a national market can be traced back to this informal system of itinerants. Prior to the mass-distribution era, warehouse salesmen traveled about, making calls on rural storekeepers. Sometimes called "drummers," they distributed samples, took orders, negotiated credit, collected bills, and gave product demonstrations in local hotels. (They were also looked on as good sources of regional news and gossip. People were curious about what was going on up the road a ways.) Over time, the road culture they created served as a vehicle to deliver mass-produced goods. Manufacturers' reps duplicated the role of their predecessors, the wholesale drummers. Taking to the road, working a territory, using telephones and driving cars, the twentieth-century salesmen helped replace the Main Street culture by delivering the modern corporate culture through marketing and merchandising.

More competition prompted an increase in corporate sales departments. The roles and responsibilities of salesmen increased, and their job may have been difficult. They had to sell to retailers who could be unresponsive or even hostile to new products and the changing times. Salesmen not only introduced new items and a new system, they also helped retailers to modernize their selling methods. They lobbied storekeepers, steeped in the traditional, local way of doing business, to adapt the modern way. They solved problems with delivery. They defended the quality and reliability of brand-name goods, and lobbied accounts to favor their brand names over the traditional stock of generic, bulk items. They also had to outsell private-labeled products and later, other trademarked merchandise. In larger stores, salesmen often visited the floor clerks making similar pitches, providing practical information on display, selling points, and passing out promotional freebies.

Consider the Coca-Cola Company as an example. Atlanta druggist John S. Pemberton created Coca-Cola on May 8, 1886. He had been living in Atlanta for seventeen years and had a local reputation for his homemade soda fountain drinks. His cola concoction was a recipe for a nerve tonic, a drink that could settle the stomach. Pemberton's bookkeeper, Frank M. Robinson, called the beverage Coca-Cola, and scripted its logo. That day in May, they sampled their latest batch, mixing the syrup with plain water. As they prepared a second helping, the fountain clerk, Willis Venable, inadvertently mixed the syrup with carbonated water. Eureka![7]

About a year later, Asa G. Candler bought the Coke formula. The beverage originally sold at the soda fountain for five cents a glass. It was advertised to get people to ask for it first by name. Around 1900, Coke was advertised as a refreshment; a drink of active, healthy, happy people. Its national slogan: "Drink Coca-Cola Delicious and Refreshing." Candler had a zealous devotion to Coke. He began distributing and advertising it nationally by 1904. He constructed a successful sales network, whose personnel sold the syrup to soda fountaineers and bottlers.

Sales training occurred in Atlanta, where reps learned the product, the company, and how to sell coupled with advertising. Once trained, salesmen were assigned to a district and region. Out in the field, Coke salesmen sold their product obsessively. Repetitive visits were their strategy and their goal was to make an impression by frequency. When they called on their accounts, they used a variety of selling methods: giveaways such as dispensing urns and wall clocks; samples, couponed rebates. They combined such premiums with product education. A visiting salesman taught the retailer how to dispense the beverage, proposed a selling plan, distributed advertising, and instigated his customer to post signs and posters. The idea was to place the logo and trademark ubiquitously in any and every locale. Their goal was to make people think Coke first when thirsty and choose their product over everyone else's, all the time.[8]

By 1920, Coke monopolized the soft drink market. That year, Coke syrup was manufactured in thirteen plants in the United States and in Canada and Cuba. It was warehoused at thirty-eight sites and distributed to 105,000 soda fountains, and 1,500 bottlers supplied 100,000 retail outlets. Nine years later Coca-Cola was sold in seventy-six countries.[9]

Indeed, the heart of the market was retailing. In rural areas, the nineteenth-century country store contained a hodge-podge of stuff, displayed randomly and sometimes sold for negotiated price, haggled. Barter and extended credit were still standard practices. Inventory was inconsistent, varying with what was available from wholesalers. Customers bought irregularly, paying high prices for goods that moved at low volume. Neither the customer nor the retailer knew or heard of the producer. Products were usually sold in bulk and generic, that is unpackaged.

Urban shops were not that different from rural retailers. In cities, street corner or sidewalk shops were common into the twentieth century. General stores carried a variety of goods and specialty shops limited their stock to particular items. Usually, general stores were the norm in country towns and specialty shops were mostly city.

Both town and country stores bought their inventory from wholesalers through traveling salesmen. The shopkeeper relied on the warehouse supplier. This meant that his supply depended on what was available locally at a particular time. Regularity was not normal. Most shop owners could not expect a steady or consistent inventory of goods. Quality was a similar problem.

Retailers could not control their inventory effectively, its quality, or their purchasing. All the particulars of supply were ad hoc at best and chaotic at worst. Shopkeepers rarely bought directly from manufacturers. They did not generally have any contact with the producer. There were not any trademarks, packaging, or brand-name items to ask for. Whatever the wholesaler bought from the producer was pipelined into the market through an established itinerant sales system. Localism at all levels pervaded: production, warehousing, wholesale, retail. The product flow was segmented, usually in two's above. The whole system was inefficient, unreliable, and expensive. Eventually, it was replaced by mass marketing and distributing.

The first way around this system was mail order. It brought the bounty of mass production deep into the core of the American market more effectively. In the age of print media, catalogs became an effective way to market products to nonurban areas. Mail order opened the hinterland to mass consumption, enjoying peak success from 1908 to 1925.

Although the first mail-order companies were small direct-sale firms, selling through monthly pulp magazines, the business took off after it assumed a corporate form. Montgomery Ward was the first modern mail-order company. It began in 1872, supplying Grange co-ops. Aaron Montgomery Ward was a traveling salesman based in Chicago, working for a dry goods store. He got the idea to start up a business from conversations he had with farmers. They did not like general stores because of high prices, limited inventory, substandard merchandise, and credit problems. Aware of the Grange movement, Ward decided to sell to them directly, bypassing both wholesalers and retailers.[10]

Mail order was the solution, and Ward started up a company in 1872 with a one-page price sheet of offerings to the Grange. At first, he struggled doing business part-time while he held a day job at the Partridge Dry Goods Company. Surviving the Panic of 1873, Ward avidly pursued business with the co-ops, and in 1875, he offered them goods from a 375-page, pocket-sized catalog. In it, Ward wrote that he could sell good stuff at low prices because of low overhead. With factory-direct purchasing, the savings could be passed on to the customer.

The next year, Ward offered a money-back guarantee in his catalog, now stocked with 3,899 items. This offer, even over great distances between producer and consumer, may have been the underlying reason for Montgomery Ward's success. Even though the co-ops went out of business, Montgomery Ward continued to serve the hinterland market. The company garnered $1 million in sales in 1887. From 1886 to 1889, Montgomery Ward received over three million letters and shipped 800,000 packages.

By 1890, Montgomery Ward was a ubiquitous presence in rural American culture. In many schools, the Montgomery Ward catalog was considered a reference book. When catalogs arrived, for many families it was greeted with almost holiday-style exuberance. Customer loyalty often lasted decades. By 1900, the Montgomery Ward catalog included just about any item most people could want; rural or urban. It was a $10 million business, and its corporate headquarters in Chicago was the tallest business building in the world. The 1901 catalog had more than 1,000 pages of merchandise.

In *New and Improved*, Richard Tedlow concluded that Ward was the first to create trust over distance between seller and buyer. He also successfully overcame the traditional relationships built up between local shopkeepers and their customers. Ward success in competing in this once closed market was revolutionary. In addition, Ward was one of the first to cast a favorable relationship between a large, distant corporation and its customers. This foundation was critical in supporting the expansion of a national consumer society during the 1920s.

The strengths of the mail-order system fostered its success. Catalogs marketed products nationally and deeply into the hinterland. Thus, manufacturers' reach extended much farther then local over-the-counter sales. Catalog order-filling was more efficient, even at a distance from the point of sale. Large inventories, systematic processing, and regularized delivery made mail-order more reliable than the small-town retailer, who simply did not have the strength and depth of resources to effectively compete with large enterprise. Big catalog corporations had vast resources, centralized and available on a regular schedule. The result was that mail order became a reliable and constant source of supply for rural consumers. Large corporations like Montgomery Ward and Sears ended a long-term era of rural scarcity by introducing mass distribution that in turn, precipitated mass consumption.[11]

Montgomery Ward and Sears overcame the traditional localism of the market. Selling at a distance, unknown and unseen, necessitated breaking the bond between the local merchant and their customers. Both mail-order houses did this through product guarantees and liberal refund policies. They also successfully used innovative mass-distribution techniques to deliver orders on a regular and timely basis. Adopting the large-scale corporate form enabled this. As a result, Montgomery Ward and Sears were fundamental catalysts in the construction of a national mass-market that eventually spawned an entirely new society, one based on consumption spending.

The market framework first established by mail-order houses was further developed in urban areas by department stores. In time, they evolved to become fantasy lands of plenty, "cathedrals of commerce," emporiums of largesse, and flagships of large-scale enterprise, corporate capitalism.

The department store industry emerged over the years, 1860 to 1910, and established itself around 1880. By 1900, these stores gained a popularity after outcompeting the traditional small specialty shop. From 1905 to 1930, the era of department stores flowered.[12]

A combination of economic factors prompted this industry's success. People began to cluster in cities, and they eventually created a demand for convenient, nearby shopping. All-in-one grand emporiums fit in perfectly with the new urban environment. City industries created more reliable job opportunities and family incomes, generally, stabilized and for some, actually increased. More people with more disposable income spurred retail competition. Market entry became an exciting proposition during this era, congruent to a general modernizing social trend.

Department stores also made inroads into the rural market. Some of them set up in small towns prior to 1900. Evidently, local loyalties and buying habits changed from exclusively patronizing neighborly shopkeepers, to the uniformity, regularity, and system offered by department store/chain store retailers.

Alexander T. Stewart opened one of the first department store prototypes. Arriving in New York City from Ireland, Stewart taught school then took over a dry goods store in 1823. In 1848, he built his Marble Palace store. It was the first large store devoted to retailing and designed for women. Stewart employed male clerks who sold prepriced, quality, stylish goods in a friendly, courteous manner. The store evolved to a department store after it was moved to Broadway in 1862; called the Cast Iron Palace. It had eight levels, and two and one-half acres of floor space. By 1870, the store had 19 departments, 9 cashiers, 25 bookkeepers, 30 ushers, 470 floor clerks, 200 cash runners, and 50 porters. Amenities included organ music and full length mirrors. It was avidly studied by other businessmen.[13]

The structure of a large department store developed, combining elements of general merchandise selling and warehousing. General stores prevailed in rural areas and specialty shops were typically nineteenth-century urban. Take the variety of the general store, enlarge its holding capacity and display its inventory in specific areas, or departments and a new form of retailing results.

Typically, a large variety of prepriced goods, and later packaged brand-name items were for sale, systematically and often handsomely displayed on an open selling floor where browsing was encouraged. The interior design of stores was systemized during the 1890s. Shelves and display cases were lowered so sight lines were opened. Glass showcases replaced wood counters. Merchandise was displayed systematically, cleanly, neatly, and tastefully. (Inventory was stored elsewhere.) Indiscriminate stacking and piles of stuff and cluttering were eliminated. Customers could see what was available and find an item easily.

Quick access was a selling strategy, and store clerks soberly hawked their wares under the pretense of friendly conversation and customer service. The sales transaction usually was cash and carry, although some customers were invited to set up charge accounts. Keeping a tab, like in a general store, was no longer acceptable. Cash was tendered to the clerk who had the money delivered by a runner to a cashier. That clerk recorded the transaction and the purchaser, made change, and issued a receipt. Eventually, runners were replaced by pneumatic tubes and later by cash registers.

Selling and buying became a ritual surrounded by atmosphere and ambience. Displays were tidy, at the very least, and opulent and ornate in the extreme. High-end display furniture and fixtures prevailed. Floors were often carpeted. Lighting was eventually designed for effect, not just illumination.

Modern, contemporary accouterments were incorporated into the store's interior design: electric lighting, elevators, escalators, public telephones, forced-air ventilation, and later, air-conditioning. Some of these technological advances were in place prior to 1900. (Air-conditioning was first tried at Schlesinger-Meyer, in Chicago, in 1903, and in Filene's Basement store, in 1912.)

By 1929, more than half of the industry offered a large mix of in-store amenities as part of doing business. These were designed to attract business and create repeated visits: clean attractive bathrooms, sitting rooms, restaurants, post offices, telegraph and telephones, lost-and-found, reading rooms, and public lectures. Customer service eventually included charge accounts, telephone ordering, and home delivery. Both exteriors and interiors became effective mechanisms of persuasion, inducers to buy.[14]

Department stores became a new, popular thing to do. In particular, shopping became entertainment. Customers could shop, attend a music program, visiting the ladies parlor to write letters and meet friends. Make purchases in the art gallery.

Nationwide, department store companies freely imitated each other. High volume, low margins, ambience, and customer service became the method. Erecting impressive edifices to house this modern world of goods, became *the* selling place. Displaying this cornucopia of plenty elegantly and presenting merchandise as representative of class and status became a widely accepted industry practice. Store clerks became an increasingly important part of selling.

Establishing and maintaining demand became the basic reason for this entire store atmosphere. Staff was trained to manipulate shoppers to buy more than they intended. Individual transactions, conversations, and socializing were supposed to promote this. Developing and cultivating repeat business and establishing a convivial acquaintanceship with regulars had a similar purpose. By using appeals to fashion and style, store clerks manipulated a customer's sense of class. By fostering and promoting buying good stuff—wrapping it in an aura of elegance and sophistication—urbanity and modernity could be attained.

The department store became a public place, a social setting for its clientele where shopping was an excursion that included amusement and diversion. Customer amenities and ambience became strong attractions to the modern consumer. At the same time and similar to the shop floor and the modern corporate office, the selling floor became a place of socialization. Those who interacted there were acculturated to this emerging modern ethos. In the process of selling goods, class, image, and urbanity, store personnel were absorbed into the middle-classness of a consumer society. Many of the working-class store clerks were schooled in selling, etiquette, and good public manners. Taught customer service skills then included product knowledge, persuasion techniques, and deference to the customer. Department stores first informally and after 1900, formally schooled their personnel. By the 1920s, in-house training including general education in math, English, homemaking, and Americanization became industry standards. The foundations for this attempt to reeducate their workforce were middle-class values, taste, urbanity, and contemporary fashion. Store management believed that uplifting their personnel would enable staff and customers to better relate and interact.

The successful marketing package that department stores created molded shoppers into happy spenders. Simultaneously, chain stores brought a similar culture to Main Street. A consumer society based on these new social habits resulted by 1930. The formal structure of the urban-based grand eloquent department store became the model for a smaller-sized, diffused version that would spawn a derivative retail industry especially in rural areas, the chain store.

During the 1920s, chain stores were revolutionary. They brought urban, downtown-style emporiums into outlying areas. By 1930, there were more than 7,000 of all sizes doing about 20 percent of total retail business. The largest and first of its kind was the A&P food stores.

The creation of a chain-store system first occurred at the regional level. Urban food selling was similar to dry goods and general-store retailing. The market structure was small in scale and inefficient. Small stores sold at low volume and high prices. Refrigeration was not yet common to households until the 1930s, so food shopping was a regular routine. In some places, grocery orders were phoned in, picked by the store clerk, and then held for pickup or delivered. Since stores often specialized, a full shopping cart as we know it, then, required several stops at different stores in a shopping district or central market.

After the turn of the century, a new food-marketing innovation occurred, again, the chain store. George F. Gilman started the Great Atlantic and Pacific Tea Company in 1859. His store specialized in imported tea until 1862. At first focusing on high-margin, high-priced mail-order sales, Gilman eventually expanded his retailing to eleven stores in New York City by 1870. He added a line of groceries ten years later. At the turn of the century, there were two hundred A&P stores, scattered in twenty-eight states, and growth continued. Selling goods like a general store, they took phone orders, and then began to offer premiums such as food stamps, and occasionally extended credit.

In 1913, they started a new kind of store they called "economy stores," one that was cash-and-carry, and staffed by only a manager and assistant. The general-store arrangement was eliminated. Their inventory was warehoused, and they offered brand-name goods, cheaper, as a result. They used a new selling strategy—high volume, low margin. Low operating cost resulted, and consequently, competitors soon imitated A&P's method. As a result, the grocery-store industry skyrocketed during the 1920s, and by 1930, A&P had over 15,700 stores; Kroger had 5,165; Safeway had 2,675. A&P quickly became the industry leader.

These chain stores generally sold cheaper than independents because they could buy and sell on volume. Their specialized management structure enabled them to better monitor and control their inventory, advertising, and profit margin. In merchandising, they emphasized price and location over traditional retail services as delivery and credit.

A&P sustained its leadership and became one of the most significant twentieth-century retailers because it developed and successfully managed a vertically integrated selling system. It revolutionized food distribution at the retail level by selling at high volume and low profit margin; eliminating middlemen, and using and integrating successfully house brands (also known as off-brands) with nationally advertised brand-name goods. Its system was widely copied by all kinds of chain store companies. Meanwhile, A&P persisted as a leader until forced to compete with supermarkets during the 1930s. In response, A&P adapted this new format, which was a hybrid of chain-store marketing method.

The grocery supermarket arrived during the 1930s, competing with food market chains. Enlarging on the chain store concept, supermarkets specialized in high-volume, low-margin, brand-name products. Michael J. Cullen conceptualized the idea in 1930. He worked for Kroger grocers in downstate Illinois. He proposed to Kroger a store concept that included using cash registers at the point of sale; shipping foodstuffs directly to the store instead of warehousing; placing stores away from urban central markets where land would be cheaper and automobile parking could be easily provided. Food purchases would be in cash, and no credit or delivery would be provided. The store would be stocked with a wide variety of brand-name goods prepriced and arranged so that the purchaser picked out what they wanted. Clerks would no longer be necessary.

Kroger never responded to Cullen's proposal, so he took off on his own and opened King Kullen Grocery Store, in Queens, New York, in August 1930. Six years later, he had fifteen stores. That year, when he died, he was one of the first to succeed in this evolutionary grocery store venture. Consequently, imitators followed and supermarkets became a trend.[15] Big Bear Supermarkets appeared in 1932 and added dry goods such as electrical appliances and car supplies to their stock. Even industry leader A&P followed the trend in 1938 and so too Safeway and Kroger later.

The chain-store trend proliferated to other retail sectors. By 1929, there were 159,638 chain stores nationwide. Of these 114,882 sold food and the rest a wide array of consumer goods: drugs, candy, apparel, shoes, cars, gasoline, and furniture. They were successful because they offered low prices, a variety of products, and convenient locations; they appeared organized, neat, and clean.

Thus, chain stores and mass distribution complemented each other. Volume-buying lowered retail prices, enabling profit from high volume sold at low margin. Professional management used administrative practices successfully applying contemporary scientific management principles within the emerging standard large-scale corporate form. In combination, chain-store strategy executed within that structure fortified each company's market position in both the short and long runs. Investment credit was readily available and losses could be absorbed.[16] The industries' short-term successes during the 1920s strengthened them for the economic onslaught in the 1930s.

Manufacturers began to advertise in order to influence the purchaser before they walked into the store. One of the first nationally advertised brands was Royal Baking Powder. Through repetitive advertising, Royal influenced demand for the product by its name. They were successful, becoming a model for bringing the concept of brand-name loyalty to the market.

All the methods of mass marketing—mail order, department stores, and chain stores—were dependent on advertising for their market success/survival. Successful competition meant recruiting new purchasers and holding on to regular customers. To maintain and improve market strength, manufacturers and retailers used advertising and sales departments to manage demand at the selling floor level. Advertise a brand-name product so that its demand increases. The retailer orders it from the wholesaler in response to customers asking for the product by name. Thus, the control of distribution has just been reversed. The producer controls it through the consumer demand that advertising generated.

The key factor, the foundation to this system, was advertising, and popular magazines were advertising's first great mass-communications vehicle that delivered the notion of mass-production goods, and the concept of corporation to the public. The *Ladies Home Journal*, *Saturday Evening Post*, *Munsey's Magazine*, *Harper's Weekly*, and *McClure's Magazine*, among others were so-called general-interest magazines, and they were our first mass-culture medium. They were successful and economically viable because of advertising revenue.

These magazines defined, explained, and disseminated the content of American culture. They contained written pieces of general interest, fiction, poetry, and nonfiction. Authors such as Hamlin Garland, Conan Doyle, Stephen Crane, Jack London, Upton Sinclair, and Willa Cather wrote for these companies. Some magazines such as *Munsey's* and *Cosmopolitan* focused on urbanity, high culture, and famous people. Some, like *McClure's*, became muckrakers. Each magazine constructed its own style and attitude toward levels of culture and progress. For example, *Munsey's* took the lowbrow approach and *McClure's* the middle path, while *The Century* styled above, and *Cosmopolitan* combined elements of all three. Indeed, popular magazines delivered contemporary America into people's homes, and that included consumption spending and its corporate providers.

General-interest magazines became popular and affordable during the 1890s. A new era began in 1893 when *Munsey's* sold for ten cents a copy. An increase in readers followed and other publishers imitated *Munsey's*. These magazines became cheap to buy, garnering a large and national audience. In the days before broadcasting, reading was entertainment, education, acculturation, socialization, and leisure all in one.[17]

The *Ladies Home Journal* (*LHJ*) was an industry leader; a trendsetter for other publishers, women's interests, advertising, and consumption spending. It was particularly aimed at middle-class women, but it appealed to readers of all stations. It was like a TV show that was must-see. The magazine's contents idealized middle-class life and proselytized consumption spending by integrating and connecting text with ads in its layout. Its articles often promoted wise shopping decisions in the context of accepted standards of taste and fashion. The ads were often distributed, to be read in tandem with specific pieces.

Before 1900, these magazines generally carried over fifty pages of ads; after the turn of the century, ad pages increased to over one hundred per issue. At first, ads introduced new brand-name products on the emerging modern, national market and attempted to stimulate demand. Soon ads were designed to sustain that demand; to convince spenders to keep buying what they had already been sold and to buy more different things. Thus, the ads started out informing. They evolved to create desire.

At the same time, the popular-magazine industry became an effective and ubiquitous instrument of acculturation and socialization. They promoted the fundamental value of American progress. Industrial advancement and consumption spending were parts of this package. Modern machine-age progress and the conquest of scarcity became new American values. General-interest magazines proselytized this within their literary content and subtly—or blatantly—in their ad copy.

Their reach was widespread. There were magazines for every household member. For example, women read the ads and purchased, based on that information, or the impressions the ad made. Her daughter used the ads to contrast images of her social reality. The son prefers *Youth's Companion* or *Popular Science Monthly*. The father perused *Munsey's*, but preferred *Cosmopolitan*. Thus, this appeal of print material was significant. Out in rural areas, advertisers delivered their messages to spend in *Southern Planter*, *Country Gentleman*, and *American Farmer*.

Magazines were "a potent and powerful force shaping the consciousness of millions of Americans."[18] Many of these magazines favored and proselytized the new industrial, technological, political, social, and corporate order. Their publishers viewed themselves as facilitators of change for those willing to read.

The *Saturday Evening Post* (*SEP*) reflected this. Cyrus Curtis bought the *SEP* in September 1897. The magazine targeted the average American man, defining that group as essentially middle class and business. Their message was wrapped in private-sector progress. The ads that accompanied the text were also male oriented, focusing on investments, office supplies, business clothes, and schooling. By 1908, the *SEP*'s orientation and advertising moved toward general consumerism and away from its original male orientation. Instead, it became a family periodical, proclaiming its dedication to common-sense Americanism, and loaded with ads that took up 60 percent of its content.[19]

In total, popular magazines of this era delivered a message promoting an achieving culture, progress, and the new abundance.[20] As Pendergast wrote:

> the magazine became the first true vehicle of mass culture in America, a medium that reached people of all classes all over the nation. Produced, even manufactured, by increasingly large corporations, edited by sharp businessmen attuned to the public interest, filled with reading matter intended for the broadest possible audience, and stocked with ads for nationally branded products, these magazines were the perfect expressions of the emerging modern corporate capitalist culture.[21]

In effect, they created a new national ethos based on contemporary improvements and the standardization and organization of life. Corporate organization structured and mass production, distribution, and consumption fueled the newly emerging paradigm. Formulated late in the nineteenth century, the new model emerged and solidified prior to World War I. It blossomed during the 1920s, and was delivered as a complete package right into the home via literary content and ad copy in these popular magazines.

Popular magazines were the main medium until the 1920s, when radio broadcasting first appeared. In the spring of 1920, a Westinghouse executive noticed a Pittsburgh department-store ad promoting a radio receiver which could be used to listen to an experimental Westinghouse broadcast station. The idea occurred to him to develop radio as a broadcasting medium. Later that year, November 2, 1920, station KDKA began broadcasting from Pittsburgh. During the next five years, local, independent radio stations went on the air. For example, in 1923, 180 of 573 stations were owned by electric appliance stores or radio sellers. The rest were operated by local banks, newspaper publishers, stores, theaters, etc.[22]

Radio-set ownership increased too. In 1922, there were an estimated 60 thousand radios being used; 1925, 4 million; 1930, 12 million; 1932, over 16 million.[23] By 1932, Herman Hettinger wrote that over 17 million people listened to radio broadcasts and half the nation's households owned a radio. That year there were 604 stations nationwide, which meant that day-programming was available to 94 percent of the country, and night-broadcasting reached 89 percent.

Radio's appeal was universal and it was initially considered a modern miracle of technology. Live sporting events, instant news reports from far away, and big city entertainment, were some of the new features that captured huge listening audiences. These innovations were organized and fostered by large corporations. They marshaled their institutional resources to improve the technical requirements to broadcast, organized and systemized a broadcasting infrastructure, and financed the equipment and programming necessary to go nationwide.

Radio corporations took broadcasting from its local beginnings to a national level. The first radio stations were local, small-time operations, broadcasting to its home locale. They were often funded as adjuncts to local businesses. Consequently, their spending budgets were small so they could not afford continuous programming. Being insular, most stations could only draw on nearby talent to create entertainment. In response, radio manufacturers, especially Radio Corporation of America (RCA), estimated that centrally managing, controlling, and distributing broadcast programs was feasible and potentially lucrative. If they offered good shows, people would buy their radios.

The fruition of this idea was centralized broadcasting, what we today call networks. In 1926, the first national network, NBC, began broadcasting; CBS started in 1928, and by 1932, there were 171 nationally affiliated radio stations. NBC had 76 and CBS 95. Networked affiliates soon dominated the airwaves because they offered regular, expensive, and sophisticated programming: music, comedy, drama, variety; children's, religious, sports, educational, and farm programs. No longer decentralized, most radio shows were the syndicated creations of large corporations.

Radio advertising began with local and regional broadcasting where specific shows were sponsored by specific companies. National Biscuit, Wanamaker, Royal typewriters, Ray-O-Vac, Everyready, and B. F. Goodrich were original sponsors. Because broadcasting costs were high, radio too, relied on advertising revenue to survive.

AT&T introduced national advertising in 1924. They created a package offering radio stations a set of programs with advertising. Although the response was tepid, the institutional trend toward commercial radio began. Acceptance of commercials was slow. There were many critics declaring ads as home invasions. Admen and broadcasters feared advertising would cause resentment and audience loss. Print ads were trusted, successful methods. Radio advertising was new, untested, risky. Few advertisers wanted to be pathfinders. In 1922, an editorial in *Radio Broadcast* magazine suggested that listeners would lose influence on broadcast content should advertising become acceptable. There was a fear that programs would become adjuncts to commercials.

Nevertheless, commercials were integrated into programming. At first, direct advertising was unacceptable. Only sponsorship was allowed; the company name was mentioned but not the product. On December 4, 1923, the National Carbon Company sponsored the "Everready Hour," the first time a syndicated program was company sponsored. That same year, station WEAF in New York City aired an ad from a Long Island real estate firm.

Once radio broadcasting expanded nationwide, the format became a strong avenue for advertising. As a source of news and entertainment, radio was popular, the way television was later. Writing in the 1930s, Hettinger suggested that radio ads might be more effective than print. He argued that good programming would attract loyal listeners who would hear the commercials specific to each station, creating an exclusive and repeat audience for the advertiser's pitch. He suggested that the repetitive commercials would be very effective, being listened to as part of the program and absorbed indirectly. Others suggested that half-hour programs held an audience and offered more exposure to commercials then print ads. Radio brought products right into the home, often to several family members at once. Even those who could not read were exposed to it. Program content eventually wrapped itself around the commercials. Particular programs attracted the targeted audience, held their attention, to hear the sales pitch. Even the program scripts were written to sell specific products, as part of the story line or complementary to it. The idea was to fit the commercial seamlessly into the program the same way ads were integrated into magazine text.

Homemakers became a specific target of advertisers once daytime broadcasting began. Experts such as Betty Crocker did how-to programs, and soap operas began in 1932 as a way to sell soap, among other things, to women during the day. Children's shows sold cereal and the like.

Thus, the use of radio advertising increased during the 1930s; food, drug, and toiletries makers were huge users. Price advertising began in 1932. Promotions were already part of the sales pitch. Large corporations especially hawked their wares. Even though many small producers discontinued advertising during the Great Depression, big business dominated commercial airtime, to the extent that the advertiser often was the radio program's producer. By 1940, the concept of corporation financed, nationalized standardized, systemized, and sustained the broadcast industry, creating commercialized radio as its end product. Popular magazines and radio broadcasting delivered the message of mass-consumption abundance, in part through the advertising industry. Admen helped create modernity, and were sustained by it, all at the same time.

The modern advertising industry began during the popular magazine era. At first magazines were supported by subscription price alone. When general circulation magazines, beginning with *Munsey's* in 1893, dropped their prices, they eventually turned to advertising revenue as their chief means of support. The relationship supported the magazine and later the broadcast industry, introduced the abundance of mass production, spawned the ad agency industry, and created a revolutionary society based on consumption spending.

Advertising had more than one purpose. Besides announcing product availability, ads attempted to educate the public about mass-produced goods and in some instances how to use them. Ads also attempted to create familiarity with a product through association with a trademark or logo.[24] By 1920, admen created a dialogue that attempted to connect spenders with the product and its producer. Ultimately, during that decade, the ad industry went beyond providing information. They now attempted to create demand and manage it, by stimulating desire; a want to possess stuff, and to spend money to get it. To accomplish this, they equated happiness, social status, and household tranquility to consumption spending. As early as 1901, one contemporary observed: "Each individual tries to outdo his neighbor in the goods he consumes and to increase the distance between himself and his inferiors."[25] Perhaps even then, the label was the thing?

Brand-name advertising began during the 1880s.[26] The first nationally advertised products were cereals, soaps, baking ingredients, and food. The earliest ads were for: Royal Baking Powder, Sapolio soap, Ivory, Pear's soap, and Lever Brothers.

For example, soap makers Enoch Morgan & Sons, of New York, introduced Sapolio scouring soap, advertising it in 1869. It eventually became a nationally used brand and was pitched using slogans such as: "Be clean" and "Sapolio scours the world." In 1900, they started a series of related ads called "Spotless Town." Its cartoon characters praised Sapolio in the context of everyday serialized vignettes. In all, twelve characters lived their lives in these commercials. They became quite popular and "Allusions to Spotless Town soon became a familiar site in newspapers, on the streets, in public speeches, and even on stage. Cartoons, toys, books, plays, and political speeches borrowed the Spotless Town phrases and scenes."[27] The campaign lasted about six years.

As other companies advertised, a new national, informal dialogue developed. Ellen Garvey suggested: "As the national distribution and advertising of goods by brand name shaped a national vocabulary, the cultural shorthand they created enabled people across the United States to understand a reference to a brand of soap or a joke about an advertising slogan."[28] She went on to write that referring to ad content became both popular and trendy.

Another example of an early success in product advertising was teaching the public to eat oatmeal. Henry P. Crowell was a pioneer in marketing a packaged cereal with a specific name. He created Quaker brand oats, packaging it with a logo and a recipe. Then, Crowell advertised in newspapers first in 1888, extolling oatmeal's healthful effects. Next, Quaker Oats appeared in magazines, booklets, and billboards and on streetcar signs. His company gave away samples, included coupons on calendars and in cookbooks. Their efforts were successful. Quaker Oats became a national brand, and oatmeal was no longer considered food for those sick in bed.

Quickly, other companies advertised similarly: Campbell's, Proctor & Gamble, Borden, Levi-Strauss, Hires, Hills Brothers, Carnation, Cream of Wheat, and Pepsi Cola, among others. Their brand-name products invoked a belief in their safety and reliability, a sentiment that became a permanent association among the buying public.

At the same time, trademarks helped to personify corporations. The earliest of trademarks were likenesses of the company owner, say the Smith Brothers. Turn-of-the-century, pioneer trademarkers included Quaker Oats, Woodbury Soap, Lipton Tea, and Underwood Ham. Later, gimmicks such as the salt girl and animals were adopted as corporate symbols. The object was to dilute the social distance between an unseen, often distant producer and its product users. Even back then, corporate anonymity was a problem.

During the 1890s, packaged foods began to change lifestyles: cereal and coffee for breakfast; canned soup and ham for lunch; a Swift roast for supper. Over the next few decades, preparing food, rather than cooking from scratch, prefaced what became a new sense of modernity. The novelty of using packaged foods and preparing them quickly and conveniently with new-fangled kitchen appliances probably kindled the interests of many homemakers. This attitude, no doubt, expanded in response to the promptings from advertisements.

The underlying force was the marketing of technologically driven innovations translated into everyday life as convenience products. Modernity's appeal was often based on the elimination of household drudgery and the newness and novelty of possessing and using these new things. Buy the product; use it; break up the routine; reduce tedium; it's easy, convenient; and the food tastes pretty good considering! The products made you feel better. It was also a way to be up-to-date, modern, and contemporary. Advertising played to these notions, if not in fact created them. During the

1920s, ads for such products increased even more. Soon, some brand-name products became household names.

This availability changed our material culture by introducing new things and ideas, and common/homogenized ways of doing things. As it developed over the next decade, this advance in technical, social, and cultural conceptualization and perception was revolutionary. Such a series of changes expanded social horizons and sensibilities. We call this trend modernization. The changes of mind and then mindset were instigated in part by advertising agencies and their corporate clients.

The first advertising agents were space brokers, working in small partnerships typical of the pre-corporate private sector. They were middlemen who provided services to both advertisers and publishers. The early expansion of regional markets necessitated product-availability announcements in different local newspapers. Simultaneously, publishers realized that ads paid overhead and often kept the newspaper afloat. The ad agent thus filled a niche by connecting the advertiser to the newspapermen. The agent bought ad space wholesale and resold it in smaller increments to product advertisers. The agent thus provided the producer with ad copy in several places at one time.

One of these agents was Volney B. Palmer. He started his business, in 1841, in Philadelphia. By 1844, he expanded his firm via offices in Boston, New York City, and Baltimore. His agency sold ad-space for newspapers, delivered the copy, and collected fees. Palmer's company also helped the advertiser to pitch appropriate newspapers, and he offered assistance copywriting. He called himself a newspaper agent because he considered himself to be working for the publisher, soliciting ads from producers and retailers. This kind of middleman business worked. Publishers did a lot of business with Palmer, and his success spawned imitators and competitors.

One was Francis W. Ayer, who in 1868 worked for the *National Baptist Weekly*. The next year, Ayer went independent, forming a partnership with his father Nathan W. Ayer. Operating out of Philadelphia, N. W. Ayer was the typical storefront nineteenth-century business, in this case a two-man operation.

Their first accounts were religious weeklies such as *Catholic Standard*, and *Episcopal Register*, two among eleven accounts total. These two were lucrative because religious weeklies were widely read, being precursors to popular national magazines.

F. W. Ayer solicited ads from product producers and placed them in the space he bought. His middleman responsibilities included copy delivery and follow-up collections. They were successful and by 1872 had 324 accounts and a third coworker. By 1877, success followed success and the Ayer agency bought out a competitor, Volney B. Palmer, the pioneer of the agency business.

While building their market position, the Ayer agency also expanded their services. In 1874, they published an advertising manual that included their accounts and rates. Two years later, they enlarged the manual to include what we today call a public relations booklet. It was filled with short pieces, humor, and sales pitches to advertise through Ayer.

More significantly, in 1875, Ayer added a printing department and began their own graphics production. In 1879, they did a prototype market-research analysis. In order to solicit a new account away from a rival, Ayer was challenged to determine where Nichols-Shepherd could best sell their threshers. Ayer compiled county-level data on agricultural production and newspaper circulation figures in farm areas. Their report garnered the account and eventually this first-time, coordinated, in-depth market-research method became standard procedure by 1900.

However, Ayer was not what we call today a full-service agency. It took a few decades for Ayer to evolve into a comprehensive, systematic corporation. Composing ad copy and graphics for the clients began after 1880. In 1884, Ayer did, for the first time, a complete ad campaign for a tobacco company: media selection, ad copy, scheduling, and promotions. Permanent copywriters and graphic designers eventually came aboard. By 1900, Ayer was positioned as an innovative, pioneering comprehensive, and for then, a full-service agency. Their accounts included: Wanamaker, Montgomery Ward, Whitman's, Singer, Standard Oil, Hires, National Biscuit (Nabisco), *Godey's Lady's Book*, the *Saturday Evening Post*, *Philadelphia Inquirer*, *New York Herald*, *Baltimore Sun*; after 1900 they added Heinz, Steinway, New York Life, A.T.&T., and Western Union.

During the next few decades, Ayer maintained itself as an ad-industry innovator and leader. It reorganized internally and brought in outside management prior to World War I. They resisted using negative and what they considered degrading appeals to emotion in their copy. When radio happened along, Ayer waded in being the first to organize a broadcast program in 1923. As the radio industry developed, Ayer was there, albeit reluctantly at first, studying it, and then attempting to control program content. The ad industry followed their lead.

N. W. Ayer and their competitors such as J. Walter Thompson (JWT), trumpeted themselves as advertising experts—professionals like lawyers and doctors—prior to 1890.[29] Both companies created the advertising profession as they developed.[30] For example, JWT was one of the first to target-market. Thompson favored magazines over newspapers and placed ads designed to reach the better sort and women who they believed controlled household spending.

A campaign for Woodbury soap was one such example. John H. Woodbury created a face soap in 1885 and at first successfully marketed it. However, sales dropped and Woodbury sold his interest to the Andrew Jergens Company in 1901. To improve sales, Jergens hired JWT, in 1910, and they developed a campaign over a six month period. Staff used the soap; read books on skin care; did lab tests, and visited retailers to analyze consumer behavior, consulted a doctor, and did house canvassing. Their first ads described the therapeutic value of Woodbury soap. The ads repeated the brand name, encouraged regular use as a skin treatment, and added a slogan to the graphics. Sales immediately increased.[31]

The Woodbury effort conformed to the general strategic trend ad agencies followed. At first the ads appealed to reason, the so-called reason-why method. By 1920, the sales pitch emphasized emotion. Woodbury soap was a good thing to use regularly for its therapeutic and hygienic value. However, its use also improved one's appearance and attractiveness. Self-esteem and confidence building as a result were implied.

One of that campaign's auteurs was Helen Landsdowne, who originally worked in JWT's Cincinnati office. In 1910, she was assigned the new Woodbury soap account. For the ad campaign she coined the slogan, "The Skin You Love To Touch." The ad was a sensation, and Woodbury soap sales increased exponentially. Jennifer Scanlon credits Landsdowne with creating the association of selling a product through sex appeal. The ad became a precursor to using emotional appeals, which became standard procedure during the Roaring Twenties.

Thus, Woodbury was successfully sold through an emotional appeal, a style of ad and system that was refined by psychologists. They entered the ad industry about 1901. By the 1920s, behavioral psychology was a fundamental part of advertising strategy.

The emerging profession of behavioral psychology became a foundation of advertising psychology. Since persuasion, and creating desire for products was advertising's goal, scientific method became part of their design. Advertising corporations hired psychologists and John B. Watson was a formidable figure in that field.

Watson formulated many of Behaviorism's tenets and proselytized the field as a modern science.[32] Admen joined with behaviorists over a common goal: to predict and control human behavior.

Watson hailed from South Carolina, schooled at Furman, and the University of Chicago where he specialized in experimental psychology. There and later at Johns Hopkins, working with lab animals, Watson transferred behavior theory from these experiments to people. He suggested that humans were more mechanical in their behavior, and he sought methods to predict and control it. During the spring of 1913, Watson began to publish his findings and coined the term Behaviorism. He theorized that both human and animal behavior was based on reactions to the environment via the integration of genetic adaptations and habituation. Individual and group behavior was then predictable, manipulatable, and controllable.

After a time, his publications significantly influenced the field of psychology and Watson eventually rose to almost celebrity status among his peers. In 1916, he started consulting work so to test his theories. In 1920, he left Johns Hopkins to work at the JWT agency. There, he applied behaviorism to advertising psychology successfully, as part of JWT's efforts to systematize their organization and strategies based on contemporary scientific methods.

The use of advertising appeals was, in part, developed based on Watson's theories on human emotion. In effect, the consumer market became the laboratory and the spender the test subject. Watson used symbols in graphics, testimonials, and indirect emotional appeals. For example, use toothpaste and attain popularity and social approval. More directly, selling baby powder meant instigating a mother's fear of irresponsible parenting. Overall, Watson helped to integrate contemporary psychological expertise into advertising strategy, and he concocted ad campaigns that relied on appeals connecting product use with self-improvement.

Watson and his contemporaries worked in the ad agencies prior to World War I. From 1900 to 1920, the ad industry moved away from informing the public about products, to influencing them to buy. Psychologists were used as experts to develop strategies to place products into the collective American mind. Their goal was to inculcate consumption spending as a permanent, ongoing behavior.

Early on, the admen and their psychologist consultants were not quite sure how, but they concluded anecdotally that advertising was a powerful method to create demand. Scientific, psychology-based advertising theory was available in the literature even before Watson. One of the first, *The Theory of Advertising*, by Walter D. Scott, was published in 1903. It and others became textbook method for copywriters. Ironically, many businessmen were initially ambivalent about advertising. Some questioned its effectiveness; others used it anyway. Most advertisers accepted some efforts to systemize its use. Applied psychology became the foundation.

Advertisers began to follow general principles. Everyone assumed that ads had to gain and hold attention and draw interest to a product competing with others. At the same time, ads must stimulate an association; an intense sensation toward the product, and its symbolic value, must be aroused. The graphic content of the ad was designed to achieve this in combination with the ad's written sales pitch or appeal. Illustrations had to be novel and immediately contrasting to competing ads. The accompanying text should be obviously understandable. Together, the ad must be repeated.[33] Scott wrote, "The advertisement with a constant recognizable feature that varies in detail from time to time allows for both change and repetition, and is to that extent the best advertisement."[34] To meet these standards, admen created logos, characters, slogans, and graphic symbolic representations of the product and its producers.[35] (Today we consider some of them as pop culture icons: Coca-Cola, the Morton Salt girl, the G.E. logo, etc.)[36]

To accomplish this, psychologists and social scientists determined what strategies were effective. Understanding psychological association was fundamentally important to creating successful, stratagems. Connecting a product purchase to some desire or personal satisfaction prompted spending. Thus, the whole package of the ad—text and graphics—had to convey a want for the product.

Perhaps most important, ad psychologists fostered the use of emotional appeals. The ads must provide more than just product information. They must induce feeling, arouse sensation, and cause an emotional symbolic reaction. Even though then, they did not know quite how it worked, they believed that attention-getting involved grasping an idea and feeling it and hence wanting it, the product. Arousing interest, then attention and want became the goal. Using positive and even negative, anxiety-based reactions was the accepted method. Ironically, creating positive associations toward the product was the purpose.

To do this, the emotional appeal strategy replaced informative, "reason-why" sales pitches. Psychologists theorized appealing to emotional, irrational behavior was more effective. They suggested if living habits were not rational choices, then appeals to imagination and desire were more important than individual rationality. Involving reason inhibited spending. Connecting products to feelings and intangible social constructs such as appearance, reputation, popularity, elegance, taste and domesticity, promoted spending. The goal was to equate happiness with consuming and to induce the purchase of goods by creating a constant interest and desire. Thus, the good life was translated in terms of acquiring good stuff.

Repetition would inculcate the desire, and the association of a thing with its brand-name version. That such an approach would work was based on the foundation premise that people did not normally rely solely on rationality and logic in their decison-making. Instead, they were products of their surroundings and their thoughts and actions were the sum of a variety of factors. Scott wrote: "A man's occupation, his age, his environment, etc., make a difference in his manner of thinking, and in the motives which prompt him to action."[37] Admen and their consultants applied these principles, from the book and anecdotally by trial and error, effectively to market the abundance of the new industrial age, its corporate providers, and modernity in the process.

As professionals, the ad industry believed they were capable of shaping attitudes. By 1925, product producers were paying large sums of money to advertise. Effectively, the ad agencies created these markets by filling periodicals with ad copy, billboarding town and country and by flooding the airwaves.

The specific strategies they used varied with the circumstance. Generally, they theorized that successful ads slipped into everyday thoughts and imprinted persuasive and friendly messages about products. The trademark, logo, and brand name were the transition devices. Scott asserted that ads had to appeal to emotions more than reason. Favorable associations between the ad and the product would be remembered and cause the person to buy it.

Early on, beginning with magazine ads, women were targeted as the principal household spenders. A dichotomous relationship immediately developed. Convincing women to spend was the goal but: "These men saw their audience as female; fickle, debased, irrational, possessing a natural inferiority complex; having inarticulate longings, low intelligence, and bad taste; and being culturally backward."[38] Consequently, admen believed that women were especially susceptible to emotional appeals. Ads often constructed scenarios that manipulated female emotional desires to be pursued; to be clean/hygenic; to be popular; to be respectable; to be a good mother and household provider. Playing on guilt became a constant undercurrent in ad text/graphics.

Admen attempted to influence women to seek perfection in their lives, and to emulate sound middle-class standards by using modern products. A clean house was as important as a clean body, and products became available, by 1920, for both. Cleanliness for everyone became a marketing concept. Personal care products were the solution to body odor and bad breath. Cosmetics promised to improve appearance, sustain youth, and attract men. Women's deodorant debuted in 1919, and Listerine in 1922. The latter was advertised as a remedy for bad breath. Listerine ads became the model for creating a feeling of personal anxiety that a product could cure. Thus, create a problem in order to sell a product to remedy it. Above all else, the spender had to be convinced that positive social attributes were associated with purchasing these remedies and conveniences. Buying things became a proper thing to do.

Even children could be taught to become spenders. Scott suggested that ads could shape their future buying habits. He believed that childhood associations were especially strong and persistent. Childhood habits would affect adult behavior. Thus, trade cards introduced brand-name advertising to them and from there what they learned would be enhanced when they started reading magazine ads.[39]

Besides gender and age, ads often appealed to social status. Especially during the 1920s ads aimed at adults praised the image of the sophisticated individual who attained success through the use of consumer products. Good hygiene and eating habits, appearance, and style were all purchasable, respectable, social attributes, associated with products.[40] In total, "advertising men undertook to conceptualize the cognitive and emotional make-up, the life situations, the social aspirations, the capabilities and the inadequacies of citizens, the better to create needs among them"[41] in order to sell them products to remedy or satisfy the wants they created.

Thus, the scientific systematization of advertising based on psychological tenets, proliferated during the 1920s. As a result, advertising rose to new levels of influence on America's economic and social behavior. Over the ensuing decades, advertising pervaded contemporary mass communications/media and its importance and influence was well understood, if not accepted.

As early as 1909, Samuel H. Adams wrote: "We live surrounded by the advertisement. There is no hour of waking life in which we are not besought, incited, or commanded to buy something of somebody."[42] The trend continued, and in 1933 Herman Hettinger commented that radio advertising had "one fundamental purpose: To induce the sale of a given commodity, service, or proposition by successfully appealing to the consumer to purchase it."[43]

Conceptualize modernity in terms of its foundations in mass-produced, technically innovative goods. Advertising became the prime method of teaching the public the new world of goods and in convincing them to make contemporary consumer products a new cornucopia of plenty, and significant parts of their lives. The public's acceptance of this created our modern consumption society.

Whether or not advertising was effective, a consuming society evolved during the 1920s. It formed because of a combination of factors: change in distribution of goods, of popular reading and listening habits, and advertising.[44] This new, emerging consumer society was built on the incomes and values of the upper classes and more importantly, on the nascent white-collar middle class consisting of professionals and their support staff. Many of these households could immediately afford the relatively higher-priced, brand-name goods. The urban middle class, especially provided enough spenders to nuture and sustain a consumption-spending culture. Their purchasing habits influenced public taste and they became the trendsetters, in turn affecting how others spent.[45] In effect, they became the harbingers of change.

In 1924, Christine Frederick wrote that wages generally tripled since 1900 and had outpaced the cost of living.[46] As a result, family budgets now can allocate spending to a greater variety of categories, including more on leisure. In this day and age there was more spending than saving: "We are a markedly consuming nation; we may be said to be in an era of family money-spending, to develop absolutely new standards of living, in keeping with modern science and modern outlook on life."[47]

In her analysis, Frederick asserted that bathtubs, cars, phonographs, telephones, and radios are now necessities. She suggested that many more families could afford normal things. These increases in household income allowed them to become "regular American families," now able to buy personal care products, appliances, and more and better-quality clothing. For them, the ability to spend beyond bare necessities was a new thing.

Available numbers seem to agree. After the Great War, consumer prices dropped during the 1920s, and wages trended upward after 1922 for skilled and unskilled workers.[48] From 1900 to 1926, the average increase in real wages for that entire period was 4 percent. That same year, 1926 the average hourly earnings for fourteen million workers was 125 percent greater than the 1914 average.[49] In 1922, the average wage was forty-eight cents per hour; in 1929 it was fifty-six cents.[50] In 1924, 40 percent of American households earned $2,000 annually.[51]

TABLE 3.1
Consumer Prices, 1914–1948

Year	*Price*
1915	72.7
1920	146.5
1925	124.0
1930	113.9
1935	96.9
1940	100.9
1945	128.2

Source: Sayre, *Consumer Prices*, 35–41.

TABLE 3.2
Annual Average Weekly Wages for all Manufacturers.

Year	*All*	*Skilled/Semi-*	*Unskilled*
1914	12.54	14.16	10.71
1920	29.37	33.23	27.09
1925	26.93	30.89	23.74
1929	28.24	32.58	25.49

Source: Ada Beney, *Wages in the United States, 1914–1929*. (New York: National Industrial Conference Board, 1930): 45–47.

If so, then as Benson suggested, women consumers from skilled-labor households began to afford spending in department stores. At the same time, these stores began to structure their price strategies to include more of the shawl trade. A credit revolution in the form of time-payment plans simultaneously occurred and further opened up the world of goods to those who normally could not afford to pay in full. Average household debt during the 1920s increased noticeably: 1900–1916, $70.31; 1920–1929, $175.85; 1930–1939, $185.75.[52] Such consumer credit enhanced buying power and if the standard of living decreased, then, as Frederick Lewis Allen observed, a comfortable standard of living was potentially available on less money.

Many department stores were staffed by what we would call lower-middle-class and working-class clerks. The store as a public place was open to all social classes. In many of them, staff members were directed to give the shawl trade their sense of dignity too. Thus, through working in these stores or browsing, the lower orders were introduced to the notion of acquiring stuff and to the idea of consumption spending. Even though most working-class people could not afford what was on the main floors, department stores sometimes adjusted prices to do business with them. That's where the bargain basement or budget department came from. There, an occasional purchase could be made. The wealthy may have led the way to the spending ideal, but some working-class people participated through seeing the merchandise displayed; viewing ads in public places; watching other people acquire things, and making purchases if credit was available or at reduced prices in the bargain basement or in neighborhood chains like Woolworth. Regardless of means, the ends were similar. The world of goods beckoned, and its call was answered by many. As time went by during the 1920s, that call reached further down the socioeconomic ladder to include the immigrant working class, at first through advertising in pulp magazines and later via radio.

Seemingly, consumption spending appealed to all classes.[53] Covetousness in all forms is perhaps primal behavior. If so, then wanting something and not acquiring it may result in similarly priming and inculcation of attitude. In this case, the attitude was consumer product affiliation and association with its corporate producer. Regardless, whether the item was affordable, its continual and repetitive advertising had the same effect for those that could afford it and those that could not.

The same message went to rural areas via mail order, chain stores, and advertising. By 1930, rural participation in the new society was significant. This process may have begun with mail-order monthlies. *Ladies' World*, *Comfort*, *People's Literary Companion* were tabloids full of product ads, giveaways and some content. Targeted to rural areas, these magazines may have helped set the stage for the later arrival of nationally advertised goods. Mail ordering may have kindled the interest of rural households and whetted their appetites for mass-produced consumer goods. Women's magazines, especially the *LHJ*, actively promoted modern living based on consumption spending. Buying ready-made dry goods and brand-name groceries was pitched as contemporary living. Those that did, as we would later say, were "with it."

The availability of products helped end persistent localism by diluting rural self-sufficiency. The advertised world of goods effectively enticed many country people. Contemporary studies revealed the hinterland farm family was willing to travel to shop, and was acquiring a sense of brand-name recognition. Modernity here meant at least a modest dabbling in the new world of regularly available, reliable, affordable goods, mostly provided by large corporations far away and culturally removed.

In everyday life, the reality of a new consumer society appeared in the results of the Middletown study, done in 1924–1925, by a team led by Robert and Helen Lynd. Their community analysis of Muncie, Indiana, was one of the first attempts to systematically study a community's culture.

The Lynd team considered Middletown to represent homogeneous, small-town, White America. In 1920, less than 5 percent of Muncie's 38,000 people were foreign born. The town was a county seat, contained a college (Ball State), and had a mixed economy hinged on the manufacture of glass products, metalworking, and car parts manufacture.[54]

Sociologically, Middletown reflected a consumer society in microcosm. Although, not to be overgeneralized as typical to every American town, in the least, Muncie offered at least a snapshot of daily reality within that new social ethos.

First and foremost, Middletowners defined themselves by how they made a living and what that income enabled them to buy. The rationale for steady, secure work was utilitarian. The "calling" itself was not as important as the income potential of any given occupation. Both the business and working classes there considered hard work as a means to make enough money to buy good stuff. Working hard to consume was viewed as more important even then leisure time. Making money became the foundation of Muncie's culture.[55]

Since Middletown was mostly working class, installment buying was ubiquitous, and an important means to improve one's standard of living. Attainable things above one's current station in life were held in high esteem. This attitude was defined by striving to obtain the accouterments of middle-class life: a household with car, modern plumbing in the home, "ample" furniture, electrical appliances, telephones, radios, ready-to-wear clothing, "silk underwear and hose," canned and packaged food, and cigarettes.

Clothing and fashion were especially important to Muncie's women. It was considered a significant item in family budgets and an indicator of social position. "Dress to impress" was important to both genders. What was worn in the movies was often imitated.

Advertising delivered the messages of a consumer society to Muncie, and its residents considered it a normal part of everyday life. Women's magazines, especially the *LHJ*, were popular throughout and given credit for introducing modern food preparation and housekeeping methods. The Lynds commented then: "Through these periodicals, as well as through the daily press, billboards, and other channels, modern advertising pounds away at the habits of the Middletown housewife."[56]

By 1930, a consuming society was in place in Middletown and considered normal. Five years later, during the Great Depression, a follow-up analysis by the Lynds concluded that the consumption-spending ethos persisted in Muncie as it was in 1925 with only moderate adjustments caused by hard times.

Middletown author Robert Lynd remarked in the 1933 *Recent Social Trends* that traditional mores had been changed. The Puritan tradition of abstinence and the sinfulness of leisure and spending had been diminished. Family savings and paying cash as common practice was changing to spending more and purchasing on installments. Living within one's means and accepting one's lot in life were being replaced by a desire to make more money in order to spend more.[57]

These changes in the social web that occurred in Muncie were all grounded in the rise of a consumer society. Its particulars were almost entirely constructed by the American corporate sector.

At the time, corporatism's immediate impact was blatantly economic and its social and cultural impact adjunct, complementary. Big Business eventually established the foundations of a consumer society, mass production, and mass distribution, which in turn delivered the concept of corporation to American homes nationwide. It was packaged subtdly as part of the emerging modern consumer society. It was a process that began in the late 1880s, lasting into and surviving the 1930s, and culminating during the consensus decade after World War II. Salesmen, mail-order companies, department and chain stores fueled by national advertising of brand-name products, were its delivery vehicles.

Modernity and its message were accepted during the Roaring Twenties. It was an era of change from the old order to the new, and consumerism defined and accelerated it. Big Business, delivered good stuff and job opportunities. Through mass production and distribution, corporations changed the national economy from a mechanism that labored under scarcity, to a system that conquered it. In the process, the public accepted both the message and its messengers to an extent that the corporate institution survived the Great Depression relatively unscathed.

By 1940 two synergistic processes had permanently altered American society. Workers were taught to accept industrial discipline and to function in an organizational framework. They were also persuaded to become consumers and to participate in a mass culture, defined as a consumer society. These two major constructs, created, managed, and sustained by large corporations, formed the new paradigm for everyday life, modernity.

Notes

1. Philip Scranton reminds us that several industries used batch and custom manufacturing methods instead of the assembly line process.

See "Manufacturing Diversity: Production Systems, Markets, and the American Consumer Society, 1870–1930." *Technology and Culture*, 35(1994): 476–505.

2. Richard S. Tedlow, *New and Improved: The Story of Mass Marketing in America* (Harvard Business School Press, 1996 [1990]): 14.

3. Timothy B. Spears, *100 Years on the Road: The Traveling Salesman in American Culture* (New Haven: Yale University Press, 1995): 56–57; Glenn Porter and Harold C. Livesay, *Merchants and Manufacturers: Studies in the Changing Structure of Nineteenth Century Marketing* (Chicago: Ivan R. Dee, Inc., 1989): 2–4, 162, 224–27; Susan Strasser, *Satisfaction Guaranteed: The Making of the American Mass Market* (New York: Pantheon Books, 1989): 18–19, 59–60.

4. Spears, *100 Years*, 57; Tedlow, *New and Improved*, 14; Ellen G. Garvey, *The Adman in the Parlor: Magazines and the Gendering of Consumer Culture, 1880s to 1910s* (New York: Oxford University Press, 1998): 17; Richard Ohmann, *Selling Culture: Magazines, Markets, and Class at the Turn of the Century* (New York: Verso, 1996): 87–88; Christine Frederick, "New Wealth, New Standards of Living and Changed Family Budgets," *Annals of the American Academy of Political and Social Science* 115 (September 1924): 220.

5. Porter & Livesay, *Merchants and Manufacturers*, 169–172, 176–95, 228–229; Strasser, *Satisfaction Guaranteed*, 83.

6. Porter & Livesay, *Merchants and Manufacturers*, 163–64.

7. Tedlow, *New and Improved*, 23–35; Juliann Sivulka, *Soap, Sex, and Cigarettes: A Cultural History of Advertising* (Belmont, California: Wausworth Publishing Company, 1997): 74–75.

8. Tedlow, *New and Improved*, 36–39, 48, 63, 66–67; Strasser, *Satisfaction Guaranteed*, 184–186.

9. Tedlow, *New and Improved*, 63, 66–67.

10. Strasser, *Satisfaction Guaranteed*, 212; Robert Hendrickson, *The Grand Emporiums: The Illustrated History of America's Great Department Stores* (New York: Stein and Day, 1979): 207-09; David Blanke, *Sowing the American Dream: How Consumer Culture Took Root in the Rural Midwest* (Athens: Ohio University Press, 2000): 189–99.

11. Tedlow, *New and Improved*, 285–86; Strasser, *Satisfaction Guaranteed*, 204; Jackson Lears, *Fables of Abundance: A Cultural History of Advertising* (n.p.: Basic Books, 1994): 205.

12. Hebdrickson, *The Grand Emporiums*, 30, 33, 58; Susan P. Benson, *Counter Cultures: Saleswomen, Managers, and Customers in American Department Stores, 1890–1940* (Urbana: University of Illinois Press, 1986): 13–15, 31.

Note: The term "department store" was first used around 1880 to describe the new kind of store. In 1887, the H.H. Heym Department Store was the first company to use the term in its name. (Hendrickson, *Grand Emporiums*, 33.)

13. Hendrickson, *Grand Emporiums*, 34–38; Pamela Laird, *Advertising Progress: American Business and the Rise of Consumer Marketing* (Baltimore: The Johns Hopkins University Press, 1998): 26–27

14. Benson, *Counter Cultures*, 17–20, 39, 75, 85–89, 102; Bronner, *Consuming Visions*, 110–115, 119–120, 127–128; Norris, *Advertising Transformation*, 18; Strasser, *Satisfaction Guaranteed*, 209; Leach, *Land of Desire*, 133.

15. Note: Silvuka claims that the first self-serve grocery store was Piggly-Wiggly in Memphis, opening in 1916. Customers picked their own groceries from open displays and paid for them at a checkout counter. (*Cultural History*, 9. 145.)

16. Lebhar, *Chain Stores*, 98–101.

17. Schnierov, *The Dream*, 2–6, 75–77; Garvey, *Adman*, 9; Norris, *Advertising Transformation*, 38, Ohmann, *Selling Culture*, 28–29.

18. Schnierov, *The Dream*, 4.

19. Tom Pendergast, *Creating the Modern Man: American Magazines and Consumer Culture, 1900–1950* (New York: Columbia University Press, 2000): 51–58; Martha L. Olney, *Buy Now, Pay Later: Advertising, Credit, and Consumer Durables in the 1920s* (Chapel Hill: University of North Carolina Press, 1991): 138–139, 183.

20. Schneirov, *The Dream*, 103–104, 123–124, 255–259; Norris, *Advertising Transformation*, xvi–xvii.

21. Pendergast, *Creating*, 30.

22. Herman S. Hettinger, *A Decade of Radio Advertising* (Chicago: The University of Chicago Press, 1933): v, 173–174; Susan Smuylan, *Selling Radio: The Commercialization of American Broadcasting, 1920–1934* (Washington: Smithsonian Institution Press, 1994): 13–14.

23. Hettinger, *Radio Advertising*, 42.

24. In 1870 there were 121 trademarks registered; 10,000 in 1906 (Ohmann, *Selling Culture*, 101.)

25. Emily P. Meade, "The Place of Advertising in Modern Business," *Journal of Political Economy*, 9(March 1901): 231.

26. A brand name derived from the use of labels on crates of tobacco, a practice similar to livestock branding. (Silvuka, *Cultural History*, 48)

27. Silvuka, *Cultural History*, 72.

28. Garvey, *Adman*, 7.

29. Laird, *Advertising Progress*, 170, 284–286, 311–112.

30. Ohmann, *Selling Culture*, 96.

31. Scanlan, *Inarticulate Longings*, 202–207.

32. John M. O'Donnell, *The Origins of Behaviorism: American Psychology, 1870–1920* (New York: New York University Press, 1985): 203–26; Kerry W. Buckley, *Mechanical Man: John Broadus Watson and the Beginnings of Behaviorism* (New York: The Guilford Press, 1989): x, 74–75.

33. Walter D. Scott, *The Theory of Advertising* (New York: Garland Publishing, Inc., Reprint edition, 1985 [1903]): 6–12.

34. Scott, *Theory of Advertising*, 26.

35. Kuna, "Suggestion," 347–51.

36. For example, in 1939 copywriter Robert L. May created a Christmas promotion for Montgomery Ward. It featured a red-nosed reindeer first called Roll, then Reginald, and finally Rudolph. (Hendrickson, *Grand Emporiums*, 230.)

37. Scott, *Theory of Advertising*, 204.

38. Olney, *Buy Now*, 177–78.

39. Scott, *Theory of Advertising*, 43, 53–54; Garvey, *Adman*, 16–19, 25–26, 44–50.

Note: Ad agencies were aware that World War I testing revealed a relatively dumb general adult population. The agencies also held the notion that the general public lacked initiative and was lethargic, conformist, and culturally deficient. Typically, these groundlings, rarely contemplated more than what was in front of them; seeking mostly immediate gratification. (See Roland Marchand's *Advertising the American Dream.*) Reflecting back while typing this, the typical American seems certainly to be an expert in two things: eating and spending money.

40. Pendergast, *Creating*, 144, 148; Silvuka, *Cultural History*, 149, 163–164, 204; Norris, *Advertising Transformation*, 168.

41. Ohmann, *Selling Culture*, 116.

42. Samuel H. Adams, "The New World of Trade: Part I, The Art of Advertising," *Collier's*, 43 (May 22, 1909): 13.

43. Hettinger, *Radio Advertising*, 17.

44. Samuel Strauss, "Things in the Saddle," *Atlantic Monthly*, 279 (November 1924): 577–78; Daniel Horowitz, *The Morality of Spending: Attitudes Toward the Consumer Society in America, 1875–1940* (Chicago: Ivan R. Dee, Publisher, Elephant Paperback edition, 1992 [1985]): xx.

45. Lynn Dumenil, *The Modern Temper: American Culture and Society in the 1920s* (New York: Hill & Wang, 1995): 78–79; Benson, *Counter Cultures*, 75; Garvey, *Adman*, 18.

46. Frederick worked as a columnist and consultant at the *Ladies Home Journal* from 1912 to 1919, specializing in Taylorizing households (Scanlon, *Inarticulate Longings*, 61–62).

47. Frederick, "New Wealth," 80.

Indeed, the average saved percent of disposable income decreased during this era: 1869–1897, 3.2 percent saved; 1898–1916, 5.5 percent; 1922–1929, 3.9 percent; 1930–1940, 2.6 percent (Olney, *Buy Now*, 50).

48. Robert A. Sayre, *Consumer Prices, 1914–1948* (New York: National Industrial Conference Board, Inc., 1948): 35–41; Albert Rees, *Real Wages in Manufacturing, 1890–1914* (Princeton: Princeton University Press, 1961): 4; Paul H. Douglas, *Real Wages in the United States, 1890–1926* (Boston: Houghton Mifflin Company, 1930): 108; David Brody, *Workers in Industrial America: Essays on the Twentieth Century Struggle* (New York: Oxford University Press, 1980): 62; Ada M. Beney, *Wages, Hours, and Employment in the United States, 1914–1936* (New York: National Industrial Conference Board, 1936): 44–47, 52–55; Whitney Coombs, *The Wages of Unskilled Labor in Manufacturing Industries in the United States, 1890–924* (New York: Columbia University Press, 1926): 99, 116, 119; David M. Kennedy, *Freedom From Fear: The American People in Depression and War, 1929–1945* (New York: Oxford University Press, 1999): 22.

49. Douglas, *Real Wages*, 581–86.

50. Brody, *Workers*, 62.

51. Silvuka, *Cultural History*, 142.

Of Note: As counterpoints, Elizabeth Cohen, in *Making a New Deal*, suggested that the prosperity of the 1920s did not necessarily trickle down the social scale (p. 102). Jurgen Kocka, concurred, in *White Collar Workers in America*, stating: "The prosperity of the 1920s has undoubtedly been exaggerated by contemporaries and historians looking back from the vantage point of the severe depression that followed . . . broad sections of the population lived on less than contemporaries defined as the minimum necessary for existence, the poverty line, or an 'American standard" (p. 166).

52. Olney, *Buy Now*, 87–89.

53. Most historians and social scientists seem to accept the belief that good times after 1921 were widely available to all social classes. However, many of them have not explained what happened to those tenement dwellers of the Jacob Riis and Jane Addams era. Did wage increases enable them to spend and did advertising, catalogs, and department and chain stores create desire? For a dissenter, see Elizabeth Cohen's essay in *Chicago History* 18 (Summer,1989): 22–39, titled, "On Their Own Terms: Mass Culture and the Working Class World."

54. Robert and Helen M. Lynd, *Middletown: A Study in American Culture* (New York: Harcourt, Brace & World, Inc., 1956 edition [1929]): 8–9, 21, 39, 93.

55. Robert and Helen M. Lynd, *Middletown in Transition: A Study in Cultural Conflicts* (New York: Harcourt, Brace & World, Inc., 1965 edition [1937]): 7; Lynds, *Middletown*, 21, 49, 73–76, 80, 84, 87.

56. Ibid., 158.

57. *RST*, 867.

4

Seated Around the Monolith

The Organized People of Plenty—1950s

American life, defined in the 1920s, as "only yesterday," teetered during the Great Depression. As the national economy spiraled down, many Americans lost jobs, small businesses, farms, domiciles, families and self-respect. Hard times rocked the very foundations of our way of life, and our belief in a strong economic future and progressive destiny. By 1932, Hoover's *laissez faire* state and its foundation ideology had failed. The body politic turned it aside. A few months later, in March 1933, "a man who couldn't walk was about to carry a crippled nation." That year, the state of our nation was not so good.

In 1929, the unemployment rate was 3.2 percent. When the economy bottomed out during the winter of 1932–1933, there was at least 25 percent unemployment; an estimated range of 8–20 million people were unemployed during the decade. In 1939, the unemployment rate was 17.2 percent; 1940 it was 15 percent. William L. O'Neill wrote: "In 1940 there were 9 million men still out of work, and it was not until 1943 that they were fully absorbed.[1]

For the employed, many had their wages and hours slashed. The lives of many on the lower rungs, shattered, by futile job hunting, eviction, malnutrition, and destitution. Higher up the socioeconomic ladder, retrenchment accompanied befuddlement. Those who could've known what was wrong, didn't, and the public- and private-sector powers that be did little. Consequently, President Franklin D. Roosevelt and his New Deal programs slowed the negative spiral, ameliorated hard times for many, and helped mass society, and perhaps capitalism, survive. Mobilization and war, as the depression decade drew to a close, became the final cure for our moribund economy.

The ability to survive and cope with the all-consuming ravages of the downturn, depended, generally, on one's economic power and social status. At the top of the socioeconomic pyramid, Big Business rode out the economic storm effectively in most cases. Our largest corporations sustained themselves, and in many instances, profitably, after 1933.

An example of this was Gulf Oil. In 1929, it had assets of $340 million and revenues of $246 million, from 90 million barrels of oil products. Sobel reported:

> The firm was well integrated and strong. Gulf service stations were in all parts of the nation, and its petroleum sources, both domestic and foreign, were more than adequate for its refinery runs. Thus, the company was able to absorb a 23 million dollar operating loss in 1931 and continue research and exploration activities even though sales, production, and prices had declined.[2]

Using other tactics, several corporations resisted price slashing when demand declined. Instead, they attempted to maintain prices, cut production, and lay off workers.[3]

Overall, Corporate America, financially fortified and institutionally established, weathered the Great Depression, surviving it more so than succumbing. It was, as Frederick Lewis Allen observed: "The monster corporation had a bigger place than ever before in the dim sun of American business."[4]

At the same time, Americans, generally, by then, were hooked on consumption spending, thus, the economic downturn did not destroy their affiliation with big businesses' products. By then, corporations provided things that were often technological wonders, both big and small, such as automobiles and radios respectively.

Corporations appealed to our innate sense of curiosity for the new, the novel, and modern. Big business offered a greater degree of job security. It provided satisfaction to our sense of acquisitiveness, as promoted by their advertisers. As a result, when economic conditions worsened, culpability was not overtly directed toward the producers of all this change. Instead, financiers failed, and businessmen did take their hits, but the relationship between people and the concept of corporation suffered less.

For example, by 1930, Sears, Roebuck & Company catered to the American middle class by supplying their demands and aspirations for household basics and nice things. As a result, the firm gained a loyal following, and apparently, some people were still spending. Consequently, Sears experienced a one-year loss in 1932. For the rest of the decade, its sales value and profits increased. Throughout the depression, Sears expanded its operations. In 1930, they had 338 stores; 428 stores in 1935; 595 stores in 1940. Richard Tedlow observed: "It was the allegiance of this customer that helped Sears weather the depression so well and that positioned it for its explosive growth after World War II."[5] In hindsight, during the Great Depression, as Sears went, so too did the rest of corporate America.

From another perspective, consider Middletown reflecting the national ethos. There, they still wanted what the corporate sector provided. The Lynds observed that the depression did not significantly change aspirations and desires. In fact, they wrote that American culture was a "culture hypnotized by the gorged stream of new things to buy."[6] That desire to spend, became the impetus to sustain what was available and to look to the future for better times. Americans seemed willing to work pragmatically within existing institutions.

During the Great Depression, Americans did not attempt to dismantle their economic system. By then, they had accepted the monumental changes in business. Corporations provided jobs and desirable products. Americans wanted more of both, a return to the new, modern normalcy.

Mobilization and world war finally conquered the Great Depression. It made many Americans believe the good times would hopefully continue in peacetime. The chronic unemployment and seasonal discontinuities of the early twentieth-century world of work and the devastation of the Great Depression vanished. During and after the war, steady employment became more and consistently available, and, as a result, wages and earning power trended upward. During and after the war, steady work became more and consistently available. Unemployment significantly dropped, and wages and hours increased. Incomes and spending power went up.

TABLE 4.1
Family Income Levels as a percentage.

$ Annually	*1935–1936*	*1941*	*1944*	*1946*	*1950*
Under $1k	43.5	29.0	10.7	8.8	7.6
1k to 1,199	34.2	29.9	19.8	17.6	15.1
3k to 3,999	4.4	9.8	18.9	19.8	17.4
5k to 7,499	1.6	2.8	11.7	13.0	17.5
More than 10k	0.9	1.3	3.0	4.1	5.6

Source: Compiled from, Selma Goldsmith, "Size Distribution of Income Since the Mid-Thirties," *The Review of Economics and Statistics*, 36(February 1954): 4–11

At war's end, Americans wanted consumer goods, houses, and cars. In *American High*, William L. O'Neill boldly proclaimed: "When peace came, spending would replace saving, launching the greatest period of sustained economic growth in history and physically remaking the nation."[7]

During the war, 16,354,000 Americans served in the military. In its last months, there were 12,123,455 on duty. As the Rising Sun waned, through the smoke, fire, and ash of atomic destruction, the "war without mercy" abruptly ended. As Americans vacated a war-torn world, they were steeled by depression and war. Together, they would become optimistic, ambitious, hardworking and determined. Again!

As the new American sun dawned in 1946, those millions of Americans came home. They didn't know they were already on a journey that would make them the greatest generation, for reasons then, they couldn't imagine, and for us today, almost too bewildering to contemplate.

At the same time, during the late 1940s, another kind of citizen, the big business corporation, was also on the move. The evolution of a corporate-fueled modern society resumed. As Americans demobilized, they did not know they were on the brink of a new dawn of prosperity and consensus, a new era that would be based on consumption spending.[8]

Early in the twentieth century, economist Simon N. Patten was one of the first to suggest abundance could replace scarcity. He suggested the emerging industrial order could potentially produce enough goods to eliminate want, to provide for all people.[9] Patten wrote:

> Here is the basis of a new civilization; here is evidence that economic forces can sweep away poverty, banish misery, and by giving men work bring forth right and enduring character within the race.... Economic forces—if dynamic—should form steps by which men would readily mount from low planes of well-being to higher ones.[10]

However, what Patten prophesized did not happen during the Roaring Twenties because incomes for all did not increase enough to enable ubiquitous, continual, mass-consumption spending. Instead, the national economy, driven by speculative growth and overproduction, crested, teetered at the top of the wave, and then tumbled deeply into what became the Great Depression. For many, it took mobilization and war for the U.S. economy to provide jobs and increased income sufficient to reconcile scarcity and want. The abundance Patten envisioned emerged during wartime. Its cornucopia poured forth afterward, during the 1950s. The postwar boom positively affected all but the bottom social stratum. The average unemployment for the 1950s was 4.6 percent, and recessions occurred during 1953–1954, and 1957–1958, with less deleterious effects. That postwar prosperity did not supply a utopic uplift for all, but, it did transform American life, pushing it in directions hardly envisioned from the bottom of the economic trough, in 1933.

As a prime mover, firmly established, the technologically modern, mass-producing corporate sector offered lots of jobs. High production levels fueled by advertising's mass-consumption ethos, created and sustained steady employment and relatively secure incomes. Consequently, standard of living, overall, increased. Many households had more disposable income, cash to spend, and good stuff was more than available to buy. The middle and upper strata gorged themselves while those still mired in racially caused or rural poverty looked on from the outside. Those who could spend, did. The resulting boom was fueled by purchases for housing, cars, and durables.

As flush times occurred, and prosperity persisted, we became a nation of consumers more than ever before. Now, the largesse formerly available only to the better off and well-to-do, finally trickled down the socioeconomic ladder, almost as Simon N. Patten and Edward Filene envisioned. What had been luxuries to previous generations became necessities, as the average family income doubled between 1941 and 1969. For many, a chance of prosperity arrived at their postwar doorsteps; the front stoops of immigrants and their children, and even some of the other urban masses.

Consumption spending increased. For after all, acquiring things might be more a human instinct than cultural construct. If they weren't buying modern stuff for the first time, they were replacing what they already had with bigger or better good stuff. Big business provided lots of things to buy. Electric appliances became passé because everyone had them now. Thus, the contemporary kitchen, for example, became an advertiser's dream, and a modern status symbol for the contemporary household. In 1950, four of five households had refrigerators; seven of ten had stoves; seven of ten, washing machines; three of five, vacuum cleaners. Americans bought 75 percent of all appliances produced worldwide. New stuff became available: vinyl floors, telephones with buttons, stereos, washer-dryer sets, electric blankets, floor polishers, and electric can openers, among others. Those with smaller incomes bought smaller things: alcohol, packaged food, personal care products, cigarettes, etc.

If something cost more than what they had, they got it anyway, on credit. Regardless, they got it, and that's what made them happy, to have and to hold, to acquire. To possess became the new national pleasure and pastime. In 1958, David Riesman wrote:

> Americans resent being deprived of the things they are supposed to have, and advertising tempts us with the halo of association rather than with the objects per se . . . a quite expensive 'standard package' of durable goods has now become a necessity . . . the basic stockpile on which our society's dynamism has rested—the stockpile of new and exhilarating wants.[11]

In the process, consumption spending also became a significant factor determining and indicating stratum, status, and social class.

In these new, modern times, it no longer mattered if a current desire was affordable. There were means to acquire, to satisfy that desire. Credit! Installment buying became the open door to the good life; the treasure house of good stuff corporations provided, despite the fact that disposable income might not be keeping up with the managed demand of a consuming society. From 1946 to 1960, consumer debt increased from $8.3 billion to $56.1 billion, and from 1952 to 1956, consumer debt increased from $27.4 billion, to $42.5 billion. From 1954, to 1960, installment debt increased from $14 billion to $43 billion. Spending was now more important than saving, and lenders abounded.

The modern concept of consumer credit developed during the 1920s from its nineteenth-century roots when commercial merchants did business on credit. Also, in 1857, Singer Sewing Machine company offered installment purchasing terms: five dollars down payment and three dollars per month. Later, during the Roaring Twenties, installment buying was a contemporary marketing innovation, a privilege, and modern convenience offered by certain retailers, car manufacturers, and banks; personal finance companies did direct loans. Prior to World War II, these businesses cautiously increased the amounts of credit extended to the general public. This trend continued into the 1930s despite hard times. Then, the credit industry, and retailers such as Montgomery Ward, catered to those who still had jobs. For example, aggregate loans for household durable goods increased from $199 million, in 1933, to 1.6 billion, in 1939. In 1929, 208 banks made such loans; in 1935, 685 banks loaned money. Four years later, banks surpassed small-loan companies in lending, and one year later, the banking industry passed installment-finance companies. Ironically, no less, as Lendol Calder wrote:

> Thus, during the black years of the Great Depression the logic and legitimacy of consumer credit was perfected, not destroyed; the popularity of consumer borrowing was enhanced not diminished; and consumer credit acquired the institutional make up that after the Depression and another war, would make so many American dreams come true.[12]

During those bleak years, consumers generally tried to keep up payments. Large-scale defaults and repossessing did not occur. In fact, by 1940, the U.S. Census Bureau reported the general public sustained a good effort to pay off outstanding debt, but then, in turn, bought some more.

After wartime, credit controls ceased, and installment buying became a basic, and more than respectable means of enjoying a good life through consumption spending. (Credit cards also became available: Diner's Club, in 1950, and American Express, in 1958.) Calder suggested that consumer credit became the cement that held the components of a consumer society together.[13] Historian Daniel Boorstin concurred: "It was hardly an exaggeration to say that the American standard of living was bought on the installment plan."[14] Also, Gary Cross suggested the time between 1950 and the early 1960s was "the golden age of American commercialism."[15] And Sivulka: "This was a time when consumers could be persuaded that a lifestyle might be bought on credit, and they were encouraged to own two cars and several television sets and to shop excessively."[16]

Thus, the Greatest Generation engaged the new normalcy during the 1950s. They participated in a renewed, refreshed, and invigorating civilian life, now fortified by steady employment, opportunity, and consistent and greater income levels; access to a cornucopia of consumer goods, and eligible to have it all, assisted, if necessary, by lines of credit. Thomas Hine delightfully declared:

> The decade from 1954 to 1964 was one of history's greatest shopping sprees as many Americans went on a baroque bender and adorned their mass-produced houses, furniture, and machines with accouterments of the space age and of the American frontier.[17]

For that generation, and their children (the first Boomers!), it might have been indeed, an "American High," brought to their doorsteps through advertising, especially on television, and by the castle on the hill, the big business corporation.

Early in the corporate century, during the 1920s, retailer Edward Filene wrote prophetically about mass production and consumption spending:

> The business man of the future must produce prosperous customers as well as saleable goods. His whole business policy must look forward by creating great buying power among the masses. Otherwise, mass production cannot succeed. The business man of the future must fill the pockets of the workers and the consumers before he can fill his pockets.

And from there, on businessmen:

> They control the progress of the country simply because this is an industrial nation and their hands happen to be on the levers of power. . . . What business men think and do about production, distribution, and consumption is therefore the most important single factor to be considered in any study of the possible arrest or advancement of social progress. . . . the key to social progress lies in their hands.[18]

Corporations fulfilled the role, Filene described, providing mass-produced goods and jobs for what Bensmen and Vidich labeled, a "New Society." (Even during the depression, Keynesian economist Alan Hansen predicted that increased consumption spending would foster prosperity. Its importance was the subject of public comment. For example, Herbert Gold wrote in 1957: "The life of consuming requires a neuter anxiety, and the pressure to conform, to watch our cues, to consume, makes us all the same—we are customers—only with slightly different gadgets."[19] Business-oriented observers, such as

Fortune, huzzahed this new, strong, American market. They claimed, "The U.S. is becoming a one-class market of prosperous middle-income people."[20] Indeed, "middle," seems to be the buzzword of that decade. Writing in the Consensus ethos, public commentators en masse extolled the concept of middle income and middle-class life. They created this huge new bell-curve-like hump, where blue-collar union tradesmen or assembly-line operators making scale, "good money," could own a home in Levittown; stock it full of good stuff; own a car or two, and use one of them for a drive-to vacation. In the contemporary public view, "working class," "lower socioeconomic status" occupations and concomitant lifestyles have now flowed upward to what was becoming a nebulous, fuzzy-bounded, all-encompassing, ubiquitous middle class. Burleigh Gardner, writing in *Industrial Man* (p. 483), near the end of the 1950s, defined the "middle majority" to include white-collar workers, small business proprietors, and semiskilled and service workers. At the same time, professionals like doctors and engineers, the traditional, original middle class, labeled themselves in the same category. The army of clerical workers whose wages were probably at the lower end of the income scale also displayed the trappings, lived the life, espoused the same consensus values, and asserted themselves as middle class.

IBM engineers, GM assembly-line workers, or Mutual of Omaha receivables clerks: They all considered themselves to be middle-class, average Americans (especially if they lived in the suburbs). A bell curve representing this attitude and self-perception would probably not have discernable tailing edges.

Postwar prosperity broadened the label "middle class," destroying its previous definition in the process. (The connotations, though, forcefully and confidently persisted.) Now, in the 1950s, middle class was a cultural and economic label and social construct. More money per household meant more consumption spending; acquiring a greater amount and variety of goods. Status from possessions clumped together an accountant, a foreman, and an assembly-line worker. Regardless of the blue or white collar, an occupation's real income defined class position.

This socioeconomic melding of different occupations fostered a more universal, cultural clumping. Both "collars" could often afford the same status-producing things, thus aspiring and seeking common, similar products, their symbolism, and the psychological satisfaction they provided. In common, they sought, learned, and often acquired similar values, norms, protocols, and behavior, just like accumulating the cornucopia of plenty available that decade. The cultural, social behavior might have been subtly, subliminally, indirectly acted on. The display and use of good stuff, manifestations of that common prosperity, was overt. All of this was corporate derived.

Peter F. Drucker asserted in *The New Society* (1949) that corporations created two new social classes: a ruling elite of corporate and union executives, and a new middle class consisting of, "technicians, professions, foreman, accountants, middle-managers, etc., a class enjoying both considerable power and great social prestige, yet employed, dependent and subordinate."[21] The latter group, he predicted, would "be the decisive social development of mass production society."[22] Writing later, in 1959, in the *Status Seekers*, Vance Packard credited corporations with creating the new social-class parameters via its increasing levels of managers and their accompanying status. He also commented that by the mid-1950s, there were more people wearing white collars than blue.

Regardless of nomenclature or classification, this idea during the 1950s became truth and imitative to most Americans. Consequently, this belief in the new middle class became, in hindsight, an economic, social, cultural, and political revolution. Behind the curtain, driving it forward, the engine was the big business corporation.

Over the ensuing decades, the American public assigned an affilial relationship with the corporate institution, the monolith, because like the gods of the past, it too, provided security, prosperity, and plenty, fulfilling the wants, needs, and desires of those who cast their allegiance in that direction.

The desires corporations fostered in the American public were fueled by advertising, as mentioned in the last chapter, during the 1920s. Adding television to print and radio broadcasting, advertising agencies created an American lifestyle that revolved around the world of goods available on the now fully reconverted civilian market.

During the 1950s, the advertising industry was a significant part of the corporate, private sector. Much of it centered in New York City: J. Walter Thompson; Batten, Burton Durstine & Osborn (BBDO); Young and Rubicam; Leo Burnett; Oglivy & Mather; Doyle, Dane & Bernham (DDB), and others became that industry's most famous agencies.

Their job was to sell to the public and they considered this hard work, despite their glamorous and controversial reputation. (The industry debilitated the health of many who stayed in it.) Creating ad campaigns was time consuming, nerve-wracking, and crisis-ridden. New ideas must be constantly created, and that process extended beyond an eight-hour workday. The best admen were always working; always thinking about information and how to use it to produce new or improved ideas to persuade people to buy.

Ad agencies provided services mostly to producers of groceries, soap, toiletries, cigarettes, cars, and alcoholic beverages. For, example, in 1956, the largest product advertisers were GM, Proctor & Gamble, Ford, General Foods, GE, Colgate-Palmolive, Lever Brothers, Chrysler, National Dairy Products

(Kraft, Parkay, Sealtest, Hydrox, Breyers), RCA, Westinghouse, and Distillers Corporation. These companies accounted for 15 percent of total advertising billings that year.

Advertising agencies used a variety of established, controversial, and risky methods. The Bates Agency used teams of admen and specialists, and emphasized product-testing to verify manufacturers' product claims. The Ogilvy agency specialized in prestigious products, so they used snob appeals in their campaigns. The Norman agency used motivational-research techniques, which sought hidden value that products could bring to people; so did the McCann agency. Some ad companies used a certain method or philosophy exclusively, adopting the particular campaign to the method. Other agencies did the opposite, attempting to pick a method compatible with the product.[23]

Keep in mind, these are large, sophisticated, institutions, using a variety of disparate talent to create psychological methods designed to effectively persuade a mass audience made up of a wide variety of individuals to buy, to affiliate to a brand name or a cause and a corporation.

During the 1950s, increasing their use of social-science experts, these agencies offered a world of goods, an American lifestyle based on the accumulation of good stuff. The text and images they used to sell consumer products, at the same time, conveyed and impressed upon their audience, the idea of using consumer goods to add lots of twigs to the nest, to enhance home and hearth. Both print and broadcast advertising presented an American life based on homeownership, cars, and possessions, as means to supposedly express and announce individuality, style, status, and happiness. In doing so, the ad agencies both shaped and reacted to the reality they were creating and living in. Socialized by the ideas they created, the admen seemed to be constructing a culture that wound up reflecting the ideas they were selling to the market. As this process accelerated after World War II, the culture they were making and selling became the "American Dream." The mirror and its reflection became reality.

Recall that ad agencies used social scientists early on, such as John Watson as a prime example. This trend continued over the decades. By the 1950s, psychologists worked in agency research departments with other professionals such as marketing and media specialists. They all worked together, trying to figure out human nature, and to use those secrets to develop a persuasive method of selling. They target-marketed to specific groups. They took Lloyd Warner's advice and tried to deliver an effective message to "Mrs. Middle Majority." She was a methodological composite of white and blue collar, now calling themselves middle class.

The ad agencies were grandly successful. (Again, look around you and recall your past. How many jingles can you remember? How much commercial syntax do you imitate in your speech? "Been there, done that.") They are orchestrating consumption spending during the prosperous postwar era. In the long run, beginning in the 1920s, they succeeded to the extent that "ads even altered peoples' lives down to the smallest details, shaping such daily habits as drinking orange juice; brushing one's teeth; taking a bath/shower, and using deodorant."[24] From hindsight, the advertising industry might have been second to mass-production manufacturers in creating and shaping the American Way of the 1950s.

Advertising corporations used a variety of scientific and anecdotal methods to create campaigns. For part of the1950s, Motivational Research became a controversial trend. This method emphasized the unconscious process that might influence buying behavior.

What John Watson did for Behaviorism, Ernest Dichter did for Motivational Research (MR), becoming its chief advocate and spokesman. Dichter suggested that human emotions were a normal part of thinking and cognition, and that to label emotion as a negative social construct was a distortion of reality. He did not fear emotions. Instead of trying to control emotions, Dichter considered them when expressed through desire, as "raw material." He accepted the importance of emotion and believed it could be worked to persuade people to change attitudes and beliefs; to vote certain ways; to advocate causes, and to spend money on good stuff, among others.[25] Dichter was unabashed in his defense of MR, when Vance Packard (*The Hidden Persuaders*), and others, questioned its use. Dichter argued that persuasion was a normal social process, and "educating" people to buy, even to spend freely, was not negative. He asserted consumption spending enhanced and "fulfilled life," and that was good. (As a spokesman, he was an advertiser's dream, apparently.) Rightfully so, he insisted that spending, more than not, positively affected the individual, the community, the economy, and society. All these things were, thus, good.

When admen used Dichter's version of Motivational Research, they attempted to discover the raw, basal causes for making decisions. They interviewed test subjects to try to figure out what caused people to buy what, assuming the real reason were rooted in the unconscious and often unknown to the individual. They used depth interviewing. Test subjects were not asked a battery of questions. Instead, they were encouraged to talk; to give their reaction, their opinion about the topic being tested. The discussion technique usually consisted of: first-time use, best and worst comparisons, and descriptions of routine, life experiences. Test subjects were also asked to associate feelings toward everyday objects such as office equipment and to differentiate normally used products. Throughout, the test subjects were encouraged to express themselves freely.

Agency researchers examined material culture (stuff!), and tried to determine what meanings these had to the interviewees. The things we use everyday have meaning and they elicit reactions.[26] For example, when setting up a campaign to sell baby food, they interviewed 350 mothers and determined that convenience and the food's taste were more important than the nutritional value. Appealing to the latter would have been insufficient to effectively sell the product. Convincing the mother that the child would like the food—not spit it out—thus making feeding easier, was the predicted correct way to promote baby food products. Researchers believed that convenience was more important than motherly love (nutritional value).

In 1954, George H. Smith's book, *Motivation Research in Advertising and Marketing*, summarized some of the published findings from MR. Some examples: Many people like to go to see movies besides watching TV, because at the movies, the big screen and uninterrupted play made the story more real and thus made it easier to role-play, inserting oneself into the film's plot by relating to one of its characters.

Also, packaged food should be sold as a way to improve homemaking, especially efficiency. Surprisingly, convenience eliminated negative feelings about inefficient homemaking. Within that context, instant coffee, for example, caused mixed reactions. It was convenient, caffeine-free, and easy to make iced coffee. However, it *was* fake coffee, not as good as the real thing, and it implied lazy housekeeping.

Home appliances influenced self-satisfaction, status enhancement, improved home life, convenience, and a way to be creative. Flour must be white, a sign of purity. Wine symbolized celebration and luxury. The sterling silver next to the wineglass was also a luxury, particularly a way to show off status. Its prestige value was more important than its utility.

All of these conclusions came from testing the emotional reaction to the object, gleaned from analogy, the syntax and posture of the respondent. Researchers then asserted that successful ad campaigns had to assign and imply emotional value and subliminal, unconscious symbolic appeal to the prospective buyer. This included feelings of sex, security, social acceptance, success, fashion, style, taste, luxury, etc.

For examples, the then, "eye-popping" ads for Maidenform bras were supposed to appeal to women's latent tendencies toward exhibitionism. Also, women didn't like to admit to dying their hair, hence, "Does she or doesn't she." Cake mixes originally were just-add-water. Researchers found that such suggested laziness. It was too easy and connotated poor cooking ability. Instead, cake mixes were redesigned to add milk and eggs. Hathaway shirtmakers advertised only in the *New Yorker*, using an eye-patched male, set in sophisticated scenes. The latent image sold the shirt. It was successful when measured by sales increases after the campaign started.

As the industry did its work, the trend over the decade emphasized the image of the product more so than its features. Over time, ad agency researchers concluded that the symbolic value or emotional appeal a product evoked was often a greater influence on the public's decision to buy, then the product's usefulness. Once advertisers figured out these connections to the objects, then, they used that knowledge to associate a brand name to a human emotion.

Indeed, these images and the symbols they invoked, or even created, became icons of American life: homeownership; a house filled with good stuff, cars, fashionable clothes, and backyard accouterments.

Motivational Research was a new trend for a while. Eventually it garnered followers and detractors, and wound up as another available resource competing with already established methods such as reason-why/rational appeals and hard-sell techniques.

Then, was the advertising industry successful? Ask Betty Friedan. She wrote in *The Feminine Mystique*:

> They are guilty of persuading housewives to stay home, mesmerized in front of a television set, their nonsexual human needs unnamed, unsatisfied, drained by the sexual sell into buying things. . . . They have done this so successfully, employing the techniques and concepts of modern social science, and transporting them into those deceptively simple, clever, outrageous ads and commercials, that an observer of the American scene today accepts the fact that the great majority of American women have no ambition other than to be housewives. . . . They are responsible for keeping them there [in the home] . . . they have seared the feminine mystique deep into every woman's mind, and into the minds of her husband, her children, her neighbors.[27]

Another contemporary observer, Vance Packard, critiqued advertising's implications even further; a potpourri of quotes:

> Advertising in general is a manipulative force. It has become a major instrument of social control in much of the western world. . . . The massiveness of the behavior-molding effort of advertising can be seen in the viewing of television commercials. . . . (Ads) modify the life-style and attitudes. They seek narcissistic, more status-conscious, and more prone to live against the future. The goal is to create more insatiable consumers. . . . Control is being achieved over human actions, moods, wishes, thoughts. . . . The reshaping of man now under way can occur within a few decades.[28]

In *The Hidden Persuaders*, Packard asserted:

> Sell the children on your brand name and they will insist that their parents buy no other. . . . The potency of television in conditioning youngsters to be loyal enthusiasts of a product, whether they are old enough to consume it or not, became indisputable early in the fifties . . . the merchandisers sought to groom

> children not only as future consumers but as shills who would lead or 'club' their parents into the salesroom.[29]

Thus, big business ad agencies institutionally marshaled professionally trained resources to create ad campaigns. Pooling the talent of psychologists, nutritionists, product specialists, cooks, scientist-specialists, marketers, writers, designers, etc., how would they not be successful in the long run? Why wouldn't the typical consumer be easily swayed by one of these agencies to pick a product instead of some other? The institutional application of talent and experience would most likely consistently create ad copy and campaigns that would be successful.

The advertising industry was also successful on another level. Ad agencies significantly contributed to the construction of postwar American culture.

Using mass media, the ad industry fostered the acceptance of an American lifestyle based on the use of trademarked, brand-name goods. (As you read this, look around you and recall your home as you were growing up.) The admen succeeded, using a combination of systematic, social-scientific persuasion techniques that associated lifestyle and other social attributes to corporate consumer symbolism.

Throughout this process, contemporary eggheads debated consumption spending as a trend, behavior, and value among other issues. They questioned among themselves (up in the ivory tower where few could hear or notice them), the changes from a production to consumption ethos. They worried about advertising manipulating people to spend their money for stuff they didn't have, or in many cases, didn't have to have. All the while, the concerned critics did not recognize as David Potter did in *People of Plenty*, that acquisitiveness and possessing are human constants, perhaps even genetically imprinted, base drives. If so, the world of goods that big business laid at our doorsteps, front stoops, and driveways, was so immediately appealing because the attraction of good stuff was not necessarily completely manipulated, or manufactured, or managed, rather, it was a natural human desire. The social scientists working in the ad industry might have missed this idea, or refused to accept it. Nevertheless, their success even in the 1920s, was immediate. Advertising good stuff worked because it tripped deeply embedded human constructs, and previously learned inclinations to acquire and possess.

As a result, the American Character was also altered, a psychological and social revolution that went deeply beyond the obvious economic change. The admen intended only to sell goods. They probably were not aware or concerned with the indirect results, or latent changes, that consumption spending fostered.

During the 1950s, the advertising industry also forged the filial relationship between the individual, as consumer, and the provider of good stuff, the big business corporation. This relationship originally emerged during the 1920s, survived the Great Depression, and ascended to new heights during the 1950s. It is true, as David Potter suggested in *People of Plenty.* He wrote then:

> Advertising now companies with such long-standing institutions as the school and the church in the magnitude of its social influence. It dominates the media, it has vast power in the shaping of popular standards, and it is really one of the very limited groups of institutions which exercise social control . . . advertising has joined the charmed circle of institutions which fix values and standards of society.[30]

In the long run, admen created and successfully fostered sets of aspirations and notions of identity that would dominate American culture and society. The advertising industry's image of reality they created to sell products, became *the* reality for many Americans. It contained organizationally orthodox values: prosperity, progress, consuming satisfaction, among others.

Throughout these decades, advertisers and their admen effectively used contemporary mass media to deliver their selling messages to their audiences. During the 1950s, the advertising industry added a new resource to their institutional inventory. As the decade dawned, the "ultimate medium" arrived, television. As an advertising medium, it furthered this new consumption-spending socioeconomic revolution.

Television design began before World War II. In 1927, A.T. &T. debuted the concept, showing an image of commerce secretary Herbert Hoover. Television prototypes were displayed at Chicago's Century of Progress Exposition (1833–1933). In 1939, NBC did the first television broadcast from the New York World's Fair and started an experimental station later that same year. In 1941, the F.C.C. sanctioned commercial broadcasting; about six stations went on the air thereafter, reaching into about ten thousand households in the New York area. Televisions sold retail; even kits to assemble. The Durant Corporation began to advertise TVs in 1943. Even then:

> The corporation conveyed the message that television and the American future of material and spiritual progress were synonymous and this rhetoric, in part the legacy of Protestant millennialism, was now applied to television as it had been used to evoke the utopian goals of electrification and radio.[31]

Despite television's immediate potential, World War II priorities delayed further development.

Radio networks developed the television industry, in fits and starts. There were channel allocation problems (VHF had only twelve channels.), prompting an F.C.C. permit freeze from 1948 to 1952. During those years, television broadcasted to sixty-three metro areas. About three-fifths of the total population had access to these TV orbits. In those areas, TV use increased. After the freeze ended, the television industry boomed. There were more channels (70), available via UHF, thus fueling the expansion.

Thus, the television industry progressed and expanded during peacetime. In 1946, .02 percent of American households had a TV; by 1950, 9 percent did. By January 1948, there were 102,000 TV sets in use; that April, TV sales doubled. Then, televisions were luxury items, most often bought for public use in public places such as taverns. Eventually, prices became affordable for those with less disposable income. By 1948, some already viewed television use as significant. The July 1948 *Architectural Forum* reported:

> Where the television set has come into the home the separate dining room has disappeared. The family has begun to eat its meals where it has put its television set. It has postponed dish washing, until the favorite program has faded from the screen. Some families have even taken to sleeping in relays in order to look after the large number of firmly rooted guests who come over to look at the television.[32]

Beginning in 1949, the television industry accelerated when corporate sponsorships significantly increased, and about three million TV sets were sold; in 1950, 7.5 million sold. In 1952, there were 108 broadcasting stations, and by 1955, 441 stations broadcasted into thirty-two million households. That year, 1955, about 67 percent of total U.S. households had televisions. This included about 48 percent of households in the lowest income quarter. In contrast, 81 percent of the top quarter, had televisions; the second quarter equaled 76 percent; the third, was 69 percent. *Business Week* boasted that 95 percent of American households had access to television. Thus, TV sales and presumed use, spread significantly through American society, regardless of social class or income level. Over thirty-three million households used thirty-eight million televisions; annual new TV sales were about eight million. In 1956, *Business Week* claimed:

> In less than a decade, the home screen has absorbed so important a part of our lives that it's already difficult to remember how our living patterns may have changed. There are very few places in the U.S. that are still "TV-free"—and it's almost impossible to find substantial numbers of people who haven't been influenced to some degree.[33]

Even though television use concentrated in metropolitan areas, TV was in the majority of households throughout the country, so they claimed then. By 1960, almost 90 percent of American households had a television, and average daily viewing equaled five hours.

During the 1950s, Leo Bogart attempted to synthesize current research findings about television. His book *The Age of Television*, published circa

1956, offers a contemporary snapshot of how television affected his times. By then, television was the new centerpiece in the American home. (Three of four households had one TV, and broadcasts reached 97 percent of the country per Bogart.) People stayed home and adjusted their off-hours to accommodate television programs. Many believed, even then, that TV watching was habit forming. Bogart wrote: "Evening viewing is for most people, a full-time and absorbing occupation."[34] This was okay according to Bogart. *Business Week* concurred, asserting that the longer people had televisions, the more they watched it. Television dominates leisure time; watching four hours per night was the average per family. Despite this, Bogart did not see television as the "monster" as others did. He did recognize its significance:

> TV is More Powerful. Because it mobilizes more attention and attracts more time from its audience, television is a more important force than radio ever was in the cultural, social and economic life of the nation. Television is more spectacular as a medium, because its productions are grander, supported by advertisers on a larger scale than radio knew in its prime. TV provides its audience with more bedazzlement, whether or not it offers more entertainment. Like radio, television can make reality seem more dramatic than it really is, but it can do so with stunning effectiveness.[35]

Thus, at that time, what we today consider as normal television fare was back then, new or experimental: sports events, public occasions, political conventions, situation comedies, plays, and melodramas, all debuted then. As the networks expanded to daytime broadcasting too, programs diversified. Morning shows targeted family members home during the day, women and children, especially women during the workweek. After school, the programming focused on children. What we call prime time today, back then, was called the family hour.

Within these broad parameters, the general target audience, or typical viewer, was the middle class. Bogart then observed:

> Television and radio programs are for the most part directed to the psychological and cultural interests of the average, middle segment of the population, since this approach presents the greatest promise of attracting the largest number of people to the audience.[36]

In particular, the middle-class family became the message and the audience simultaneously.

Program content presented a variety of options even then, ranging from news and sports, to action-adventure dramas. The core was family fare, what we call today, sitcoms (situation comedies). Like its audience, the TV family was usually white, suburban middle class. Setting and audience, image and reality matched and reinforced each other. However, television's reach was ubiquitous toward all races, ethnics, and social classes. A middle-class ideal consisting of nuclear-familied, homeowning, white-faced suburbanites living and loving their uncontentous lives with much time spent together watching television, underlie significant amounts of programming. Television shows like *Ozzie and Harriet, Father Knows Best*, and *Leave it to Beaver* exemplified this idea.

The message they carried was subtle: family consumption, postwar consensus, progress, the good life, and wholesome family life. The good life manifested in a steadily employed, stable, suburban family, complemented the underlying advertisers' message to buy this product and don't stop spending. ("Harriet Nelson" did commercials right from the television studio kitchen.) Well-dressed, presumably well-off, families lived near-perfect, consensus, consumer-based lives, in almost-perfect suburbia. These families rarely fought. Everyone was healthy. Women loved homemaking, and their men loved their work and family. There were few family crisises, or personal scandalous vices. Their children were more adjusted than not; none were on medication. Siblings could get along. Life was pleasant for all, most of the time, and optimism ruled. Contentiousness and conflict situations were used for plot/comedic devices. This image became the ideal type, the aspiration to imitate, for a broad cross section of Americans.

Behind the curtains on the studio sets, the industry professionals who wrote the scripts were probably organization men injecting their corporate cultural attitudes, beliefs, values, and behavioral protocols into the subtext and tone of each show. Thus, the archetype and the ideal type that television presented to the public of organizational culture and all its trappings, was transported to the family under the guise of consensus All-Americanism.) The scripts that the "Andersons," "Cleavers," and "Nelsons" acted out reflected the corporate-organizational work and idealized domestic ethos that underlay the thinking and beliefs of its writers. The images we viewed on our televisions were the direct reflections of what corporate institutional culture expected of its constituents, of what kind of national character it was influencing.

Did the message, back then, get through? Probably, whether we wan't to admit to that now.

In the May 24, 1948 issue of *Time*, editors predicted that television would: "change American life more that anything since the Model T." It seems from hindsight this prediction was well on its way to becoming true during the 1950s. Already in 1952, Ashley Montagu observed:

> Indeed television represents the most vital of all living miracles. . . . Television is capable of moving men to thought and action as no other medium. . . . There can

> be not the least doubt that television has within its power to become the most important of all agencies of social change.[37]

Thus, during the 1950s, as television evolved and expanded, it became a popular, ubiquitous, pervasive, and persuasive social construct, and it was brought to you by?

Just like the radio industry, television broadcasters relied on advertising revenue. That is, sponsors' advertising paid for program production costs. Nationwide, advertisers spent $453.9 million on television commercials in 1952; in 1955, they spent over $1 billion. Those spending the most: Proctor & Gamble, Colgate-Palmolive, Chrysler, and R. J. Reynolds. In 1956, *Business Week* asserted: "One thing is certain. Television does sell goods."[38] One corporate executive suggested that he believed television commercials would be very effective in persuading people to work hard to make money and then spend it.

Again, using Bogart as a contemporary observer, he commented, in 1955, that television was considered a powerful new, "advertising vehicle." Then, studies indicated that the audience did remember the content of commercials and that advertising was effective. ("Chairs ain't the only thing with legs. Look at you, you got two; stick 'em in your Kazoos; listen to the Ewwwwws. Kazoos is lean-age pants.")

Although all family members and all types of people were sales-pitched, women and children were priority targets. Women were especially hosannahed in their expected role as homemakers and mothers. Commercials glorified a woman's abilities to use products to provide for her family and to assert her womanly and motherly skills in her all-important social environment, the home. Appliances and food products enhanced the hearth.

Admen also understood television's powerful influence on children. Sponsors of kid's programs recognized a child's influence ("Mommy, I want . . .") on family purchasing: snacks, breakfast food, toys, and soda, for example. All these products made their way into the home via television. (Anecdotally, their commercials were probably effective. Recall your parents' or grandparents' kitchen pantry and refrigerator contents during the days of your youth. Which Kraml milk vignette was your favorite? Corn Flakes or Rice Krispies?)

Broadcast content and commercials combined to pack a multi-faceted wallop, promoting consumption, capitalism, and American culture. (The latter being created as it was sold.) Regardless of home—city or suburb, town or country—television, as the center of domestic social activity, became a mass social arbiter, proselytizing a consumer ethic, and a homogenized, standardized middle-class-based American Way.

Not only did television influence thinking and language. Its messages offered the American corporate cornucopia of plenty, prompting spending throughout the socioeconomic system. That world of goods defined the American material culture, which in turn, offered new parameters for the American way of life, our American Dream that led to fundamental change in the American Character. In August 1959, the *Saturday Evening Post* presented a panorama of this on one of its covers.[39] A young couple stargazing into their futures together visualize their world as constellations: suburban house, two cars, two children and a dog, television, transistor radio, power tools, refrigerator-freezer, washer-dryer, toaster, Hoover vacuum cleaner, steam iron, cake mixer, coffee percolator, electric fry-pan, rotisserie. Good Stuff! During the 1950s, big business directed American society around the final turn toward the nirvana of unlimited and unfettered abundance.

Thus, television and its culture gradually became ubiquitous in America during the 1950s. Coupled to advertising content, the industry shaped its audiences with its dramatic portrayal of society, culture, and daily life. As a result, television both fostered behavior, values, and attitudes, and evolved, based on its own social creations, which became social constructs, in the process. Life created art, and art influenced life.

During that decade, advertisers began using television, targeting their messages to what appeared to be a new, potentially lucrative market: "middle-class suburbia." The advertising industry effectively utilized their resources and capitalized on the immediate popularity of television out in the suburban boondocks. Harry Henderson, investigating the suburban phenomena early in the 1950s, observed how important and valued television was in suburban households.[40] The advertising industry caught on and quickly followed, easily inviting themselves into suburban homes with the greeting: "brought to you by."

Their target was as new as the medium they were using. The suburbs like television, were the latest thing. The American housing industry was moribund before World War II. The Great Depression destroyed the building boom of the Roaring Twenties, when Americans built four million houses between 1921 and 1925. From 1931 to 1946, housing starts averaged 330,000 annually, part of a decline that began after 1925. That year, there were 937,000 starts; in 1933, 93,000. In 1938, the yearly average units constructed per firm equaled 3.5, with 86 percent of the total industry building only two houses per year, and 60 percent just one.

The housing sector of the economy was a localized industry, entrepreneurial; not big business in size, structure, and method. Despite its decentralized makeup, it wasn't competitive in each local market.

Building costs were high because contractors didn't buy materials direct, and they used high-priced, inefficient, union labor. To compound the problem, builders did not use "modern" home construction methods. Instead, they viewed house building as a craft, and used guild-based construction techniques. Such construction companies were mostly small businesses, and used a multiple-contractor system. *Fortune* described it as: "a succession of unconnected handicraft operations of masons, carpenters, electricians, plumbers, and painters."[41] All were subcontractors, and each worked at the mercy of the efficiency of the work group preceding them at the job site. If the framers, for example, started late, or had to stop or slow down because of material shortages, then all work scheduled to follow was delayed. Generally, this meant one firm could build about five houses per year.

Fortune labeled the housing industry as unaffected by the industrial revolution, downright feudal. The magazine recommended change: "Efficient house production requires firms big enough to mobilize capital and organize production in systematic, repetitive operations."[42] They suggested eliminating the subcontracting system, lowering labor costs, and selling cheaper to the buyer.

As America demobilized (six million in the military discharged in 1945; four million in 1946), many returning veterans began to attempt to resume a normal civilian life. This meant finding a job and getting a wife. These aspirations blossomed into a national trend, and as a result, the demand for housing rapidly increased. In spring of 1946, *Fortune* reported an expected demand for three million housing units. Although federal government programs provided financial assistance, the private sector inadequately responded to the demand. As a result, a nationwide housing crisis greeted many returning veterans. People took shelter where available: Quonset huts; unused trolley cars in Chicago; unfinished bomber fuselages in California; abandoned mining tunnels; cars; newlyweds often stayed with relatives.

Despite the lucrative demand, few residential construction companies were capable of building houses rapidly and in large volume. Material shortages compounded the problem, and the houses, actually built, were traditional, high-priced (eight to ten thousand dollars), and out of the price range of most veterans.

Between 1944 and 1947, 1,056,771 veterans received home loans via the G.I. Bill. In contrast, there were 114,000 housing starts in 1944, and 937,000 in 1946. Construction-industry response to this demand would permanently alter house-construction method. Assembly-line style produced a standardized product, built wherever open land was available. Some contractors adopted methods they used to quickly build war-worker housing, for example, William J. Levitt's company built 2,500 units around Norfolk, Virginia. After the war, when Levitt returned to civilian life, he took up his old trade. That pursuit would make him a legend and revolutionize the way Americans lived.

The Levitt brothers played a significant role in creating, in the East, the new postwar suburbia. Halberstram, in *The Fifties*, asserted that the Levitts made the American Dream and middle-class life possible for many who didn't think it was available. The Levitts applied mass-production methods, successfully modifying them to an outdoor work-site environment, and effectively building cheap housing quickly.

The Levitt brothers systemized the single-family residential construction process into twenty-seven steps, employing a nonunion work team for each. Using an adaptation of the piecework method, the Levitts offered a base salary, plus productivity incentives, that resulted in good money for the construction workers, averaging $100 per week, during a nine-month building season. This was pretty much equivalent to union scale.

The Levitts formulated this process just in time for World War II to interrupt their civilian life. Bill Levitt enlisted in the U.S. Navy, and was able to experiment with, and refine his ideas doing construction as a Seabee. There, in the military, he learned effective mass-production techniques, and he anticipated using them in his own business at war's end.

When peace retuned, Levitt, began (with his father, who started the business), to experiment on land near Hempstead, New York, where they had bought land before the war. He firmly believed that he would succeed, making houses available similar to going to the store to buy ready-to-wear clothing. He attempted, and succeeded, on land twenty miles from Manhattan Island, where they called the project, Island Trees. Today, we remember what they did there, as Levittown.

The Levitts began building single-family, 4½-room, basementless houses, on lots 60 by 100 feet. Each unit had called a Cape Cod model, sold for $7,990, at $65 per month. A larger version went for $9,500, and sold initially as a rental, with option to buy. All these first domiciles included a TV and washing machine.

Marketed at first to veterans only, the Levitts advertised in the *New York Times* on a Monday. The next morning, thirty people showed up to inquire, and more arrived everyday that week. When the Levitt sales office officially opened in March 1949, they sold 1,400 houses in one day.

To build at a rate to fulfill demand, Levitt adopted Ford Corporation's River Rouge assembly-line method. They took the factory system outdoors, where semiskilled workers, using different components, some preassembled, but not prefabricated, built the house on a slab of concrete. Armed with only the recently introduced "power tools," they constructed a community in what was once a potato field.

Most of the construction occurred on-site: warehousing components, cutting wood, assembling pipes, and prefabricating concrete. Trucks delivered a house in pieces (but not prefab, they insisted), depositing piles every sixty feet. Teams of workers then swarmed over each site, following a set method and sequence. They embedded the concrete floor with heating coils. Frames went up, roofed, walled, windowed, etc.

Peak production estimates don't agree. They might have approached thirty units per day. Regardless, by taking the turtle-speed, crafts-guild method out of the process, the Levitts could build efficiently and cheaply. Also, they succeeded in keeping costs low through vertical integration. Corporate subsidiaries provided lumber, appliances, nails, and concrete, all bought at wholesale; pretty much all construction material, wholesale, too. They were heavily capitalized, bolstered by a large line of credit.

The Levitt corporation's big business method worked. They successfully answered *Fortune*'s 1947 clarion call to build housing cheaply and quickly to satisfy postwar demand. By July 1948, they could construct 180 houses during a five-day workweek, eighteen per shift. (Sometimes they could build into the wintertime on foundations when frames were already in place.) By fall, they built 6,000 units since their initial start-up. From 1947 to 1951, Levitt built 17,450 houses. The first Levittown wound up containing 17,450 units, occupied by 82,000 people. Then, it was an unprecedented accomplishment. As a result, the Levitt corporation became a trendsetter and industry leader, eventually building 146,000 units in the East. The housing boom that followed in 1952 grossed $11 billion. Between 1946 and 1949, there were 3,476,000 units built; in 1950, 1,396,000. From 1956 to 1960, 1.5 million houses went up annually. Thus, during this time, the house construction industry resurrected itself to become a leading industry. In 1940, 41 percent of Americans were homeowners; in 1957, 59 percent.

The Levitt corporation built durable communities then, from the foundations up: including roads, water and sewer lines, publicly controlled schools, church buildings, swimming pools, etc. The homeowners that flocked in created what became postwar suburbia, a contemporary, brand-new version of the American Dream. Others followed.

Suburban subdivisions proliferated during the 1950s, finally alleviating the postwar housing shortage. As these suburbs bloomed around our cities, these new communities quickly drew public attention and social scientists' curiosity, among others. Two such studies present a snapshot of 1950s suburban life: Levittown, in New Jersey and Park Forest, Illinois.

The third Levittown built in New Jersey, seventeen miles from Philadelphia and later called Willinboro, became a classic suburban sociological case study in 1958. Herbert Gans moved there and stayed until 1960. Using a team, and participant-observation techniques, they provided a contemporary picture-like analysis of suburbia, similar to what the Lynds had done in Middletown decades earlier.[43]

The Gans team was particularly interested in learning how this phenomenon of suburbia affected social behavior. The team lived in and analyzed what we call a suburban bedroom community from October 1958 to September 1960. They also did fieldwork there until June 1961. While they were on-site, Levittown continued to grow, newcomers constantly arriving.

Gans' study focused on the original 3,000 residents there when he arrived. Many of them were already suburbanites, 46 percent; from cities 33 percent, and 19 percent, from "Main Street." First-time homeowners equaled 53 percent; second-home ownership was 32 percent. They were mobile, more on the move than persistent to any community. Most of them moved to Levittown to have a place of their own and more room, at a good price. Gans concluded that just owning a house, somewhere, anywhere, underlie their reasons for moving to a new place, and not primarily the place itself. Apparently, Levittown offered a deal more acceptable then elsewhere. In fact, house ownership and the belief in what "having a place of our own" could do for lifestyle, was the most mentioned reason for moving there. At the same time, home life was expressed as more important than community life.

Spatially, Levittown, New Jersey, was a planned community made up of a landscape constructed as defined neighborhoods. Conceptualized by William Levitt, this version was a hybrid of the previous two. In response to critics and their negative stereotyping, all the houses were not the same, and they were higher-priced and designed differently than before. This Levittown was packaged and targeted to the middle-middle-class buyer, instead of loan-bearing vets. Those that moved there were mostly under forty years old, married, with children. They lived diversified lives based on their ethnicity, income levels, and occupational class. Lifestyle and routine were more heterogeneous than alike. Family composition and unity, child-rearing, education aspirations, church participation, public behavior and appearances all varied by social class, more so, than what would be expected if the suburban stereotype was the testable hypothesis.

Once a suburbanite, many of them assumed the position. Everyone maintained their front lawn to look nice, while the backyards were nobody's business. Original friendships formed among neighbors, and then branched out. They also joined clubs, based on individual interests or hobbies. By 1960, there were about one hundred ongoing voluntary associations. There, leadership maneuvering brought out the community's small business professionals, who sought these roles.

Voluntary associations, that is, clubs and social groups, are very effective means of socializing its participants. There, groups, seemingly typical to the new suburbia, might have been effective means for the organization man to proselytize his corporate-culture values away from the workplace. The behavior patterns someone learns at work—a place where people spend more conscious hours awake than at home—would inevitably filter out of the workplace and into the off-hours routines of most people. Within group activities, on their driveways, backyards, and living rooms, besides the formal groups, the ways and means of the corporate culture found their way to a new home away from home.

Within any group, a pecking order usually develops. Those at the top impose or influence an order and behavioral method on the rest of the group—both formal and informal situations. Also, if socializing was as widespread as observers suggested, then the new suburban social environment was fertile ground for incubating and nurturing these specific behaviors. This group process occurs within corporate culture similarly. That interaction in the workplace will spill over into other interactions away from the time clock. The psychological and sociological process in both situations is similar. Ideas, values, opinions, can be disseminated and integrated in group activity when done on a regular basis. It is conditioned learning, an accepted constant in understanding human behavior. Thus, the suburban culture of the 1950s that drew so much contemporary media attention and social criticism, was a lawn and garden derivative, a version of, or transfer of corporate culture to the neighborhood regardless of locale, suburban or urban.

In the workforce, 56 percent of Levittowners were white-collar workers; 18 percent were labeled professionals; 20 percent were blue-collar workers. Some of them worked in nearby Philadelphia, Pennsylvania, and Camden, New Jersey. The white-collar workers were petite bourgeoisie, and the blue-collar were mostly skilled tradesmen, foremen, and technicians. Gans labeled them as mostly lower-middle class, some working class, and even upper-middle class.

Gans eventually asserted that this Levittown was not typical to the suburban stereotype. Mostly lower-middle-class and working-class people lived in this one, not exclusively the white-collar organizational man and his "Harriet Nelson" wife, and "Beaver" children. Instead, Levittowners worked at different occupations from white-collar managers, to blue-collar trades. Their ethnic backgrounds varied, as did their religious faiths. Political party affiliation remained fixed by social background. This particular suburb remained politically diverse without either political party monopolizing the vote. When Gans lived there, Levittown was more heterogeneous than homogeneous in social composition.

Most importantly, Gans disagreed with most of the media criticism. There was actually less controversy and negativity within suburban living than publicly alleged. Gans did not believe the suburban physical landscape and location was cathartic: Nor did suburbanites view themselves living the phony lives critics accused them of. Lifestyle and life ways out there either weren't the way the critics said, or suburban residents accepted and coped with the ethos, including its good and bad components.

Despite the variations from the believed suburban norm, Gans suggested a common, significant link between his neighbors in Levittown and the prevailing suburban model:

> People like them are the principal market for the consumer goods offered by big national corporations, the entertainment and information provided by the mass media, and the political appeals that come from Washington. They are the customers for whom these agencies create their product—and they are the people who converse about soap and aspirin in the television commercials. . . . In short, they are the people whom the major creators of America's products, services, and ideas believe to be most important or most typical.[44]

Thus, even in Gans's Levittown, they too, were constituents of that grand consensus-based consumption communities in the world according to Boorstin, who wrote of Americans:

> Americans were now held together less by their hopes than by their wants, by what they made, and what they bought, and by how they learned abut everything. They were held together by the new names they gave to the things they wanted, to the things they owned and to themselves. . . . Men were divided not by their region or their roots, but by objects and notions that might be anywhere and could be everywhere. . . . Now men were affiliated less by what they believed than by what they consumed.[45]

Successfully creating a Levittown, or a Park Forest, spawned clones nationwide, accelerating the population flow even more away from the central city. In 1920, the suburban population was about fifteen million; in 1930, it was sixteen million; in 1941, it was 31.1 million people; by the late 1950s, 47 million, and in 1960, there were 60.1 million suburbanites. Already in 1955, suburban towns were almost fifty miles from New York City.

The newness of postwar suburbia, its seemingly sudden occurrence, its popularity, and the idea it represented as a new way of life, brought its culture to the forefront, and attracted widespread media attention. Frederick L. Allen, writing his last effort before he died, observed that suburbia was "one of the major changes of our time, which seems destined to alter the face of the land and affect our national way of life for generations to come."[46] Business, academia, and media institutions, among others, all took interest in what was happening out there, in these new towns on the "crabgrass frontier."

So just what was it like, at least in the popular mind, to be a 1950s suburbanite? Typically, you were married, with at least two very young children. The husband was the breadwinner, who usually commuted to a job in the city, where he spent a lot of hours being the organization man, fitting into the corporate culture. There, he quickly learned that he had to not only work hard but also to fit in.[47]

His wife managed the home and raised their children. Her life, as a housewife, centered around the hearth and the kitchen. Homemaking and mothering, encouraged through advertising, was her calling. Everyone then knew—especially advertisers—that a woman's place was in the home; that became her office, her factory, and the place where she showed off all their good stuff. Cooking, cleaning, and raising children were a wife's expected role and socially mandated occupation. When not ensconced in her home, behind the white picket fence (figuratively) or driving to do errands, her time was spent creating a web of acquaintances and friends as she established neighborhood networks, often instigated by her children's friendships or acquired through socializing or group affiliations.

Indeed, associational behavior became important for both genders, probably placing third behind their children and television. Suburban couples often participated in the structured, organized, scheduled leisure-time group activities that were based on hobbies, particular interests like card playing, and car clubs, for examples. They also participated in civic activities: school board meetings, political causes, homeowners' groups, veterans' clubs, booster clubs, etc.[48] Henry Henderson observed that group participation and especially seeking leadership roles and working hard at it were widely approved ways to gain community prestige. He also noted lawyers and salesmen dominated these roles.

The concept of conformity rose to the top of the list of all things observed to be suburban. It seemed endemic to all suburban locales, and it manifested in a variety of behavior. Proper living protocols seemed to spontaneously generate. Too much conspicuous consumption, contrary clothing styles, being too smart, acting too much beyond what everyone else was, all drew informal negative sanctions. Even the condition of one's front lawn was subject to peer review. Suburbanites reinforced appropriate behavior by gossip, giving hints, sarcastic remarks, poking fun, ridicule, sending a message through the children, talking behind someone's back, and sometimes, even ostracism. William Whyte observed: "The sanctions are not obvious, indeed people are often unconscious of wielding them, but the look in the eye, the absence of a smile, the inflection, a hello can be exquisite punishment.[49]

To be suburban meant, at least superficially, to be like everyone else. By all appearances, conformity on the job and off, was expected and considered normal, positive behavior. It was evident to Henry Henderson:

> Nothing less than super-conformity satisfies. Generally, in my interviews with men and women who live in the new suburbs, the drive to conformity was acknowledged, sometimes laughed at and often defended.[50]

That same year, 1953, *Fortune* concurred:

> Suburbanites are growing more than ever concerned with the opinions of others in their group. . . . The fact that almost everybody has similar ideals, standards, and incomes, strengthens rather than weakens the groups' hold on the individual.[51]

William H. Whyte Jr., observed similarly, when *Fortune* had him investigate four suburban sites. Whyte wrote: "There is a remarkable similarity in attitudes, toward politics, education, economics, sex, religion, from suburb to suburb. Almost a new way of life is in the making in these communities."[52]

An omniscient observer would reveal that our American suburbs of the 1950s varied in social composition, cultural competition, and individual community ethos, from place to place. However, the nebulous pattern, composite image of all of those places would resemble the standard stereotype these investigations presented. In hindsight, I would project that back then, the more the suburb was occupied by white-collar, managerial, or clerical workers, the more likely the community exhibited the tendencies stereotyped as the 1950s suburban milieu, because they were the occupational groups most influenced by corporate culture. They were the organization men, the Keatian drones in the gray flannel suits who were the most significantly indoctrinated by organizational culture. It was that ethos, ingrained by 1960, that they helped create, and then adhere to. Only through the media and corporate culture did their values trickle down to the ranks, to the working-class or blue-collar trades. It wasn't the physical suburban infrastructure causing the suburban culture. The people that moved there created it, and many of them had been socialized urban and corporate. Perhaps they thought they were "clever and classless and free."[53]

Under the scrutiny of academia and the press, an image and derivative stereotype emerged of life outside congested cities. Hence, whether they wanted to, or cared, suburbanites became famous; their lifestyles became the perceived and believed leading edge; social, political, and market trendsetters. From 1948–1958, twelve million people moved to the suburbs, making them now the statistical average. At the same time, Robert C. Wood, noted:

> The most fashionable definition of suburbia today is that it is a looking glass in which the character, behavior, and culture of middle class America is displayed . . . (and it) reflects with fidelity modern man, his way of living, his institutions and beliefs, his family and his social associations.[54]

Thus, suburban living, based on middle-class, white-collar employment, middle-income purchasing power, supplemented by often-overextended installment buying (and now available to lower-middle-class and working-class people in the nation's Levittowns), family and child-centered home life, casual, informal conformist public behavior and dress, conservative politics and dedicated and inconspicuous consumption spending, became the new American way, the new American Dream.

Figuratively speaking, up on their corporate hill, overlooking the paradise they helped create, was big business. Already, in 1953, William H. Whyte wrote that corporations were largely responsible for suburbs because these communities were corporate residential way stations, dormitories of the next managerial class.[55]

Recently, Lizabeth Cohen asserted that a prime factor in shaping postwar America was consumption spending.[56] (Eventually, the consumers' republic spread through much of our social system.) If so, consider how corporations provided the incomes for many, to purchase their heavily advertised products, the good stuff this new suburban middle class displayed in their homes, on themselves, and on their driveways.

After they moved into suburbia, they spent money in amounts that seemed unimaginable before the war. Consumption spending became a fundamental aspiration, almost an achieved right. They purchased, then filled their homes with good stuff. If indeed, postwar consensus America evolved to become Boorstin's consumption communities and Cohen's consumers' republic, the epitome, leading-edge archetype, and model for this consuming ethos was the new suburbia. Back then, *Fortune* claimed the new suburban lifestyle created new trends. Suburbia, they wrote:

> will more than ever set the nations' standards and styles. . . . For it is Suburbia, teeming with new wants and appetites, taking prosperity, for granted, borrowing easily, and saving (when it does save) only to facilitate spending, that has exalted spending better into a way of life.[57]

Hence, by creating a consumption-spending ethos, combined with the influence of corporate culture, a new modern corporate America happened.

Corporations thus wielded a double-edged sword. Through role expectations and subtle, soft-pedaled white-collar industrial discipline, corporate culture shaped the workaday public, political, and even leisure-time behavior of its employees. As time marched on during the 1950s, the suburban life became the stereotyped life, "the people of plenty," and its concomitant corporate life, became publicly perceived, hailed, ridiculed, but believed true, manifested then by such labels as: the organization man, the man in the gray flannel suit, and the other-directed commuter robot submerged within the teeming middle-incomed, consumption-spending masses, the lonely crowd.

This was the contemporary model, seemingly what literate America believed was their social reality. Even though American middling life, that great hump under the normal distribution, had more variation and exceptions to the norm, truth becomes what the people believed it to be. Many Americans, by decade's end, believed that the new, modern suburbia was *the* America, the new American Dream. Many of them, often, regardless of social class, occupation, ethnicity, and, in some cases, even race, adjusted their behavior accordingly, conforming to this new ethos and its rules and protocols, rituals and expected behavior. The social forces emanating out of the image of suburbia may have powerfully influenced the shaping of reality for many. Whether they wanted to or not; whether they were conscious of it, or not, it was the new, common, expected way to live. Many believed it was the way it was supposed to be, and they attempted to participate, to do their part, and get their share; their share of the new American Pie. But all did not seem right to many who eyewitnessed the changing and prosperous 1950s. Recently, Thomas Frank reminded us that:

> Author after author warned in the 1950s that long-standing American traditions of individualism were vanishing and being buried beneath the empires of the great corporations, the sprawl of prefabricated towns, and the reorientation of culture around the imperative of consuming, homogenized mass-produced goods.[58]

To them, something seemed off. The trends started by the suburban exodus and the new lifestyles seemed too good to be true. Could a modern utopia be developing there, in the land of the picture window, out on the crabgrass frontier? Was this new, suburban life all that it was supposed to be, or were there cracks in those picture windows?

A pattern developed portraying suburban life as different from expectations and traditions. Observers attributed those new social constructs to a general change in American social values, and to the nature of the suburban milieu. This stereotype depicted suburbanites as bland conformists, living packaged, routinized, regimented lives analogous to the similarity of each new subdivision. Conformity reigned supreme, as Harry Henderson mentioned. In suburbia, women ruled the roost and set the social tone in each community while their spouses remained in the city, chained to their desk jobs. Behind the white picket fence, families were riven by a hidden contentiousness and strife: family dysfunction, infidelity, alcohol abuse, depression. Observing at the end of the decade, Herbert Gans wrote:

> In unison, authors chanted that individualism was dying, suburbanites were miserable, and the fault lay with the homogeneous suburban landscapes and its population . . . and some critics charge that suburban life is socially, culturally,

> and emotionally destructive, and that the causes are to be found in the nature of suburbia and the move from the city.[59]

The "problem" of suburbia that so attracted the egghead's attention was the manifestation of more fundamental and institutional changes.[60]

Suburbia mirrored, reflected outward what America became economically, socially, and psychologically, within the evolution of metropolitan industrial modernity. It seemed to have permanently altered the nature and structure of institutions, the economy, people, and ultimately, the American Character.

Among these observers, journalist William H. Whyte was first and foremost. In his book *The Organization Man* (1956), Whyte argued that large bureaucracies, especially big business corporations, shaped behavior and indoctrinated its employees to an institutional, organized ethos, manifesting in specific attributes. Although the corporate culture was a ubiquitous environment, it affected its constituents differently. That is, it wasn't defined by any particular occupational class. An organization man could be an executive, other managers, or even support staff. However, most likely, they are of that nebulous, bell-curved hump cohort being somewhere in the middle, as Whyte opined:

> They are the ones of our middle class who have left home, spiritually, as well as physically, to take the vows of organizational life, and it is they who are the mind and soul of our great self-perpetuating institutions.

Only a few are top managers or ever will be; . . . they are of

> the staff as much as the line, and most are destined to live, poised in the middle area that still awaits a satisfactory euphemism. But they are the dominant members of our society nonetheless . . . but if is from the ranks that are coming most of the first and second echelons of our leadership, and it is their values which set the American temper. . . . The corporation man is the most conspicuous example, but he is only one, for the collectivization so visible in the corporation has affected almost every field of work.[61]

To be an organization man meant surrendering to the institution, accepting its job demands by working hard, striving for constant achievement, and adapting to the rules and protocols of its internal culture. It meant absorbing and inculcating bureaucratic institutionalism, and integrating its values into one's own, and forming a strong, personal identification with the job provider.

Whyte considered this a major ideological change in American society, and attributed it to those who worked in corporations. He referred to this as a new social or organizational or bureaucratic ethic. It imposed loyalty and demanded devotion and affiliation to the organization similar to a secular faith.

To believe in this system meant to think along with and for the group; not to be too creative or too different or mavericky. Conformity was an expected obligation. an expected belief was active participation in the group process, thus, fortifying the group's strengths. Giving one's talent, time, and ultimately, one's self, were expected, that is, to succumb and accept participating in the "rat race," as they called it then, or getting on and staying on the treadmill.

William Whyte suggested that adherence to these beliefs was similar to a spiritual union between the organization and its members, and acceptance of organization was moving to a level of idolatry. Also, during that decade, journalist Vance Packard observed that these corporate behavior patterns extended from the top, down. He wrote:

> If the publicly owned, pyramidal-type corporate power structures are producing more and more blandness at the top, what is happening to the managers who are still lower down? Many evidences of manipulation, dehumanizing and de-individualing suggest that the pressures toward blandness are even stranger below than they are at the top.[62]

Combine aspiration, achievement motive, and the desire to make money, a hybrid of Whyte's organization man developed. I suggest the organizational ethic was not limited to the workplace. Once absorbed and accepted, or acquiesced to, organization man transmitted the corporate ethic outside of the job to his family, peers, and neighbors. It especially took root in suburbia, what Whyte called, "the packaged villages that became the dormitory of the new generation of organization men."[63] Out there, in the land of tabula rasa, where the situation was receptive, new communities lacking ethnic neighborhood tradition, or entrenched social resistance, delivery of the organizational ethic created social conformity, group mindedness, group-centered activity, and deference to one's neighbors. Just like being at work, neighbors learned to try to get along, fit in, pitch in, and go with the flow. Out there, at home, family and friends garnered loyalty similar to affiliation to the job, authority, and coworkers. It was a near-exact, thorough translation, transmutation of corporate culture, to the home and hearth, and it was not merely limited to suburbia. Wherever the organizational ethic was taught, whether in big cities or in places like Muncie, Indiana, it was transmitted like a spreading virus from its host, the typical corporate employee.

This social-class cohort became the vanguard society, establishing its operational norms, values, living standards, and lifestyles, similar to their group forbearers, who set the social tone during the 1920s. Then, the white-collar managerial classes could do this because their occupational and corporate affiliation provided them a significant measure of power, privileges, status, influence, and prestige. Decades later, during the 1950s, few Americans were immune unless they avoided or lacked access to mass media. Both print and broadcast media directly delivered the same corporate ethic to the home via programming and advertising. Ubiquitous television was especially effective delivering corporate organizational life ways into many living rooms. The American Way they presented was really the Corporate Way. The big business advertising and broadcast industries effectively socialized their audiences through the ideal type presented in sitcoms, and by the positiveness of consumption spending in its commercials. To laugh along with Ozzie and Harriet, or with the Cleavers, also meant to learn and imitate the consensus/organizational life that television scripts subtlety propagated, using the mechanism of familial domesticity. Through television, the organization man was fully embodied in recognized, famous faces; as friendly and familiar as the trademarked Morton Salt containers on many kitchen tables, or better still, on our TV trays. Thus, the Consensus Ethos, that marked the 1950s, and its attributes of conformity, blandness, deference, etc., was really a corporate-directed consensus.

Our collective relationship to work and its derivative values and attributes might be related to a change in the overall personality of industrial man and the new society he lived in. Sociologist David Riesman and others addressed this in *The Lonely Crowd*, published in 1950. The authors postulated the emergence of a new, national social character, the other-directed person, challenging the already established, traditional man, and the next recent, inner-directed man. Generally, the cues traditional man conformed to were often coerced or imposed by powerful state- or church-level institutions, as in medieval times. The inner-directed man learned to conform to prevailing norms by his family and kin.

Writing in his own times, Riesman suggested that this character emerged out of the urban upper-middle-class milieu. (It applied to both individual and society.) These people seemed to be altering their public behavior in response to new social cues, expectations, and learning. More and more, they behaved in the way they believed was expected by others. Church and state still had influence on inculcated beliefs, and so did the effects of family and kin association. However, Riesman suggested that a new, more contemporary force added to the prevailing social mix. Now, those in formal and informal associations, peers at the workplace, in public, and where people spent their increased leisure time, influenced an individual's public behavior and social character too. This change manifested itself publicly by people seeking peer approval and shaping their own behavior in anticipation of others' expectations.

Let's apply Riesman's paradigm to the changes observed during the 1950s. The other-directed man was made for consumption spending and persuadable by advertisers' content, especially their emotional appeals. Being like everyone else was important, and that meant getting married and having children, buying a house and filling it with good stuff to display to others, to get their approval, while showing that they were just like them. Keeping up the lawn and keeping up with the neighbors, was expected and approved behavior. Living alike, looking alike, that is—clean, casual, and smelling good—and residing alike, were derived behavior consistent with an other-directed personality. Writing during the 1950s, Robert Wood observed:

> Suburban culture and the pattern of suburban life are designed to intensify the pressures on the individual. They encourage conformity, and subtly rearrange use time and space, the relations of the family, the activities of social and political organizations for the purpose of 'the group.' Each characteristic and institution of suburban life bears witness to the fact that David Riesman's lonely crowd is everywhere.[64]

In 1952, the editors of *Life*, opined that conformity was "being elevated into something akin to a religion."[65] Considered on a national scale, other-directedness embodied the Consensus Era.

Back to Riesman's paradigm, the other-directed man was *the* organization man. That is, the reasons for much of organization man's behavior was his other-directedness. Those socialized to perform to the expectations of others, were perfect fits for the demands of the modern corporate culture. Becoming a company man was the logical and inevitable destiny of someone attuned to behave in anticipation of others' expectations. As a result, the corporate culture could easily influence individual transactions and group behavior.

The corporate industrial order promoted a dual loyalty among its employees. They were expected to form associations and affiliations within and to their corporate cultures. Simultaneously, the good employee was also the good family man and consumer. He provided a home and hearth, building both by purchasing and producing the corporate world of goods.

If so, how did this occur during the 1950s? The other-directed man, being the organization man, both twins, were progeny of the corporate culture, originating in the 1920s, and evolving, thereafter, this hybrid personality, a new social construct, formalized, and became entrenched, during the 1950s. It was the result of an immersion into a cultural and commercial ether, a corporate miasma, of its own design. Thus, the corporation through its employment opportunities, new forms of industrial discipline, its institutional culture, advertising, and providing good products and services, synthesized a new social, industrial, and economic man during the consensus prosperity, and very fertile ground of the 1950s. Vance Packard approached this in *The Hidden Persuaders*. He wrote:

> The trend in American society to the other-directed man—the man who more and more belonged to groups and played on teams—was welcomed and abetted by a large segment of United States industry. People who coalesce into groups, as any general knows, are easier to guide, control, cope with and herd.[66]

Packard went on to observe that group orientation became accepted practice and standard operating procedure, then, for business, government, and labor. In corporations, team players were the most desired types, the most sought-after corporate commodity.[67] Later, Packard wrote in *The Naked Society:*

> as far as conformity is concerned, personnel managers of large bureaucracies—who are in a better position than most of us to help shape society—are much more interested in identifying and selecting conformists than non-conformists.[68]

Elaborating further in *The Pyramid Climbers*, he wrote:

> What is commonly wanted by corporate leaders is the appearance of individualism by basically polite, well-broken in team players.[69]

Overall, conformity and control became an obsession, as large corporations grew in size. Citing contemporaries, Chris Argyris and Absalam Maslow, Packard continued in *The Naked Society:*

> Their findings in general support the view that many managers have been digging themselves into a deeper and deeper hole by their suspiciousness, their careful splintering of responsibility, and their devising of ever-tighter controls on the individual employee whether he is a line worker or an accountant or middle manager[70] . . . (and) . . . A good many social scientists have found that by employing their insights they can point to ways of attaining some degree of control over human behavior. They have shown marketers how to play upon the human subconscious in order to move goods; they have shown management how to spot, conformists who will be good team players.[71]

This meant exerting control at the start: Hiring the right people included the use of background checks and personality tests. In the case of corporate-executive job candidates, even their wives were investigated. Could she be a respectable member of the corporate family? Would she actively and responsibly promote her husband's career by offering her complete support of his work and the firm?

In 1952, a *Life* survey suggested a good corporate wife supported her husband by not complaining about him working late or transferring to a new location.

> They do not behave in a controversial manner or meddle in their husband's work. They maintain the home and hearth for their corporate husband bread-

> winner. They must support and nurture their spouse so he can sustain himself before the rigors of business. Corporate wives must also be sociable when entertaining, be a good "mixer," and be involved with the community.[72]

Even though published in 1952, what was this foreshadowing? In the same issue:

> Today's young couples not only concede their group-mindedness; they are outspokenly in favor of it. They blend in with the group not because they fear to do otherwise but because they approve of it.[73]

With whom were they concurring, and were their responses typical? The 1950s Consensus was a well-publicized and analyzed phenomenon during that decade. "By the middle of the 1950s, talk of conformity, of consumerism and the banality of mass-produced culture were routine elements of middle-class American life." Sloan Wilson wrote a novel, *The Man in the Gray Flannel Suit* (1955), a story drawing on the organization man and how he and his family coped with business and suburban life. In this story prosperity delivered its promised goods and also discontent.[74]

John Keats viciously parodied the organizational-suburbanite relationship in his 1956 novel, *The Crack in the Picture Window*, targeting commercial developers as villains creating a suburban hell behind the white picket fence. Keats' tone in this example typifies his judgments throughout his book:

> More insidious and far more dangerous than any other influence, is the housing development's destruction of individuality. We live in a time of mass terms . . . and we're constantly being badgered to look around us and make sure we're doing and saying and thinking what the mass of our neighbors will accept. The closer we huddle together, the greater this pressure for conformity becomes and today's housing development gives impetus to this pressure in every way.[75]

During these times, by the way, while those in the know were railing away at the dangers wrought by the industrial order, consensus families were buying good stuff from their corporate benefactors, when not glued to the television.

Nevertheless, this decade drew attention from many different perspectives. Professor C. Wright Mills examined two significant components underlying postwar prosperity: the white-collar middle class and power elites.

In *White Collar* (1951), Mills postulated the importance and influence of the new middle class. They rose slowly but persistently to prominence during the twentieth century, acquiring influence and power in the process. By the beginning of the 1950s, Mills asserted the "white collar world" was "characteristic of twentieth century existence" and that their lifestyle changed the "American experience."

Their power and influence as a group, a mass society, was profound. However, as individuals alone, each one was merely an insignificant cog, especially at the workplace where individuals were reduced to bit parts often waging internecine petty, competitive games. Mass media and consumption preys on the individual's wallet and directs his public and in some cases his private behavior.[76] Mills and his followers believed, according to David Halberstram:

> The new threat to the human spirit came not from poverty but from affluence, bigness, and corporate indifference, from bland jobs through which the corporation subtly and often unconsciously subdued and corrupted the human spirit.

And where the white-collar work culture lost control of their lives:

> Here was a world where individuality seemed to be threatened and the price of success might well be greater conformity.[77]

Later, in *The Power Elite* (1956), Mills contended:

> The life-fate of the modern individual depends not only upon the family into which he has been born or which he enters by marriage, but increasingly upon the corporation in which he spends the most alert of his best years.[78]

Some of Mills's contemporaries concurred. In 1953, Chris Agyris pointed out that corporate culture fostered dependency, passivity, subordinance, and loss of workplace control. He likened this process to a role reduction from independent adult to childlike dependency.[79] Erich Fromm opined in 1955, that industrial capitalism created automatons, alienated workers, perpetuated consumers, and men who hate their jobs, "because it makes him feel like a prisoner and a fraud."[80] Later, Robert Theobold, referring to *The Organization Man* and *Life in the Crystal Palace*, asserted:

> These and the many other books on the subject all illustrate the fact that one of the basic conditions of freedom is not fulfilled for the individual who works in a corporation today. . . . Our social system demands such a high standard of material wealth that most men must work, and, as work normally requires set hours, man has little freedom to organize his life as he wishes.[81]

Together, these social observers correctly dissected how our corporate, consensus culture evolved, as it was happening. They focused on its symptoms too much perhaps, and each author exaggerated on certain points of argument. However, diagnosing problems is the purpose of social criticism and intellectual analysis. In hindsight, their collective assessments bore significant truths, despite their sometimes curmudgeon tone, their controversial findings, and their anti-consensus postures. They all offered valid and valuable analysis of their own times. In particular, best-selling author Vance Packard might have had the most complete body of work. A Packard biographer, Daniel Horowitz, asserted that Packard's books, in total, based on decades of public involvement, presented a challenge to the status quo.[82]

So why did rugged, individualistic (victorious in world war), Americans assume the role of conformist organization man? First, they had to make a living and aspiring for a good-paying job in a big company became the norm in at least metropolitan America. To many, a white-collar job became the ideal career path; others wore the blue collar as industry reconverted to civilian production.

Once on the clock, they were expected to accept the rules and norms of corporate culture. These included what became the stereotype: other-directedness; devotion to the organization; lots of time spent on the job; diminishing one's sense of self for the company or the job; conformity to expected behavior both on the job and off. This observable behavior created the stereotype. Thus, the man in the gray flannel suit, also known as the suburban organizational man, embodied the 1950s, becoming the new archetypical American: A people of plenty, living and working and spending money in an affluent society, exercising a strong achievement motive, often shaped by hidden persuaders and other organization men. They set the tone, both in the office and on the shop floor, where the corporate ethos trickled over.[83]

Since American society strove for consensus during the postwar ascent to prosperity, the corporate conformist was its perfect ideological and practical component. The creation of the organization man by corporate culture was psychologically logical. Simply stated, immersing oneself into the corporate bureaucracy and accepting its norms and protocols is natural. We are associative, so becoming an organizational man is similar to being accepted into a tribe or group. The procedure and psychology is similar, but the scale is vastly different.

During the 1950s, the organization man with his inculcated loyalty to the corporation and its values married the consumption-spending woman, who also had an affiliation to the corporate sector that provided her with good stuff. Together, they moved into the suburbs and out there, on the crabgrass frontier, often behind their crack in the picture window, they forged a new middle-classed, standardized, homogenized and widely accepted new lifestyle for themselves and their children. In the process, American society transformed despite the critics, including Main Street, America, its urban and rural have-nots, and racial underclass, were all swept up in its gigantic powerful flow.

What directed and coalesced the disparate economic, institutional social, cultural, and behavioral forces to produce what we look back on as the Fifties? Alfred Chandler wrote:

> As modern business enterprise acquired functions hitherto carried out by the market, it became the most powerful institution in the American economy and its managers the most influential group of economic decision makers. . . . Indeed, years after World War II mark the triumph of modern business enterprise.[84]

The big business corporation, a large economic, social, and political institution, was the vectoring engine that converged these social forces into what became the Consensus and Plenty Society of our postwar years. It was an acceleration of a process began in the 1920s, interrupted during the 1930s. The process continued during and after World War II, and by the end of the century, corporations effectively usurped significant degrees of institutional sovereignty.

Notes

1. Robert Sobel, *The Age of Giant Corporations: A Microeconomic History of American Business, 1914–1970* (Wesport, Connecticut: Greenwood Press, Inc., 1972), 123; John A. Garraty, *The Great Depression* (New York: Anchor Books, 1987), 13–16, 86 (Note: Garraty also wrote: "No accurate counts were made either before, or during the depression," p. 100. Experts studied employment, but could never adequately figure out its extent, p. 104); Charles R. Hearn, *The American Dream in the Great Depression* (Westport, Connecticut: Greenwood Press, 1977), 56; Gary Cross, *An All-Consuming Century: Why Commercialism Won in Modern America* (New York: Columbia University Press, 2000), 68 (I've heard some suggestions that in 1933, the unemployment rate, when part-time work was not counted, reached 44 percent. See Ellis Hawley, *The New Deal and the Problem of Monopoly*, and in, *The New Deal*, Anthony Badger wrote: "The unemployment statistics were notoriously unreliable. It is quite likely that one third of those available for work were jobless," p. 18); William L. O'Neill, *A Democracy at War: America Fights at Home and Abroad in World War II* (New York: The Free Press, 1993), 25,75, and quote on 202.
2. Sobel, *Giant Corporations*, 125.
3. Sobel, *Age*, 123, 152; Pells, *Radical Visions*, 46–47; Garratty, *Great Depression*, 124, 134.
4. Frederick L. Allen, *The Lords of Creation* New York: Harper & Brothers, 1935, 462.
5. Richard S. Tedlow, *New and Improved: The Story of Mass Marketing in America* (Boston: Harvard Business School Press, 1996 [1990]), 300.
6. Quoted in Daniel Horowitz, *The Morality of Spending: Attitudes Toward the Consumer Society in America, 1875–1940* (Chicago: Ivan R. Dee Publisher (1985), Elephant Paperbacks, 1992), 160–161.
7. O'Neill, *A Democracy at War*, 7.
8. See Lizabeth Cohen, *A Consumer's Republic: The Politics of Mass Consumption in Postwar America*, New York: Knopf, 2003.

9. See Simon N. Pattern, *The New Basis of Civilization*, Cambridge: Belknap Press (reprint edition, 1968), 1907, and *The Consumption of Wealth*, Publications of the University of Pennsylvania, 1901.

10. Patten, *New Basis*, 72.

11. Davis Riesman, "Abundance for What?" *Bulletin of the Atomic Scientists*, 14(April 1958), 136–137.

12. Calder, *Financing*, 262.

13. Ibid., 11–12.

14. Daniel Boorstin, *The Americans: The Democratic Experience* (New York: Random House, 1973), 426.

15. Gary Cross, *An All-Consuming Century: Why Commercialism Won in Modern America* (New York: Columbia University Press), 2000, iii.

16. Sivulka, *Soap, Sex*, 245.

17. Thomas Hine, *Populuxe*, New York: Alfred A. Knopf, 1986, 3.

18. Edward Filene, *The Way Out: A Forecast of Coming Changes in American Business and Industry* (New York: Doubleday, Page & Company, 1925), 201, 34, 45–46, respectively for the three quotes.

19. Gold, "Happy Problems," 59.

20. *Fortune*, August 1953, 98.

21. Peter F. Drucker, *The New Society: The Anatomy of the Industrial Order* (Westport: Greenwood Press, reprint, 1982, [1949]), 38.

22. Ibid., 40–41, 43.

23. Ibid., 50–69.

24. Sivulka, *Soap, Sex*, 426.

25. Ernest Dichter, *The Strategy of Desire* (New York: Doubleday & Company, Inc., 1960), 13–17.

26. Ibid.

27. Betty Friedan, *The Feminine Mystique*, New York: W.W. Norton & Company, Inc., 1963, 228.

28. Packard, *People Shapers*, 128–129, 12, 3

29. Vance Packard, *The Hidden Persuaders* (New York: Pocket Books, 1957), 136–138.

30. David Potter, *People of Plenty: Economic Abundance and the American Character*, Chicago: University of Chicago Press, 1954, 167–168, 177.

31. Cecilia Tichi, *Electronic Hearth: Creating an American Television Culture* (New York: Oxford University Press, 1991), 12.

32. *Architectural Forum* July 1948, 7.

33. *Business Week*, "Cyclops," 76.

34. Bogart, *Age of Television*, 105.

35. Bogart, *Age of Television*, 35.

36. Bogart, *Age of Television*, 62.

37. Ashley Montagu, *The American Way of Life*, New York: G.P. Putnam's Sons, 1967 (1952), 44–46.

38. *Business Week*, March 10, 1956, 91.

39. Marling, *As Seen*, 255. For the illustration, see *The Saturday Evening Post*, August 15, 1959.

40. Harry Henderson, "The Mass Produced Suburbs—Part I, How People Live," *Harper's Magazine* 207 (December 1953), 28.

41. August, 1947, 65.

42. Ibid., 66.

43. Herbert J. Gans, *The Levittowners: Way of Life and Politics in a New Suburban Community* (New York: Pantheon Books, 1967), vii–viii, xvii–xviii, 27, 44.

44. Ibid., vii.

45. Boorstin, *Americans*, 1, 89–90.

46. Frederick L. Allen, "The Big Change in Suburbia," *Harper's Magazine*, 208(June 1954), 21.

47. I wrote the second draft of this chapter during 2003 and the other chapters thereafter. In 2007, AMC's *Mad Men* debuted on cable. I was dumbfounded by how well it portrayed (circa 1960–61, the first season) the workplace and suburbia, reflecting the stereotypes and what was observed during those times. I'd be curious to know if its producers and writers read some of these books, *The Cliffdwellers, The Hucksters*, and *The Man in the Gray Flannel Suit.*

48. I synthesized these last few paragraphs from what I read. Harry Henderson examined suburban life over a three-year period, investigating six towns. His conclusions, similar to my composite, appeared in the November and December 1953 issues of *Harpers Magazine.* See also the May, July, and August 1953 issues of *Fortune.*

Here's a synopsis of his investigation. At that time, Henry Henderson observed similar patterns in the suburbs he visited; where he interviewed residents in six suburbs, over a three-year period. The average age of the men was 31; women, 26. Income ranged from four to seven thousand dollars per year. The male occupations included managers, professionals, salesmen, skilled workers, GIs, and small business owners. Commuting for one to one and one-half hours, the men worked and the women didn't. Pregnancy was ubiquitous. During the day, the women created a subculture based on home visiting; especially the coffee klatch.

Houses cost between seven and twelve thousand dollars. Each place visited, looked the same, but there were few complaints. As similar as each house looked on the outside, there was lots of effort expended on interior design. They cozied the nest using examples from magazines.

Henderson found that suburbanites were joiners and actively participated in group activities; much of which was centered around home visiting and neighborliness. The women and children gathered during the day; families during off-hours and weekends.

However, television was a significant competitor for free time. Henderson observed that these places were the first where TV's influence significantly affected daily life. He opined that TV shows drew viewers together by providing a similar experience for all.

These residents were, typically, casual, non-snobbish, friendly, warm, outgoing, bouyant, and willing to help and cooperate regarding common problems. It seemed like the opposite of long-established big-city coldness and indifference.

Henderson also noted that these communities had few problems; lots of room; countryside atmosphere; "good" neighborhoods; centrally located stores.

They also had a weak, local political infrastructure; no established neighborhood, and essentially, no clearly defined, traditional, urban-based class structure. These 'burbs were all new and didn't have the problems that cities do: blight, vacant lots, congestion; old garish business districts.

In retrospect, one could say that Henderson hit on a prevailing attitude that underlies the ubiquitousness of this new lifestyle. He noted an attitude of unbridled optimism toward the future, and confidence about attaining success in their blossoming careers, regardless of having to live on a budget, or for the lack of savings. The success ethic ran deep and translated in terms of income achievement.

An omniscient observer could say that this pattern repeated itself elsewhere, and that stereotypes are often based on observable behavior. (Source: *Harper's Magazine*, November 1953 and December 1953)

49. William H. Whyte, "The Outgoing Life," *Fortune*, 48 (July 1953), 158.

50. Harry Henderson, "Rugged American Collectivism—The Mass Produced Suburbs, Part II," *Harper's Magazine*, 207 (December 1953) 81.

51. *Fortune*, November 1953, 131.

52. Whyte, Jr., William H. "The Transients," *Fortune*, May 1953, 113.

53. John Lennon, "Working Class Hero."

54. Robert Wood, *Surburbia: It's People and Their Politics*, 1958, 4.

55. *Fortune*, May 1953, 113, and July 1953, 84.

56. Lizabeth Cohen, *A Consumer's Republic: The Politics of Mass Consumption in Postwar America* (New York: Knopf, 2003).

57. *Fortune*, October 1956, 128: Note the lack of worry about saving for a rainy day.

58. Thomas Frank, *The Conquest of Cool: Business Culture, Counterculture, and the Rise of Consumerism* (Chicago: The University of Chicago Press, 1997), 10.

59. Gans, *Levittowners*, xvi, 153

60. Since 1996, when I finished my PhD in American history, at age forty-five, I too, consider myself as a card-carrying egghead. Was not this the term first applied to those in the know during the 1950s?

61. Whyte, *Organization*, 3.

62. Vance Packard, *The Pyramid Climbers* (New York: McGraw-Hill Book Company, Inc., 1962), 272.

63. Whyte, *Organization*, 10.

64. Wood, *Suburbia*, 5.

65. *Life*, January 7, 1952, 36.

66. Vance Packard, *The Hidden Persuaders*, New York: Pocket Books, 1957, 173.

67. Ibid., 173–177.

68. Packard, *Naked Society*, 287.

69. Packard, *Pyramid Climbers*, 299.

70. Packard, *Naked Society*, 99.

71. Ibid., 286.

72. *Life*, January 7, 1952, 32–34.

73. Ibid., 36.

74. The man in the gray flannel suit can symbolize the corporate institutionalization of the Protestant ethic within American society. The ethic provided the moral motivation to both improve and accept the new, more subtle system of industrial discipline, which was manifesting itself within corporate culture. Indeed, the tenets of the

ethic easily fit into the organizational paradigm. (Other-directedness; group instead of congregational obligations; deferred gratification to organizational gratification; outward manifestations of deference to hard work, self-reliance, etc.)

Whyte's organization man embodied and modernized the Protestant ethic, but did not destroy it. The organization man worked hard; dedicating himself to his job and to the firm. He strove to get ahead; to make money; to outwardly display his accomplishment through consumption spending. He deferred to authority; learning his place within the corporate culture. See Max Weber, *The Protestant and the Spirit of Capitalism*, and R. H. Tawney, *Religion and the Rise of Capitalism.*

75. John Keats, *The Crack in the Picture Window* (Boston: Houghton Mifflin Company, 1956), 193.

76. Mills, *White Collar*, xiv, 24, 69–71, 74, 161–166, 186–188, 259, 363–264.

77. Halberstram, *The Fifties*, 528–529.

78. C. Wright Mills, *The Power Elite* (New York: Oxford University Press, 1956), 6.

79. Chris Argyris, "The Individual and Organization: Some Problems of Mutual Adjustment," *Administrative Science Quarterly*, 2 (June 1957), 13.

80. Eric Fromm, "The Present Human Condition," *The American Scholar*, 25 (Winter, 1955–56), 29–32.

81. Robert Theobold, *The Challenge of Abundance* (New York: Clarkson N. Potter, Inc., Publisher, 1961), 156.

82. Daniel Horowitz, *Vance Packard and American Social Criticism* (Chapel Hill: University of North Carolina Press, 1994), 2–5.

83. My own corporate experience fits Riesman's model. My first adult job was in the corporate office of a Fortune 500 company, one famous in the clothing industry. They at first didn't want to hire me because I had a master's degree (history), and they were afraid I would take over the department (at twenty-four years old and essentially with little serious work experience). They promptly christened me, "The Dummy," which became my informal nickname. After a year or so they wanted me to go on the union track instead of management. I declined. After more wheel spinning, now working for a third management team in less than two years, someone remarked that showing up to work everyday and doing a good job was not enough to get ahead. I wouldn't unless I became one of the boys. I didn't lunch with the right people, and I never stayed after hours or went to happy hours, like the rest of them. In hindsight, without the nine years I worked in the corporate sector, I probably wouldn't have done this book.

84. Alfred D. Chandler Jr., *The Visible Hand: The Managerial Revolution in American Business* (Cambridge, Belknap Press, 1977), 1, 477.

Of note: Essayists George D. Smith and Davis Dyer, writing in Carl Kaysen's *The American Corporation Today* (1996), commented on Chandler: "All who sought to explain the nature of post-industrial American culture had to concur with the broader implication of his argument: that as its economic development came increasingly under the control of large corporations, the United States became a managerial society," (chapter 2, p. 34).

Interlude

The Organizational Synthesis

BY 1950, THE AMERICANS' social relationship with their cultural paradigm had been forever altered by the corporate sector. Indeed, a new model evolved from this interactive process among individual, group, and institutions. Sociologically and psychologically speaking, a new paradigm could be called the Organizational Synthesis.

The old order of the nineteenth century ended with the emergence of mass production, distribution, and transportation. The corporate sector of the economy directed this. Extrinsically, this was the creation of the modern urban-industrial order, that derived an organizational and consumer society. Indirectly, big business ushered in a new social paradigm. The new corporate order replaced the nineteenth-century rural and agrarian model.

The paradigm in Robert Wiebe's *The Search for Order* spawned the hypothesis of this book. Within its parameters, the social order of American society included a series of relationships characterized by autonomy and individualism, small group interaction, associationalism, and persistent localism. Lumped together, these were some of the parts of Wiebe's island-community model. In that world, autonomous, and probably, typically, inner-directed individual exercised and engaged their American freedoms, in a Turnerian and Jeffersonian agrarian psychological, social, and spiritual paradise. Here, the belief elevated individual freedom and citizenship to baroque levels. The yeoman farmer, westering pioneer, conqueror of the red man and of nature and a continent, characterized that idea, ideal, value, and belief.

While the autonomous individual occupied his little house on the prairie or riverbank, his affiliations ranged from neighborliness to small, insular community relations. Almost all normative group activities, the nineteenth-century, automaticity of everyday life, was small-group interaction: family, kin, neighbors, townsfolk, the church, the community school; a local market entrepreneurial craftsmen and retailers.

Everyday life was simple, local, and insular. Reality was often defined by the horizon; civically by the township or county. Households were independent, self-sufficient, subsistent, isolated from the larger world. Outlook went as far as neighbors, townsfolk, and local interests. There wasn't much interest in reality beyond the horizon. Congress to most nineteenth-century Americans meant attending church, a town meeting, or socializing around the store or in a saloon. Association was informal and local.

This America of de Tocqueville, Jefferson, Hawthorne, and Turner persisted to the Civil War, and then slowly changed, fostered by new socioeconomic and technical catalysts incubating in American cities and factory towns.

Technology and innovation energized the paradigm shift. The factory system became more mechanized, expanding as a result. As the nineteenth century ended, social, economic, and scientific forces coalesced. Out of this synthesis emerged the urban-industrial order and its principal manifestations: mass production, distribution, and consumption.

The resulting revolutionary change would eventually alter the old order, creating a new, evolutionary social model. Anonymity and consensual homogeneity replaced autonomy and individualism. Large group association superseded small. Interdependent complexity overwhelmed simplicity and localism. Corporate institutionalism replaced traditional associationism as dominant reality.

The nineteenth-century American individual—frontiersman, pioneer, entrepreneur—became the assembly line worker, the organization man in his gray flannel suit, and on weekends, his suburban dungarees and sports shirt. The twentieth-century typical American did not stand out, or alone from most of his contemporaries. As parts of a greater urban-industrial machine, they became stereotyped and interchangeable, and over the long run of the century, consensually homogeneous, no longer as important as their fittability into a greater systemized, nationalized whole: the city, the factory, the office, the monolithical corporation, the target market. Thus, anonymity and homogeneity trumped autonomy and individualism.

Lost in the crowd, became the new social normalcy. Mass society seemed fueled by large-group action. Large factories with large worker populations, produced large amounts of goods to be distributed to large numbers of people, living in large cities and growing-large suburbs. Everything associated with the big business corporation seemed to enlarge in size, shape, depth, range, and complexity. Mass production, distribution, consumption, transportation, communication, entertainment, leisure, all of grand scale and scope, necessitated systematic organization, management, administration, and execution by masses of people, working together, in large massive institutions. Again, the corporate form and culture led the way. Thus, the small-group infrastructure and methodology of the old nineteenth-century order succumbed to the large-group orientation of mass scale.

That agrarian, rural, small-town, small-group associationalism gave way to the absolute and irreversible large-scale institutionalism of the corporate industrial order. What could be accomplished on an individual or local small-group scale in the nineteenth century, now could only be managed and accomplished by massive, monolithical, systematized organizations. Mass communications and transportation connected the nation; shrinking distance and time simultaneously. Mass production and distribution delivered, via that system, to a nationwide, mass market. Mass society imploded upon itself in large cities, spilling over eventually into suburbia, exurbia, and sprawlurbia. Mass media forged an almost instantaneous homogeneity, and political and social consensus, at least for a while.

After mid-century, nothing seemed simple anymore. American life was large, plentiful, complex, and subtly interdependent more than ever before. The growth and expansion of the American socioeconomic system, driven to behemoth levels by corporations, fostered a lattice of increasingly connected, interdependent complexity. Transportation, communication, distribution, media: All developed and expanded in relation to and fueled by each other. By the end of the twentieth century, most of the myriad anchor points of the system were connected and interlocked.

This new, twentieth-century American system, can be seen by its emphasis on individual anonymity. (We're all just a number, parts in a greater machine.) Is is a society and economy controlled by large group behavior, operating on a complex institutional, bureaucratic, level, tied together anonymously, but interdependently over distance.

It became a new social universe, culture, and nation-state that couldn't have been envisioned by those that lived under the old order. The new world of twentieth-century America transcended, perhaps, the wildest dreams of long-dead empire builders, utopian visionaries, and even power-mongering tyrants and demagogues. They couldn't attain what the new American Century accomplished because they lacked the institutional fuel, resources and organizational infrastructure necessary to launch a society to its baroque limits. It was accomplished in twentieth-century America by a monolithic, big business corporation.

Part II
CORPORATE BAROQUE

Throughout much of the twentieth century, big business influenced the lives of most Americans chiefly by providing job opportunity and good stuff to buy. Over those decades, this influence increased in strength and depth. As William G. Roy wrote,

> Few features of contemporary American society are more far-reaching or awesome than its large industrial corporations, the largest of which command more resources than the majority of nations in the world, employ more people than live in many cities, and shape our daily life more thoroughly than previously dominant institutions such as religion.[1]

Ultimately, the corporate sector of our political economy and socioeconomic system became its most significant force. Its influence on twentieth-century America is similar to Frederick Jackson Turner's frontier on the nineteenth.[2]

The interaction of the corporate institution with individuals and groups, and the level of influence the corporate sector had on our nation's economic, social, and psychological development, was the general subject of the first section of this book, chapters 2 through 4.

Here, in part II, chapters 5–7, I focus on the big business corporation, collectively, and that sector of the economy, as plenipotentiary institutions. That is, how corporations function on the level of our civilization's most powerful institutions: the federal government, the nation-state, and society. We are about to enter the top tier, where the institutional participants operate on the highest level; where the men in the high castles create, administrate, manage, and direct large-scale socioeconomic, and social factors that fuel the very core engines that push our society.

This is done on the institutional level, monolithical, as in the artist Thomas Cole's series "The Course of Empire," his portrayal of the life course of civilizations.[3] At the center of this are the big business corporations, where they help shape policies, practices, and the life course of society.

Thus, in part II "Corporate Baroque," I will attempt to explore the relationship between big business and big government, in chapter 5; the corporate sector's role in lobbying, interest groups, influence peddling, political action committees, and campaign finance, in chapter 6. Chapter 7 is about multinational corporations and globalization.

Notes

1. William G. Roy, *Socializing Capital: The Rise of the Large Industrial Corporation in America* (Princeton: Princeton University Press, 1997), xiii.

2. See Frederick Jackson Turner, *The Frontier in American History* (New York: Hill & Wang, 1986 [1920]).

3. There are five paintings: *The Savage State* is raw nature, the howling wilderness. *The Pastoral State*, represents man's first encounters with it, similar to the first years of our colonial history. *Consummation* depicts the nation at its height. (Think of ancient Egypt, Greece, Rome; nineteenth-century England; and the United States during the twentieth century.) *Destruction* shows the inevitable decline and failure of the above. *Desolation* pictures the ruins and return toward its natural beginnings.

5

The Dance of the Titans

Business/Government Relations and Power Elite Governance

BUSINESS/GOVERNMENT RELATIONS operated on more than one level. This chapter will examine how the two institutions evolved a plenipotentiary relationship and then sustained it throughout the twentieth century. Essentially, it occurred through interaction at the elite/executive/managerial level, in response to a series of events beginning before the start of World War I.

Most analysis and interpretation of business-government relations (B/G), clusters around political, economic, administrative, policy analysis, and legislative history. A lot of it factors in political ideology regarding capitalism, communism, socialism, conservatism, liberalism, and, recently, globalization.

In this already complex mix, I would like to emphasize the role of institutions and group action. It includes some of the above. However, I'm attempting to add additional factors, including the interaction of informed and interested characters, operating within their respective organizational systems and institutional cultures. My overall purpose is to add to the preexisting analysis, not contesting or refuting what is already published. Instead, my presentation angle comes from a different direction, seeking a place for the organizational synthesis at this high level.

In this chapter, I've strung together points of contact and repulsion, to show a long-run pattern. In itself, a history of business and government relations is a book-length study. Here, I can only survey this interaction, zooming down across the years, for a closer look at specific times and its participants. Hence, the chapter format.

Early in 1902, a newspaperman told financier, J. P. Morgan, that the federal government intended to prosecute his holding company, the recently formed

Northern Securities Trust, for Sherman antitrust violations. Morgan's immediate reaction was dismay. He opined to some of his associates that President Theodore Roosevelt should have contacted him, stating what he wanted, and allow Morgan to re-craft his company to conform to the government's requirements.

On February 22, 1902, J. P. Morgan met with President Roosevelt, in the White House. During their very formal conversation on the Northern Securities issue, Morgan said: "If we have done anything wrong, send your man to my man and they can fix it up." To which, Mr. Roosevelt replied, "That can't be done." At the president's side, Attorney General Philander Knox added, "We don't want to fix it up, we want to stop it." Morgan responded: "Are you going to attack my other interests, the Steel Trust and others?" Roosevelt, replied: "Certainly not—unless we find out that in any case they have done something that we regard as wrong."

Business-government relations were more than just powerful individuals making deals and negotiating. These men were players, acting on behalf of two, emerging, evolving, and powerful institutional behemoths.[1] Through individual effort, group effort, and insider arrangements, big business and the federal government cooperated, conflicted, and created modern America. At times revolutionary in their efforts, the reality they made, was, over the long run, more pragmatically successful than they knew at the time.

In retrospect, we know these efforts as: The Progressive Era, mobilization for two wars, Normalcy, The New Deal, and the Cold War. The historical details were often the result of different levels of conflict or cooperative effort between business and government.

Today, we know about some of these details from studying corporate liberal reform, the War Industries Board, President Herbert Hoover's associative state, the National Recovery Agency, the Arsenal of Democracy, and the military-industrial complex, among several others.

These episodes in American history were the results of the work of several enabling groups, made up of influential individuals who together formulated public policy: The Committee on Economic Development, the Business Advisory Council, and the Council on Foreign Relations, as examples, were all nongovernmental organizations created to come up with public policy. They advised on, or made public policy recommendations at the federal level.

Through these groups interacting with the federal government, men of the private and public sectors attempted to forge a manageable and persistent political economy, nation-state, and society, within the established legal, political, and believed boundaries of a capitalistic democracy. Over time, and through a consistent effort, big business and the federal government, two giant institutions, interacted, a dance of the titans.

They created a new modernity as they lived it, and within it; creating as they go. The resulting economic, political, and social realities necessitated adaptation to changing conditions, caused by this newly emerging urban-industrial order and mass society.

Both big business and government attempted to interact with each other and manage the political economy by group dynamics and institutional action, in a linked, interdependent manner.

As previously seen in chapters 2 and 4, managing a large corporation had to be done by groups of experts and specialists, linked in a systematized institutional framework. (This too, became standard procedure for federal government policy making and rule.)

Both institutions increasingly relied on networked thinking, utilizing groups of experts. Thus, big corporations produced good stuff as the result of group effort. Engineers, accounts, lawyers, paper-shuffling managers, all specialized in specific tasks, and all interlocked, to pool their talents in order to effectively manage businesses that mass produced, mass advertised, and employed large numbers of people, often working in geographically dispersed sites. Corporations such as Standard Oil and General Electric, in order to successfully compete and manage large-scale manufacturing plants, typically used the group approach more so than the jack-of-all-trades, individualistic system. The old, small-shop model could not be applied.

The federal government also adopted the corporate organizational model, as it, too, increased in size and complexity. Using similar personnel and knowledge resources, it governed applying business methods. As its role in the economy and society enlarged, it made policy, and governed by using groups, specialists (often from the private sector), who worked together formulating policy on advisory committees, public commissions, and within the federal bureaucracy. Similarly, group thinking and policy execution superseded much independent, individual decision-making. The government secretary or his support staff often used the same corporate methods to manage that their corporate counterpart used to produce goods and services in the private sector. Hence, the organizational model includes both of these institutional giants.

Even as the two titans danced, the organizational pattern persisted.[2] Examples in this chapter, ranging from the War Industries Board to the Committee on Economic Development, were groups that applied methods developed by big business, used by both, and part of the organizational revolution as it evolved prior to 1950.

Although often at odds with each other, big business and government, decade by decade, more or less conformed to this new operational model. This chapter attempts to show how.

The changing times caused by the emergence of monolithical corporate capitalism prompted action by contemporary those-in-the-know. The rapidly changing political economy quickly drew public attention. Those in both the private and public sectors attempted to address new social conditions, with a combination of old and new ideologies and methodologies.

Their contemporary world changed dramatically due to mass communications, production, marketing, and distribution. American society was now morphing into a truly modern, national, coast-to-coast political economy, linked by technology such as the telegraph and railroads; later, the telephone and radio, movies, and cars and airplanes. Corporate, standard, mass-marketed and distributed consumer products, and a new, mass media, began to influence a changing American culture.

Thus, prior to World War I, the American economy and culture rapidly, if not abruptly, changed, causing socioeconomic situations that stressed traditional methods of doing things. In response, stakeholders associated together, using group strength and collective resources, to address the social problems that, too, immediately occurred as by-products of this new modernization. This group response is the Progressive Era. Their attempts to adapt society wound up setting precedents that persisted deep into the rest of the twentieth century.

The Progressive Era was the first time that business and government confronted each other over what America was becoming. Robert Wiebe suggested that B/G relations, were like each sector controlling spheres of interest, similar to sovereign nation-states. Big business often viewed the federal government as another form of competition. Tacitly, corporations did not recognize or accept government's police power. Rather, they viewed government as an equal. Big business preferred government in friendly hands. When controlled by unfriendly politicians, say, William Jennings Bryan, government became a foe, similar to labor unions and reformers and socialists. Hence, business was almost always wary of government, at any level.

Some of their interaction created and sustained precedents that would influence their institutional interaction for the rest of the century. The dance they began, then, included the role of government in the economy, the level of citizenship big business would be expected to fulfill, the use of government countervailing power, and the roles each institution played in addressing very public social issues.

During the late nineteenth century, business rose up unfettered during the Gilded Age. Starting with railroad expansion across the continent, corporations began to emerge and grow, nurtured by what we call the captains of industry: Rockefeller, Carnegie, Harriman, Gould, Fisk, Morgan, etc.

They sailed an economic sea essentially devoid of ships of state. Classical laissez-faire economics prevailed, enabling industry to steer itself on the highest seas of capitalism. Even as the nineteenth century ended, as the frontier closed, the federal government seemed content in its all but invisible role. Except for tariffs and promoting foreign trade, the general government had little interaction with the private sector.

This relationship would change as one era ended, as one paradigm shifted. At the century break-point, new socioeconomic forces gathered strength and quickly coalesced, rapidly expanding in influence and power. Modernization in terms of mass-production technology, mass communications, and mass distribution together precipitated a new socioeconomic synthesis, the rise of big business.

During the first twenty years of the new century, the power and influence of this new socioeconomic force burst forth into the political economy, vigorously asserting its market power and noticeably its institutional presence.

The engines of big business, quickly created, fired up and began to steer American society, consequently startling all three levels of government, from town, state capital, and Washington, D.C. The emergence and rise of big business directed and shaped the political economy by providing new institutional models of economic strength, technological innovation and applications, business-administrative system, and new legal issues. While influencing most of American society, it too, spawned a new, hybrid of itself—big government. Thus, in the years prior to World War I, the new American titans debuted, and their century-long dance was about to begin.

The first round occurred during the Progressive Era. From about 1900 to 1915, the concept of corporation moved beyond revolutionary. To some contemporary observers, it became threatening; to others, a curiosity; to many, modern reflections of man's technological know-how, and an indicator of progress and modern system. There was even a sense of hope that this new urban-industrial order might provide new opportunities if fully integrated into society.

At the same time, corporate size, wealth, and power became a perceived threat. The changes occurring in contemporary society were blatantly evident, manifested in the products corporations produced and distributed; the size of manufacturing plants; the six-day workweek they imposed; the adaptation of work to machined mass production. Then, the nearby, emerging factory, mass-production world of work became the subject of public debate, and for the first time, a significant concern of public policy at the three levels of government.

The impact of big business on society would be the root cause of what became Progressive Era reform. The reconciliation of the economic, legal, social, and political status of big business played out as the three governments responded to public calls for some sort of civic response to the new conditions the new industrial order presented.

These conditions included a comparatively abrupt change in social reality from the old nineteenth-century to the new urban-industrial ethos. This new order superseded the traditional Jeffersonian and Jacksonian America, replacing it, in a few years, not decades, with the worlds of Alexander Hamilton, Andrew Carnegie, John D. Rockefeller, and J. P. Morgan. Under this new social order, everyday life translated itself into wage earners replacing small farms and craftsmen and mass-production work obsolescing most skilled labor.

In response to these changing economic and social conditions, and to the rise of big business, government, especially the federal government, wound up revolutionizing its public role.

Our courts made corporations legal citizens, thus quickly generating questions about their political and socioeconomic status, influence, and responsibility. A reform impulse soon followed. That notion, addressing the problem, and attempting to influence and control this new, modern industrial order, sparked the federal government to institutionally grow and intervene in the corporate dominated economy.

Thus, it is true, to view the rise of big business as the catalyst for the evolution of big government. In response to the institutional force of big business, the administrative, policy making, and coercive involvement of the federal government increased, directly influenced by the socioeconomic changes caused by the corporate sector.

Despite their laissez-faire rhetoric regarding free markets, the captains of industry preferred and attempted to control competition through combination, prior to 1900.[3] Consolidation included most of the burgeoning corporate sector, from materials supplier to product producer. This trend continued into the twentieth century despite the Sherman, and later, Clayton antitrust acts. By 1917, the American economy, was characterized by concentrated and consolidated monopoly power.

The federal government's first response was the Interstate Commerce Act, of 1887, and the Sherman Anti-Trust Act, of 1890. Consider these two acts the debut of the federal government on the top-level playing field, one already being staked out by the emerging titan, corporate capitalism. The federal government's initial moves were largely ineffectual. Already, corporate combination consolidated into monoliths well in advance of the federal government's attempt to become a countervailing power.

Despite government's efforts to enforce, at first, Sherman, later Clayton, the results were, in hindsight, negligible. Gabriel Kolko assessed their antitrust efforts as merely social sanctioning. I see it as laws that weren't adequately enforced, or twisted in its purpose, to instead, control and suppress labor organizing. The Sherman Act was too general in text, and lacking in a set of specific sanctions.[4] It could be applied and adjudicated widely, depending on the situation and the ideological belief of the player. Would the U.S. Justice Department apply the law to all combinations, or simply not enforce it? Would the courts uphold its enforcement? Even then, the federal government was mostly business-friendly and already influenced (see chapter 6), by corporate wealth. At the same time, contemporary belief favored unfettered capitalism over a new-fangled regulatory state. At this time, the political economy, although rapidly evolving, was still grounded in nineteenth-century, preindustrial ideology that favored the position of business trumping government. Then, an interventionist state was not considered normal.

Thus, the federal government's interaction regarding the first question, was at least situational, superficial, and lacking in system, organization, and strength. Then, the federal government, respectively commanded by Theodore Roosevelt, William H. Taft, and later, Woodrow Wilson, had not acquired the necessary institutional strength to exert effective, let alone, overpowering influence over and significant control of monopoly power.

They did not know it then, and neither did their successors, that a prime moving force, operating within the system it created, cannot be effectively controlled because it has already influenced the legal and political process to an extent that the power necessary to control it had been subverted, co-opted, and rendered ineffectual. By and through the Progressive Era, big business already accomplished this. The result for the federal government, as it too, pieced together its new, modern institutional makeup, could only hope to contain a power that already was too advanced to stop or roll back. The rest of the corporate century attests to this unequal dance.

We shall see throughout this chapter how these public and private groups worked to analyze contemporary socioeconomic and political issues; publish public-policy proposals, recommendations, and statements; to execute administrate, and manage subsequent policy actions; to supply expertise in the administrative bureaucracies of the private and public sectors; and most important, to see the managing role that major players in big business had in influencing federal government policy formulation and execution.

President Theodore Roosevelt was the first president to wrestle with the concept of corporation and its position in the political economy, and before the public. As a main player, Roosevelt assumed a conservative role, maneuvering between internecine political conflict within his own political party, and within the federal government. He also had to respond to the public call for some sort of response to contemporary socioeconomic conditions.

Roosevelt's response was pragmatically conservative. For after all, he was born of privilege. Thus, his perceptions of reality prismed through what he was.[5] He opposed socialism and was not friendly to radical labor. At the same time, he had that upper-crust, patrician sense of noblesse oblige.

These personal attitudes influenced his role and actions as a pilot of our ship of state. He participated in shaping the modern roles of government, directly, and of big business, indirectly. He successfully rode the storm he helped create, emerging from it subtly triumphant, setting government and big business on a course that became our modern, corporate liberal state and political economy. It perhaps was his greatest, albeit seldom heralded, accomplishment.

Theodore Roosevelt assumed the presidency on September 14, 1901, after President William McKinley was assassinated. The new president pledged to maintain his predecessor's programs. The McKinley administration, supported by big business, was entirely business-friendly. The replacement president, too, initially stayed the course as he began to run the gauntlet between the old order and the new. Roosevelt supported big business, accepting its emergence and growth, but at the same time, he believed that the federal government should also grow, empowering itself to what we call today a countervailing power to corporate power. Thus, simply stated, if big business was to grow, and become powerful, then the federal government in response, must follow the same path. Hence, de facto, big business spurred the growth of big government.

In May 1905, President Roosevelt said:

> I believe in corporations. They are indispensable instruments of our modern civilization; but I believe that they should be so supervised and so regulated that they shall act for the interest of the community as a whole.[6]

This meant that Roosevelt had to interact with powerful corporate executives, who were already aligned with their political allies in the Republican Party, the United States Congress, and corporate-friendly state and local governments. Hence, the gauntlet.

Roosevelt positioned himself at two different points on the political spectrum simultaneously. He did not hesitate to suppress labor unrest, for example.[7] Remember, he was upper-crust in heritage, status, education, and belief. Hence, the masses were the masses, and could only be allowed to go so far. Thus, his sense of noblesse oblige had limits.

Although Roosevelt recognized what the captains of industry accomplished, their risk level now changed. Investing in new, untested production methods succeeded, garnering corporate industrialists outstanding and well-deserved profits. Since then, however, that risk had decreased, calling into question the prevailing high corporate profit levels. This success enables big business, simply put, to pay their help better. Roosevelt believed this was both the next practical step in the new order of things and a necessary measure to prevent working-class uproar and violence by labor's most radical elements. At the same time, Roosevelt did not worship at the corporate altar. John M. Cooper suggested that by the 1912 election campaign:

> Roosevelt implicitly accepted three propositions: that the biggest corporations had for the most part achieved their stature through efficient competition, that large corporations were here to stay, and that present economic conditions represented progress. But for him those were not the most important concerns. When he expounded on such matters as "conduct not size," how businesses treated workers and consumers, and putting "the hand of government" on them, he was voicing his true concern. He believed that the main economic task of government lay in protecting the victims and clients of large-scale enterprise through greatly strengthened regulation and supervision. Some might hold that he was anticipating John Kenneth Galbraith's concept of "countervailing power" between big business and government. Actually, Roosevelt wanted an overwhelming governmental supremacy that did, in a nonpejorative sense, deserve the designation "paternalism." His vision of public supervision and protection forecast much of the twentieth-century welfare state.[8]

And, as a politician, Roosevelt was well aware of Bryanite opposition in that wing of the Democratic Party. Later, in 1940, Matthew Josephson wrote that Roosevelt was a reluctant, hesitant reformer, who was prodded into response by public pressure, instigated by Democratic Party opposition.

At the same time, Roosevelt had a penchant for reform, which he had already manifested when he served as a New York state assemblyman, as governor, on the New York City police board, and then at the federal level, on the civil service commission. Thus, when he assumed the presidency, his mindset and attitude were already in place, and his track record could have been used as a predictor for what occurred next.

For example, when Roosevelt replaced McKinley, the trust problem was already a significant public policy issue. As a typical northeastern conservative, the new president accepted the notion of what big business was. Yet, at the same time, he believed that the federal government had to respond to contemporary change. Because big business, corporations, grew to unprecedented levels of socioeconomic power and influence, the federal government must have a hand in making sure corporations acted responsibly. In 1901, soon after assuming office, the now President Roosevelt said:

> Great corporations exist only because they are created and safeguarded by our institutions; and it is therefore our right and duty to see that they work in harmony with these institutions. . . . In the interest of the public, the government

> should have the right to inspect and examine the workings of great corporations. . . . The nation should, without interfering with the power of the States in the manner itself, also assume power of supervision and regulation over all corporations doing interstate business and in 1902: The great corporations which we have grown to speak of rather loosely as trusts are the creatures of the State, and the State not only has the right to control them, but it is in duty bound to control them wherever need of such control is shown. . . . (Applause) The immediate necessity in dealing with trusts is to place them under the real, not the nominal, control of some sovereign to which, as its creatures, the trusts shall owe allegiance, and in whose courts the sovereign's orders may be enforced. (Applause) In my opinion, this sovereign must be the National Government.[9]

Thus, limited regulation within the existing framework of a newly evolving corporate capitalism would be his policy response, and the foundations he helped put in place established precedents and prompted trends that pushed the federal government out of its old paradigm and toward the new, what became the regulatory, state.

From this perspective, consider President Roosevelt as a bricklayer, putting in the foundation level for an increased role of the federal government (not yet big government). His efforts, fueled by the very muckrakers he maligned, and by his own personal willpower to take command, butted up against already entrenched corporate influence in both the United States Congress (especially the U.S. Senate), and the federal court system.

His own political party was not a consistent supporter of his programs. John M. Cooper suggested that Roosevelt was unsuccessful in moving the conservative Republican Party back to the platform it stood on during its formative years. Consequently, Roosevelt's reform impulse, became a hard fight between competing policy interests, ideologies, and institutional change.

At the helms of their ships of state, presidents had to grapple with the politics of their own parties, and the opposition, while governing and interacting with big business. When attempting to govern within these parameters it doesn't matter what one believes in or says while politicking to get elected. Once in office, the slate is usually clean and the elected official now must attempt to govern despite what he believes or had said. Regardless of intentions, once governing, everything becomes even, with checks and balances, the Congress, and the judiciary, becoming countervailing political forces within one's own house, let alone when attempting to govern for the rest of the national constituency. Thus, opposition can spring up from one's own political party besides from the other, in addition to the roles of competing interest groups.

For many politicians, the ability to govern is hindered by political considerations. This is an uncontrollable fact or flaw in our system of democracy. Hence, effective government is often dichotomous policy making because it is based on compromise and half-measures caused by often-ideological brinkmanship.

Thus, Roosevelt's programs, often diluted in substance, nevertheless set the pattern and built the foundation that enabled the federal government to evolve in response to contemporary change. Theodore Roosevelt steered the ship of state through the stormy seas that change wrought. A paradigm change is usually a stormy course.

As a result of this dichotomy, Roosevelt's legislative initiatives varied in type and substance. The Elkins Act of 1903 barred railroad rebates to large corporations. The Hepburn Act of 1906, enabled the Interstate Commerce Commission. The Pure Food and Drug acts of 1906, also a once-moribund reform initiative, long buried in the business-friendly U.S. Senate, eventually resurfaced as a result of the public outcry prompted by Upton Sinclair's *The Jungle* and Roosevelt's subsequent political maneuvering.

In contrast, the business-friendly U. S. Congress ignored Roosevelt's calls for an inheritance tax (later enacted), an income tax (ratified in 1913); a national, federal incorporation chartering law; an expanded eight-hour workday law; mandatory labor dispute investigations; federal employee liability and worker compensation; and a ban on labor injunctions, among others. Roosevelt also wanted to strengthen the Sherman Anti-Trust Act, redirecting it toward controlling so-called bad trusts.

Despite these political dichotomies in Roosevelt's domestic policy agenda, as chief executive, he trod new ground, fostering arbitration in the Pennsylvania Anthracite Coal Strike, 1902–1903; the U.S. Justice Department won the Northern Securities case before the U.S. Supreme Court, in 1904. Trust-busting followed: American Tobacco Company, Standard Oil, DuPont, and the so-called beef trust; for a total of over forty cases. Ironically, Roosevelt preferred regulation to litigation. It's been said that Roosevelt resorted to his justice department as his only recourse since the U.S. Congress refused to enact legislation.

From another viewpoint, Burns and Dunn suggested that after Roosevelt became president, he eventually attempted to shape the federal government into a regulator and ultimately a restrainer of big business and the plutocratic class it represented. They wrote:

> little by little, TR would evolve from the mild regulator of megacorporations and the neutral umpire in labor-management disputes that he was during his first term to—in the last year of his presidency and beyond—a militant foe of those he called "representatives of predatory wealth" and a committed supporter of the rights of labor.[10]

Furthermore, these two authors maintained that all along, Roosevelt wanted to adhere to the spirit of his reform-minded past of the 1880s.

Similarly, Arthur Link suggested that toward the end of Roosevelt's second term, he, "set forth his developing concept of the federal government as a dynamic force in the social and economic affairs of men." Later, presented in the 1912 campaign as the New Nationalism, Roosevelt, by 1909, then out of office, "had adopted a program demanding broad federal economic and social regulation."[11]

Theodore Roosevelt's and Woodrow Wilson's programs, then, fit into the model Herbert Croly suggested in his *Promise of American Life*, published in 1909. There, Croly suggested that the federal government act out Alexander Hamilton's original plan, instead of adhering to Thomas Jefferson's. Croly asserted that an active federal government in the political economy was a suitable, modern change, and one that could foster progress. In a way, Croly proselytized a new order whereby the federal government used Hamiltonian principles to attain Jeffersonian ends. This philosophical foundation became, de facto, one of the underpinnings of the federal government's increased role in the political economy as it transformed prior to 1929. Exigencies of war and economic depression pushed the federal government further in this direction and the Croly-Hamiltonian Progressive model was gradually applied, and by World War II, institutionalized. Along the way, for the most part, big business opposed and fought this change. Occasionally, they acquiesced and went along.

In that light, these, landmark pieces of legislation were the exceptions to a consistent anti-government attitude of big business and their U.S. Senate allies that persisted throughout Roosevelt's terms of office. The corporate sector remained a defiant participant in the political economy, unwilling to yield its strength when confronted by federally promoted social reform efforts. They maintained this position past the Theodore Roosevelt era, and throughout the rest of the century.

The dance of the titans continued when presidents William H. Taft and Woodrow Wilson joined the fray.

President Taft was not a friend of, or crusader for, reform. Conservative in his beliefs, he was not a state-builder like his predecessor, nor was he a friend of organized labor, especially when they turned violent. At Yale University, William G. Sumner taught Taft his laissez-faire dogma, and Taft persisted in those beliefs.

Typically, what Taft believed on paper became necessarily adjusted as office-holder, politician, and statesman. For example, Taft eventually recognized a degree of peaceful labor organization and collective bargaining. Oft suggested, Taft might not have been an original thinker or a robust activist. Perhaps he merely went along with what Roosevelt left him. However, wrapped around his persistent affiliation with capital, Taft attempted to foster business-friendly policy: He recruited five corporate lawyers for his cabinet just as a starter.

Yet, despite his philosophical leanings, he fostered further railroad regulation resulting in a revision of the Elkins Act, in 1910. Taft supported other reforms: railroad safety improvements, a government-contractor employee liability law, and an eight-hour workday for government workers. Taft also believed in the traditional value of business competition, and asserted that effective enforcement of the Sherman Anti-Trust Act was the way to control monopoly. Hence, his willingness to trust-bust, despite his favorable attitude toward the private sector. Thus, with Taft's approval, the justice department successfully prosecuted, using Sherman, more so than during Roosevelt's terms.

These examples of federal government intervention are events played out at the top level. Contemporary times create circumstances that both institutions respond to. The corporate sector tries to maintain its sphere of influence, while acquiescing to and sometimes acknowledging the federal government's arrival on their playing field.

As the federal government responds to contemporary calls for action, law and policy formulation became a complicated process involving private-sector lobbying, executive branch action, congressional lawmaking/politicking, and judicial decision-making.

During these times, the federal government, too, begins to operate on a more systematic, sophisticated level, similar to modern, contemporary, corporate bureaucracy. Now the foundations are falling into place.

Within the federal government, the bricklayer's trowel is passed to the new president, Woodrow Wilson. He will further the process of activist state-building, becoming a significant participant in the still-evolving modern political economy.

Woodrow Wilson was a reluctant Progressive, compared to Theodore Roosevelt and Herbert Croly. Instead, Wilson was a states' rights Democrat who believed in the traditional values of Jeffersonian, small-scale competition. In that system, typically, the federal government should promote the general good, fostering competition over monopoly. It should also be restrained in its support of labor. Government paternalism wasn't necessary in any regard. On the other hand, John M. Cooper suggested that Wilson abandoned his philosophical roots by jumping on the Progressive Movement's bandwagon, even before he entered politics. Whatever the case, once engaged, President Wilson promoted legislation that was similar to the Progressive Party's 1912 campaign platform.

Furthermore, Wilson institutionally inserted the federal government into the political economy, as an active, ongoing, participant, promoting competition as a countervail to the monopolistic status quo.[12] Acting on this viewpoint,

President Wilson fostered a domestic policy, the New Freedom, which Cooper assesses as spectacularly successful, and on the same level of the New Deal and Great Society. Wilson's great triumvirate included the Federal Reserve Act, Clayton Anti-Trust Act, and the Federal Trade Commission Act.

Creating the Federal Reserve System was a response to the congressional Pujo Committee hearings, 1912–1913. Those revealed the magnitude and depth of monopoly in the banking industry. Also, testimony revealed that several major trusts in the transportation and manufacturing sectors were the creations of a few banks that placed their personnel on boards of directors, thus creating a system of monopolistic control of other monopolies, through corporate interlocking directorates.

The Federal Reserve Act of 1913 placed, for the first time, the federal government, as a regulator, squarely in the center of the money and banking industries.

Similarly, the Clayton Anti-Trust Act of 1914, attempted to clarify the legal ambiguities resulting since Sherman. Clayton's refinements, among others, included banning: sweetheart price and contract arrangements; divvying up markets and customers; manipulating production and supply to cause scarcity, and price-fixing.

In tandem with antitrust legislation was the Federal Trade Commission Act of 1914. Rather than codification, some reformers advocated a trade commission, designated to determine unfair trade practices on a case-by-case basis, or specialized basis. Theodore Roosevelt favored this method, but Woodrow Wilson opposed it during the 1912 election campaign. Later, after looking into existing antitrust law, Wilson, decided to reconsider the commission idea; especially when business elites preferred the commission type, rather than the Clayton bill. Other participants preferred dealing with regulations and established standards beforehand instead of prosecuting litigation afterward. Wilson went along with this option.

The result was the Federal Trade Commission Act, 1914. It created the Federal Trade Commission and its supporting bureaucracy. They were empowered to look into, and act, regarding unfair trade methods or unfair competition. The commission could hold hearings and render cease-and-desist orders. The goal was to monitor big business practices in order to promote competition and stifle monopoly.

This was a significant increase in the federal government's involvement in the political economy. Historians disagree on big businesses' position during this time. It would seem the corporate sector opposed federal intrusion unto their turf. Others suggest a bit of cooperation, if not acquiescence, in order to use government action as a way to rationalize the economy by controlling and limiting cutthroat competition.

President Wilson promoted Clayton and the F.T.C. bills as common ground between government and business. Thus, like Theodore Roosevelt, President Wilson believed these measures fairly and, effectively addressed public concern about corporate power, and, simultaneously, establishment fears regarding social unrest. (The latter was a dark, underlying thought current that was in the back of the minds of all participants during these times.)

However, others studying that era disagreed. In contrast, big business attitudes remained, privately, consistent regarding Wilson's reform programs. Essentially, the corporate sector preferred otherwise, but reluctantly went along when public circumstance and political momentum necessitated it. Ultimately, both the corporate sector and its patron, the Republican Party, repudiated and then ended Progressive reform during the Normalcy of the 1920s.

This relationship between business and government was a public issue, before World War I. Politicians, including Woodrow Wilson, publicly postured against government's all-too-cozy relationships with big business. For example, in his book *The New Freedom*, Wilson wrote:

> the degree to which government has become associated with business. I speak for the moment, of the control over the Government exercised by Big Business. . . . Our Government has been for the past few years under the control of heads of great allied corporations with special interests . . . it is an intolerable thing that the Government of the Republic should have got so far out of the hands of the people; should have been captured by interests that are special and not general. . . . The masters of the Government of the United States are the combined capitalists and manufacturers of the United States. . . . Every time it has come to a critical question, these gentlemen have been yielded to and their demands have been treated as the demands that should be followed as a matter of course . . . private monopoly is indefensible and intolerable. . . . A trust is an arrangement to get rid of competition, and a big business is a business that has survived competition by conquering in the field of intelligence and economy. . . . I am for big business and I am against the trusts.[13]

Adding to these public comments, Woodrow Wilson connotated that big business believed they were the guardians of, or the trustees for, the nation. In retrospect, one can surmise that at the same time, and over the decades, the American ship of state was often co-piloted, unseen on the bridge, by captains of industry.

From what I've read so far, I see the Progressive Era as a time of accommodation between big business and the federal government. As each institution evolved to its next level, big business led the way. The government, at the same time, reacted to this change, expanding its role and institutional depth, in response.

This dance of the titans was not limited to government officials and their corporate counterparts. Wrestling with modern institutional change also occurred outside the halls of government and the corporate boardroom. As the public and private sectors maneuvered over their institutional roles and the resulting policies, another problem-solving method emerged.

Formal and informal groups also began to grapple with public policy issues. These groups, usually composed of a combination of businessmen, academics, and civic and government elites, operated in tandem with the U.S. Congress, the White House, and the courts.

Often working out of public view, these groups became influential policy formulators and were the catalysts of a new trend of formal and informal, ad hoc, and often-systemized interaction between the private and public sectors.

Players from both began to associate formally, creating groups of interested and informal stakeholders and experts, who were determined to address contemporary problems. Their efforts, forming specific groups to examine a social or economic problem, and then to rectify it, fit the modernization model. One of these pioneering associations was the National Civic Federation (NCF), formed in 1900.

This organization attempted to sponsor a partnership between the public sector and the private sector to formulate economic and social policy at both the local and national levels. They fostered the idea that government should have a defined and positive role in ameliorating contemporary socioeconomic conditions. At the national level, this included increased involvement by the executive and legislative branches.

Overall, the association was pragmatic, embracing traditions of American federalism, while integrating new, systematized, and government-centered approaches to problem solving. It became a significant vehicle for voicing public concern and subsequent policy recommendation and formulation, prior to World War I. Typical to the times, the National Civic Federation evolved from the Chicago Civic Federation (CCF), founded in 1894. During the economic depression following the panic of 1893, several Chicago clerics and reformers, organized by journalist William T. Stead, met, to examine the social costs of hard times. Spurred by its secretary, Ralph M. Easley, the CCF became a way for those concerned city dwellers to pool their resources and use a group approach to work for civic, local, municipal reform.

This included attempts to systemize local, private relief efforts for the unemployed and to seek the causes of the economic downturn, and then formulate public policy. Their goals were to relieve social strain and then attempt to avoid future economic problems.

Early CCF members included the local banker (and rebuilder of Chicago after the 1871 fire) and U.S. treasury secretary Lyman Gage, social reformer

Jane Addams (a pioneer in the settlement house movement), industrialist Franklin MacVeigh, and social scientist Edward Bemis.

Once formed, the CCF tackled local unemployment relief, organizing, and fundraising. During the 1894 Pullman Strike, the CCF offered to mediate, thus moving unto the path that took it toward addressing greater, national-policy issues. From that effort, during the rest of the decade, the CCF examined election reform, foreign policy regarding Cuba and the Philippines, and trusts.

They organized and convened national conferences to do this, using that format to associate different people and their divergent perspectives. From such systematic, social-science-based collaborations, the federation hoped to instigate political and social reform. The federation believed that objective policy analysis promoted positive, workable policy reform in contrast to partisan considerations, which usually resulted in bad public policy. The basis of this formulation was to apply current social-scientific methods to assessing a policy issue, then recommending analysis-based policy recommendations, derived from discussion and compromise.

Over the next six or seven years, the Chicago Civic Federation morphed into an organization with a national perspective. In the course of examining a wide range of policy issues, the association became the New York–based, National Civic Federation (NCF), with Ohio senator and president-maker Mark Hanna as its first chief executive, and Samuel Gompers, of the American Federation of Labor, its first vice president.

By 1912, the NCF had about five thousand members, a mixture of people from big business, organized labor, academics, and the interested general public. The latter, consisting of a conglomeration of local and state government officials, journalists, reform groups, charities, and research foundations.

The NCF was heavily funded by the likes of Andrew Carnegie and August Belmont. They also managed the organization by serving on its executive council. Throughout, corporate interest was significant. Inevitably, these executives injected a special-interest agenda into the council's work. After awhile, their tactics drew public criticism.

Despite this, the NCF made a genuine effort to maintain its multifactional agenda. They set up research and analysis groups that used their subject expertise to analyze policy problems and then to attempt to design solutions. Their efforts often triggered attention from the top operating levels of the political economy.

Complementing their basic methods, the NCF began publishing research imprints and the *NCF Review*. Such literature was aimed at libraries, other organizations, and to interested parties in the private and public sectors, including both groups and individuals.

During its formative years, even before Mark Hanna's involvement, the NCF focused on labor issues. After, Hanna died in 1904, the federation, now guided by August Belmont, broadened its scope to examine a greater range of policy issues: trusts (again), workmen's compensation, immigration, social welfare, and public utility regulation were immediate concerns, in an attempt to recognize, analyze, and ameliorate contemporary social conditions that were the results of this newly emerging urban-industrial order. In response, the council's mission became promoting gradual reform, working within the existing system as it evolved.

Thus, the NCF positioned itself in between the extremes, of what they believed to be outmoded laissez-faire capitalism, and from socialism, which they considered unacceptable to American tradition. The result was a general attitude that promoted a moderate approach to reform issues. On one hand, they were suspicious of the emerging power of the federal government, and only accepted some government interaction into the economy. On the other, the council fostered the idea of responsible corporate management and citizenship. The NCF became a policy-reform association. The NCF viewed current reality, positively, embodying the very spirit of the Progressive Era, a time when many in the know were willing to address contemporary change, to see it for what it was, and then do something about it.

The NCF helped initiate a trend of using consortia of informed, interested participants, willing and able to associate in order to address contemporary public issues. Perhaps not intended, the NCF and its work, was the beginning of a pattern of formal and informal associating, where interested parties, representing different interests and constituents, allied with contemporary experts and government officials to address national situations.

This method of using system in an organized format became standard operating procedure for policy analysis, formulation, and execution, for the rest of the century. Thus, the work of such organizations as the National Civic Federation and their Progressive Era state and local counterparts, established precedents.

Despite its reform efforts, then, historians have not viewed the NCF entirely in a positive light. They criticized the NCF as a prime promoter of big business special interests, proselytized through the efforts of its corporate members. If so, then even during the formative days of the associational and organizational society, big business already had influence in policy formulation.

These critics have a valid point. Even then, there was evidence of a different state of affairs. The U.S. Commission on Industrial Relations, composed similarly to the NCF, but with big business personnel and trade unionists dominating its membership, published findings with different conclusions. Their portrait of contemporary America wasn't as optimistic. Their trend showed a decline in the status of the American workingman, as the result of potential unemployment problems and loss of labor organization. This commission was not optimistic about the middle-of-the-road potential, if business and labor cooperated. Whenever the NCF postured optimistically about the future, the industrial commission's findings suggested otherwise.

Overall, from my point of view, the work of the CCF and its national progeny, the NCF, is a very early example of using contemporary, evolving, systematic method to address current policy issues. Here, at the outset, and later, during the Progressive Era, beginning with local commission-level civic reform, interested participants operated within my organizational paradigm. Then, applying what they considered to be modern, neutral, and social-science-based criteria and methods, they associated together to use group resources and talent to address contemporary social, civic, and economic policy issues.

As time marched on into the first decades of the twentieth century, this method of associated professional talent working together in groups became standard operating procedures, setting precedents for attempting to confront local and national issues.

As the twentieth century proceeded, this method used by business, government, and interest groups forged the political, economic, and social reality that they lived in. All the while, they operated within the parameters of the modern organizational paradigm, associating when relevant to their interests, forming interdependent, complex, networked, connections among the people with different ability, experience, education, biases, and ideologies. Applying pooled resources, they attempted to address current public issues within established civic, economic, social, and governmental parameters. This method, spawned as a product of the new corporate-industrial system, wound up providing a method acceptable to those applying it in each their own time, often in response to situations caused by the very system they created and were sustaining as they lived.

The reform ethos during the first two decades of the twentieth century was stormy. The titans' dance was an institutional fight at times, but it was also marked by privately maneuvered cooperation between big business and the federal government.

The root cause of this was big business, opposition to what it considered government interference in the economy. It was a new, but unwelcomed role by the federal government. Publicly, big business clung to its laissez-faire roots, expecting the federal government to promote trade and control labor unrest. Privately, sending their men to see government men, together, sometimes eagerly, but more often reluctantly, they attempted to address the changing social conditions, as they were still creating them and living within them. (Roughly, compare everyday life, then, being changed by the corporate-industrial order, similar to how the Internet changed life during the 1990s.)

Antipathy to the changing role of government far outweighed their willingness to cooperate. This collective mindset probably began during the Gilded Age when what became the modern concept of corporation began.

In 1953, Chester M. Destler suggested that even in the Gilded Age, there was a significant public demand for government regulation of business, because of perceived corporate abuses. For example, criticism wasn't just aimed at large producers. Farmers disparaged the railroads out in the country. In cities, street railroads, food and drug producers, and lumber cutters drew public criticism.[14]

Then, captains of industry were scornful of any criticism, and the federal government was still operating within the old institutional model: hands off the private sector and maintain distance from market involvement.

At the state level, existing regulations, often, were not enforced or were effectively neutered by state or federal courts. Also, even then, the opposition to potential government regulation prompted the affected business interests to manipulate the press and the general public on their own behalf. When the federal government attempted to intervene, big business often became publicly defiant. As examples: Executives of meatpacking corporations ignored subpoenas. Standard Oil management couldn't remember during testimony, or invoked the Fifth Amendment. Critics and the opposition were often maligned. Inspectors were bribed. Laws and court decisions were disregarded. Corporate attorneys for Cornelius Vanderbilt and J. P. Morgan had to find out how to effectively get over on the law.

While doing the bob and weave when confronted by activist, interventionist government, corporations postured rhetorically and often fell back on their time-cherished beliefs in rugged individualism and laissez-faire, combined with social Darwinism and the gospel of wealth, in an effective public defense of their own business practices. Back then, the robber barons might have established precedents for future corporate executives, and no doubt helped lay the foundations of corporate culture recalcitrance in the face of government intervention into the economy. Thus, within this corporate nirvana, the rhetorical, platitudinous public posturing these first large corporations offered in their own defense served as the foundation, and often an automatic reflex, for seven decades following, when a response to public criticism or government action was necessary.

Convinced by the absolute truth of their market culture, big business was determined to do their business and to mind their own business, and they expected the federal government and the general public to do the same.

The market economy was their turf, especially becoming corporate turf, and they vigorously defended it from such unwelcome intrusions. The Great Barbecue they created, the arena they functioned in, was theirs alone. The "No Trespassing" and the "Do Not Enter" signs were posted, and they devotedly walked the perimeter, patrolling the boundaries of their turf. The market economy was the corporate sector's sphere of influence.

As the war clouds from Europe appeared on the American horizon, President Woodrow Wilson and the federal government mobilized for war. The war provided a catalyst for a new kind of business/government relationship, a temporary arrangement in the face of a threatening national crisis. Sort of similar to the Progressive Era, these two juxtaposed, yet naturally repellent institutional forces could somehow spin closer into complementary, cooperative orbits. On those occasions, their dance became synchronized. This happened briefly, but significantly, during the national mobilization for war.

It was an extraordinary and unprecedented exigency that neither the federal government nor big business was prepared to immediately meet. The resulting institutional response was ad hoc, tentative, and it remained so for the duration. Both economic sectors quickly realized that the free market system was not compatible with a national mobilization for total war. For example, with no central planning, federal government bureaucracies purchased munitios, as if on the day after Thanksgiving. The result was economic destabilization. Massive war orders spurred inflation. Supply of raw materials was unorganized, thus hampering the mass-production process, and at the other end, the existing transportation infrastructure couldn't handle the volume effectively. Consequently, the federal government had to step in.

Their efforts were, at best, noble. Rather than creating a synchronized, smooth-running Tayloresque system, the architects from the public sector and private sector threw together a delicate, unstable institutional war production and distribution system that eventually managed to produce war matériel that in the short run about adequately kept the Allies supplied. By November 11, 1918, when hostilities ended, this effort, at first, a reluctant business and government partnership, accomplished a war effort that was not sophisticated, mistake-free, or viable for the long term. Their effort was still evolving, in November 1918, when the war ended. The duration was not long enough for the system to be rationalized and systematized thoroughly.

The process of war mobilization began America's active participation in 1917. After the European war began in 1914, our military began to look at possible contingencies, including involvement and mobilization. Thus, preparedness began earlier, consisting of a series of group efforts involving business, the civilian government, and the military. The army and navy analyzed war routinely, but so too did the civilian sector. After 1910, this informal effort eventually led to Congress forming the Council of National Defense, in August 1916. It was a group composed of cabinet members, the military, and businessmen. An advisory commission (AC), became part of the council. The AC contained business and engineering executives who attempted to promote and implement Taylorized standardization, scientific management, and professional research to the preparedness process. Council members such as B&O Railroad president Daniel Willard; financier Bernard Baruch; Hudson Car executive Howard E. Coffin, and union leader Samuel Gompers, among others, together, attempted to assist the council, in managing mobilization, even though they didn't know how a government bureaucracy worked, and didn't, according to War Industries Board member Grosvenor Clarkson, fully understand what should be done to marshal "the untrained strength of the sleeping giant of America," in an all-out war effort.[15] Nevertheless, in the months preceding the April 1917 war declaration, the council and commission members started out as advisers on how to manage the logistics of the war production industry. At the end of 1916, they began to contact private-sector industry leaders about preparedness. They also attempted to set up a procurement system for war matériel. Producer committees formed to represent different companies seeking government defense contracts. Overall, they attempted to recruit, quality, private-sector managerial and administrative talent, who also had good reputations with and connections within the private sector.

By March 1917, they already realized that modern war necessitated national-level planning and coordination of procurement with war production. Later, that summer, the council agreed to create another organization, what became the War Industries Board (WIB), again a group of civilian federal government officials, military representatives, and businessmen. The WIB became the clearinghouse, organizer, and arranger of industrial war mobilization. It marshaled the private sector's participation in total war, a national mobilization of the domestic economy, managed by civilians in government and business.

After entering the war, the domestic war production industry was chaotic. American companies competed for war matérials. The military branches still purchased separately. America's European allies also were purchasers, thus causing raw-materials scarcity and high production demand. Without central planning or national coordination, unfettered market capitalism resulted in some firms being overwhelmed with orders. Thus, there was very little system.

The WIB attempted to ameliorate the problem. De facto, it was a go-between, middleman, and mediator for government buyers and private industry suppliers. The board attempted to coordinate government and Allied countries, demand; created and managed a production priorities system; organized supply based on that system, and controlled prices.

The board's institutional life began in 1917, immediately getting involved with internecine conflict among military procurers; having to overcome private-sector indifference to the war effort and the federal government's administrative inadequacies. As a result, the board struggled to do its job, barely surviving along the way. Its task was daunting. It was charged with organizing and integrating the disparate private sector into a modern, national, war production machine.

The effort of mobilization on such a scale necessitated utilizing corporate managerial skill and production resources. To do so, a business-government partnership evolved as a necessary response. It was at first, a reluctant relationship, with many firms resisting conversion to a war footing, because among other things, they were suspicious of any organized federal government action that could lead to more intervention into the private sector, or more government regulation, such as restrictions on consumer goods production and distribution or price controls.

Nevertheless, businessmen were expected to cooperate, in a common, greater, and national effort, instead of what they were used to—competing with each other, and at the same time, as they were accustomed to, avoiding scrutiny by the burgeoning, meddlesome, federal government. With them, the private sector was expected to form what they considered an unnatural partnership. They preferred to keep government at an often unfriendly distance.

Thus, in a sense, our entire mobilization process became a sojourn into uncharted and unfriendly waters. Both business and government were used to their own spheres of influence, and up to this time, their interactions were more marked by contention and avoidance (i.e., trust-busting and regulation), than by cooperation.

Despite this, the two reluctant institutional associates managed to marshal this first great arsenal of democracy, providing more than four million tons of war matériel within an eighteen-month duration.[16] All the while, operating upon a sea of contradictions, they attempted to create an organizational system for war mobilization, while balancing different views, methods, ideologies, and policy preferences. Indeed, this partnership remained ad hoc, a learn-as-you-go effort, where applied pragmatism became the guiding hand. Early in March 1918, President Wilson ordered the WIB to manage mobilization, thus forcing the civilian and military sectors to formally wage war in tandem, together, as partners. This reined in the military to conform to WIB decisions. At the same time, the board finally forged some positive working relationships with much of private industry. These presidential mandates addressed the nagging weaknesses of the toothless committee approach that caused the board's difficulties at the outset.

Formally, the WIB was supposed to control the allotment of material necessary to produce war-related goods, foster efficient war production and distribution, and manage Allied procurement logistics. The director of the Council of National Defense, Grosvenor Clarkson, went on to assert that the WIB effectively managed our war effort. He attributed this to the business management talent available from the private sector.

The war effort was formidable even though the federal government was not prepared to effectively manage mobilization.

To be successful, a first-of-its-kind government and business partnership was necessary. Effecting such a working relationship would not be easy. The two sectors had more not in common and doing business together would be inherently difficult.

The public-sector bureaucratic culture differed from its corporate counterpart. For example, the two military branches competed with each other for procurement. There wasn't much system, so this meant the private sector had to do business with a decentralized, unorganized, unsystematic purchasing system. Also, keep in mind that both institutional systems were enlarging and simultaneously evolving, working out their infrastructure and culture as they did business.

The private sector did do business with the military. But the relationship was ad hoc; procurement was not systematic. Instead it was small in scale because individual military departments did the purchasing, similar to shopping in the local market.

Corporate managers did mass purchasing, production, and distribution. (Recall chapter 3.) Thus, they were a logical and pragmatic choice to manage war mobilization. For example, in 1916, Hudson Car Company executive Howard E. Coffin suggested a mobilization partnership. Industrialists had to join with the military to successfully wage modern war. He believed that businessmen and engineers were the only ones capable of successfully running a wartime economy effectively. Hence, they could potentially rationalize military procurement, successfully melding it to contemporary mass-production and distribution logistics.

Doing such business was their job. They knew how to get these things done. Corporate managers and specialists knew how and where to purchase raw materials and understood production processes and product turnaround time, for example. They knew where the supplies and parts producers were and how to get them raw materials and how to ship the related goods. They could move materials, parts, components, and finished products effectively.

They also knew cost accounting and pricing factors. These were the necessities of doing business, and for a relatively short time, at least, they brought their private-sector expertise into play. After the war, business management was applauded for its work with the WIB. Thus, one could say, big business was a prime mover in orchestrating and managing its own mobilization. Clarkson agreed, asserting that the private sector was successful in managing this, and fairly representing government interests when negotiating contracts for them with their private-sector colleagues.

At the same time, in order to wage war, the federal government was willing to do so within big businesses' parameters, that is, essentially within a private-sector controlled economy. Becoming a consumer, the federal government, sought a close business relationship with its corporate suppliers and logistics handlers, a necessity when waging war on a mass scale, an ocean away.

At war's conclusion, it seemed that big business wasn't a slacker. It did its part, rallying around the flag, helping to supply and manage wartime production. However, Clio, the muse of history, proves to be a harsh mistress, and in hindsight, all was not what it then appeared to be.

Soon after, the veneer began to peel off the luster of America's mobilization effort. In the U.S. House of Representatives, the Nye committee knocked the icon off its pedestal during their investigation, from 1934–1936. The committee examined our war effort, and found private-sector participation in mobilization was not entirely acts of self-sacrifice and patriotism, as propagandized. Despite lots of genuine patriotic effort, the committee discovered conflicts of interest pervading the WIB's work that resulted in extraordinary profits for war contractors, at the cost of the federal government and the national effort as a whole. Since then, historical assessment has been equally critical, albeit considering the circumstances then, that controlled just how much government and business could accomplish together.

I also interpreted this first attempt in public-private cooperation with a jaundiced perspective. Back then, doing business was an ethos that significantly stressed the perceived voluntary cooperative tradition. Within the market mentality of corporate capitalism, government was a significant foe, i.e., trust busting and regulation.

To effectively mobilize, these areas of suspicion had to be overcome. When it came to competing, making money, protecting spheres of influence, preserving market and political power, the market-place ethos was more important to businessmen than patriotic cooperation. This clash in institutional cultures was the root cause of the problems both sectors had when they tried to forge two disparate ways of doing things into a unified, effective, efficient, war-making whole.

Persistent laissez-faire traditions and the emerging corporate institutional ethos, created a collective mindset that insulated big business from effectively sharing power and responsibility with government, in mobilization against a greater common threat. Instead, the corporate sector maintained their principles that substantiated what was good for them economically and politically. The onus of cooperation was then back to the federal government. Through it all, big business managed to maintain a publicly fortified position, mobilizing its resources for the war effort while orchestrating the process more on its terms and conditions (and for profit over patriotism), then the government.

Thus, early on, the pattern of corporate recalcitrance is already evident. Whenever the two institutional forces draw near to each other, breaking their self-imposed barriers of mutual repulsion, the ensuing interaction will likely be tilted toward what's good for business, regardless of the interests of, and costs to, the other constituents in the commonweal. Nevertheless, mobilization for the Great War was the beginning of an institutional relationship trend, that would over the ensuing decades, broaden, expand, and deepen, and eventually entrench itself into our political economy.

Big business and the federal government both institutionally fortified themselves through the process of mobilization. Not only did big business receive an increase in profits through government contracts, but more importantly, the corporate sector had a direct managerial partnership with the federal government in prosecuting the industrial phase of total, national warfare. As a result, a permanent conduit and precedent began that weakened the wall of separation between business and state power. Once in, the corporate virus was there to stay.

Government too, morphed itself larger and more powerful politically through its absorption of corporate systematization of mobilization and the use of corporate management to pilot the domestic war machine. As a result, both institutions would propel themselves ahead, feeding on each other, indeed, bursting out, taking off from their initial emergent phases to positions of ever rising, sustaining levels of power during the following decade to 1930.

In addition, war mobilization by big business and government fits into the organizational paradigm. It was a national, institutional-level effort made up of several interdependent and often disparate smaller parts. Led by some public figures such as Bernard Baruch and technical experts such as Herbert Hoover, mobilization of a war industry was a group effort of anonymous private-sector managers and administrators, working together with federal officials, who would become those "faceless bureaucrats" of later infamy.

The process of mobilization, its awesome complexity and fluctuating conditions, created a demand, a necessity for, group effort. They pooled their talents to manage a vast, burgeoning domestic cornucopia of material and experience, working to control a complex network of private-sector producers and sellers with the federal buyer-bureaucracy.

Within the organizational paradigm, these large, anonymous groups of teams accomplished this effort. They did this through an interlocked, interdependent system of partnershiped management, melding the producing private sector, with the buying/consumer federal government. This was an institutional effort carried out, managed, and administrated on the top tiers of the political economy. In the process, a disparate, pluralistic, scattered, private sector, organized itself into a complex, large-scale mobilized domestic production and distribution machine. It functioned as a sum of many parts, just like contemporary mass-production methodology, meshing into an integrated, interlocked large-scale system, and managed rationally, anonymously, by people functioning in group settings.

The whole effort, an expansion of the administrative state on the federal side, and a newly formed partnership with the private sector, established precedents and methodology pushing these two separate spheres into new orbits that during the rest of the century, spun them closer and closer, institutionally, in a more convergent manner than disparate. The dance of the titans became a tighter circle when the action of one sphere of influence affected the other as never before.

After November 1918, the war clouds dissipated and America returned to Normalcy as the new decade dawned. Business and government parted ways, each following a different institutional fork in the road. Their paths diverged from each other with business rising to the forefront, and the federal government masked in the monolith's ever enlarging shadow.

During the 1920s, business reigned supreme as the private sector fostered a prosperity decade. Many worshipped at the altar of the free market, laissez-faire, unfettered capitalism. Indeed, Robert Sobel noted, that contemporary economists observed, during the 1920s, that big businesses' power grew unencumbered, and during that decade, we became "a business civilization."[17]

Despite movement into modernity, the private sector tenaciously clung to the values and beliefs of the old nineteenth-century order, to the old laissez-faire paradigm. Big business was unaware or unwilling to grasp the indicators of institutional change they were fostering. The synchronized, cooperative effort of business and government during the Great War established institutional precedents that served to guide both sectors for the rest of the century. Associating in one form or another, group thinking, and collective action became standard operating procedure to address exigencies of the day. This method included commission fostered municipal, state, and national government reform.

It also became an institutionalized system within governments and also within corporate culture. Governments used this system to govern within a bureaucratic system, and to examine social and economic problems. Non-governing organizations such as the NCF and trade associations like the National Association of Manufacturers and the United States Chamber of Commerce, similarly worked within the new associational model.

This new system and the continuing dance of the titans moved to a new level during the 1920s. Business-government relations took a favorable turn toward the interest of business, and later in that decade, Herbert Hoover attempted to forge within the federal government, a corporate structured culture, as the associative state.

As the 1920s roared, a sort of modern, electrified version of the Gilded Age Great Barbecue happened, and the corporate sector, in the forefront, continued to evolve as a socioeconomic institutional force. Part of that development was an ad hoc attempt to professionalize and organize business as a formal entity.

The agent of this trend was the trade association. Nationwide, and within local markets, both small and large businesses organized into these formal associations. Joining such groups was a new thing in the private sector. The trade association's rise in prominence might have been helped by their participation in war mobilization. For example, the U.S. Chamber of Commerce used existing trade associations to organize each war-goods producing industry, serving as an intermediary between the public and private sectors.

By 1929, there were more than 13,000 trade associations (at all levels—local, regional, national), listed with the United States Chamber of Commerce (USCOC). In 1919, there were about 700 national trade associations; 1929, over 2,000. Although some industries associated before the Civil War, the movement significantly accelerated right along with the rise of big business.

Businessmen formed these groups ostensibly to promote learning and applying contemporary, systematized business practices; to distribute information, and to foster policy interests locally and nationally. Published in 1930, Joseph Foth's book asserted that the trade association movement exemplified a new era of cooperation among people interested in group effort to effect common ends. Another observer of the time, in 1925, F. Stuart Fitzpatrick, wrote:

> Men form themselves into groups because through collective action they may achieve results or obtain satisfaction out of reach of the individual. . . . These groups are establishing a new governance of industrial and commercial activities. They are an important social phenomenon: Businessmen have organized trade associations for the purpose of meeting circumstances which were curtailing the operation, impairing the profits, or threatening the existence of their particular industries or branches of commerce.[18]

In contrast, there were critics. They asserted trade associations were organized, subtle efforts to carve up local markets, control supply, and collude on prices. Also, then, it was commonly understood that trade associations were effective hedges against the Sherman Act, and in some situations, de facto cartels. Later, John Hicks offered this comment:

> Another principal function was to scrutinize the regulatory proposals of both state and national legislative bodies, and to make sure that laws unfavorable to the interest of the particular group they represented failed of passage, while laws that might be helpful to its members went on the statute books.[19]

In hindsight, it is likely that trade associations did all this and more, in an ongoing battle to wrestle with the specter of uncontrolled competition.

As trade associations evolved, they took on attributes of modern system by promoting standardized administrative business practices such as uniform cost accounting, shared production and distribution information, attempts to self-regulate, and ultimately (see chapter 6), lobbying all three levels of government. By 1930, both business and government recognized their importance, aiding in administrating the logistics of market capitalism, and influencing policy issues regarding the political economy.

Most trade associations began simple. They were small-scale, niche-specific to local markets, business-professional and social organizations, that, in some cases, dated back to the mid-nineteenth century. By the end of that century, many of these groups expanded their reach, becoming national in size and scope, generally in response to how the economy expanded. (Recall, chapter 2.) Foth placed the trade association movement's ascendancy from 1900 to 1918, with World War I a significant catalyst.

Despite legal questions involving the Sherman Act, the trade association movement continued, fostered by a favorable U.S. Supreme Court decision in 1925, its private-sector adherents and participants, and the U.S. Department of Commerce (USDOC), during the 1920s. In fact, the federal government promoted trade associations as a means for the private sector to self-regulate, unfettered by an activist federal, administrative state. Cotton manufacturers, insurance companies, bankers, car manufacturers, oil producers (American Petroleum Institute, 1902), lumber, canners, cocoa, sugar, and chocolate manufacturers, coal mining companies, and chain stores formed trade associations.

Market competition created a series of unacceptable business practices that were legislated illegal at the state and national level: price collusion, production controls to keep supply low in order to jack up the selling price; distribution irregularities, such as rebates and nonuniform freight charges, to name a few.

Trade associations attempted to address these market problems by fostering uniform trade practices, using arbitration panels, cooperative committee work, professional conferences, written and unwritten business ethics and trade codes, litigation, and even cooperating, under certain situations, with the Federal Trade Commission, and more so, with the USDOC.

Their public goal, at least, was to form their own rules for doing business, to voluntarily regulate their own turf, in order to keep the ever-looming federal government at an acceptable distance.

For most of the 1920s, the federal government went along. They interacted with trade associations usually through the USDOC, then managed by future president Herbert Hoover, and through a relatively hands-off attitude by the FTC. It was as if the intended temporary war-fostered truce between business and government continued by the business-friendly presidential administrations of Warren G. Harding and Calvin Coolidge. Normalcy prevailed and that meant fertile ground for big business to grow in wealth and subsequent power and influence.

During the 1920s, accepted business practices, in (the future New Deal chief NRA administrator) Hugh Johnson's view included: child labor, farmer exploitation, anti-unionism, speculative banking and stock and bond trading, anti-statism, anti-old age, unemployment, and disability benefits for workers; and adherence to cutthroat competition and methods, including monopoly practices, among others.

Back then, however, there were underlying systemic problems. Modernization, specifically mass production, increased production capacity, causing epidemic overproduction, which in turn, fostered cutthroat competition. Market survival became a vicious fight, and collusion and monopoly were the remedies of choice.

At the same time, this new form of corporate capitalism remained wrapped in the drapes of laissez-faire individualism, when indeed, it was about the opposite in reality. This was capitalism's dark side during the 1920s, throwback attitudes from the previous century. However, right alongside these perceived deficiencies, American capitalism was also modernizing.

Contrary to American heritage myth, corporate capitalism might not have returned to its nineteenth-century roots. Instead, big business was now modern. At its core was mass production and mass distribution, systematic management, and professional marketing. It was a new capitalism, based on the efforts of inventors, engineers, educated business administrators, stock market investors, and entrepreneurs combined with the old order of finance capitalists. Together, during the Roaring Twenties, they were still forging what would become the new synthesis: institutional, managerial, corporate capitalism, and as an economic, social, and political institution, big business increased its interaction within the political economy well beyond the range that its laissez-faire-oriented Gilded Age forebears, those robber barons and captains of industry, could have envisioned.

The Great War provided a reason, a common end for big business and the federal government to cooperate. Later, as the new decade began, top-shelf elites like Herbert Hoover saw a future where business and government operated as a cooperative, but separated partnership. With government's positive sanction, big business self-regulated, adopting modern, scientific, professional business administrative practices, in order to successfully and honorably compete within a new, systemized market economy. Government would be there to lend its assistance when called upon.

This new arrangement, an updated version of send-your-man-to-see-mine, became the trend in business/government relations with commerce secretary Herbert Hoover managing policy and promoting and using the USDOC as a connecting point to the private sector.

The popular engineer and hero of the recent war relief effort became secretary of commerce in 1921. Soon after, he began to foster a policy that promoted smooth relations between the private sector and the federal government. Back then, Hoover brought to the job deeply held beliefs, including in the virtue of individualism and a distaste for big government. He also believed the old ways could be melded to the emerging, new, modern order. In particular, he saw good in applying scientific method, but without diluting inherent individual effort. He believed that this meld could be effectively applied to current policy issues.

Regarding the business world, he viewed trade associations as an important means for business to self-regulate and progress within the political economy, while remaining free from the heavy hand of federal regulation and active intervention. He even believed this new organizational order was naturally evolving as America modernized. It also had a place for the federal government, albeit an associative one. Indeed, the federal role was different: advisory, emphasizing/promoting conferences; forming cooperative committees and panels of experts, instead of exercising police power as in the recent past, that is, regulation and legal coercion. Ellis Hawley called this attempt the associative state.

Hoover attempted to apply his vision of an associative relationship between government and business through the recently created USDOC. It was not yet an entrenched bureaucracy, but Hoover successfully influenced the department's development, expanding its administrative practices and visibility, and used it as a mechanism to foster business interests.

He added to, and deepened the scope of, the department's structure, creating: the bureau of foreign and domestic commerce, bureau of standards, building and housing divisions, and the census bureau, for example. In 1921, the USDOC first published the *Survey of Current Business*, using lots of statistics provided by trade associations. Whenever he could, he drew in other agencies, or functions, such as absorbing the patent office, and taking over the collection and publication of mining statistics, for example.

Secretary Hoover nurtured and developed the department as he managed it. He believed he was successful in upgrading it to become a productive provider of information and policy influencer within the federal government, while at the same time, fulfilling his plan to promote private-sector interests. All the while, the department functioned within his philosophic framework, of cooperative association rather than statist intervention.

Using War Industries Board precedents, Hoover formed different commodities groups, staffed by industry experts, who provided information on applicable business practices, statistics, and research. Thus, Hoover, through the mechanism of an associative state, attempted to form a cooperative alliance between government and business, by applying system and modern management and business administrative practices. At the same time, Hoover hoped that each industry group could set trade standards and then essentially self-regulate.

The success of this system, in hindsight, might have been like beauty in the eyes of the beholder. At the end of the decade, Foth observed, that despite concerted efforts by trade associations to control or eliminate unfair trade practices, the problem persisted. So far, most of their methods didn't solve the problem. Evidently, self-regulation wasn't working and neither were federal government efforts. In reality, the private sector could not live up to its own standards.

During the 1920s, the failure of the private sector to self-regulate within the auspices of the associative state, was perhaps the last great triumph of nineteenth-century social Darwinism, before the arrival of the new monolith, the regulatory state. If this is true, then, because of human nature, restraint often must be imposed or coerced. The larger and more powerful the institution, i.e., the typical big business corporation, the greater the amount of imposed restraint necessary, as applied by an equally strong countervailing force, i.e., the federal government as an interventionist, regulatory state. That time was about to arrive.

As time marched on, around the bend lurked the monster of recession and economic chaos. There, the new system would be challenged to its breaking point. Together, from the exuberance of the Roaring Twenties, the two titans would now dance to, and almost topple over, the brink, as the Great Depression forcefully made its presence known.

Normalcy came to an end when the dark clouds of recession conspicuously arrived during the months after the October 1929 stock market crash. This economic storm persisted through the next decade. Its wrath pummeled contemporary corporate capitalism; affecting most the labor force that enabled it, and least those who were its creators and managers.

As institutions, corporations survived and ironically, in the face of this storm, the emerging, activist, federal government, became even bigger, and more incident into the political economy, society, and in the ordinary lives of everyday people.

As indicated in chapter 4, the Great Depression wreaked havoc in America throughout the 1930s. From the fall of 1929, and through 1932, the economic downturn devastated American society. National income and wages steeply declined. There were no jobs for millions. Although estimated national unemployment was about 25 percent, this masked the demoralized situation locally: Cleveland, 50 percent; Akron, 60 percent; and Toledo, 80 percent, as examples.

Although institutionally and financially fortified to weather and survive the onslaught, the corporate sector did little to address the chaos. Prior to 1933, clinging to their myths and philosophy of nineteenth-century laisez-faire capitalism, the corporate sector chose to ride out the storm until the cycle, like the weather, would improve by itself.

The federal government did similarly, steered by Herbert Hoover and his devotion to the old order and tradition. It couldn't be rectified using the methods based on the ideologies of the old order and its nineteenth-century model. The new, modern mass economy worked differently, and when it broke down, it could only be fixed using applicable methods.

In 1932, our toolbox was empty. Laissez-faire was inadequate, and so was rugged individualism and its voluntaristic-based associative state. These fundamental principles of the old order, so clung to by those that called themselves conservatives (both then and now), failed. The world they believed in wasn't working. As a result, American society, by 1932, was moving toward the brink.[20]

Ironically, calls for business-government cooperation during the Hooverian phase of the depression, arose by some of those involved in the previous war mobilization. Most economists favored some sort of working relationship between the public sector and the private sector.

However, neither business or government were sufficiently, institutionally developed to effectively address the massive economic disaster, While the Great Depression occurred, both institutions were still growing and evolving. Both were at stages that were still inadequate to significantly adjust to a collaborative effort.

Ultimately, and in hindsight, the efforts of those in President Franklin D. Roosevelt's administration were based on pragmatic Progressivism and were the federal government's first concerted efforts to address this disaster.

The New Deal attempted to ameliorate what the depression wrought. This federal program provided a new, temporary, top-shelf arena for the two institutional titans to dance. There, the relationship became a struggle, almost a fight, as business and government, grappled with each other over what to do to keep the system going, while, seemingly, the arena's walls were cracking, and the floor beneath them buckling.

One of its early efforts was the National Industrial Recovery Act, signed into law on June 16, 1933. It was a first attempt to address this national economic emergency. The program sought to rectify problems of unemployment and market competition without changing the accepted and prevailing capitalist order. This meant controlling wages, hours, and rules of production and market competition via a business/government partnership. The private sector was to create and manage the program, with federal government assistance.

The program had to adjust wages up, so to increase purchasing power, and working hours down (Note: This was a time when fulltime work meant six days per week.), in order to spread out jobs, increase opportunity, and stop overproduction. Price minimums prevented selling below costs. Other parts of the law included limiting the time production machinery could be used to make things. Some industries were prohibited from expanding plant capacity. The act also mandated uniform accounting standards and the publication of production figures. Also, statistics were to be collected, and prices published. No new machinery could be purchased, which was an attempt to curb industry expansion. Unionization and collective bargaining were permitted.[21] Some things were prohibited: shipping on consignment; rebates, and varying contract terms.

The core of this program was code making. Businessmen and government bureaucrats created and managed the process. For example, the first completed industry code was for cotton textiles, July 13, 1933. The code abolished child labor; reduced the workday from three shifts to two, in a forty-hour workweek. Wages were increased to 1929 levels, which were based on a longer workweek. The minimum weekly wages equaled ten dollars in the South and eleven dollars in the North.

The federal government relied on trade association expertise to construct the industry codes (which the government administrator approved), and managing implementation. The federal government did not have the resources or experience to do this alone.

Circumstances fostered business controlling the code-making process. They had the knowledge, resources, expertise, the associations and their connections, and economic power to influence and garner participation and cooperation, thus, hopefully, creating workable public policy that they could effectively manage.

The deputy administrators were usually recruited from the private sector. Most of those pseudo-government employees were either associated with business or agreeable to its viewpoint. One contemporary observed that this working relationship meant that program participation was negotiated by businessmen for themselves, with business representatives working for the federal government, but with attitudes favorable to business interests, more so than any others. A deputy administrator was assigned to negotiate with each industry group. These were recruited from industry with the understanding that they would perform with a sense of obligation to the public, more so, than out of self-interest. Those who had a large stake in an industry group could not do that code. The first batch of codes was done this way. It was assumed that industry knew more about their problems and how to fix them. There were also rumors that many of the deputies were deliberately inserted into that role so to look out for, or fix, the codes for the benefit of the trade group or corporation. After all, they were loaners to the public sector from the private, and, as temps, their loyalties were necessarily with their providers.

Despite good intentions, the code making struggled from the outset. It took them two months to complete eight codes; hundreds were pending.[22] The task was arduous because it was difficult to find common ground among competing interests, beliefs, and attitudes, among participants: businessmen, lawyers, economists, union reps, skeptical reporters, etc. Thus, after one year, Bellush asserted, the NRA was a large, poorly managed, and ineffective federal program.[23]

Once engaged, the code assemblers disagreed among themselves, and government administrators had to intervene and referee, because the negotiating wasn't necessarily based on mutually cooperative attitudes. It seemed that the business experts commissioned to making codes, were better at code breaking (especially when tried-and-true self-interest prevailed over the public good). Even with trade association participation, private-sector participants struggled. Code proposals often conflicted.

Code supervision varied by industry, often, ad hoc to the negotiating parties. These were called the code authority, consisting of a combination of administrators, and or, industrial representatives, each with varying degrees of autonomy regarding interpretation and implementation. Trade associations were used where available; about 218 of 400 code groups had trade associations in dominant positions. Labor and consumer groups usually played diminished roles. Individuals selected, varied from group to group. There was no pattern or emphasis on uniformity or system. Thus, imagine this process, where the NRA officials had to arbitrate negotiations that resulted from melding the interests of three disparate groups: industry, labor, and consumer.

The whole program, once in place, was undermined continually (despite cooperation from big business), by so-called chiselers, code breakers. They abounded nationwide. Many were still looking to get an edge on their competitors, especially among small businesses and those in local markets.

In overall context, the process of code making and subsequent compliance was complicated by the degree to which its participants were willing to compromise on their own favored interests. It was as Peter A. Gourevitch wrote: "The characteristically conservative notion that self-administration by businessmen freed of politics would overcome conflict proved illusory."[24]

Also, in this instance, corporations dominated the procedure, being more institutionally powerful and influential than their partners: small businesses, organized labor, and do-gooders. Furthermore, when the federal government could have been the logical referee or arbitrator, that role couldn't be adequately executed because it contradicted the very beliefs, the old paradigm, that fostered and sustained the differences and hence the problems they were trying to solve. The role of an expansive, interventionist state was emerging for the federal government at this time. Thus, an overtly activist, heavy-handed role was not then considered the correct thing to do. As a result, during the depression, the acceptable way, like during the World War I mobilization, was to agree to give business de facto power to organize, construct, and administer the program. Government believed that business could self-police. Turns out, they couldn't, and Washington wouldn't.

In hindsight, the task they undertook, due to the disparate nature of the economy, might have been a Herculean, if not impossible undertaking. Success might not have been possible. There were too many regional and market-share differences. Competitors had to cooperate, a new thing for those who hadn't previously colluded. Cooperation, concessions, self-regulation are all antithetical to the fundamental driving force behind market capitalism—self-interested greed based on competition, and social Darwinism—capitalism's dirty little secret.

Even if they didn't like the program, many businessmen believed doing something was better than nothing. So they made the best of it, participating in order to get what they wanted out of the deal, with government support thrown in. (Ironically, the NRA program provided corporations with much-sought-after relief from trust busting and cartel regulation.) Because the program was similar in method and attitude to war mobilization, this might have prompted some cooperation.

Not surprising, contemporary investigations revealed that usually the large corporations benefited the most. In particular, the more economically powerful the firm, the more likely it was able to dominate competition within its market. In a portent of things to come within the corporation nation, the big guy held sway over the little. Thus, under the guise of industrial self-government, the feds partnered with big business, operating perhaps only as the referee, signing off on the codes when they were submitted for official approval. The orchestrator of or facilitator for the bulk of the process was big business. This was the beginning of a subtle process whereby business assumed influence and power in governing. Contrary to popular notion, big business might have been more institutionally fortified by recovery efforts than the federal government. From there, their institutional position enlarged, later, especially after 1940, during the next mobilization.

Controversies aside, the Blue Eagle (the NRA symbol was a blue figure adapted from the Navajo eagle), lived a short life, succumbing to Supreme Court examination resulting in being declared unconstitutional, in May 1935. It wasn't a surprise decision because many, including its architects and participants realized its dubious constitutionality. By then, however, it might have been a moot point because as believed then, much of the private sector already stopped participating. Remnants of the program might have informally lasted into 1937.

Big business responded in kind. The struggles over creating and managing the NRA caused the two titans to once again spin away from each other. By 1936, business generally was against the New Deal, resenting taxation, the public dole, huge amounts of government spending, regulation, trust busting, and the perceived federal government's statist/interventionist philosophy and action. Organizations such as the United States Chamber of Commerce, the National Association of Manufacturers (both self-proclaimed mouthpieces for business interests), and the Liberty League (LL), insisted that President Roosevelt's version of government was an impediment to economic recovery. Efforts by the federal government to reconcile, 1935–1939, with business, were largely unsuccessful. (During the winter of 1938–1939, President Roosevelt realized privately that the New Deal was over.) Ellis Hawley wrote that President Roosevelt:

> grew increasingly disillusioned with businessmen, increasingly resentful over the continual carping, their lack of social responsibility, and their apparent willingness to block any measure of social reconstruction[25]

Gerald Nash suggested that some of this reform impulse resulted from President Roosevelt's Progressive-Era past. Responding as the national crisis deepened, the president looked more and more to long-term system change, instead of temporary stop-gap measures. Increasing the federal government's role in the economy was one result, and from 1935 to 1937, this translated into the Wagner Act, the Glass-Steagel Act, Social Security and the Tennessee Valley Authority, among others.

With the demise of the Blue Eagle, the problem of business-government relations reappeared in earnest. There was a resurgence of calls to return to the days of laissez-faire beliefs, trumpeted loudly by the likes of the USCOC, NAM, and LL. Their calls for the good old days of leave-it-alone drowned out those few who were still interested in continuing the business-government partnership. They postulated this even though once again the private sector failed to self-regulate, similarly to how they failed to fix prices through collusion and cartelization efforts during the Roaring Twenties. The legacy of greed and self-interest left over from the Great Barbecue was still effective.

Thus, after 1935, business-government relations entered an institutional interregnum, marked by drifting apart to pursue their own interests. Business maintained efforts to control its own markets through informal and illegal collusion and price-fixing. The federal government increased its influence in pragmatic attempts to ameliorate the economic conditions that business caused.

From the resulting impasse, the federal government evolved a new strategy and created a new role that today we call countervailing power. The government's programs and posture toward big business shifted formally away from cooperation, to one of active institutional competition and conflict. What would become Big Government started out promoting and protecting the interests of the economically weak: organized labor, small businesses, and the agricultural sector. For the time being, the duration of an unstable peace, the business-government partnership was over, in earnest.

Despite the flat-earth logic of the right wing, then and now, it was as Bensmen and Vidich opined:

> Though business rejected Roosevelt with hatred, it was Roosevelt who rescued business from its own greed and incompetence and, at times, even furthered the role of business in national policy making.[26]

President Roosevelt would have concurred. According to Herman E. Kroos in his *Executive Opinion*, the president:

> did not need the votes of the businessmen. (1936) He was overwhelmingly re-elected without them. Yet, it annoyed the President to be unpopular with any group. Hs felt terribly persecuted. "Never before in all our history," he said, "have these forces, business and financial monopoly, speculation, reckless banking been so united against one candidate as they stand today. They are unanimous in their hate for me—and I welcome their hatred."[27]

Even war did not ameliorate Roosevelt's belief. Neil Smith offers this vignette, in *The Endgame of Globalization:*

> In 1945, Franklin Roosevelt wanted the world but he knew before he died that he would not get it all. At home he had been supported by many industrialists—a

good number of them signing on as "dollar-a-year-men"—yet many more among the ruling class detested his "liberal" policies.

One day he was visited in the White House by "a rich man" and Roosevelt, anticipating an attack on his New Deal reforms, pre-empted his visitor: "You hate my guts," he opened, "for bending to the demands of workers and the poor, don't you?" The rich man admitted that was true, and FDR proceeded to explain why he had established the welfare state. "I was convinced we'd have a revolution" in the U.S. "and I decided to be its leader and prevent it. I'm a rich man too," he continued, "and have run with your kind of people. I decided a half loaf was better than none—a half for me and a half for you and no revolution."[28]

The big business response to the downturn, from the beginning, was a desire to control their own marketplace unencumbered by government. It turned out to be an all-or-nothing arrangement. For whatever reason, they attempted to work with government, but true to their grounding in competitive self-interest, they were unable or unwilling to yield ground, to make short-run concessions for long-run gain. They didn't believe in giving some, to get some later. As a result, a cooperative business-government partnership to deal with the economic crisis they confronted was doomed from its conception. Effective governance over time has proven to be a function of compromise and concession. In simple terms, to get some, one must give some. In the face of the depression, big business was incapable of taking this posture both within its own market sector and in its managerial and administrative partnership, albeit, short-lived with the federal government.

They attempted to control an economy that they didn't effectively understand. Their actions, policy formulation and execution, attempted to address modern problems using attitudes, beliefs, ideologies, and learned behavior from the old order, that in hindsight, we know now, couldn't work.

Nevertheless, operating with what they knew about the economy, and what they believed should be the roles of business and government, the NRA was an attempt to apply components of the new way of doing things, coupled with what they thought was true of the old. It is likely that all contending participants believed in their own cause and the mutually exclusive truth in what they fostered, despite the overall veneer of cooperation in 1933.

Here's an example of their basic philosophical differences. Then, Simon N. Whitney suggested the private sector believed that overproduction was a cause of the depression. That is, there was more stuff available than could be bought. Big business viewed this from a production perspective. Overproduction caused price-cutting, then also known as cutthroat competition. Their remedy was to agree to control production and maintain prices. This was adherence to classic economic belief of equilibrium. At that time, many realized this idea and method didn't work, and some believed production controls had to be mandated.

In comparison, the federal government asserted that under-consumption, lack of purchasing power, was the depression's root cause, and that the NRA programs addressed this. Whitney, perhaps representing the business viewpoint, disagreed. They viewed purchasing power, necessarily, raising wages to do so, only as a cost (raise wages and increase the cost of doing business); a negative.[29] Thus, their perspective remained wrapped around their own self-interest, an attitude entirely grounded in the supply and production side of economic thinking and practice. It was standard procedure then, before the appearance of the Keynesian paradigm. It was also wrong.

Overall, these problems resulted from the incompatibility of laissez-faire, social Darwinism, and classic capitalism with the contemporary realities of the newly formed corporate order and interventionist state. Because modernity meant new situations, neither business nor government were ideologically or methodologically prepared to meet them. The American political economy was evolving away from what it was when it spawned its ideology. This meant its two main institutions, had to feel their way within it, utilizing what they believed (laissez-faire), avoiding what they feared (socialism), and forming partnerships that the private sector did not want, and accepting government intervention when it was on business-friendly terms, all necessary when facing the threat of social unrest, war mobilization, and economic catastrophe.

Participants in big business and in the federal government could not reconcile the incompatibility of the free market ideology with contemporary exigencies that suggested an attempt to try new methods of control and planning. Increasing the role of government in the economy, was just too distasteful to significant portions of American society. The concept of increased federal regulation, at best, was a suggestive, but questionable alternative to accepted beliefs about how the political economy worked. They were just emerging from the darkness of their pre-Keynesian worldview. It was as George A. Steiner quoted Arthur M. Schlesinger:

> The great achievement of the New Deal was to introduce the United States to the twentieth century. Roosevelt redressed the defects of the Jeffersonian tradition by equipping the liberal party with a philosophy of government intervention—a belief, as he put it, that "the government has the definite duty to use all its power and resources to meet new social problems with new social controls."[30]

Franklin D. Roosevelt left no doubt by his intention to use the powers of government to combat the depression. He directly abandoned and ridiculed the "let-things-alone" philosophy in stating:

"From the days of the cave man to the days of the automobile, the philosophy of 'letting things alone' has resulted in the jungle law of the survival of the so-called fittest. The philosophy of social action results in the protection of humanity and the fitting of as many human beings as possible into the scheme of surviving." He, in other statements urged, "bold, persistent experimentation" as a technique for curing the depression ills. This included "restoring farmers' buying power, relief to small banks and homeowners, and a reconstructed tariff policy." He displayed an intense interest in and sympathy with the problems of the common man. On one occasion he declared that "the issue of Government has always been whether individual men and women will have to serve some system of Government or economics, or whether a system of Government and economics exists to serve individual men and women." He went on to observe in the same speech: "As I see it, the task of Government in its relations to business is to assist the development of an economic declaration of rights, an economic and constitutional order"[31] (At most revolutionary; at least, genius.)

This introduction was an unplanned and difficult set of relationships as the political economy heaved and lurched during the depression decade. The two institutions were founded on dramatically opposite philosophies and evolved and maintained subsequent belief structures. The federal government rules and exerts its police power for the commonweal; for the greater good of its citizens, at least in theory. Thus, self-interest is not part of its body of knowledge and method.

In contrast, big business is grounded in self-interest and survival of the fittest, and because it has never effectively shaken off its foundational heritage, it will never fully accept the role of the countervailing role of government in the political economy. In fact, big business has been more effective in usurping privileges of citizenship (see chapter 6), and in acquiring the power of institutional sovereignty.

In addition, there were some economists, basing their suggestions on a book by Adolf Berle and Gardiner Means, *The Modern Corporation and Private Property*, asserting that the contemporary corporation was now controlled by a managerial class that often lacked a sense or obligation of responsibility. If so, then it was government's job to control the newly acquired economic power of corporations: "The modern corporation, they claimed, had become a semistate and required more regulation than in the past," so wrote Robert Sobel.[32]

Newly emergent beliefs in the corporate culture further fostered this unwillingness to cooperate with their market-sector peers and the federal government, organized labor, and consumers. Such would then be consistent with the institutional selfishness corporatism fostered. Regardless of the magnitude of the national crisis, the prerogatives and presevational institutional instincts of the corporation still dictated their disposition to cooperate, compromise, and when necessary, make concessions. The previous ideal of cooperative voluntarism, when applied in this evolving ethos, was doomed to failure.

If there was a path toward economic enlightenment, another crisis, another war, detoured that journey. As the decade ended, the two titans were once again confronted by a threat that would forever change the arena of their grapple. World War II mobilization became the death knell of the old order. It swept the two titans into a dance whose embrace became a permanent clinch.

The economic maelstrom of the Great Depression still overcast America in 1939, when new trauma arrived in central Europe and east Asia. War would both threaten American civilization and bring relief from the decade's economic tribulations. The ultimate test of whether the economic world of John Maynard Keynes worked was about to begin.

The Japanese attack on Pearl Harbor was a spectacular success.[33] In a Hollywood case of artistic and literary license, the screenwriter, Larry Forrester, in the 1970 movie *Tora! Tora! Tora!* attributed this prophetic quote to Japanese admiral, Isoroki Yamamoto.[34] In the days after raid, the admiral said: "I fear all we have done is to awaken a sleeping giant and fill him with a terrible resolve."

Indeed, that giant was, until December 7, 1941, a reluctant participant in international events. Nevertheless, as Europe and East Asia descended into the maelstrom, the United States slowly began to prepare for another war, essentially, rearming during the eighteen months prior to Pearl Harbor. Like before, the federal government did so hesitantly, haphazardly, using pragmatic experimentation with little help from the private sector. The government understood that this war would be drastically different from the Great War. Lessons learned from the depression might have limited application in what they guessed would be a national campaign of long duration and higher intensity, and one with greater demands on all resources.

There were some sobering lessons learned from World War I. Recall, mobilization was ad hoc, disorganized, and done with not much system. Free-market capitalism wasn't necessarily compatible with war procurement. Then, war mobilization was based on voluntarism, patriotism, and cooperation, more so than state coercion. Bernard Baruch and the War Industries Board successfully walked the line between them. Despite problems and the short duration, they learned from it.

The National Defense Act of 1920, was one result. It enabled the War Department to do advance planning for future war. The root of those plans was to, once again, rely on a WIB model, creating temporary federal agencies to organize and manage preparedness and subsequent mobilization. Its bottom-line objective was to control procurement outside the military, so to avoid repeating the chaotic conditions in 1918.

In 1931, the U.S. War Policies Commission created an analysis of the Great War's mobilization. Their Industrial Mobilization Plan (IMP), called for a civilian advisory council of industrialists and others to manage war mobilization. The report also suggested that preparedness was necessary and contingency plans were a contemporary fact of life.

Although a back-burner contingency during the 1930s, awareness and alertness, leading to preparations, persisted, even though it was peacetime, and we were preoccupied with domestic dysfunction. Nevertheless, vigilance persisted through the depression decade, with the military studying contingencies and revising the plan every so often.

The IMP, revised in 1933, 1936, and 1939, was to be a guide, a contingency plan if a crisis occurred. A War Resources Administration (WRA), again, another group effort, composed of experts from the private and public sectors, would manage a war economy. In August 1939, FDR set up the War Resources Board (WRB), assigning it to study how to manage a total-war economy. Based on the IMP findings, it was in response to what was happening in Germany during the fall of 1938. The U.S. goal was to quietly prepare for the exigencies imposed by the looming threat of another European war.

The board's membership was mostly corporate, including: Edward R. Stettinius, Jr., U.S. Steel COB; Karl T. Compton, MIT president; Walter S. Gifford, AT&T president; John M. Hancock, Lehman Brothers partner; Harold G. Moulton, Brookings Institution president; John L. Pratt, G.M. director; (General) Robert E. Wood, Sears, COB. It was chaired by Stettinius.

While Western Europe succumbed to the German holocaust of fury ("When the Blitzkrieg raged and the bodies stank, pleased to meet you. . . .") FDR reconvened the National Defense Advisory Commission (NDAC), in May 1940.[35] As during World War I, this group represented the private and public sectors, and attempted to work with the Council of National Defense. The latter consisted of the heads of the war, interior, agriculture, commerce, and labor departments. This advisory commission examined mobilization logistics and made policy recommendations. A former vice president at Sears, Donald Nelson, described the council as "the first full-bodied governmental group formed to study and consult and act on defense production.[36] It was staffed by major corporate personnel, such as: William S. Knudsen, president of GM; Edward R. Stettinius, Jr., COB of U.S. Steel; and Ralph Budd, president of Chicago, Burlington & Quincy Railroad. (There were also representatives from labor, academia, and the government.)

Although limited in what it could actually do, the NDAC was the first significant attempt by the federal government to move the political economy toward a war footing. It reviewed defense contracts, created a priorities system, inventoried on-hand resources, designated locations and fostered defense plant construction, determined which firms should be exempted from antitrust consideration, and created sections that were forerunners of full-scale war agencies, among others.

The federal government mobilization process continued that year, when the Roosevelt administration created the Office of Production Management (OPM), in January 1941. Led by William Knudson, of GM, and Sidney Hillman, of the Amalgamated Clothing Workers Union, the agency was charged with fostering production increases from depression levels and managing the labor supply. However, expediting, but with no police power, and overlapping with other bureaucracies, immediately diluted it effectiveness.

At the same time, its advisers, a small coterie of corporate volunteers (so-called dollar-a-year men), were reluctant to lobby, let alone coerce their private-sector counterparts to switch over to producing war matériel, instead of consumer goods. They also resisted overt governmental efforts to formally assert managerial control of national mobilization. Later investigations (the Truman Committee), revealed corporate volunteers dominated upper management policy decision-making positions. In the process, they fostered business interests, often at the expense of mobilization progress. Some critics viewed their participation, at least at this early stage, as a significant hindrance. At the same time, an informal system developed where committees took to meeting away from their government counterparts, where deals could be cut and policy influenced.

Nevertheless, by the fall of 1941, American industry assisted in supplying our European allies and a growing U.S. military, now expanding to 1.5 million in service. Raw material shortages had already occurred the previous spring. Now resources such as aluminum were mandated to war production. Things continued to heat up.

The federal government accelerated building up the army to a wartime footing during 1941. That summer, the government began to finance plant expansion and mandated conversion of some industries. The gears engaged and the industry's wheels began to turn, albeit slowly, ultimately greased by the attack on Pearl Harbor.

Not everyone, then, saw it the same way. Some contemporary critics believed, generally, that the OPM carried on ineffectually through 1941, eventually replaced by the War Production Board (WPB), in January 1942, with former Sears executive, Donald Nelson, its head. Now mandated toward full mobilization, the WPB, was to enforce it, and manage it, at least in theory. The board functioned similarly to the WIB, including making many of the same mistakes. War management was tremendously different because of the nation's complex and diversified industrial infrastructure. Consequently, waging war using industry caused significant stress on both the public and private sectors. A trial-and error process followed, searching for workable methods.

Management and administration where already systemized within both business and government. Companies especially had honed this science as a necessity to doing successful business in the overheated economy from 1900 to 1929. Successful management meant applying method to effectively execute strategy. It was supposed to work this way too, during mobilization, but it didn't, and they learned its difficulties as they worked within it.

They thought small groups of policy makers could effectively manage the job, delegating its execution down the chain of command, similar to how they worked in their own corporate cultures. This was common among all those serving on the WRB, NDAC, and now, the OPM.

Circumstances overwhelmed them. Mass mobilization thoroughly disrupted the civilian economy. Shortages, everywhere, occurred quickly and lasted the duration. The size of total-war procurement at first, overwhelmed, even our highly touted mass-production and mass-distribution system. Its size and depth made it only partially manageable, even by those who were considered corporate managerial elites.

Throughout the preparedness process prior to Pearl Harbor, the federal government assumed that they would create policy that would be executed by their agencies working with ongoing procurement methods set up by the military.

As it turned out, what they believed would work, in theory, when applied on an unprecedented scale, was inadequate. Mobilization after December 7, 1941, included a rapid escalation of economic conversion. Mistakes resulted typically, but at the same time, experimentation was necessary. The reality of war production dwarfed expectations. Waging war on this scale went beyond their range of experience regarding administrative management and logistics.

Thus, the effects of national mobilization reverberated throughout our market economy, and shook our society and culture to its core. It taxed all our collective physical, social, and psychological resources, seemingly, all at once, as the smoke from Pearl Harbor wafted away in the breeze. Over the next twelve months, war affected almost all Americans. Men and women went into the military; others as civilians in war administration, and others helped create this version of the arsenal of democracy.

Confronted by war on two fronts within days after December 7, 1941, defense mobilization eventually expanded in size, scale, and depth. It would have to be a massive, national response, for an undetermined amount of time, in order to succeed over two very determined and so far, successful, foes. Succeeding at mobilization meant solving enormous logistical problems after the contracts were signed: overcoming scarcity, working within the priority system, weathering shipping bottlenecks, competing with the military for personnel, refitting industry for a war footing, and building plants. As Bruce

Catton observed: "this was going to be a war of steel mills and copper mines, of power plants and laboratories, of mechanics and technicians; a mobilizing and using of the *total* strength of the country."[37]

In response to this threat, as in the past, the federal government attempted to organize and then manage a vast pool of material and human resources, within a political system that still hinged itself on its simple past, while at the same time, took on the institutional trappings of modern corporate-administrated management and an increasingly powerful national state.

The result of using a combination of the old and the new typically led to a rough go, for what could be called a marriage of necessity between government and business. From the disaster at Pearl Harbor in 1941 to the triumph in Tokyo Bay, in 1945, once again, a circumstantial partnership between government and business succeeded in creating, indeed, President Roosevelt's arsenal of democracy, an "American Colossus," that enabled the Allied military to defeat the Axis and, in the process, push the United States upward past the Roman Empire as the greatest of human civilizations.[38]

Business and government accomplished this together, but, all the while, they continued to wrestle with the nature of their institutional identities. This process could destroy philosophical and ideological underpinnings.

Wartime exigencies exacerbated this fundamental difference by imposing new sets of rules, procedures, and methods. Industrial production must swing away from normal market situations toward a different set of objectives. To provide war products, the private sector must cooperate with government and conform to its way of accomplishing national security goals. These times were exceptions to custom and practice. Nevertheless, there was resistance. (At the same time, this marriage of necessity, this extraordinary arrangement, subtly led to a permanent bond and working arrangement.) This wartime triumph and relief from the deprivations of a depression decade was the culmination of what we, today, call the American Century.

This ascendancy was not easy, 1941–1945. The effort by the civilian federal government and the private sector supporting the military waging war, was fraught with mistakes, conflicts, contentiousness, and more revolutionary institutional change. Yet, they eventually succeeded in creating, organizing, and managing an economic behemoth that produced war matériel in unprecedented amounts; a magnitude of industrial might that only could have been accomplished through an organized mass systematization of resources that American corporate capitalism had at that time.

After the war, Elliot Janeway wrote that once mobilized, American industry produced big-time. He especially lauded production-level management for what they accomplished, stating they showed a "genius for production."[39]

Concurring with Janeway, Luther Gulick offered this contemporary assessment, published in 1948:

> The total development of our war production from 1939 to 1944 was an industrial feat of the most stupendous order, unmatched by anything in economic history.[40]

He stated that war production peaked two years after Pearl Harbor, the result of improving the effectiveness of private-sector production and distribution. A result caused by a combination of factors: leadership, organization, management, discipline, and the elimination of unemployment. Gulick wrote:

> Perhaps I am unduly impressed by this experience because I was in the midst of it. But it strikes me now, as I look back with some perspective over the record of what Donald Nelson and the businessmen, the professors and career administrators did, as one of the major miracles of the war and one of the reasons for our final victory.[41]

It bested, mightily, the call to arms declared by President Roosevelt in January 1942. Indeed, the president's arsenal of democracy, a joint business-government effort, produced enough to enable the Allies to win a global war. A grand total of over $300 billion of government spending.[42]

TABLE 5.1
U.S World War II Production

Military posts	3,700
Aircraft	295,959 (58,000 to allies)
Air craft carriers	27
Escort carriers	110
Battleships	8
Cruisers	48
Destroyers	349
Destroyer escorts	412
Submarines	203
Liberty ships	2,695
Landing craft	79,125
Tanks	88,410
Artillery	400,000
Mortars	100,000
Rifles	6,500,000
Carbines	6,100,000
Submachine guns	2,000,000
Small arms	3,000,000
Motor vehicles	2,700,000
Railroad cars	95,000
Locomotives	7,500

Source: "U.S. War Production 1941–1945, in Roger A. Baumen, Quantum Increase: The MIC in the Second World War," in Cooling, *War, Business, and American Society*, 126

Indeed, the sleeping giant did awake. Consider, in December 1940, the Army Air Force had 63 bombers, 30 medium bombers, and 193 pursuit fighters.[43] And once it gathered itself up, rising up angry, and went to work, it produced a cornucopia of war goods, never before marshaled in the history of human conflict and aggression.

American industry, dependent on a domestic consumer economy, successfully switched its collective gears, and focused on producing goods for death and destruction. Richard Polenberg wrote that it took eighteen months, mobilizing, converting to a war economy. The process included physical plant conversion, building new factories, procuring raw materials, relocating labor supply, and coordinating production and transportation. (It would later include price controls, rationing consumer commodities, more taxation to pay for the war, and war bond drives. A war-regulated economy affected most people.)

Here are some examples of conversion. Once cut off from East Asian natural rubber supplies, American industry successfully developed synthetic rubber, a product necessary for tires. The federal government financed fifty-one synthetic rubber factories, then leased them to producers. A U.S Rubber Company factory in West Virginia sprawled over seventy acres, capable of producing 90,000 tons of rubber per year. This industry, by 1944, produced over 800,000 tons of rubber annually.[44]

Another example, Henry J. Kaiser, switched from dam construction to boats. Heavily financed by the federal government, his company produced destroyer escorts, landing craft, troop transports, and tankers, and the famous Liberty Ship. (This was a mass-produced cargo ship that became the lifeline to the Allies.) In 1941, it typically took one year to build a cargo ship. Kaiser's company reduced construction time to fifty days. Their record for one, was fourteen days.

Mobilizing the automobile industry was critical to the war effort. As a leading industry in the private sector, civilian economy, carmakers were contracted to produce heavy war goods: airplanes and tanks, besides trucks, jeeps, half-tracks, etc.

Their mass-production capacity and their management and workforce were at the heart of applying modern manufacturing technique to national industrial mobilization. Yet, prior to Pearl Harbor, the auto industry was reluctant to prepare and then convert to war matériel production when first requested to do so by the federal government. War planners projected this industry producing 20 percent of total war production. However, regardless of what the federal government wanted, automakers were enjoying an increase in the domestic market, and were content to focus on this revived consumer product, instead of converting to war matériel production for our European allies. Thus, carmakers produced more autos in 1941 than in 1939. In April 1941, the auto industry agreed to allocate 20 percent of its capacity to military contracts. General Motors expressed a willingness to curtail production of its 1943 models, but not their 1942's. I. F. Stone then remarked that despite government's attempt at preparedness, the car industry instead, was more interested in producing more cars per year than ever before. So much for corporate patriotism, Stone opined:

> In the midst of the greatest defense emergency in our history, the automobile industry increased the production of cars by 20 percent. . . . These announcements of sacrifice are confessions of shortsightedness and greed.[45]

Note that when first approached by the federal government to cut domestic production, expand plant capacity, and increase military vehicle production, the auto industry declined. This occurred early on. Consider that successful mobilization, as Donald Nelson then asserted, depended on the auto industry's cooperation because of the size, capacity, and industrial strength of these corporations. It was a leading industry. In aggregate, this sector's assets totaled over one thousand factories, 850 companies of various size, that included subcontractors and suppliers. De facto, it was crucial that automakers switch to producing military durable goods.

Eventually, the auto industry converted. Packard Corporation began to produce Rolls-Royce engines in 1940. Chrysler commenced tank production. Ford built a plant at Willow Run, thirty-five miles from Detroit, and then started airplane assembly. It was the epitome of what mass-producing American corporate capitalism could accomplish once committed.

After April 1942, the auto industry had to go on a full wartime footing when the federal government suspended domestic car manufacturing. Writing after the war, Donald Nelson suggested the whole automobile industry, which included all sizes of firms, producers and suppliers, might have been enough by themselves to manufacture what was necessary to win the war. Even during the depression decade, the car industry's total production capacity was greater than most other countries. There were about 1,050 factories among approximately 850 car and parts companies, spread across forty-four states, employing about 7.5 million people. A behemoth industry indeed.

Once mobilized, this disparate industry quickly coalesced into a nationwide, institutional machine, marked by a quickly acquired ability to cooperate with each other regarding the war effort (via the direction of the American Automobile Council for War Production), rather than competing with each other as they normally did.

Indeed, the now wide-awake giant, a corporate-led institutional behemoth, once up, manufactured war matériel in the aforementioned amounts. Besides setting these production records, this corporate production monster innovated, managed, and controlled as they went, prompting Nelson to opine:

> Probably the world has never witnessed such a powerhouse of technical brilliance, training, and inspiration.[46]

It was like this in other sectors of the economy too.

In 1939, the airplane manufacturing industry employed 48,638; in November 1943, it employed 2,103,000, 12.4 percent of the total industrial workforce. There were 41 plants in 1940; 81 in 1943. In 1939, they produced 5,865 planes; 1944, 96,369. During March 1944, the industry produced 9,117 military aircraft. From January 1, 1940, to August 14, 1945, the aircraft manufacturing industry produced about 303, 317 military airplanes.[47]

Aircraft manufacturers too, worked cooperatively together pooling resources, technical information, and manpower, integrating into a nationwide, interconnected manufacturing colossus.

Nelson concluded this production litany by recalling how controversial President Roosevelt's prewar call for 50,000 airplanes was in the days prior to Pearl Harbor. Looking back, from our time, decades later, could the manufacture of aircraft, vehicles, guns, rifles, and ammo have been accomplished without the manufacturing infrastructure already in place, a creation of our industrial corporate capitalistic system? Hardly. Even though the Greatest Generation did indeed win the war on the battlefield, could they have done this without the cornucopia of destruction being created for their use?

This spectacular production success came from a forced business and government marriage. At first, and despite government's good intentions, the private sector, generally a foe of the Roosevelt administration, and still mired in an economic-depression mentality, was not about to extend itself to another cause on government's behalf. Once again, their collective, institutional mindset, grounded in self-interest, prevented the corporate community from assuming a leading-edge position as the war clouds moved closer to our shores.[48] They didn't take the initiative and weren't proactive. They were reluctant to shift their gears to assume a war footing, to, on one hand, losing their consumer base, and on the other, being uncertain about what would happen in the postwar economy.

Also, during 1941, the consumer market improved, thus there was little incentive to take up the federal government's call to arms. Conversion, thus meant losing this newly acquired, resurrected, consumer market, retooling plants, retraining workers; entering a continuing business arrangement with a single buyer, and then subject to a sudden dead market at war's end. If the situation suddenly blew over, then what? Who will buy all this military stuff? Who gets stuck with all this? What kind of incentive was there?

At the same time, even in late 1941, prior to Pearl Harbor, many in the private sector turned away from the federal government because of their antipathy to New Deal programs and the concomitant rise of the activist state. Big business feared government would usurp more power and expand its political influence (including more social reform by the accursed and hated New Deal), under the guise of mobilization. Perhaps they feared aiding and abetting an enemy? For after all, they seemed to be at philosophical and policy odds with the federal government, especially since the end of the NRA program. They weren't about to offer unfettered cooperation when it wasn't on their terms.

As a result, the federal government had to lead this latest dance of the titans, manipulating and then forcing the participants into a closer, more coordinated choreography. It was done largely on the private sector's terms, offering tax breaks, covering plant expansion costs, suspending antitrust enforcement, and offering lucrative war-contract terms, among other incentives.

Many of the participants realized that mobilization for war still had to be done within the already established formal and informal precedents, rules, and protocols of a free enterprise system. Thus, the federal government had to extend profit-enhancing terms, while at the same time, offering financial assistance for production development costs, including plant conversion and expansion. The federal government also had to limit some regulation, thus muting its political role as a coercive power, interventionist state.

Within this partnership, business and their corporate inventory of production resources and personnel enabled our mobilization success. After reluctantly converting to a gradual wartime footing before Pearl Harbor, the private sector (including all sizes of firms), once mobilized, succeeded in providing the arsenal of democracy for victory.

They did this by applying contemporary institutional corporate capitalism to war production. Mass-production companies now made airplanes, tanks, and weapons, instead of cars and other consumer products. They then used their transportation and distribution systems to move matériel and military personnel across continents and oceans. Coupled with an already established institutional knowledge base to develop war products, they did so using mass-production and distribution methods that only large-scale corporations could muster. Thus, once reined in by the threat and exigencies of global war, American corporate capitalism finally answered the call to arms.

This supposedly temporary partnership between business and government, was once again, set up and executed within contemporary standards, beliefs, and methods of corporate capitalism, by its own creators and managers.

Big business managed the economic home front during World War II. It was a business-oriented, market, consumer-producer relationship between the warring federal government and its private-sector suppliers, well within the parameters of traditional corporate capitalism instead of state socialism or fascism.

Business management personnel and government bureaucrats formed the core of this partnership. Each group most likely brought with them, cultural baggage peculiar to their own pasts and organizational training. Each had their own ideas, beliefs, and methods of doing things. These oft-disparate values and knowledge systems had to be blended together, in order to get the job of war production done. They don't naturally mix. However, there were many in both sectors who believed that cooperation was possible. Beginning with prewar preparedness, this attitude evolved and prevailed in response as the international crisis escalated.

Large corporate institutions partnered with ever-growing federal government bureaucracies, combining their work-talents, their industrial might, and management ability, to mobilize and sustain a partnered, cooperative effort that lasted for the duration, and then eventually morphed into the Cold War military-industrial complex, which in turn precipitated a permanent working, albeit dichotomous relationship between the two institutional titans during the prosperous postwar decades. Thus, the adhesive binding the melding of these two behemoth institutions was large group associations.

At war's end, the two institutional titans attempted to return to the normalcy of a prewar status quo. Indeed, they attempted to, but once again, the times forced the two back into their partnered dance necessary to win a hot war. Now, during the rest of the 1940s, the dance of the titans once again spun toward a mutually sought center, reacting to a hot war that despite seeming to end and go away, instead, turned Cold. That, unplanned, unforeseen circumstance, the Cold War, sustained the momentum of the dichotomous, dissonant relationship of these two institutional behemoths.

Backed by the American arsenal of democracy, war goods aplenty, the Allies, in time, rolled back the Axis Powers in Europe and Asia. War production surged, especially during the first quarter of 1945. The American war machine hummed, now in tune with military might, it equipped and enabled. It *was* as someone once said long ago, to Thomas Jefferson: "Your people sir, is a great beast." Indeed, as Bruce Catton put it into historical perspective:

> This was the high noon of the world's greatest democracy. The people had been asked for more than any people had ever given before, and—in mine and in factory, on the farm and in the forest, at home and in the training camps—they were doing all that had been asked of them. They were justifying a belief, a legend, and an inheritance; for this the immigrant ships had sailed west and the wagon trains had crossed the plains, forests had been cleared and cities had been built, traditions had been created out of death and faith and courage, strength had been drawn from the air and the soil of the richest, proudest land on earth. They

> were waging war on the seven seas and three continents, they had the power to say what the future would be like.[49]

It was, as Norah Jones sang in Ken Burns's *The War*, "America, America, I gave my best to you."[50] It was simply beautiful, beautiful, beautiful.

And then suddenly, the war ended, first in Europe, in May 1945, then later, in August, on the other side of the globe, in the heat of nuclear destruction.[51] During those subsequent months, civilian, domestic economic controls eased, and war contracts canceled. Workers lost jobs, rationing stopped, war production ended, and the militiary personnel of who would later be called the Greatest Generation finally came home.

The political exigencies of global war, and its effects on daily life, thus ended, within months. The quick switch to a peacetime footing was deliberate by the federal government. It hoped that the private sector would quickly return to doing what it was so reluctant to stop in 1940, producing for a newly revived domestic market. Many government officials and policy planners believed (perhaps hoped more so than not), that prosperity could continue once consumer products became readily available again. Maybe another return to the good ol' American normalcy would sustain the prosperous times that a war economy brought to the home front.

However, there were leaders in business and government who feared what direction the economy would take. Could prosperity be sustained or would we return to the depression decade? Also, along the same lines, what kind of economic problems could reconversion cause?

Thus, as victory celebrations waned, we stopped and took a sobering look around, as Bruce Catton wrote:

> The end of the war did not leave us on a high mountain top, looking ahead to a limitless vista, with horizon lying beyond horizon to the end of time. Instead it left us in a mysterious valley, cloaked by an eerie fog and swept by confused alarms. We came out of the war timorous, uncertain, confused, not quite clear just what it was that we had done and everlastingly perplexed as to exactly what we ought to do next. We had won the war but we had done nothing more than that, and we began to see that a good deal more than that was urgently required.[52]

While still deeply immersed in the maelstrom of global war, federal government policy makers began to look to a postwar future, and typically, they formed a group of experts to analyze this situation and look to ways and means to convert wartime prosperity to peacetime.

For example, in 1942, commerce secretary Jesse Jones started promoting an independent association to do this. Others, such as Paul G. Hoffman and William Benton, sought an alliance with businessmen and academics, to study the economy. They were willing to examine and even question traditional, often considered sacrosanct, business beliefs. They thought their efforts could cause positive change. Perhaps collective economic education could produce a better society.

Thus, during the spring of 1942, the USDOC created the Committee for Economic Development (CED), made up mostly of members of the Business Advisory Council (BAC). The committee was supposed to find ways to prompt a prosperous peacetime economy.

The CED operated on two levels. At the top, it set up groups to examine national policy issues. At the local level, the committee established about 2,900 branches, decentralized, autonomous, and managed by local businessmen. These were designed to analyze local business conditions; forge, ad hoc working relationships with civic leaders, professionals, and politicians, and then together, attempt to make relevant policy recommendations. (Many of these locals were operating in 1944.)

Back at the top, the CED's role was mostly advisory. Originally convened as another, temporary, war-emergency agency, it persisted after the war and eventually separated from the USDOC. The committee continued on its original mission, using a combination of business elites and academic professionals, to influence federal government policymaking. Over the ensuing decades, it published a plethora of policy papers and analysis.[53]

Although typically and mostly favorable toward standard corporate policy positions, the CED didn't fall into lockstep with other policy-advocacy organizations such as the United States Chamber of Commerce and the National Association of Manufacturers.

Brian Wadell asserted:

> The experience of war mobilization had convinced many corporate leaders to value the compensatory role played by the national state and to appreciate a national state apparatus tamed by the wartime influx of corporate executives. Many of these men, including those who organized the CED, preferred a new era of economic growth based on a business-oriented Keynesianism to either a return to a mythic laissez-faire economy or a redistributive welfare state. Of course, the CED's endorsement of a positive role for the national state did not entail acceptance of and any reduction of corporate privileges and prerogatives. The CED, while liberal, opposed any replacement of corporate control with governmental direction. . . . The CED hoped to counter the predatory, antistatist, and inherently anarchic character of the U.S. business community by organizing positive, business-centered solutions to imminent economic problems and by delineating and advocating a limited Keynesian role for the national state.[54]

To accomplish this, their idea was to represent the entire business sector via a consortium of informed managerial elites working in tandem with academics.

Together they attempted to analyze policy issues and then make recommendations that fostered anti-interventionist federal policy, friendly to corporate interests, but scientifically based, and thus, less ideologically limited.

Some general examples of CED policy advocacy include: support of and influence on policy that eventually became the Employment Act of 1946; advocated no corporate taxation, and some tariff reduction; refuted the federal government's balanced budget orthodoxy; accepted some situational government intervention in the economy; policy recommendations at the Bretton Woods conference, and on what became the Marshall Plan.

Concurring with Waddell, Karl Schriftgiesser pointed out that early on, the CED was a proponent of government using Keynesian economics when attempting to fine-tune the economy (stabilization), thus, attempting to control the business cycle and in the process, establishing a persistent precedent that would underlie the committee's future policy recommendations. Schriftgiesser went on to claim that many in the CED camp were willing to accept policy considerations that were contrary to orthodox economic thought. In this contrarian view, the federal government had a role in influencing the economy. He wrote:

> They were not afraid of the power of government but were determined to use it, on their own terms, to make the private enterprise system work in the way they knew it could. . . . From its inception CED accepted the fact that government was big and was constantly growing bigger and that there was no returning to a simpler, happier past in this respect. It believed that the question was not *how much* government should do but *what* it should do, and once this was determined how it could be done most effectively.[55]

Furthermore, Schriftgiesser also asserted that by 1946, the CED showed its value and mettle in analyzing the economy. By 1950, economist John K. Galbraith agreed, stating the CED was:

> the newest and in respect of ideas the most influential of national business organizations, [and] from the beginning has had a deep though unproclaimed commitment to Keynes.[56]

Thus, the CED sustained itself after World War II, and during the next decade, proceeded to actively participate in the federal government's policy making, when President Dwight Eisenhower tapped two of its members for cabinet posts, and some undersecretaries too. (Eisenhower was a CED trustee when he was president of Columbia University. During its first fifteen years, 38 of 150 CED trustees were either elected to or appointed to federal government positions.) The now ten-year-old CED was especially influential within the Eisenhower administration. (Prior to taking office, Dwight Eisenhower received a packet of policy concerns from the CED.)

During those years, having published about twenty-seven policy statements, the CED proceeded to publish another twenty-five. Schriftgiesser remarked that the committee built and expanded on its good reputation among the informed by examining fiscal and monetary policies, urban renewal, agriculture, underdeveloped countries, foreign trade and investment, balance of payments, and the Common Market. He went on to write that the CED reflected the views of our economic elites and that the committee was a unique partnership between business and academia.

Back then, *Business Week* labeled the CED as progressively conservative. When reviewing the committee's literature, it appears that the CED expected the private sector to take an increased interest in public policy and for business leadership to be a consistent and persistent proselytizing agent and asset. Robert Collins likened the CED to the efforts made by the National Civic Federation. I see the CED as an upgrade in effort from past precedents established by the civic progressives, the associationists as Collins suggested, and the New Dealers, who are really original Progressives. The CED expanded their reach into public policymaking on the foundational precedents and examples these precursors provided. Since the CED consisted of corporate insiders and informed academics (thus, according to Shriftgiesser, it was a unique organization), it is likely their policy analyses and recommendations influenced federal government decision-making.

After World War II, this interrelationship became more the rule than wartime exception. Relying on outside, systematic expertise began to become standard operating procedure. Corporate executives were now in favor, and they were in the know. The Eisenhower administration especially welcomed their input. Furthermore, using contemporary system and scientific analysis to formulate and execute public policy, gained wider acceptance during this decade.

The hot, global war ended, resulting in a new institutional synthesis: an American diplomatic, nation-state, and economic titan that immediately had to confront a new challenge, not of its making. The hot war didn't die with its progenitors. Instead, its victors created a new form of war—cold war—consisting mainly of ideological, diplomatic, and economic competition (and intermittently military conflict) at the plenipotentiary level. In turn, this affected entire civilizations and set the life courses of nation-states for the remainder of the century.

As the new global titan, the postwar United States of America advanced, carrying with it into the realpolitick arena, its greatest asset: the economic, institutional, organizational, and cultural resources owned, operated, and proselytized by our own corporate-dominated private sector.

The domestic dance of the titans was about to spiral into an ever-closer, more mutually dependent orbit, in response to a new global war, a cold war that would pervade and dominate the rest of civilization over the next fifty years.

The relationship that business and government forged in response to war crisis sustained itself by confronting the fear of postwar economic calamity, and the diplomatic specter of Soviet imperialism. Thus, as the depression-and-war era ended, the two institutional behemoths continued the trend of commonsense marriage, out of necessity. Uniting to confront a common peril, the two worked together toward a common end, while remaining ideologically and politically separate and apart.

After 1945, our Arsenal of Democracy morphed into a national security state, in response to a newly polarized world, divided between the economic systems of capitalism and communism, and the political systems of the free world versus despotism.

In our country, this dance emerged as what we now call the military-industrial complex (MIC) and its adjuncts.[57] As this new crisis evolved, the federal government response became as Robert Sobel suggested: "Increasingly big government and big business came to resemble each other,"[58] and Benjamin Cooling: "It may have been inevitable. Marriage between two strong American institutions—national government and the business community was meant to be."[59]

From approximately 1949 to 1989, the federal government, more or less, fought world communism successfully, spending vast sums of money rebuilding Western Europe, through the Marshall Plan; controlling Japan via occupation and aid, and influencing its internal politics; suppressing the spread of political and economic communism, through overt, covert, and military measures, and engaging in hot wars (police actions), in Korea and Vietnam.

While exercising its role atop the Free World, wearing the white hat (the ultimate Dodge Boys), fighting tyranny, the federal government, was also consuming huge quantities of war matériel (including the development and deployment of a new arsenal—nuclear), that in turn continued, de facto, wartime, overall, prosperity at home via a persistent consumer/producer relationship with the private sector, i.e., defense spending.

This quasi-war arrangement was its own dichotomy. Even while retaining a semi-war footing, the domestic economy did reconvert back to its consumer-products base, while a separate war economy persisted. The latter pushed the two institutional titans back into familiar war patterns, while the former, kept them clinched in a serious grapple. The view of their arena, was now parallax, akin to a psychedelic case of distorted double vision.

This relationship on the war side, was different from previous. It was not a marriage of convenience and necessity, as before: World War I, the New Deal, World War II. Now, forging a cooperative, customer-supplier relationship, in response to the cold war, was enthusiastically sought and sustained by both parties, albeit limited to defense-related industries.

The subsequent, evolving relationship during the 1950s, might have been unique to its participants. The federal government's military and the private sector did not spill over into what had been an antagonistic business-government situation. Countervaliance was not part of the MIC.

Domestically, for the U.S., the Cold War footing, sustained war readiness; kept government spending at high levels; promoted more prosperity via a surging, robust domestic economy, and significantly fostered continued collaboration between business and government as they maintained their wartime partnership within a market relationship through the mechanism of the MIC.

Thus, defense spending played a significant role in fueling overall domestic prosperity during the 1950s. (Recall chapter 4.) Together, guns and butter resulted in the People of Plenty. Then, big business provided good stuff for citizen-consumers and their government. The creation of this new synthesis from 1946 to 1960 persisted when new catalysts were added to the mix: the Space Race, nuclear armament escalation, and storm clouds gathering in southeast Asia. The dance of the titans would spiral in even closer than before.

The Cold War economy coalescing during the 1950s expanded during the Vietnam era (here defined from the Kennedy through Nixon administrations), becoming an institutionalized production system. Steven Rosen called this, Pentagon Capitalism, a permanent war economy. By then, Rosen claimed, the U.S. Department of Defense did business with 20,000 firms and 100,000 subcontractors.[60]

Place this development in the context of the United States, now, as a world sovereign, a new Rome, with its dynamic, soon-to-be globalized (see chapter 7), economy, absorbing and institutionalizing a new derivative, a carryover from World War II. The permanent war economy now defined by large amounts of guns purchased through Defense Department contracts, became thus formalized, institutionalized, and permanent. Thus, originally fueled by anti-Soviet and anti-(worldwide)-communism, and then escalating during the Vietnam War, our political economy formalized defense spending as a permanent component.

By then, in a thirty-year, evolving process, it was no longer a wartime exigency. It was now normalcy and seemingly permanent, at least then, for after all, ideologically, communism, and the Soviet Union and China, were all perceived to be permanent foes. In order to compete in the world arena of power politics, maintaining that dynamic tension (See Henry Kissinger's

A World Restored), it was necessary to wield a strong, technologically superior military, even though the war was not hot.

This effort, this decades-long buildup was supplied to the federal government by American corporate capitalism.

Following the fall of Saigon and during the post-Watergate era of the Ford and Carter administrations, the Cold War consensus sustaining a permanent war economy, somewhat eroded. The political and social turmoil fueled by the Vietnam War caused a public policy reassessment of America's world position, and of the negative consequences of such a war-like economy.

This was only a temporary retrenchment and criticism because the cold war simmered on all fronts. When a flashpoint cooled (Korea, Cuba, Vietnam), another one was likely to take its place. Consequently, the war economy persisted. Vigilance and preparedness were now permanent parts of federal government policy making in a new world where isolationism was now a concept on the museum shelf. Thus, in order to maintain world sovereignty, the tandem producer-consumer relationship between big business and the federal government continued, flourishing in its strength. Now, perhaps more than ever because of the culture resulting from the emergence of the Cold War national-security state, big business has a permanent say in how the federal government does its business.

This trend continued and accelerated during the 1980s because rearmament surged during the Reagan–Bush I regime; the MIC and its corporate clients benefiting from government's largesse. Somewhere along the line, all participants concerned—big business, the civilian federal government and their military—realized a permanent war economy was mutually beneficial, thus becoming reluctant to quell their collective grasp on the cornucopia of good stuff the MIC offered.

Thus, business and government together, as the MIC, forged a separate economic and political relationship parallel to the main civilian domestic, consumption-spending economy. Here in this important aside from tradition, business and government operated on an entirely different plane. In what was a niche, albeit an important, lucrative, and influential relationship that eventually did spill over, somewhat, into the domestic sphere. That confluence was limited, in that business antipathy for government, as a matter of principle, prevented copasetic and formally friendly relationships.

Thus, the cold war footing, and especially its anti-communist ideology and rhetoric, opened doors for big business to establish, and then fortify, a foothold in influencing the policy, regulations, administration, and management of the federal government. Forming a collaborative alliance to fight a common, perceived enemy, one, a threat to the existence of our nation-state because of nuclear war or World War III, and the other, as a threat to corporate capitalism, resulted in a final morphing when big business and the federal government handcuffed themselves together in perpetuity.

In this context, the MIC is an operational economic and political system, composed of people in business and government, together, associating, to formulate policy, and creating economic and political precedents and protocols, that help sustain the system as a whole, simultaneously, with its parts and stakeholders.

At the same time, this is also institution building, interaction among behemoths—the corporation and the nation-state. (Now, de facto, sovereigns dealing with sovereigns. See chapter 7.) The overall arrangement is based on mutual dependence, fulfilling concomitant priorities. The corporate sector wants to do business and get big contracts from their customer, the military. In turn, the federal government wants good stuff too (in this relationship—airplanes, ships, bombs, weapons, etc.), as a means for it to promote its foreign policy, and political goals. Some say defense spending is more than national security, it is vital for economic prosperity.

As mentioned, a separate niche-sector grew from this: defense contractors. They became an important component for, especially, the private sector's largest corporations, but at the same time, it was not the sole source of profit for much of the *Fortune* 500. Many of those in the know suggest that big business is not solely dependent on government spending for their main source of income. Regardless, the customer-producer relationship is crucial, especially when coupled with the ongoing plenipotentiary association between the two institutions.

Before 1989, it was lucrative for the private sector to produce what the nation-state wanted for its Cold War crusade. The result, our Arsenal of Democracy, synthesized into a National Security State. What were once referred to as the Merchants of Death became simply defense contractors. They made fighter jets, the B-47, the B-52, the B-1 and Stealth. They made nuclear-powered and missile-carrying submarines such as *Nautilus, Thresher, and Scorpion*, to name the most famous. They made nuclear-powered aircraft carriers. They made Inter-Continental Ballistic Missiles (ICBMs), medium-range ballistic missiles, and cruise missiles. They also made rockets that put people into space and sent Apollo 11 to the moon and back safely, "in a single decade." They were mostly big corporations: Boeing, Lockheed, Electric Boat.

Defense spending includes a wide variety of products and programs: large and small, mundane and esoteric, very simple and vastly complex, ranging from aircraft carriers to toilet seats. Regardless, of what kind of commodity purchased, it *is* consumption spending, and as Lizabeth Cohen, and others, suggested, it *is* the lifeblood of our economy. Thus, when a large and rich consumer such as the federal government spends, and has the ability to sustain purchasing, a significant market sector develops. As a result, big business did what was necessary to cater to and nurture this very lucrative profit source. Corporate capitalism, thus fueled the marketing relationship, besides foreign policy decisions. Hence, the MIC sustained itself and indeed, grew in significance for most of the second half of the twentieth century. It will remain a significant market sector as long as we maintain our Romanish status as world sovereign, and as long as we sanctify state tribalism over scientific advancement.

In the decades of the Cold War, the institutional culture of the big business corporation successfully influenced its counterpart more so than the other way around. Corporations, by 1950, were already large structural bureaucracies with their own institutional cultures. (Recall, chapter 4.) Through the interaction of defense contractors and their federal customers, more than just a business relationship formed. De facto, the ways of big business have seeped into the way the federal government operates, because over the decades, these linkages persisted, becoming standard operating procedure for the duration of the Cold War. By the time the Berlin Wall came down, these linkages and their trappings were institutionalized, resulting in the de facto corporatization of the federal bureaucracy.

These participants unwittingly created a new component to fit into our organizational society. This new piece, the MIC, was the catalyst that moved business-government relations permanently away from the old order, to the new. The power of individualism, characterized by the robber barons and the captains of industry, was now replaced by institutional, corporate, and bureaucratic power.

Although big business and the federal government retained their separate ideologies and institutional prerogatives and roles, the dance of the titans, after the war, remained intertwined for the rest of the century. The partnership remained dichotomous. Working together as cold war allies, the two sectors still competed ideologically and politically, with neither side willing to relinquish its prerogatives and established precedents. The federal government persisted, in varying intensity, in its regulatory role, and big business resisted them. This parallel relationship persisted throughout all the presidential administrations from Truman to Johnson.

Generally, when the Democrats governed, they favored a stronger regulatory role and promoted reform for the greater common good, thus heating up the institutional difference between the two.

In contrast, the GOP, now the party of big business, was much friendlier to deregulation, in particular, and to, generally, catering to the policy preferences of their corporate clients. (The financial and political basis for this relationship are included in chapter 6, on lobbying, interest groups, and campaign finance.)

Even though big business and the federal government actively competed politically and ideologically before the body politic and within the political economy, they still retained their informal partnership, now orchestrated by cold war exigencies and the compatible institutional cultures it promoted. Managerial elites, now with much in common, ran both bureaucracies, corporate and federal.

This, then, the last section of chapter 6, addresses the concept of elite governance, placed in the context of corporate influence as its principal vectoring engine throughout the twentieth century.

Those that study elites, generally conclude that the chosen ones have an inordinate and often publicly invisible hold on managing the American political economy and in influencing, if not determining, policy. For example, Prewitt and Stone called them "directing agents."

Often, especially in a representative government and capitalistic political economy, economic power fosters political power. In our case, this has always been so throughout our history. Even though an ocean separated colonial America from their English kinsfolk and overlords, and the frontier wilderness fostered an unheard-of attitude of individual freedom, overall, the colonial political economy was controlled by elites. They influenced and managed colonial growth, fostered and financed a war against England for independence, and created a new country.

From then on, this hold on economic and political power grew, forming a definable class structure, that we all so like to collectively and individually deny, that included sets of economic and social elites at the very top. C. W. Mills was essentially right. There is and always has been a power elite in this country, perhaps originating with the merchant class in the northern English colonies, and with the planter class in the South. From those kernels spawned a class structure that grew and evolved right alongside the republican form of government.

By the twentieth century, power began to be primarily determined by economic assets first and foremost. It manifested to the public and within the political economy as essentially large corporations.

It was this top-shelf segment of society that vectored the components necessary to sustain and evolve our nation. They managed life on several different levels, from local communities and their economies, to the whole economy and national domestic and foreign policy. This was more than evident, according to Cochran and Miller:

> Between 1890 and 1910 the investment bankers controlled more and more of the key industries of the nation, and the ruling oligarchy, as we have seen, became a smaller and more exclusive group.[61]

They continued, asserting that business leaders exerted control within high society, government, and civil affairs.

This trend consolidated throughout the twentieth century, precipitated by the rise of the urban-industrial order. This revolutionary onset of social forces created new elites that, sometimes, supplanted those from the old, family-based system. Regardless of origins, the old and the new elites sustained their hold on our political economy, society, and body politic.

The new order's elites emerged from the corporate cultures that spawned them (recall chapters 2 and 4), and then sustained their power and influence as America evolved toward a corporation nation by the 1960s. That trend persisted until century's end and will likely sustain itself for a long time to come. (See chapter 7, on multinationals and globalization.)

Our elites come from both old families and money, and nouveau and new. They have familiar names like Rockefeller and du Pont, and they are also from the nouveau elites who have as anonymous backgrounds as the occupations that created and supported their status.

They were a new elite class, consisting of corporate executives and high-level managers, scientists, engineers (later, computer people), and academics. (Many of them already had ascribed social status, and several achieved it.) They managed and administered their firms and institutions, and also participated, successfully influencing and formulating civic policy, at all three levels of government, thus having a considerable say in shaping, managing, and controlling the political economy and its body politic.

Beginning with the Progressive Era, elites evolved to control the policy-making process at all levels of government, and included, as Gabriel Kolko asserted, the power of social reform. In contrast, the masses either didn't participate, or only on an ad hoc or intermittent basis, such as the Grange promoting railroad regulation, and the union movement, in general.

Thus, elite governance occurred through formal and informal mechanisms: associations, networking, circulating among their own kind; contracting with, and working with, and in governments, and through lobbying (see chapter 6), interest groups and campaign finance.

Formal methods included active participation in organizations such as trade associations, serving on blue ribbon commissions, or working in the CFR or CED. Consider how the latter two groups recruited so many corporate elites and other top-level players, and put them to work on high-order problems and situations.

G. W. Domhoff, for example, asserted that the creation of Social Security, in 1935, was the work of a conservative coalition of corporate elites, foundation personnel, some academics within the Social Science Resource Council, and members of Industrial Relations Counselors. The latter, was a Rockefeller-financed organization that studied labor relations and attempted to address current labor-management problems.

This consortium of interested parties, including government officials, used the discussion group/policy analysis method (akin to Taylorism as mentioned in chapter 2), to determine how to make programs that would help stabilize labor-management relations in the workplace: old age insurance and unemployment benefits.

When President Roosevelt announced the effort, his administration consulted with these associations, laden with corporate elites. As a result, the policy formulation process, within, included their outside expertise. They even helped construct the formal analysis and proposals.

Within the policy-making process, as above, for example, and in the aforementioned associations, people of similar backgrounds and occupations, and with similar interests, congressed together to further their own interests, and when called upon, often joined with others, also of like mind, to analyze problems, situations, and then to offer advice and recommendations for public policies, at again, all levels of government.

While in the mix either in the private or public sphere, simply on the job or making public policy, they associated formally and informally, raised and discussed business and policy issues, formulating positions and strategies, and cutting deals in order to proceed on contemporary issues.

A part of this both formal and informal process including social activities within city and country clubs, summering together, and attending public and private functions, such as at the White House, and summer retreats at Bohemian Grove. These are events where people of like mind, interests, and social class break bread and discuss what's what. These activities and participants are not necessarily cohesive, overtly collusive, or conspiratorial. Rather, such gatherings are based on consensus with more in common on issues of the day, than not.

Power elite theorists all note how the upper class and economic elites circulate among themselves. City and country clubs, churches, charity events, etc., are all parts of their social network.

Part of this system includes formal and informal meetings. The NGO discussion groups represent one aspect, while the annual Bohemian Grove elitist retreat represents the other.

The Bohemian Club, in San Francisco, has been sponsoring annual retreats since the 1880s. It is considered one of the most exclusive gatherings of American power wielders. Privacy is guaranteed; no press allowed. The organized activities are usually not talked about publicly.

By invitation only, American elites congress together, usually late in July, at the Bohemian Grove campgrounds, about sixty-five miles north of San

Francisco. Over the decades, attendees have been a *Who's Who* of power in the American political economy. They range from CEOs to senators, and from wealthy entertainers to military generals and ambassadors. It is one of the few occasions where American movers and shakers are all together at the same time. Over the years, attendees included: Herbert Hoover, Eddie Rickenbacker, Lowell Thomas, Barry Goldwater, Richard Nixon, and Robert Kennedy, to name a few. When there, they have entertainment and ceremonies. They also have guest speakers, for examples: Robert Taft, Earl Warren, Nelson Rockefeller, Henry Kissinger, Neil Armstrong and Werner von Braun. Although doing business together is not a sanctioned activity at the grove, the lakeside presentation is an especially effective, private, not-public mechanism for testing the waters on national public policy issues.

Although the Bohemian Club sponsors emphasize the tradition and camaraderie of the event, business does occur. A place such as this, the people, and the circumstances would be a natural catalyst for some informal conversation on matters of mutual interest that could be followed up later when they all return to work.

Doing business often requires cutting deals. Interacting with others of common need, i.e., those opposing government regulations, are likely to associate, using lobbyists, position papers, and informal conversation, as an entire communications system, in order to politick in their own behalf. It varies with the situation, and the interaction isn't necessarily all done at the level of smoke-filled rooms. The country club, golf course, White House dinner or luncheon, and CEO meetings might be the more favorable scene. (So too, would the grove retreat fill the bill.) Thus, big business has a variety of avenues to use to influence public policy: NGOs as sampled; participating in task force or ad hoc advisory groups and commissions; working as federal government appointees and through lobbying and campaign finance.

Along with C. W. Mills, G. William Domhoff also dissected the reality of who wields power and how. This section, the next to last, examines what these two found out about what it is.

Leftist sociologist C. Wright Mills was one of the first to present a theory that was contrary to the concept of consensus America. His book *The Power Elite* asserted that our country's top social classes made the decisions that basically ran the country. He wrote:

> The power elite is composed of men whose positions enable them to transcend the ordinary environments of ordinary men and women; they are in positions to make decisions having major consequences. Whether they do or do not make such decisions is less important than the fact that they do occupy such pivotal positions: their failure to act, their failure to make decisions, is itself an act that is often of greater consequences than the decisions they do make. For they are in

> command of the major hierarchies and organizations of modern society. They rule the big corporations. They run the machinery of the state and claim its prerogatives. They direct the military establishment. They occupy the strategic command posts of the social structure, in which are now centered the effective means of the power and wealth and the celebrity which they enjoy.[62]

Mills emphasized individuals who function within institutions. Many of them were corporate executives. They, with other elites in the civilian federal government, asserted themselves through those institutions: the military, the civilian federal government, and corporate executives, who together, made policy for their mutual benefit. Within this triumvirate, Mills recognized the power and influence of corporate elites. Through them, corporations accrued more political power. He asserted that this merging of economic and political power pushed the corporation to sovereign levels, similar to nation-states. He even suggested that corporate executives had more influence on governing than politicians.

In his model, these institutional forces supplanted elements of the old order as movers and shakers in the political economy. In this process, the power and influence of political parties and traditional small-scale associations have been, if not superseded, then significantly diluted, relegated to a middle level of power.

Mills's analysis of power elites focused on individuals and certain social classes, performing in groups. Take his analysis and redirect it toward managerial elites in big business and the federal government, acting within their institutions. The corporate culture of big business and the bureaucratic ethos of the federal government are more influential social forces than social class and power elitism alone. Men acting within the job parameters, working in groups as part of their institutions, is an effective model to examine the interaction between the two monoliths.

People think in terms of their job roles, and those protocols and expected behavior to do business, to do what is required and expected to be corporate or bureaucratically successful, rather than thinking exclusively within one's social class or as a power elite. We think in the context of how we fit into the work, occupational, and market order, more so than social status or socioeconomic class. Class structure is European, Old World, old paradigm. A market, then corporate, business mentality is more typically American.

Thus, in my model, those at the top and their support staff operate for and within the context of their organizational cultures. Again, the organizational pattern fits, even at the elite level. Although powerful and influential as individuals, the root of this comes from their achieved status as members of an organization, as in corporate or governmental elites. They come from large institutions, where they work often anonymously as a team or as managers.

They often participate in other organizations such as the CED, CFR, or BRT. Again, this functioning within large groups, as a member even occurs for a manager or executive.

In all these activities, they are part of an interdependent process, a component in the greater scheme of things. Just as any managerial elite participates as part of the system, so too, do they function when formulating policy and making recommendations as contributors to what NGOs have to offer as they help manage governing within the political economy. Even at this level, the power of large institutions, big business, and the federal government is the ultimate direting engine.

A little later, another power elite theorist, G. William Domhoff, presented an even bleaker assessment of power in postwar America. Writing from a 1970s perspective; Domhoff asserted that power in the United States was dominated by the upper classes, and that they are the captains and principal engineers of our ship of state, and of our society, in general. In his book, *Bohemian Grove*, he asserted:

> It is my hypothesis that there is a ruling social class in the United States. This class is made up of the owners and managers of large corporations, which means the members have many economic and political interests in common and many conflicts with ordinary working people . . .

He continued, citing statistics that showed how they dominated wealth:

> and direct the large corporations and foundations, and dominate the federal government in Washington.[63]

and in *The Higher Circles*, he argued that the upper classes dominated the political process:

> members of the upper class sit in pivotal government offices, define most major policy issues, shape the policy proposals on issues raised outside their circles, and mold the rules of government. Legally, the government is of all of us, but members of the upper class have the predominant, all persuasive influence. (and that) These foundations, institutions, and associations—along with corporate board rooms and gentlemen's clubs—are the citadels wherein consensus is reached and from which natural leaders emerge.[64]

In *Who Rules America*, he continued:

> This leadership group is called *the power elite*. The power elite is composed of members of the upper class who have taken on leadership roles in the corporate community and the policy network, along with high-level employees in

> corporations and policy-network organizations. More formally, the power elite consists of those people who serve as directors or trustees in profit and nonprofit institutions controlled by the corporate community through stock ownership, financial support, or involvement on the board of directors. This precise definition includes the top-level employees who are asked to join the boards of the organizations that employ them. The definition is useful for research purposes in tracing corporate involvement in voluntary associations, the media, political parties, and government.[65]

and again, in *The Higher Circles:*

> It is true, as I believe, that the power elite consist of many thousands of people rather than several dozen; that they do not meet as a committee of the whole; that there are differences of opinion among them; that their motives are not well known to us beyond such obvious inferences as stability and profits; and that they are not nearly so clever or powerful as the ultra-conservatives think—is nonetheless also true, I believe, that the power elite are more unified, more conscious, and more manipulative than the pluralists would have us believe, and certainly more so than any social group with the potential to contradict them.[66]

If the devil is in the details, as they say, then the details can be found throughout Domhoff's books. He presents an abundance of case studies, examples, and policy narratives, including citing and summarizing the works of others. He weaves a pattern, using examples of how power elites function formally through social networking. He maintains that the true power elites are part of this persistent social class. They use organizations such as the CFA and CED. He goes on to assert in *The Powers that Be*:

> These organizations, in turn, are linked with social clubs and corporations. . . . The overlaps and clique patterns found among organizations concerned with economic, social, and policy matters suggest there is an institutional basis for the kind of generalized world view that is the very essence of class consciousness.[67]

The basic, persistent pattern he reveals, is one where elites dominate the policy study and formulation process, which includes associative relationships among those occupying top-shelf positions in business, government, and academia. He stated in *The Powers that Be*, that:

> The policy formation process begins in corporate board rooms and executive suites. It ends in the innermost private offices of the government in Washington, where reporters and sociologists never tread. In between the beginning and the end there are a handful of huge foundations that provide the experts with money for research, as well as blue-ribbon presidential commissions which legitimate

> the policies to the general public and present them formally to the President. Research institutes and think tanks also are to be found in the inner circles of the network, and influential newspapers and magazines are important in bringing the views of the policy groups to the attention of government personnel. However, the central units in the policy network are such official-sounding organizations as the Council on Foreign Relations, the Committee for Economic Development, the Business Council and the American Assembly, which are best categorized as the policy-planning and consensus-seeking organizations of the power elite. They are also the training grounds in which new leaders for government service are informally selected.[68]

Like Mills, Domhoff concurs that America, in toto, is a product of elite class culture through and through. As a comparison, the gist of Mills's work is individuals functioning in institutions as elites, with an emphasis on their institutional behavior. Domhoff, in contrast, emphasizes that such institutional behavior is a derivative of elite class culture.[69]

Domhoff placed corporate elites deeply in this top-level culture. He asserted that big business upper management strives to perpetuate their positions within the power elite core, as a definable but loose coalition, a corporate community, that actively attempts to influence policy formulation at the federal level. This includes competing with other community members on specific, niche issues, while simultaneously, joining forces when matters of mutual concern arise. Besides lobbying and political party funding, Domhoff suggested that formal associations, such as foundations, think tanks, and discussion groups, are principal vehicles for influencing federal policy formulation.

He also asserted that this corporate community has its own culture based on an interlocking network of elite social clubs and membership on corporate boards of directors. Thus, they circulate in what we can call high society, among those of their own kind. To illustrate this, he cited studies of their linkages, and provided descriptions of movers and shakers attending the annual retreat at Bohemian Grove, California, as one example.

Corporate involvement in the top managerial levels is equally significant. Citing other sources, the trend over much of the history of our nation was a federal government dominated by managerial personnel from the top social classes. Prior to the Civil War, most top government appointments came from landowners, merchants, and lawyers. The twentieth century added financiers and corporate lawyers to the personnel pool. In this, the latest editions of his book, *Who Rules America*, Domhoff, adds that the pattern persists: The Clinton administration conformed to this trend and so did the junta that followed after the Supreme Court coup d'etat of December 12, 2000.

In Domhoff's overall model, class dominance by people enables corporations to be powerful. I contend a different tack, instead, expressing dominance in terms of institutional power, more so than the power of social class and status, alone. In this context, these theories have been constructed in terms of individuals acting as a social class. Instead, look at these people acting as institutional constituents. That field of interaction presents a clearer image, or notion of what reality has been within the socioeconomic and political economy arenas over the past sixty years.

The power of institutional culture is an overwhelming influential force, greater even than power elite classes and power elitism itself. The twentieth-century big business corporation became the chief institutional means to express and implement power and influence in policy making and governance.

In contrast, social class power is more part of the Wiebian, nineteenth-century paradigm of disparate, less-connected, island communities. Once urban-industrial modernity progressed, the united power of the merchant and planter classes, was superseded by corporate power, first and foremost over social class power, and institutional ascendance over individual power.

Mills and Domhoff and other power elite theorists, and their counterparts, the pluralists, primarily and generally place power in the political economy, in the context of social class and group interaction. I see such action on policy making as interaction between managerial and policy experts, operating within the parameters, contexts, and culture of large institutions. Formulating policy thus becomes a clash of titans, in some instances, monolithical organizations where people play out in accordance of group or institutional prerogatives and objectives, more so than individual. As indicated, in previous chapters, the workplace has played a significant role in inculcating a disparate set of values in its constituents. Therefore, when big government deals with big business, those institutional values, now individual values, come into play. Those values are usually corporate values.

Also, I prefer to place both theories in the context of people and groups acting within larger, systematic arenas: corporate, formal associations and big government institutions. My two paradigms attempt to explain action—policy making, interest group competition, the essence of power, etc., within a modern, contemporary, evolving context. The old paradigms are largely based on nineteenth-century associations, beliefs, and ideologies. The course of the twentieth century altered those realities. Therefore, components of both models might still apply perhaps better, as parts of an evolving modern model, or in this case two: organizational and corporate.

Overall, it is as Bensman and Vidich asserted, citing Veblen, Berle & Means, Birnbaum, Drucker, and Robert Bradley, and going on to claim these authors:

> were able to convince some segments of the public through their writings that the giant corporation had become a dominant institution in American society. Collectively, such writers described the revolutionary impact of corporate pen-

> etration into all aspects of American life to the point where the trend was irreversible. . . . We are now at the point, whether we like it or not, where we live in a society where big business is a dominant institution. Our knowledge of this situation has come relatively late, and is repressed because it disturbs the comfort and prosperity of a middle-class America that is primarily employed by big business.[70]

Regardless of where Mills and Domhoff et al., fit into our body of knowledge about America, both hit on a series of truths we all like to deny because their assertions destroy several of our more cherished icons: egalitarianism, Horato Alger classlessness, consensus, and pluralism. For example, Donald R. Matthews examined federal government elected and appointed officials for the time period, 1877–1940. His findings revealed that 90 percent of positions were filled from those in the top 15 percent of occupations, concluding there weren't many commoners making political decisions. Generally, the more important the position, the higher the status of the official.[71]

In another study, called, *Men Who Govern*, researchers looked at the background of top-echelon federal government officials, from 1933 to April 1965, a total of 1,041 positions that included department secretaries, undersecretaries, and assistant general counsels. The resulting social profile revealed a pattern of recruitment. These officials, generally, were eastern urbanites, Protestant, well educated, and middle-aged. Their work experience was mostly: big government work, big law, and big business, with businessmen the dominant recruitment source.[72]

Thus, throughout much of the twentieth century (and probably much before), the top-shelf classes set the tone and the parameters in which the rest of the society functions. The upper classes use their values, beliefs, and protocols to create and sustain both an economy and a social system. They are the arbiters of what it is in the political economy, its government, and its process.

At both the local and national level, they shape the structure and life course of the local and national economies. They influence and steer the American ship of state. They set up parameters and influence the trappings of life that all the rest of the class structure adopts as their own—accepted, acculturated behavior that is infused into us through basic education, advertising, propaganda, the media, and even from the pulpit.

This is reality, and it has been this way since our colonial forefathers first arrived here. Over those centuries since, that culture has evolved, organically, responding to how the times change. During the previous century, the paradigm shifted as I have stated, and the old elites and the new maintained their collective hold; utilizing a totally new set of resources to infuse society with new energy, discipline, values, and behavior. Commonly called the urban-industrial order, this has been recently christened "corporation nation" by several of those I've cited in this effort.

Corporate culture, an ethos with a specific set of beliefs, attitudes, protocols, accepted practices and methods shaped new elites while simultaneously serving as a principal mechanism fostering the cultural persistence from the old model to the new. Indeed, a directing engine this monolithical institutional culture has been.

The congress of powerful individuals working together in a group format became S.O.P. to address contemporary circumstances. Organizing and associating on a formal institutional level was consistent with the contemporary processes evolving at that time. Similar to industrial systematization, so too, were human sociological and psychological processes responding to this new environmental, social force.

Their efforts, remembered in our heritage as the WIB, CFA, NRA, CFR, and not quite known in history—CED, BC, and Bohemian Grove—are all elements of the organizational paradigm. Through formal and informal association, politicians, corporate captains of industry, and even academic and technical specialists, pooled their talents together and attempted to address contemporary policy issues, in an effort to steer society as it plowed through the complicated currents of the high seas of modern life.

Envision our society as a vast ocean. Big business and the federal government combined to create a large, complicated societal ship (resembling a combination aircraft carrier and luxury cruise ship), capable of maneuvering in both calm seas and through storms of titanic proportions.

Such was the necessary response to the political economy they had created and were creating as they cruised along. The components of this ship's superstructure are our institutions and the major trappings of our social web. Power moves the ship and holds it together. Big business and the federal government provide the fuel.

Institutional power for the most part is primarily concerned with influencing policy making at that level. It is an elite level, in that it is interaction among managerial elites in both the private and public sectors. Managerial elites, in the corporate world, dominate the private sector, and the federal government, in the public sector. Making and enforcing laws and regulations; conducting foreign policy, etc., are all top-shelf, executive-level administrative and management activities.

All these elites, the movers and shakers on all levels, often derive their power from the affiliations they have; their wealth, and social class; the company they keep; the social networks they use; their occupation and its status, and particularly, the institutions they belong to and represent. In an organizational society, it is what you do through group work and via institutional influence that is most effective in controlling and managing the political economy.[73]

During the last sixty years of the twentieth century, institutional-organizational power became paramount power, superseding the importance of the old order's power of the person. Thus, in this context, the two institutional behemoths, big business and big government, interacted through their managerial elites: upper-level corporate executives with their public-sector counterparts—the president, executive branch support staff, and influential legislators on Capitol Hill.

All these participants are parts of greater institutions, and institutional power comes from sources specific to that institution. The state and its military derives its power from its coercive capacity, its ability to enforce laws and if necessary, to suppress. That is, for example, a government can enforce tax law and use police power to suppress internal unrest. As a nation-state, it can exert influence on other ships of state, and if necessary, wage war.

The big business corporation is a similar institution, except that it derives and sustains its institutional power from its economic, political, and social assets. Cardinal among these attributes is its economic power. Because is has money and production assets, and provides goods and services, it accrues power.

Within a capitalistic economy, big business moves money and products through the system. It has been the principal force directing and the major fuel to drive our economic system throughout the twentieth century. In the process of accumulating wealth, it enables power.

Since any society is supported by its economy, the corporate sector, through this process, becomes a self-sustaining, perpetuating foundation. Thus, decades later, as the twentieth century ended, we have, as Thomas Frank once commented, "high corporate baroque."

In contrast, during the nineteenth century, this was a much simpler relationship with business just doing business mostly at regional and local levels. This changed with the evolution of the new paradigm, the urban-industrial order. During the twentieth century, American society, the economy, and the political economy rapidly expanded, becoming more complex and at the same time, more interrelated and then later, interdependent.

This was fueled by institutional growth in both the private and public sector. Within the political economy, I called this process metaphorically and symbolically, the dance of the titans.

As the century progressed, this dance, a contest of institutional will and power, ebbed and flowed, in response to contemporary circumstances, and it occurred within the greater universe of American corporate capitalism and representative government.

In this arena, the two titans squared off, parlaying their assets, as they maneuvered like two physical worlds influencing each other's orbits. The corporate sphere wanted to assert itself one way, while the federal government sphere became a strong reactive, countervailing agent that responded as both a partner and promoter, and opponent depending on whatever circumstances they happened to encounter.

Because our collective value system and societal belief structure is based primarily on consensus-based, egalitarian principles, we have basically refused to believe that, power, in our political economy, governs, sets policy, and influences lawmaking and political office seeking. This power is not solely in the public sphere. It is, and has been, successfully wielded during the twentieth century at the institutional level within the private sector. It is elitist, Hamiltonian, T-Rooseveltian, and even Hooverian, associative, in part, all at the same time. Those doing this, maintain their cause, promote their interests, while publicly postering "for-the-people." platitudes and rhetoric. It is as William Greider once wrote: Corporate citizenship is first-class citizenship. (That is the topic of chapter 6.)

This manifested itself in a century-long dance, played out at the top level of our political economy. There, the corporate sphere, sustaining itself, wants to travel an unfettered orbit. In the process, it affects both positively and negatively all that it comes into contact with. On one side, it provides jobs and good stuff, thus producing the money that fuels our economy.

But on the other side, it also exerts a corporate culture that absorbs its human components, as Riesman et al. described. As an institution, it has bullied its way, the tough kid on the block, the coddled jock, the big man on campus, all in one, becoming a first-class citizen with more privileges of citizenship than responsibilities. (For example, as a producer, the corporation pollutes.) It exerts socioeconomic influence on communities where it operates and even in other countries (chapter 7) where it sets up shop. In the process of sustaining and self-perpetuation as an institution, it becomes a prime mover, a principal engine that drives American society.

But it is far from a perfectly operating engine, or acting like a perfectly responsible citizen. For examples, the twentieth-century business ethos consistently failed to respond to modern economic exigencies, exceptions to the status quo, specifically and glaringly, mobilization and economic contraction. In these instances, 1916–1917, 1939–1941, and 1929–1932, big business had to be prodded by the federal government to participate or act. Most of big business was unwilling to address these situations on their own.

Because of corporate recalcitrance or inability to act in response to economic downturn, the federal government must act, using a combination of fiscal and monetary policies. Big business has always been reluctant to take risks, to plan ahead, to consider the long run, to regulate itself. Because it is unwilling to do all this, it must be coerced or compelled by an equal institutional power: government—local, state, and national.

Corporations often whine and snivel like spoiled children or high school jocks when they don't get their way. They selfishly and heedlessly pursue what is good solely for them, regardless of its consequences on other fellow citizens. Always insisting on their prerogatives and rights of citizenship, which the courts have, indeed, granted them, they simultaneously, and shamelessly, shirk concomitant responsibilities of that citizenship.

Being responsible is right for everyone else except big business. Thus, since the corporate sector is unwilling to exercise self-restraint; a willingness to compromise; to get along with other societal constituents, for the greater common good, they have to be coerced or forced by state power. Peter F. Drucker, in *The New Society*, opined:

> industrial society requires a very strong and powerful central government. The enterprise is not an equal to the central government of the State. The power of both management and union has to be limited and their conduct regulated.[74]

Because of these shortcomings, big business spawned a countervailing, reactive force that evolved to attempt to alter their self-willed orbit. Thus, big business caused big government. In an organic context, big government becomes a controlling, reactive agent, preventing big business from becoming a rogue, ravenous, cancerous organism, such as Enron and its ilk.

This institutional test of power has played out over the course of the twentieth century. I've attempted to narrate some of these situations here. Those episodes, when viewed along a timeline, and regardless of one's philosophical beliefs on business-government relations, reveal an evolutionary process of institutional interdependence and interlock. As circumstances changed during those one hundred years, the two institutions responded and morphed as part of the process. Both grew in size, shape, structure, scale, and depth, becoming large, complicated, powerful institutions, both products of the universe they created and sustained. Indeed, they evolved to become a double-star system, whose interaction sustains each other, feeding upon, and fueling each other simultaneously.

Perhaps the ultimate irony from this study is that big business created the forces that fostered the growth of the federal government. Those in opposition to the institutional power of big government conveniently forget these first premises. They wound up criticizing an institution that their forebears, brothers in arms, so to speak, helped to create.

In this new century, those who cling to the mythos of laissez-faire and rugged individualism, are the equivalent of creationists and other flat-earth believers. The reality of the twentieth century was the emergence and acceleration, and then the institutionalization, of an organized society. A result of this evolutionary process was the creation of big government. As part of this process, if analogized as, organically, a large bureaucratized government, a natural result in a series of events that made up the twentieth century, the Corporate Century.

The socioeconomic combination of the Great Depression and World War II effectively altered the old order, permanently into the new. What began at the beginning of the twentieth century, the newly emerging urban-industrial order, and prompted by the use of organizational corporate capitalism, morphed into the modern corporate state by 1980.

The big business corporation was the structural and functional catalyst, especially during the first fifty years. It also prompted and caused the rise of big government, first as a countervailing foe or competitor, during the Progressive Era, and later, during World War II, and afterward, as an institutional, business partner, simultaneously. It was, and continues to be a dichotomous relationship depending on who controls the federal government.

Business-government relations have always been that way, even contradictory. In crisis, the two institutions flexibly altered their legal and philosophical prerogatives in order to cooperatively address contemporary circumstances. See mobilization or economic depression. However, underlying it all was what we call a countervailing relationship, or in some view, a negative, antagonistic, or distrustful one. Essentially, the two institutions were congenitally at odds with each other and the normal interactive atmosphere wasn't friendly. Each viewed the other as foes and distrustfulness and evasion were normative.

The resulting institutional relationship is the sum of disparate and similar parts. At its core is the countervailing standoff between two powerful institutions. The corporate sector retains its social and political power as a derivative of its economic assets. Fortified continually in the years since 1940, it has increased, and will continue to increase its institutional sovereignty. During that decade, Peter F. Drucker, even then observed:

> To Henry Ford the machine was the new and the important element of modern society. But in reality the new factor is not a mechanism but an institution: the modern large enterprise. In every industrial country the enterprise has emerged as the *decisive*, the *representative* and the *constitutive* institution. . . . Whether industrial society is organized under Capitalism, Socialism, Fascism, or Communism, the enterprise is its central institution, looks alike, behaves alike, and faces similar decisions and difficulties.
>
> The industrial enterprise is an autonomous institution. It has its own law and rationale in its function. It is not a creature of the State. It does not rest its power on delegation from its shareholders or from any other owner; in fact, the divorce of control over the enterprise from ownership is everywhere all but complete. Its function is essentially beyond the control of the State and largely unaffected by even the most radical changes in political system or in political

> beliefs. It is the first autonomous local institution that has come into existence in our society in five hundred years.[75]

Since then, the 1940s, corporations are close to becoming corporate, sovereign states. (See chapters 6 and 7.) The federal government evolved similarly, as a derivative of the rise of big business. It did, as Maury Klein wrote:

> The transformation of the federal government from a small, passive institution into a large, active one was another major feature of the corporate society and one that followed the corporate model of growth from a small firm to a mammoth organization.[76]

The small and simple general government of the Founding Fathers morphed its structural form and organizational ideology, and after 1933, became a significant director of American life, in tandem with big business. Hot and cold war exigencies made the federal government a permanent, big government, and at its core, it has persisted in its countervailing role, its most important, albeit controversial responsibility in our political economy. In a modern urban-industrial based society, the principal role of the federal government, in that political economy is to control the power of big business.

At the surface, this role seems unchanged, especially in the minds of those who oppose it (the flat-earthers). But in reality, big government's police and political power has been diminished due to the influence of a shared policy-making partnership between business and government, presented in this chapter, and through lobbying, interest groups, and campaign finance, in the next.

Nevertheless, this dichotomous and still countervailing relationship between the business and government institutional monoliths was a product of modern corporate capitalism, and their responses to hot and cold war, and now, its aftermath. What was supposed to have been a temporary, emergency, partnership, beginning in the winter of 1941, became permanent, persisting now to this day.

The post–World War II era was unprecedented, and the institutional changes that occurred within big business and big government are now permanent. This dichotomous partnership, forged by economic depression, world war, and a clash of economic and political ideologies, will persist until the next exigency enters the arena where the two titans still clash and dance. (That player has already entered and is awaiting its turn on the platform. It's called the multinational corporation and that will be the subject of chapter 7.)

As the American Century approached its political, diplomatic, and economic apex during the 1950s, the crest of the wave was a manifestation of the global triumph of the American ship of state, and the prosperity that resulted for most of its citizens.

At the foundation of that wave was a complex, elemental interaction between big government and big business, with both vital forces reacting and fueling each other to strengthen and drive the wave forward. By the end of the 1970s, it would achieve monstrous, tsunami-like power and force.

Together, subtly, discreetly, and definitely out of the public eye, the two titans continued their wartime partnership, that eventually imperialized most of the globe. It was a process involving cold war diplomacy, covert operations, and warfare (police actions), and the prosletization of the American corporate capitalism abroad.

The dance of the titans has about ended, and the corporate sector of the economy is the winner. The beginning of the end occurred during the 1980s via lobbying, interest groups, and campaign finance. That is what's in the next chapter.

Notes

1. An indication of the high degree of nascent corporate power, 100 years age, was J.P . Morgan's intervention into the financial sector of the economy. In 1894, Morgan and August Belmont bought over 3.5 million ounces of gold to answer a rush on federal government holdings. Macgregor and Burns wrote: "Afterward, Morgan considered himself the head of a 'fourth branch' of government." James M. Burns and Susan Dunn, *The Three Roosevelts: Patrician Leaders Who Transformed America*, New York: Atlantic Monthly Press, 70, 97.

Once again, in 1907, the corporation, the House of Morgan, used its economic power to "save" the economy, when it deposited money into financially teetering banks; reeling in the aftermath of the Knoblach Trust Company failure. At the time, President Roosevelt, according to Burns and Dunn, was, "almost powerless to act," resigned to his fate that he and not business would be blamed for the panic. At the same time, the press hosannahed Morgan as savior of the economy. Burns, asserted: "But in 1907, the health of the economy and the success of TR's presidency seemed to hinge on the vast economic resources of the gentleman financier, J. P. Morgan. TR's power to deal with a major economic crisis was limited, and he knew it." Ibid, 97.

Note in both instances, J. P. Morgan, the man, used the economic resources of a powerful corporate, financial institution, to effect a response to a sudden change.

2. To visualize this dance of the titans, imagine a large arena, high on a plateau. The floor of the arena conveys the energy of those that walk on it, to the society below. Thus, the activity at the top affects, or energizes what goes on below. Up there, the titans dance; it's more like a gladiatorial event or Greco-Roman match, in a baroque, *Heavy Metal*ish variation of the Paul Taylor Dance Company or Jules Feiffer's cartoon. As the two titans act out the theme, their movements create the basic fuel for the society they service. In this chapter, the titans are big business and big government.

3. Gabriel Kolko noted: In 1895, mergers absorbed 43 companies; in 1898, 303; 1899, 1,208; in 1900, 340. Source: *The Triumph of Conservatism*, 18.

4. The Supreme Court 1895 decision in *United States v. E. C. Knight*, essentially gutted Sherman. In 1895, *Lochner v. New York*, was anti-regulatory toward the states. (Source: John M. Cooper, *The Warrior and the Priest*, 150.)

5. Remember, as an individual, you are your past; collectively too, as citizens, participants, etc. we are our past.

6. Cooper, *The Warrior and the Priest*, 83.

7. TR also seemed dichotomous when taking executive action. His justice department sought to trust-bust forty-four corporations (including Standard Oil, American Tobacco Co., and DuPont), during his seven years as president. Despite his trust-buster moniker, TR believed in regulation of corporations rather than their dissolution. What then appeared as an inconsistent policy position, actually conforms to his personal ideology.

8. Cooper, *Warrior*, 212.

9. Morrison, *Theodore Rex*, 73–74,139.

10. Burns and Dunn, *Three Roosevelts*, 68-69.

11. Arthur Link, *Woodrow Wilson and the Progressive Era, 1900–1917* (New York: Harper & Brothers, Publishers, 1954), 18.

12. Note the contrast. Roosevelt wanted large corporations to be socially responsible (Cooper, 215), and economically and publicly accountable.

This is corporate citizenship, a tandem relationship of legal rights and responsibilities. As citizens, individuals have both. Corporations, throughout the twentieth century, consistently demanded their codified and adjudicated legal rights, but simultaneously, strove to ignore or abrogate their responsibilities of citizenship. Their most effective method of shirking those responsibilities is through interest group politics, lobbying, political action committee activities, and federal campaign financing. These are the topics in chapter 6. Stay tuned.

Corporations, like people, are selfish and prone to civic destruction. Thus, their actions have to be controlled to foster the greater common good. Similar to religious and social taboos and sanctions, responsible behavior often has to be influenced, manipulated, or ultimately coerced.

Corporate culture excels at influencing, sanctioning, convincing, and manipulating. The state's expertise is in compelling and coercing. That is the reality of our political economy, and we created it, in a century-long process of institutional interaction.

13. Woodrow Wilson (editor William B. Hale), *The New Freedom* (London: J.M. Dent & Sons, Ltd. [1916]), 23–24, 48–49, 135–136, 142.

14. Chester Destler, "The Opposition of American Businessmen to Social Control During the 'Gilded Age,'" *Mississippi Valley Historical Review*, 641–647.

15. Clarkson, *Industrial America*, 23.

16. From April 17, 1917, to November 11, 1918, the federal government spent $23,625,252,843, according to Helmut C. Engelbrecht and Frank C. Hanighen, *The Merchants of Death*, 177.

17. Sobel, *Giant Corporations*, 111.

18. Fitzpatrick, *A Study*, 1, 130.

19. Hicks, *Republican Ascendancy*, 12.

20. According to those in the know, the unemployment rate was never officially decided for 1920–1933. Since then, the rate has been pegged, estimated at about 25 percent,

during the worst of times. Some skeptics suggest the rate might have been as high as 44 percent. Others remarked that the federal government didn't have the means to collect such data, and during the New Deal, the attitude of let's-not-quantify-how-bad-it-is might have prevailed. They didn't want to know, and didn't attempt to calculate it.

Gerald Nash, in *The Crucial Era* (p. 3, 14), stated there were over 75 million unemployed from 1932–1933, with one of two workers having a full time job. Bernard Bellush, in (*The Failure . . .*), asserted: "Between 1929 and 1932 the employment level dropped from 97.5 percent to 60.1 percent. . . . Over half the population now subsisted on incomes below the minimum requirement for health and safety." (p. xiii).

Donald Richberg, in *The Rainbow*, elaborated on some ramifications:

> The existence of any considerable body of unemployed or impoverished workers in the United States today is an indictment either of the industrial system or of its managers. It will not do to make a counter charge against 'political interference' or internal or external 'trouble makers.' These are the effects of maladministration of economic powers, not the causes. No 'agitator' can agitate long or successfully without some real injustice to expose and denounce. No 'politician' can interfere substantially with an economic system that is providing all willing workers with a decent livelihood. (p. 279)

21. This was section 7a: "Every code of fair competition, agreement, and license approved, prescribed, or issued under this title shall contain the following conditions: (1) That employees shall have the right to organize and bargain collectively through representatives of their own choosing, and shall be free from the interference, restraint, or coercion of employees of labor, or their agents in the designation of such representatives or in self-organization or in other concerted activities for the purpose of collective bargaining or other mutual aid or protection." (Source: Leverett Lyon, et al., *The National Recovery Administration: An Analysis and Appraisal*, 895–896).

22. The main code making period was from June 1933 to March 1934. Lyon, pp. 48, 52.

23. Bellush said that after two years, the NRA was, "a sprawling administrative colossus." In August 1933, there were about 400 staff. It peaked at 4,500, in February 1935. In its lifetime, the NRA created 546 fair competition codes, and 185 other. It took 18 volumes, totaling 13,000 pages to contain them. There were 11,000 code interpretations. Bellush, *Failure*, p. 33.

24. Gourevitch, "Breaking," 114.

25. Hawley, *New Deal*, 153.

26. Joseph Bensman and Arthur J. Vidich, *The New American Society: The Revolution of the Middle Class* (Chicago: Quadrangle Books, 1971), 41.

27. Herman E. Kroos, *Executive Opinion: What Business Leaders Said and Thought on Economic Issues, 1920s–1960s* (Garden City, New Jersey: Doubleday & Company, Inc., 1970), 185.

28. Neil Smith, *The Endgame of Globalization* (New York: Routledge, 2005), 120.

29. Whitney, *Trade Associations*, 12–28, 38–39.

30. Steiner, *Government's Role*, 189.

31. Ibid., 160.

32. Sobel, *Giant Corporations*, 111.

33. "Yesterday December 7, 1941—a date which will live in infamy—the United States of America was suddenly and deliberately attacked by naval and air forces of the empire of Japan."

34. Tasogawa, *All The Emperor's Men: Kurosawa's Pearl Harbor*, Chapter 13, np.

35. During the summer of 1940, the German army occupied Belgium, France, Denmark, Norway, Holland, and Luxembourg; the air blitz of England pending. After the British evacuation at Dunkirk, FDR declared a state of emergency.

36. Donald M. Nelson, *Arsenal of Democracy: The Story of American War Production* (New York: Harcourt, Brace and Company, 1946), 87.

37. Catton, *The War Lords*, 100.

38. FDR used the phrase "arsenal of democracy" in a fireside chat on December 29, 1940 (Nash, p. 125); Adolf Hitler referred to "American Colossus" in *Mein Kampf* (Nelson, p. 36.).

39. Janeway, *Struggle*, 228.

40. Gulick, *Administrative*, 58.

41. Ibid., 61.

42. Adams, *Best War*, 114; O'Neill, *Democracy at War*, 205. Of note: in 1939, about 60 percent of American production plants were idle. In 1944, U.S. war matériel production was 40 percent of GDP (Adams, *Best War*, 117; Novick, *Wartime Production Controls*, 14). That same year, average industrial production had increased 280 percent since 1939. It was done with adding over six million to the civilian manufacturing workforce (Gulick, *Administrative*, 59.)

43. Eiler, *Mobilizing*, 60.

44. Winkler, *Home Front*, 8–9.

45. Stone, *War Years*, 60.

46. Nelson, *Arsenal*, 213.

47. Ibid., 235–238. Here's an example of cooperative airplane production, per Nelson, p. 236, selectively:

> B-29 Superfortress built by—Boeing, Bell, and Martin; the B-17 Flying Fortress—Boeing, Douglas, Lockheed; the B-24 Liberator—Consolidated-Vultee, Douglas, Ford, and North American; the Wildcat—Grumman, GM; Pratt & Whitney engines—Pratt & Witney, Nash Kelvinator, Buick, Ford, Continental, and Jacobs.

48. I consider this attitude and practice, then and now, as examples of corporate citizens shirking their responsibilities. The courts bestowed legal rights of citizenship to the corporation, similar to individuals.

As citizens, people all have rights concomitantly with responsibilities. Together, this results in a civil, orderly, and organically positive society. Of course, the corporate citizen-institution will first and foremost assert its rights of citizenship, while simultaneously going to great lengths to either avoid or minimize its citizenship responsibilities behind the façade of the cost of doing business, and straw-man, derisive labels of creeping socialism and government interference in the economy and private enterprise.

This unwillingness to accept responsibility of citizenship, imposed on or inculcated into the rest of us, is to me the fundamental and most significant flaw in twentieth century corporate capitalism. It is the root cause for all the tension between business and government, and the prime factor in forcing government to assert itself by using its coercive police power to countervail against the big business corporation's lack of citizenship. It is the main reason that the federal government has become a large institution. Countervailance was a necessary response.

49. Catton, *War Lords*, 226.

50. "American Anthem"

51. Bruce Catton offered this poignant, contemporary, comment abut VJ-Day:

> Perhaps that is why the wild rejoicing of VJ-Day, when it finally came, had in it more than a touch of hysteria—as if the people were using it, not merely to mark their release from what had been happening, but also to keep from thinking about what might happen in the future. (VJ-Day: day of triumph and victory and the end of the long trail, but given no great name out of the heart and the imagination, known only by a colorless alphabetical symbol borrowed from the jargon of the general staff.)
>
> Under the shouting and the cheering and the laughter there was a nameless and indefinable unease. The worst enemies the democracy had ever faced had been crushed to earth, but we kept on looking nervously over our shoulders. . . . Indeed, the strangest thing about the entire war was our reaction to it after we had won it. America did the most colossal job in history and came out of it with an inferiority complex and a deep sense of fear.
>
> (Source: Catton, *War Lords*, p. 305–306.)

52. Catton, *War Lords*, 307.

53. Here are some examples of CED publications: "A Postwar Federal Tax Plan for High Employment, 1944; "The Bretton Woods Proposals: A Statement on National Policy," 1944; "Toward More Production, More Jobs, and More Freedom," 10/1945; *Taxes and the Budget*, 1947; *Monetary and Fiscal Policy for Greater Economic Stability*, 12/1948; *The Uses and Dangers of Direct Controls in Peacetime*, 7/1949; *Paying for Defense*, 1950; *Economic Policy and Rearmament*, n.d.; *Tax and Expenditure Policy*, 1953; *Taxes, National Security and Growth*, 1954; *Britain's Economic Problem and its Meaning for America*, 1953; "Anti-Recession Policy for 1958," n.d.; *Economic Policy for American Agriculture*, 1956; *Economic Growth in the United States*, 1958; "Growth and Taxes: Steps for 1961," n.d.; *Fiscal and Monetary Policy for High Employment*, 1962; *Union Powers and Union Functions*, 1964; *Developing Metropolitan Transportation Policies*, 1965.

Approximate hand count of publications: 1943–1949=33; 1950–1959=47; 1960–1969=44.

Source: Schriftgiesser, *Business Comes of Age, Business and Public Policy*; Library of Congress electronic catalog.

54. Waddell, *War Against*, 137–138.

55. Schrifthiesser, *Business and Public Policy*, 13–14 and *Business Comes of Age*, 224.

56. John K. Galbraith, *American Capitalism: The Concept of Countervailing Power*, revised edition (Boston: Houghton Mifflin Company, 1956 [1952]), 179–180.

57. The military-industrial complex in this book, is a system based on a set of business, marketing, propaganda, and institutional-level relationships between the federal government and defense/war matériel producing companies. It grew out of the exigencies of capitalism versus communism, and persisted to the present.

Paul Koistinen offers: "the term usually refers to the partial integration of economic and military institutions for the purpose of national security." (Source: "IMC," *Bus. Hist. Review*, 378.

I see the MIC as more a business relationship than ideological or even patriotic. Anti-communism was good for business. Once realized, profit-making became of utmost importance, transcending political and diplomatic considerations.

58. Sobel., *Age*, 163.

59. Benjamin F. Cooling, editor, *War, Business, and American Society: Historical Perspectives on the Military-Industrial Complex* (Port Washington, New York: Kennikat Press Corp., 1977), 213.

60. Rosen, *Testing the Theory*, 20–22.

61. Thomas C. Cochran and William Miller, *The Age of Enterprise: A Social History of Industrial America* (New York: Harper Torchbooks, revised edition, 1961), 273.

62. C. Wright Mills, *The Power Elite* (New York: Oxford University Press, 1956, [1951]), 3–4.

63. Domhoff, *Bohemian Grove*, 82.

64. G. William Domhoff, *The Higher Circles: The Governing Class in America* (New York: Random House, 1970), 105–106.

65. Domhoff, *Who Rules America, 95.*

66. Domhoff, *Higher Circles*, 299.

67. Domhoff, *Powers that Be*, 19.

68. Ibid., 62.

69. I often find leftist ideological polemics very useful information sources because such authors research and provide a large amount of details to support their arguments. I often disregard their polemics and use some of the details.

70. Vidich and Bensman, *New Society*, 43.

71. Donald Matthews, *The Social Background of Political Decision-Makers* (Garden City, New Jersey: Doubleday, 1954), 28–32.

72. David T. Stanley, et al., *Men Who Govern: A Biographical Profile of Federal Political Executives*, Washington, DC: The Brookings Institution, 1967, 1–3, 17–19, 31–37, 78–79.

73. Historians have a penchant for interpreting history as action by people, often independent of the institutions they function in. It is important to do the opposite, at least for twentieth-century American history, to modernize perception and subsequent analysis. Within my modernization paradigm, the individual participants should be placed within the larger institutional structures they work in. After all, they were on the job, working, making phone calls, shuffling paper, negotiating, agreeing, disagreeing. Their behavior individually and collectively played out within larger interacting institutional forms.

74. Peter F. Drucker, *The New Society: The Anatomy of the Industrial Order* (Westport, Connecticut: Greenwood Press, reprint, 1982 [1949]}, 36.

75. Peter F. Drucker, *The New Society: The Anatomy of the Industrial Order* (Westport, Connecticut: Greenwood Press, reprint, 1982, [1942]}, 27.

76. Klein, *Flowering*, 97.

6

Citizen Baroque

Lobbying, Interest Groups, and Campaign Finance

CORPORATE CITIZENSHIP IS first-class citizenship, so said William Greider. If so, big business achieved this through lobbying, forming and supporting interest groups and political action committees (PACs), and financing election campaigns.

If the rise of big business is a phenomenon of the twentieth century, so too is its ability to influence local and national politics. The corporate rise is a derivative of its economic wealth and power. Corporations are dangerously powerful institutions because they determine the survival of their employees and their host communities, as well as national economies. Corporations are the principal provider in a consumption-spending-based body politic. They also wield political and diplomatic influence as a plenipotentiary-level participant.

In an organizational, institution-dominated political economy, individual access diminishes. As George Draffan wrote in *Elite Consensus:*

> Power, the ability to make decisions and control resources, is found in the dynamics of the relationships between people. Depending on how power flows and who wields it, political economic decisions are made and resources flow between individuals, groups, and corporations. When society's economic, political, and social structures become institutionalized, power tends to flow from people into institutions, but not back again. Power becomes concentrated.[1]

This trend developed during the past sixty years, and resulted in a new level of citizenship based on a corporation's ability to provide money to political machines, at first at the local level, and then later, the federal. As political power shifted from nineteenth-century localism, to modern national institutionalism, so too, did the big corporation and the corporate sector.

The old model was based on the political power and influence of the individual, operating within the old order. During the twentieth century, when the model shifted via the organizational revolution, with national politics supplanting persistent localism, the corporation filled the socioeconomic vacuum. The core element of corporate ascendance was an increased role in the mechanics of politics: lobbying, interest group, and campaign finance.

Lobbying and funding elections have been parts of our political process since the formative days of our republic. Organized, national interest groups are a phenomenon specific to our organizational society; so too, their hybrid association, the political action committee. Lobbying is an attempt by individuals or groups and their agents to influence government decision-making for their own benefit. This occurs at all levels of government.

Lobbying and lobbyists have been part of our political and governing process since colonial times. Indeed, our first lobbyists were colonial agents to the British government. Michael Kammen argued that prior to 1760, these agents were integral parts of the political relationships between England and its colonies. These agents participated in both the formal and informal procedures of colonial administration in England.

After the Revolutionary War ended, the creation of a new country wiped the political slate clean. Then, with politics truly almost all local, there was little system to grow upon. Colonies became states, and the Confederation became a republic. Governing, policy making, and politics had a fresh start with precedents established almost daily during Washington's presidency. Within the process of this original nation building, lobbying remained mostly in the shadows; confined usually to state and local governments, the latter having more to do with citizens' daily lives. Back then, the general government, later called the federal government, wasn't much bigger than its local counterparts.

James S. Young (*The Washington Community*), suggested that the general government during the early republic, 1800–1828, was relatively free of significant citizen or pressure-group influence. The new general government operated in physical, geographic, and temporal isolation.

If so, then indeed, it was functioning within the old paradigm, where independence and isolation prevailed. Reality, then, consisted of making a living in those insular, isolated communities, some of which abutted the still psychologically formidable howling wilderness. In that world, where life for many only existed to the nearby horizon, petitioning the general government was something someone else did. In a pastoral society, vying for attention, the spoils, and the power and influence of the general government, wasn't known by most Americans. At best, the common citizen wasn't that interested in political participation. It wasn't important for most of their lives. Most American citizens, then, had little or no contact with the general government. Typically, they were at home, living their good-earth life, while government was usually far away, beyond the horizon, hardly affecting daily life. In this pristine world, seeking influence wasn't important or practical.

Then, the simplicity of government included a political culture where congressional representatives worked in Washington, D.C., during the winter and spent the rest of their time at home. James S. Young suggested that the U.S. Congress was typically a collection of transients with short terms the norm. If so, there was no permanent institution-building.

At the same time, political affiliations were nebulous. (Today, we call them the Federalists and the Jeffersonian Republicans.) Instead, it was more important to them where they came from. Arriving in D.C., it was common for representatives from the same state to live in the same lodgings, to break bread together, and to spend free time among themselves. (In some instances it might have been more important to be Virginians or Carolinians than Americans.)

In a way, each state or region formed their own physical and cultural neighborhood or camp among groups of strangers. Imagine, what would a New Englander have in common, with a politician from Georgia? Thus, within this small world or where business was typically transacted informally, where would a lobbyist or agent fit in? Then, perhaps all politicians lobbied, but the process was small time.

Back in Washington, D.C., the process of legislating was simple. Prior to 1812, there were few rules of procedure, making the practice of democracy less formal. Political parties were nascent. Policy making was simple, just as the nation. There were few national issues because government and politics, were for sure, mostly local. Eventually, from within this political culture, at the state and local level, did the first American lobbyists emerge. In our political system, the term "lobbyist" first appeared, as early as 1828, in U.S. congressional records. In 1829, the term, lobby-agents, referred to those who hung around New York's state capitol, in Albany.

Later, there was some concern about lobbyists' significance in the governing process. For example, in 1852, President James Buchanan complained to Franklin Pierce that D.C. swarmed with various types of lobbyists, especially those representing the nation's nascent industrial sector. Notable too, was his concern about controlling them. Post–Civil War lobbyists typically represented individual interests, not group. Wealth prevailed among their clients, and overall, those who did the lobbying quickly gained bad, shady reputations as hustlers and sharpers.

Writing in the 1960s, James Deakin (*The Lobbyists*), suggested that as soon as the industrial age developed and expanded, lobbyists thronged D.C., promoting themselves and their industrial accomplishments to a cooperative federal government that didn't interfere during these times of gaudiness and corruption. Early on, to Deakin, lobbying increased in significance as the new industrial order emerged and increased in size and importance.

Margaret F. Thompson (*Spider's Web*), suggested that the beginning of the transition to modern forms of lobbying began during the 1870s. It was during this transition that the modern form of lobbying and, soon after, campaign finance both began to coalesce. They rode along the waves of change as the still very small federal government slowly and hesitantly began to flex its institutional muscles and increase its participation in domestic affairs and consequently, began to influence people's lives more and more.

Lobbyists and lobbying were already familiar, and so too, were their methods. Lobbyists and their work carried a social stigma of un-Americanism, because they were unelected, unaccountable, and an easily corrupting influence on both the political and governing process. Even then, it was very evident that what few lobbyists there were received attention from politicians, more so than citizens, when it came to doing the so-called people's business.

Probably with some trepidation, the Washington establishment began to accept lobbyists and their methods as part of governing. Thus, beginning in 1875, Congress attempted to place some controls on this new kind of political and civic participation: Lobbyists would have to register and report their expenditures. The U.S. House of Representative passed such a bill, but the session ended before the U.S. Senate could consider it.

The next year, during May 1876, the U.S. House of Representatives passed a resolution applicable to that session only, requiring agents, as they were then called, to register with the House clerk, identifying themselves and who they represented. Only registered agents could do business with representatives during that session.

During these times, the U.S. Senate was prominent, the controlling mechanism of the wheels of the federal government. The core of the machine's engine consisted of the senate committees, the political party in power, and the party caucuses.

Lobbying was one way to access this system, and the business sector of the political economy was led by railroad corporations. During the 1870s, the railroaders hired agents to work the Washington political culture. They actively competed with other lobbyists, peddling their influence. By the 1880s, lobbyists became a regular part of the legislative process.

Then, according to David Rothman, in his *Politics and Power*, lobbying was ad hoc, unsystemized, and inefficient. The agents actively competed among available clients and politicians alike. Other issues and their lobbyists also competed. Some used "grease" while many did not. Rothman further suggested that this chaotic, unorganized pluralism among the lobbyists' camp made them mere petitioners to legislators, rather than their dominators, controllers, or benefactors. Altogether, in the pluralist interpretation, lobbying was an ad hoc, session-by-session circus of often-inefficient effort.

Regardless of efforts and results, the rise of lobbyists at the federal level persisted, becoming the so-called Third House of Congress. As early as 1888, railroad corporations defended their agents as important participants in the governing process, since contemporary policy issues were becoming more complex. This became the model for other companies and policy interest groups.

Once the door opened, the lobbyists were in to stay. As the new century proceeded, more political policy issues drew more interests and their agents. Thus, lobbyists remained in the system and later blossomed and flourished throughout the federal halls of government for the next one hundred years.

An additional conduit between business and government was via campaign contributions. Then, it was understood, and accepted, that to do business, promoting one's interests to the government necessitated financial support, even more so than lobbying.

Corporations willingly, if begrudgingly, contributed regardless of political party. The importance here was the power and electability of each individual. Thus, both political parties potentially were fed by corporate coffers. More importantly: At this time in our history, the money tree, even then, was a paramount factor in gaining access. It was also an indicator of a continuing precedent and persistent trend, that money and the powerful perpetuated their own interests and their own social class, all at the same time, and carefully hidden behind the smoke and mirrors of an egalitarian, consensus, representative democracy.

According to the pluralist view, this was acceptable, because too many interests competed to allow any one group or sector to dominate. At times, the threat of public scandal kept a lid on overt and aggressive corruption. Consequently, greasing the wheels was considered atypical in this system.

In this changing political culture, lobbying evolved during the twentieth century and became a permanent part of the political process, and at first, an adjunct to the relationship between money and politics. Toward the end of that century, interest group power via the organizational society, permanently welded lobbying and money power via campaign finance. That bond is persistent.

In *Who Shakes the Money Tree*, George Thayer asserted that the connection between money and politics stretches back to Revolutionary times.

Then, the Federalists and Jeffersonian-Republicans solicited money to finance their own newspapers, which in turn propagandized their cause. During an era when print was the leading medium, this was a significant and fundamental occurrence. If so, then the relationships between finance and politics is foundational.

This partnership evolved slowly during the nineteenth century. Beginning with Andrew Jackson's presidency, party politics, increased campaign stumping, electioneering, political patronage jobs, campaign finance, vote fraud, and lobbying all emerged as part of the political culture.

After the Civil War, campaign costs sharply increased, corruption noticeably escalated; fundraising became a cottage industry, and, as Thayer wrote:

> the business-political alliance became permanent. . . . The rising costs of campaigning in the 1840s and 1850s forced many aspirants for high office to turn to men of wealth for funds. It was in this period of American history that the bonds between political and economic interests were first forged. They are bonds that have not weakened at all over the following 130 years. Many self-made men, beneficiaries of the Industrial Revolution and America's natural bounty, recognized that numerous decisions of government on such issues as taxes, trade, tariffs, and slavery directly or indirectly influenced the independence of their own enterprises. They realized it was in their own interests to exert whatever influence they could over the legislative and bureaucratic process of government. The easiest way to exert influence was with cash at campaign time. Business had money and the desire, candidates had the need, and, if elected, the power; it was a natural alliance.[2]

Thus, the marriage of money, wealth, influence and power goes deep and far back in our history.

In the nineteenth century, the political process emphasized the local and state levels, not to be superseded by national politics until the next century. During the second half of the 1800s, political parties were the principal mechanisms of politics and governance. Parties were also fueled by money from so-called tax-like political assessments or party taxes from individuals and corporations, and informally, through corruption. (For individuals these were euphemisms for kickbacks; work for the political party, get a patronage job, kick some of that income back to the party's coffers.) Both went together. De facto, many believed spoils, bribery, kickbacks, graft, and assessments were all part of the normal political process, and for companies, a part of doing business.

In whatever form, corruption persists, usually quietly, discreetly, away from public scrutiny. It is almost like a yoke on players within the political culture. Conformity seems to be obligatory. If these are the methods, everyone's doing it, so must I. We have to conform or lose.

Thus, a mutual dependence quickly arose between politicians and their providers. Prior to civil service reform, politicians preyed on their own members, and later, upon businessmen for operating funds. Cochran and Miller mentioned how the railroaders and early industrialists had to buy their way into the governing process, often being played by politicians through the regulatory process. Those authors gave the impression that this was common practice.[3]

They further suggested that once civil service reform cut into patronage and assessments as sources for money, both political parties then turned to businessmen as contributors, agreeing to do their business for financial support. If so, here might be one of the roots, planted during the Gilded Age and Progressive Era, that eventually grew into the lobbying, interest group, pay-for-benefits system that evolved during the rest of the twentieth century.

This interdependent relationship translated into influencing the legislative process, often free of the constraints of pluralistic lobbying. Campaign finance usually assured participation during legislative bill construction; especially at the congressional committee level, where the real work was often done. Benefactor input influenced the wording and assembly of the legislation, and almost as important, the ongoing selection of federal judges who eventually might have to interpret the law.

Within these changing arenas, both those that seek and wield political power and those who must deal with it are confronted by the attraction, necessity, and influence that money plays in the mix. In our form of democracy, money and influence always played their part, evolving their own specific trappings and methods, from era to era. At first, they became part of the system during the first half of the twentieth century. Now, they are the system.

Thus, the political competition, including getting an edge on the opposition via dishonesty, cutting deals, and greasing the wheels, were all separately and sometimes together, a hidden, discreet, mainstay of this process. This occurred through much of twentieth-century political history.

More so at the local and state levels before the Progressive Era, its mindset and some of its methods crept up into the federal level right before and during the early part of the twentieth century. The whole process played out from business-friendly state legislators appointing businessmen to the U.S. Senate, to large campaign contributions from Gilded Age industrialists. (Back then, state legislators picked the U.S. senator, so the likelihood of class elitism and cronyism was high. It was the ultimate patronage gig.)

This practice carried over into the twentieth century, persisting and advancing to Greideresque baroque levels by 2001. By then, shaking the money tree was institutionalized.

Consider American modernity beginning during the decades after the Civil War. From these origins, and even before, wealth and class were fundamental fuels of the political process. What was mostly an avocation of the upper classes during the early republic slowly changed and rose to new levels of sophistication, starting at the beginning of the twentieth century. Politics eventually became careers and professionalized, typical of those times, and simultaneously, politicians handcuffed themselves to the real powers that be, those that controlled the purse strings within the political economy.

Already 100 years ago, the interrelationship between political parties, their politicians, and wealth, and corporate-based vested interests formed concomitantly as the century modernized. Even then, the core was campaign finance and lobbying. The former was more important, because money was the lifeblood of the political system, more so than the ballot box. Candidates who wanted to be in politics had to take from those who could afford it, and who were usually ready to buy their way into influencing the system.

Once elected, these politicians were then beholden to their benefactors. Putting political pluralism aside, reality, then, meant cooperating with those who were largely responsible for getting them there; not the voters, but rather the campaign financiers.

Put this relationship and interaction into a social context: The one who pays the bills makes the rules. This simple family-management adage reflects the realities of human nature, its psychology and sociology. Rich benefactors and their corporate partners expected something in return for their money and political influence.

Despite the myths of our political system, this was the reality then, at our modern beginnings, and it persisted to our times. The Populists, the muckrakers, and other dissidents, such as Ralph Nader, and especially William Greider, were then, and, now, right on.

Big business was quick to understand the importance of controlling the political process through money. Gabriel Kolko cited a 1901 *Bankers' Magazine* prediction:

> The growth of corporations and of combinations tends to strengthen the forces which seek to control the machinery of government and the laws in behalf of special interests. . . . Theoretically, the ballot controls everything: but the spirit of political organization which has grown up outside of legislative enactment now goes far to control the ballot. Industrial and commercial organization, when it desires to control the government, either Federal or State, finds a political organization ready for its uses. The productive forces are the purse-bearers. They furnish the means by which alone governments can be made effective. They also furnish the means by which the political organization which produces the gov-

> ernment is created and becomes effective. The business man, whether alone or in combination with other business men, seeks to shape politics and government in a way conducive to his own prosperity. . . . More and more the legislatures and the executive powers of the Government are compelled to listen to the demands of organized business interests. That they are not entirely controlled by these interests is due to the fact that business organization has not reached full perfection. The recent consolidation of the iron and steel industries is an indication of the concentration of power that is possible.[4]

Thus, from influencing local and state governments during the nineteenth century, the nascent corporate sector quickly adopted their methods at the national level, perhaps beginning with supporting their senate candidates to their state legislatures, and then funding McKinley's campaign in 1896, to what could be viewed as their first great nemesis, William Jennings Bryan. At this time, big business allied itself with the Republican Party. In the process, the party of Abraham Lincoln became the party of the corporate boardroom. Since then, the corporate grip on the political process, personifying the group strength of money, has never relaxed. All the subsequent history became part of this financial relationship.

Then, since, and now, campaign contributors expected something in return for their financial support. Then, our first great captains of industry (the robber barons), expected political returns for their money. Over the rest of the century, so too, did their corporate descendents, even to today.

Thus, the idea and expectations that money given gets returns have not abated. Persisting within the political process, and surviving several attempts at control and reform, the relationship between money and political influence has not been weakened. At first, it quickly became an understood, accepted, expected, and anticipated part of the twentieth-century political process. Through social interactions—social clubbing, fundraising, etc.—this political relationship was soon institutionalized. This system successfully took control of the process, absorbing the participants as part of it. Thus, the people who created this system, establishing the pattern and precedents that manufactured a political method, once institutionalized, quickly consumed them.

Campaign finance led the dance, and lobbying followed the leader. As the century proceeded, the dance became a perpetual marathon. Money got access and the lobbyists did the contributors' work; the politicians did their benefactors' bidding.

The rest of this chapter presents this relationship in terms of lobbying, interest groups, and campaign finance, as time marched on. Today, in the twentieth century, the relationship between money and influence continues, still thriving despite recent and past efforts to control it.

After the turn of the century, it didn't take long for lobbying and special-interest politics to arrive noticeably on the political arena's stage. For example, Karl Schriftgiesser noted that the future president, Woodrow Wilson, as a student, examined the influence of lobbyists. Later, as presidential candidate, and then president, he disdained lobbyists and the special interests they represented. Schriftgiesser quoting Wilson:

> The masters of the government of the United States are the combined capitalists and manufacturers of the United States. It is written over every intimate page of the records of Congress; it is written all through the history of conferences at the White House; that the suggestions of economic policy have come from one source, but many sources. . . . Suppose you go to Washington, you will always find that while you are politely listened to(,) the men really consulted are the big men who have the biggest stake—the big bankers, the big manufacturers, the big masters of commerce, the heads of railroad corporations, and of steamship corporations. . . . Every time it has come to a critical question, these gentlemen have been yielded to and the demands treated as demands that should be followed as a matter of course. The government of the United States is a foster child of the special interests. It is not allowed to have a will of its own.[5]

and from *The New Freedom*, Woodrow Wilson wrote:

> the degree to which government has become associated with business. I speak for the moment, of the control over the Government exercised by Big Business. . . . Our Government has been for the past few years under the control of heads of great allied corporations with special interests . . . it is an intolerable thing that the Government of the Republic should have got so far out of the hands of the people; should have been captured by interests which are special and not general. . . . The government, which was designed for the people, has got into the hands of bosses and their employers, the special interests. . . . They have agreed to supply them with money for campaign expenses and to stand by them in all other cases where money was necessary if in return they might resort to them for protection or for assistance in matters of legislation.[6]

Once in office, he tried to eliminate their participation. Wishing to run them out of town, he made their activities an issue. A few left, most did not. The system remained intact and survived a subsequent congressional investigation. Despite findings that substantiated much of Wilson's criticism, a regulatory bill didn't pass. Lobbyists, and later interest groups, marched on; many decades later, to K-Street-epic proportions of power and influence.

Significant to the senator's situation was the congressional committee (and later subcommittee), system. As Woodrow Wilson pointed out, the civic problem with lobbyists was their influence on committee work, where legislators created the substance and text of the bill; where its content was discreetly negotiated, often out of the public's eye, but easily accessible to lobbying pressures. There, it was easier to influence-peddle among the few (not the whole assembly), who would be inclined to be more malleable, off the record, behind the scenes. Wilson also argued, that here, at this level of the lawmaking process, business lobbyists were especially effective pressuring legislators.

When Wilson opined about interest groups, perhaps he had one of the originals in mind, then, generally referred to as trade associations. The National Association of Manufacturers (NAM), was a leader during its early times, representing the collective voice of business prior to World War II. Businessmen organized the NAM in 1895, as a response to the economic deprivation caused by the Panic of 1893. The association originally focused on foreign trade and determining the causes of the depression that followed the panic.

The association's positions derived from a form of social Darwinism, extolling the believed gospel truth of market individualism. They considered the pursuit of self-interest a good in itself, and the collective pursuit of it resulted in progress for all.

In 1897, the threat of pro-labor legislation in the U.S. Congress, prompted the NAM to consider establishing a permanent lobbying office in D.C., which they eventually opened in 1899. This one-person lobby was their first attempt to make their presence known in Washington.

There, the NAM lobbied to put trade unionism down, and against any federal government assistance to unions, in the process, defending the believed right of an employer to control the operations, labor use, and costs.

This meant opposition to collective bargaining and the eight-hour workday; supporting injunctions against unions via the Sherman Anti-Trust Act. The NAM also promoted and presented policy positions on railroad freight rates, state taxation, patent law, parcel post regulations, and a national bankruptcy law. They also promoted trade schools.

During the subsequent decades, the NAM seldom deviated from its original, and now core, beliefs. By the 1940s, the NAM already had a reputation for its rigid conservatism.

After World War II, the NAM expanded their participation in the political arena, focusing their resources on promoting business leadership and government noninterference in the economy. This was a comprehensive attempt, coupling fundraising with public relations campaigns promoting pro-business policies and opinion. The NAM was especially interested in resurrecting business leadership, an attitude believed lost, by the public, during the New Deal. Altering these perceived, negative public perceptions was one of the NAM's active pursuits.

To accomplish this, their propagandizing included ad campaigns in both print and broadcast media; instigating people, especially businessmen, to write or call their congressmen regarding pending legislation and policy. These ads were designed to influence current lawmaking and regulating, and at the same time, stifle the leftist ethos persisting since the New Deal. The association also lobbied directly, by providing information to legislators.

Medium and small-sized companies, at first, dominated the NAM's membership, which ebbed and flowed over the decades. The association enjoyed increased popularity from 1903 to the Great Depression. Then, it switched emphasis and began to draw in big business members, resulting in significant expansion from 1935–1941. At the end of the 1930s, the NAM had over 3,000 company members. Again, in the postwar era, they enjoyed initial success. Since then, NAM membership fluctuated, decade-to-decade, while their policy positions did not. (In 1973, the NAM moved its home office from New York City to Washington, D.C.) By the end of the 1990s, the association's membership included 13,500 companies of various sizes.

Big business eventually grasped the importance of influencing the governing process without the overt taint of corruption. Thus, sending lobbyists, besides manipulating the electoral process, became a significant complement to campaign finance. Over time, lobbying too, evolved, penetrating the system as the century proceeded. Indeed, by the 1920s, Cochran and Miller wrote:

> It is probable, indeed that democracy cannot function without pressure groups. Prohibitionists, farmers, workers, teachers, consumers, all had their lobbies, their journals, their paid secretaries and expert propagandists. . . . But business associations and business leaders were so powerful in the twenties that none of these groups could withstand them. Businessmen and their associations thus overshadow all other groups in our society.[7]

To this, Schriftgiesser could add:

> As Calvin Coolidge was about to say, the business of America was business; its agents, infesting the lobbies of the Capitol, were allowed to go unmolested. In the twelve years of Harding-Coolidge-Hoover prosperity the tariff lobbyists and others engaged in futhering private enterprise and fostering the American Way had their fruitful innings.[8]

Hence, by 1928, according to Arkansas senator, Thaddeus H. Caraway, as he introduced a lobbyist-control bill, 300–400 lobbyists worked in D.C., and he suggested they should be publicly registered.

Business interests survived the Progressive Era, prospered during the war interlude, and flourished during the 1920s. Recall from chapter 5, this was the decade of trade associations. In D.C., many of these actively lobbied their positions, realizing representation in the halls of government was essential participation in this new day and age of an increased federal government presence. For some, trade associations, lobbying was a reason to be. To accomplish this, some of them started to put offices in D.C. For example, by 1924, there were lobbies for: manufacturers, farmers, wool, tobacco, fertilizer, cotton packers, railroads, shipping, prohibition/temperance and their opponents (wets and drys), equal rights for women, civil service employees, tax reducers, water power, disabled veterans, education aid, the military, and others. About 145 lobbies had headquarters in D.C., of which 60 were effective. The *Annals*, in 1929, observed: "Washington is honeycombed with lobbyists."[9]

Then, lobbying was referred to as the Third House, assistant government, or the invisible government. Lobbyists were called legislative agents, legislative counsels, and legislative representatives.

Supporting candidates and taking sides in the policy debates were tandem in the governing process. Their formal methods included tracking bills' progress and intending to influence action with the appropriate legislators. Influencing who sat on the congressional committees was also part of this.

The congressional committee was still the core of the legislative process, and prime targets of lobbyists. Congress usually accepted committee-report recommendations, so influencing the committee work was imperative to lobbyists. Supporting committee-member candidates, and promoting their committee selection, was the foundation of the influence-peddling process.

Lobbyists also attempted to influence the governing process indirectly, by appealing directly to voters. Sending letters to, advertising in, or submitting articles to local newspapers was intended to kindle interest and support for a particular policy issue. Lobbyists encouraged the public to write to their representatives, while simultaneously working the politicians on Capitol Hill.

Social lobbying was used in tandem with such direct and indirect methods. Lobbyists met regularly, informally, often over meals, to share information and get to know each other. Such social events included organized parties, car trips, and travel junkets. Here, during conversation, policy positions and attitudes emerged, and ultimately, what was sought by each interest, and in response, what a legislator could deliver. Deals could be cut, if possible.

Much of this was indirectly expressed, or understood by the parties involved. Propriety and discretion prevailed. The petitioners of government often left specifics unsaid during this social dance, or simply waltzed around the issues. Finding out if the legislator was agreeable to their interest, or on the program, was the main goals of these affairs.

After a brief respite during Normalcy/The Prosperity Decade, when business interests held sway in the halls of the federal government, lobbying became critical for the business sector during the Great Depression's economic trauma, social disruption, and the rise of the regulatory state.

Washington journalist Kenneth Crawford, in *The Pressure Boys*, provided a contemporary critical view of the lobbying industry. He claimed that by decade's end, there were about 6,000 lobbyists working in D.C., and they were essentially a fourth branch of government. Crawford summarized lobbyists' methods that ranged from face-to-face meetings with congressional representatives and committee-hearing testimony, to cocktail lounge and dinner-table diplomacy.

Pressure groups and their lobbyists were also adept at manipulating constituency politics through the use of propagandized petitioning and drumming up campaigns to inundate politicians' offices with phone calls and mail. In some instances, lobbyists wrote the text of the bill or the issue they were promoting.

Another contemporary observer, Stuart Chase, concurred, in *Democracy Under Pressure.* Basing his conclusions on, among other books, a 1941 study by the Temporary National Economic Committee, he too, viewed pressure groups with skepticism. He asserted that the lobbying industry's collective efforts were not good for democracy. Chase charged that business lobbyists typically act in their own, narrow self-interest. They also show little regard for social responsibility or the interests of other lobby groups. Competition for government officials' attention was constant and significant. Big business interests, in this competition, were the leading lobby groups.

Writing in the same decade, Vladimir O. Key, in *Politics, Parties & Pressure Groups*, could add to this critical perspective. He cautioned about pressure groups' tendencies to represent the minority of political and social competing interests. That is, not everybody belongs to these groups or agrees with pressure groups' policy positions. Hence, any given pressure group, besides not being elected representatives, are self-anointed policy formulators and petitioners of the government.

Overall, at the end of the Great Depression, Stuart Chase profiled the lobbying industry in Washington, D.C. Then, there were over four hundred lobby groups. The largest sectors were business, farmers, and union groups. There were also industry-specific associations representing, for example, commercial agriculture, commercial ranching, radio broadcasting, and telephone companies, among others. So-called professions also had lobbies, such as bankers, advertising, realtors, doctors, lawyers, and even teachers. Social reformers also lobbied.

These groups actively competed over a variety of public policy issues: tariffs, industry subsidies, federal government aid, open shop versus closed shop law, taxes or no taxes, for example. Some groups lobbied against each other's interests: Railroads against waterways and buses; insurance companies against expanding Social Security benefits; doctors against socialized medicine; the coal industry against waterpower. Chase asserted: "The objective behind these wants is usually a direct subsidy for the interest itself, or a hand grenade for a competitor."[10] Indeed, competition, the American way.

To compete to achieve one's interest, lobbying included: support and campaign funds for candidates who are friendly to their specific interests; pressure (persuade) politicians to favor one's interest; persuade federal agencies to interpret laws and regulations favorably; fight opposed legislation in federal courts.

To accomplish this, lobby groups typically used professional lobbyists and their support staff. The lobbyist set up the strategy and executed it based on the research from its staff. Also, they often wound up writing the relevant text of the bill. This occurred even in the 1930s.

If these criticisms were true already during the 1930s, or sooner, as some asserted, lobbyists were seen as purveyors for the few rather than the many. Was this to be addressed then, or now?

There have been occasional attempts to regulate lobbying. Some state legislatures were the first to try, by passing either corruption or lobby-control legislation. From time to time, the U.S. House restricted access to the chamber floor, and in 1876, agents had to register in order to work that session, or in 1936, to access the House, Senate, the SEC, and the Federal Power Commission. Overall, the federal government did little until 1946, when the U.S. Congress enacted the Federal Regulation of Lobbying Act. It required all congressional lobbyists to register and to reveal the origins and amounts of money received for their work. That is, a lobbyist or lobbying organization, or a corporation, had to identify themselves and who they worked for; what they were doing, and how much money was involved; reporting quarterly.

Opponents lobbied against this bill and railed against it after enactment. Despite that, the law was barely noticed or enforced. There wasn't a designated agency to enforce it, hence it didn't really regulate. Many still lobbied, but fewer obeyed the law and registered and reported. Since then, Congress determined lobby disclosure was acceptable but restrictive regulation was not, constitutionally. Subsequent efforts to strengthen controls failed, again due to successful lobbying against it, and aided and abetted by U.S. Supreme Court interpretations that further diluted the law's effect, weak as it was. From time to time, scandal to scandal, controlling lobbying usually escaped focused, significant scrutiny. (Watchdog groups were usually ignored.)

Despite its checkered reputation, lobbying ingrained itself into our political system. By 1952, there were 2,074 registered lobbyists, and the 1946 effort to fetter them didn't significantly affect the lobbying industry. In fact, most politicians realized the strength and influence of lobbyists and subsequent efforts to effectively analyze their potency and to control them, failed. Hence, throughout the 1950s, lobbying maintained its position within the governing process, all but uninfluenced or unabated by public opinion and unfettered by attempts to regulate it.

Operationally, an interest group is simply any association or group formed to influence lawmaking or public policy formulation and regulation, at any level of government. Thus, in the decades after World War II, lobbying acquired a new, more powerful facet as interest-group politics too, became a prime participant, by the end of the century.

By 1950, a pattern was already developing, according to Donald C. Blaisdell. He pointed out the significance of behind-the-scenes influence peddling (as I call it). Access to congressional committees and visits to the White House weren't publicized or consistently exposed to public scrutiny. An interest group's lobbyist went to committee chairmen, or other movers in the particular congress, or to influential White House staff members, or upper-level officials in the executive branch.

There, and often in private or away from the halls of government, the sales pitch and negotiation occurred. It could often be direct, one-on-one transactions, or group activity in social settings such as public events or socializing over food and drink. I would argue that such indirect methods were more effective persuaders than public committee hearing testimony, or other formal methods.

These publicly obscured methods were similar to doing business among decision-makers who cut deals on the golf course, after church on Sunday, at the local charity event, or after a tennis match at the local country club.

At the same time, business interest groups led the pack. In 1960, E. E. Schattschneider, in *The Semi-Sovereign People*, asserted that interest groups represented a small segment of the political economy. Most of these groups were from the business sector: For the time period, 1946–1949, 825 of 1,241 registered lobbying organizations were business. Here, within a narrow constituency, a pressure group has a better chance of getting its way. The narrower the interest, the more likely their efforts might be successful. If so, then the issues important to the private sector, in Schattschneider's model can be nicely catered to back then, and now.

This trend to formally associate and seek de facto representation continued into the 1960s. (It would accelerate through the 1970s and 1980s.) Besides large umbrella organizations such as the NAM and USCOC, industry-specific groups competed for federal attention. To name a few: America Petroleum Institute, National Canners Association, Distilled Spirits Institution, American Iron and Steel Institute, Automobile Manufacturers Institute, and the American Bankers Association, etc. These are some examples of a myriad of business associations of all sizes and sophistication; some new and some old.

Accompanying them were some corporations, perhaps the first pathfinders before the deluge. In 1961, 130 corporations had registered lobbyists; fifty had D.C. offices. David Vogel cited a 1964 study of the lobbying industry that portrayed lobbying as small-time and largely ineffectual. This, the Bauer, Paul and Dexter study, suggested disengagement between the corporate sector and the federal government as typical, with not much influence on the policy-making process. Vogel claimed the times before the upheaval were times of peaceful coexistence between the private and public sector. He downplayed the importance of corporate lobbying.

Vogel also suggested that the traditional trade association and generalized business-oriented interest groups were there, but too, not very active lobbying. In Vogel's view, not even long-standing associations as the NAM or USCOC had much standing.

If so, perhaps it was the complacent pleasantness of the consensual 1950s, when political competition wasn't that important, for after all, America in 1960, was more like America in 1940. Regardless of the veracity of Vogel's hypothesis, and whatever the reason, no one then could foresee what was over the horizon. The 1960s were about to roll into town.

During the 1960s, the federal government increased its regulatory role and integrated more and more into our political economy. Corporations eventually responded by increasing their lobbying efforts, which included, both corporate efforts through public relations and intensified government relations, and interest group activity. The latter especially accelerated during the 1970s. Trade associations increased their presence in D.C., and corporate public affairs/public relations departments also jumped into the political arena. Such efforts often were lead by a new participant, corporate executives, who acted as captains of this new kind of tag team.

It also became necessary to have permanent institutional representation in Washington, D.C. Being near the action on Capitol Hill and close to the regulators soon prompted more and more corporations to set up shop there. The idea was to be a productive participant, actively getting involved in the legislative, policy-making, and regulatory process. The corporate sector, were, eventually, spectacularly successful. Over the next two decades they became permanent residents in Washington: more lobbyists, trade associations, government-relations staffs, and ultimately, political action committees (PACs), and K Street.

The institutionalization of corporate lobbying was an evolutionary process. Again, America in 1960, was more like America in 1940. That ended during the next ten years. Politics changed, with lobbying and interest groups increasing their roles in the American political economy. This trend included:

increased influence by special-interest groups, led by corporate power, waging political war against the general welfare.

Even then, reporter James Deakin (circa 1966), contended that the federal government was heavily influenced by these special interests, who had the power to successfully push their wants to the forefront of the federal government's political agenda. (If so, the emerging pattern fifty years ago persisted, with these special interests, a.k.a., corporate interests, winning in the long run.)

Deakin also asserted that the lobbyist was deeply involved in the policy-making and regulatory process. This included authoring much of the prepared testimony presented at congressional hearings, and a significant amount of the text of bills being considered. Lobbyists could actually submit text for bills on issues they were attempting to influence. Deakin also charged that lobbyists often had access to congressional staff and their administrative resources.

After hours, the process continued on the lobbyist-dominated social circuit. Many of the events were public; several, private, in the homes and the exclusive clubs of the power elites. One of the circuit's participants pointed out such an event's potential:

> Don't leave out the parties. They're damned important, especially with the new Congressmen. The new man arrives in town with his wife. They're both a little awed. And what happens? All of a sudden, they are invited to a little dinner party given by the Washington vice president for (*sic*) a billion-dollar corporation. They're impressed, but there's more to it than that. Let's say the Congressman is a liberal. He's suspicious of big business. What does he find? The big shot is a darned nice guy. He doesn't have horns and a tail. He charms the wife and he's deferential to the Congressman. They go away feeling a little differently. Maybe it doesn't affect the way he votes, at least not right away. But it's a softening-up process.[11]

Thus, both during the workday and afterward, the influence-peddling process was both ongoing and ubiquitous, affecting all who were necessary to get the job done promoting one's interest over the other's. The typical lobbyist was a persistent, involved, participant in the access-seeking process necessary to get things done in D.C.

However, in contrast, again, David Vogel offered a different view. He asserted in his book *Fluctuating Fortunes* that big business influence on federal government policy making fluctuated. Specifically, he noted a distinct downturn in business lobbying successes from the mid-1960s to mid-1970s. He attributed this to dramatic change in the U.S. Congress: Its power decentralized, drawing away lobbyists ability to access key legislators. This took place during a time when interest group activity increased; when the court system increased its involvement in regulating, and when public-interest groups suddenly rose from seemingly out of nowhere.

In what we today refer to as the Sixties, a time of social change, it seemed that big business lost some of its monopoly power over federal government policy making. During those times, big business was noticeably unsuccessful in thwarting a resurgence in the federal regulatory state: environmental regulation, workplace health and safety, and cigarette-advertising limits, to name a few.

Vogel proceeded to suggest that the corporate sector fought back, resorting to different strategies, including addressing the larger issues of the political economy as they affected the private sector, in general, more so than each's own industry. A renaissance of two, older, organizations—the NAM and USCOC—resulted. Michael Useem might concur, arguing similarly, in his book *The Inner Circle* that during the 1970s and early 1980s, a dramatic increase in political involvement occurred at the level of big business. Led by an astute elite of politically aware business executives, the corporate sector successfully marshaled these disparate assets into a formidable inventory of political influence. He asserted this nuance of method added a new level of group and institutional solidarity, resulting in an increased potential to influence policy making. Also, during those times, David Jacobs, in *Business Lobbies*, suggested that the private sector coalesced in their antipathy to most social legislation.

Indeed, a new competitor entered the interest-group political arena during the 1960s. It had many faces: environmentalism, consumerism, voting rights, women's rights, government ethics, poor relief, etc. Together, public-interest lobbying burst on the scene and quickly affected the federal policy-making process.

Now, more and more, policy making affected larger parts of the private sector (i.e., pollution control, workplace safety), because of reform-oriented legislating and regulating. James Deakin suggested, that already by 1966, there was widespread political participation by various pressure groups. Many of these advocated reforms.

In *Who Will Tell the People*, William Greider wrote that these reform efforts drew the large corporations, in earnest, to D.C., to actively participate in the lobbying and policy-making process. As the corporate sector entered this arena in force, they believed they were the underdogs, competing at a disadvantage in the face of this reform impulse.

Big business believed the federal government and the public were against them. The reformers' collective efforts quickly attracted corporate attention because the former's targets were often the latter, as concepts of corporate responsibility and accountability became topics of discussion, public debate, and eventually public policy.

Within this arena, these reform groups upset the existing system by not playing by the established rules. In the process, the long-standing business-friendly lobbying system broke down. David Vogel in *Kindred Strangers* asserted that public-interest groups so effectively monkey-wrenched the system that big business faced its greatest political threat since organized labor's efforts in the 1930s. In response, corporate lobbying efforts had to increase, to keep up with, and often counter the new way of doing things.

At the same time during the 1960s, corporations increased their use of upper-level executives to lobby, a practice that persisted. Depending on the situation, a corporation sent a company president or other senior executive to Washington to directly lobby government officials. Like J. P. Morgan, a century ago, this was a modern update of the send-my-man-to-see-your-man method. Or, from another perspective, it was the interaction of managerial elites from both the private and public sectors meeting to exchange viewpoints, for the corporate executives as lobbyists to persuade legislators, regulators, and policy makers; for the men in the high castles to do business together, often resulting in the corporate sector strongly influencing the process of government for their own benefit.

More than likely, they were welcomed by the Washington community (as covered by Richard E. Neustadt in *Presidential Power*), consisting of career elites in the federal bureaucracy, and their top, politically appointed, managers; military top brass; congressional elites, diplomats, resident longtime journalists, and the lobbying industry.

These major characters interacted in a system organized and institutionally based on the modern concept of corporation and the political economy it helped to create.

This addition of corporate upper management into the lobbying mix had an adjunct when top executives became members of an elite lobbying organization. Its goal was to influence federal government policy at its topmost levels.

The Business Roundtable (BRT), began in 1972. This then-unique organization exclusively included CEOs from top-level U.S. corporations. (In 1977, it had 180 members.) They lobbied directly to the federal government. Unlike industry-specific trade associations, the BRT represented broad-based business interests such as tax law, labor law, and the perceived federal propensity to regulate.

The association's chief value was its personnel. Their members were top, annual-report-level executives who were CEOs and board chairmen, and company presidents. Their access to government officials was all but understood.

Thus, if BRT members have a position, then its likely they'll get the time to present it. It's top level, and J. P. Morgan would probably have been pleased with this organization and its institutionalization of his way of doing things.

Certainly, the BRT was an organization of contemporary titans, perhaps the epitome of interaction between the men in the high castles, in this case, from the executive suites and boardrooms, to the highest halls within the federal government. With the CEO as a lobbyist the gates of the citadel swing open, or more to the point, as David J. Saari, wrote: "What the Business Roundtable did was simple. The Business Roundtable developed more complete strategies to buy influence in Washington to more completely control the federal government."[12]

To accomplish all this, the BRT operated, discreetly, from offices in New York City, and Washington, D.C., unofficially, and out of the public eye. A small executive committee selected and managed the agenda. A policy committee analyzed issues, presented to them, and then made recommendations that the executive-lobbyists acted on. Throughout the process, Beltway-savvy consultants lent their expertise.

During the years they flourished, the BRT promoted: limits on corporate liability; limits on who controls the health-care industry; continual opposition to organized labor's initiatives; advocating Social Security privatization; tax breaks for their own kind; federal deregulation, in general; dilution of the Clean Air Act amendments; and advocated the Chrysler bailout. The BRT opposed: President Carter's wage/price guidelines; opposed creating a federal consumer protection agency; opposed an indexed minimum wage; opposed public financing of federal elections, and opposed the proposal by the U.S Commerce Department to analyze corporate responsibility. (More recently, the BRT lobbied for NAFTA and against the Clinton administration's health-care initiative.)

Business Week called the BRT the most powerful lobby in Washington, D.C., and an organization that enjoys a fine reputation in the private sector and among government politicians and officials. Despite this accolade, the BRT's success has been a matter of conjecture. They did not publish lists of their successes and failures over the decades.

Since the BRT has top execs who believe there is due democracy within a firm's corporate culture, it's doubtful much information will ever emerge about its internal workings. In that their physical plant and staff support is small, and their roles obscure, it's not likely an Ellsberg will occur. Because the days of good investigative journalism faded away during the Reagan-Bush regimes, not much of anything in depth about the BRT will be revealed. (However, over time, Mahood in *Interest Groups* contends that the BRT's significance faded, and by the 1990s, was a shadow of itself.)

That's probably just fine with those involved, since they believe these things should be kept from the public. Such is the way of these people who live and work in the high castles, who, aided and abetted by the co-opted federal government, monopolize the creation and management of public policy.

The BRT was a newcomer to the political arena, entering the fray on its own terms and actively competing with other special-interest groups. One of them was perhaps the most massive of all interest groups: the Chamber of Commerce of the United States (USCOC). Founded in 1912, its original purpose was to promote business self-regulation and present business interests in an organized manner, in the face of emerging threats of two perceived foes—the power of organized labor and the newly assertive federal government. In 1925, F. Stuart Fitzpatrick, in *A Study of Businessmen's Associations*, suggested that within a decade, the USCOC assumed a national role promoting business interests, and significant success influencing public policy. (Basically, the USCOC was anti-tax and for self-regulation.)

By 1940, the USCOC affiliated about 1,500 local groups with over 7,000 business memberships, and published *The Nation's Business*. Already, it was considered an industry leader among trade associations. But after World War II, the USCOC stayed distant from the political process and was not considered a significant factor in federal policy making.

This changed during the 1970s, probably in response to federal reform and its regulatory state. By 1978, the USCOC had more than 70,000 members that included companies and individuals. There were also more than 2,500 local and regional affiliates. By the 1990s, there were approximately 215,000 member businesses.

The chamber's main office moved to D.C., near the White House. In 1980, it had forty-five full-time lobbyists. In the capital, USCOC's activities included program development and implementation; affiliate member development; and addressing broad public policy issues such as economic policy, public affairs, legislative action, and communications.

During the 1970s, the core of this organization was lobbying, not to legislators, but rather, to the constituents, who in turn, via letters and phone calls, were usually acting on information the USCOC provided them. Using a corps of professionals and support staff, the USCOC examined, supported, and then proselytized contemporary policy issues through its members.

Using permanent and ad hoc committees, the USCOC marshaled resources that included staff experts, outside consultants, and corporate executives. Together, they examined such contemporary issues as: government regulation, agribusiness, transportation infrastructure, taxation, antitrust, consumer affairs, labor relations, employee benefits and pensions, limiting business legal liability, environmental regulations, international policy, and technology, among others.

Annually, the USCOC analyzed, then published positions to be lobbied. They also began a litigation center to fight government regulation. Since 1977, the center has sued hundreds of times. The USCOC also formed a foundation designed to fund research and programs fostering positive business public relations. Over the decades, the USCOC gained a reputation for its uncompromising efforts in defense of its policy positions. The USCOC claimed to represent all sizes of business, however, George Draffan asserted in *Elite Consensus* that USCOC's policy positions are heavily influenced by big business.

Despite these efforts, the business community, generally, believed they were collectively failing to compete with public-interest advocacy. Defeatism abounded during the mid-1970s (per contemporary surveys), and many corporate execs urged toughening up and being more aggressive in asserting their policy positions to the federal government. (Indeed, the BRT also fostered such an attitude among its members.)

As a result, more and more firms added personnel to deal directly with public and government affairs. By 1981, 361 of 400 companies surveyed, did so; greater than half of them had such offices in place in 1970, and almost one-third set up between 1975 and 1979. Also, in 1970, there were about 1,700 trade associations in Washington; by 1980, 2,000.

Thus, business in general, increased this kind of activity, despite the perceived prevailing anti-business social ethos. Big business saw itself on the defensive, on all fronts, and circling the wagons, hence, increasing their political participation became a critical necessity.

At the same time during the 1970s, perceptions of the rise of interest groups and their lobbyists took a noticeable negative turn, coincidental with suspicion of big business. This was in contrast to positive reactions to trade associations during their formative days, and then, decades later, in the early 1960s, when interest-group politics could still be seen as positive within the Consensus Era.

The media fostered this change in attitude, and politicians soon noted how quickly interest-group politics advanced to the forefront, becoming ubiquitous. Now lobbyists, grouped along Washington's K Street, went from representing large institutions to various political causes; encompassing ideologies and beliefs across the political spectrum. To many of the participants and their observers, this new set of ingredients into the political mix became a potentially poisoning agent in the body politic.

Regardless of the veracity of their groups' beliefs and opinions, this new corporate-created and fostered method of politicking embedded itself into the political society. Depending upon perception and outcome potential, this injection into the body politic's bloodstream could be considered either a new life source or a cancer. Regardless of sentiment or opinion, this new ingredient was a permanent one.

From 1968 to 1978, four hundred firms opened offices in D.C. When the NAM moved to Washington, in 1973, others soon followed. By 1978, there were almost 2,000 trade associations set up in our capital. (There were 179 companies with registered lobbyists there in 1971; by 1979, 650 firms; 1982, 2,445.) By 1980, 12,000 lawyers worked for the business sector, in D.C., along with 9,000 lobbyists; 50,000 trade association staff; 8,000 public relations personnel; 1,300 public affairs consultants (and 12,000 reporters), hired to track government policies for the private sector.

Those already there, typically, increased their size, adding specialists who had to know present policy positions and compete with other interests within the public-policy making process. Looking back to then, Kevin Phillips recalled Washington became a battleground of interest groups. David Vogel offered this analysis:

> Increasing the physical presence of corporate officials in Washington, using lawsuits as a device to influence the implementation of government regulatory policy, grooming chief executives to be comfortable when dealing with the public, organizing citizens at the grass roots, making more extensive use of coalitions and ad hoc alliances, enhancing the awareness of common interests among diverse organizations and constituencies, using the press as a forum for influencing public opinion, seeking allies in the universities, and even becoming somewhat less partisan.[13]

Thus, newly armed and invigorated, big business continued the fray, seeking to turn the reform tide away. Now, they would add another part to their repertoire, public relations, making their arsenal complete.

An important adjunct to the lobbying and interest-group process was public relations. As institutions, big business began selling itself to the public during the Progressive Era, and they generally sustained the method, to varying degrees, permanently.

As the lobbying industry emerged and persisted, corporations established a link to public relations. It was systematically in use by the end of World War II. Roland Marchand explained this brilliantly throughout his *Creating the Corporate Soul* (1998). He wrote:

> Emulating those organizations responsible for the education, health, religious practice, and cultural enrichment of the nation's citizens, the giant business corporation of the early twentieth century aspired to become an institution

> . . . becoming an institution meant more than simply acquiring the status of a customary established entity. It meant rising above mere commercialism and removing the taint of selfishness.[14]

If construed as proselytizing a sense of citizenship, big business was in the forefront of such self-promotion, a practice that continued and became more sophisticated as the twentieth century proceeded.

Corporations did this through institutional advertising (and later public relations), where they sold themselves, besides their products. The idea was to advertise themselves as engaged in the society for the common good as providers and social participants. They presented a corporate image of participatory citizenship, a family, similar to everyone. The goal was to respond to negative images and public fear directed toward the soullessness of a large, people-grinding, exploitative behemoth. These efforts became permanent, and in the process, created a new professional field, business player, and institution unto itself—public relations.

In *Keeping the Corporate Image*, Richard Tedlow proclaimed that public relations (PR) is uniquely American, and its importance and use slowly increased during the first half of the twentieth century. Largely through the efforts of Edward L. Bernays, who, Tedlow credits with pioneering the field, public relations was injected into the market arena, where big business eventually, albeit slowly, adopted its rationale and methods into their own business practices.

Associating business, capitalism, and free enterprise accompanied institutional advertising. Organizations such as the Heritage Foundation (1947), and the Advertising Council (1945), supported by big business, promoted and proselytized the virtues of corporate American values.

These and other organizations, such as the Foundation for Economic Education (FEE), fostered various levels of affection for different pro-business beliefs and values. What they promoted on the political spectrum varied. FEE was ideologically riven to the right, compared to the centrist posture of the Advertising Council. Prominent among even these groups was the NAM, which continued their campaign against organized labor and New Deal liberalism. (Promoting passage of the Taft-Hartley bill was one example of what they sought to accomplish.)

Thus, by the end of the 1950s, the field of public relations was already established and well positioned to aid and promote the corporate cause, which it did during the rise of television, concomitant with the emergence of media as a soon-to-be dominant phenomena in shaping public opinion as well as marketing products.

In time, public relations became another way to lobby and market. Edwin A. Epstein opined in *The Corporation in American Politics* that, overall, corporations successfully sold the public on their political views, similar to their success marketing products.

Perhaps this newly formed alliance of private-sector activism, corporate elite participation, the huge influx of business lobbyists to D.C., and the systematic use of PR worked. David Vogl, claimed that by 1978, business interests successfully stemmed the public interests sector's tide of success; countered organized labor's traditional access to the federal government, and even began to make significant strides in furthering its policy agenda.

In *Who Runs Congress*, Mark Green et al. go further, suggesting that business lobbies had de facto veto power over federal legislation, becoming the chief determinants of whether a bill becomes law by leaving it alone, or waging political war against it.

If so, big business' political arsenal is potent, consisting of an alliance of lobbyists and consultants, who can formally state their case during congressional hearings and upfront meetings. At the same time, the informal, country-club routine and social circuit abets their daytime efforts. Campaign contributions add a formidable weapon to their lobbying efforts. Public relations and taking their viewpoints to the general public and to legislators' constituents, round out the whole of their political assets. In 1970, only a few *Fortune* 500 companies had PR offices in D.C. By 1980, 80 percent did.

Thus, public relations became a significant asset in the lobbying and interest group process. These were important assets, especially when used in tandem with money.

Throughout the early decades prior to the Great Depression and World War II, a tandem relationship evolved between the lobbying process and campaign finance. Both were logistically and tactically separate methods, but each one had the same purpose—to influence, if not control, the political and governing process at the federal level.

Lobbying was already a well-established part of the political process. Campaign finance, evolving quickly, became a partner, if not superseding lobbying in importance as the decades proceeded.

Although campaign finance drew significant attention during the last twenty years or so of the twentieth century, it had been an evolving and significant part of the political process for much of that century. It gathered strength as it bore its way into the political economy and the political process.

During Normalcy, the new marriage of money and politics blossomed, especially for the party of the robber barons, the former party of Abe Lincoln. The very pro-business Hoover administration was a magnet for funds from the private sector.

TABLE 6.1
Percent of Total Contributions to the Two Political Parties from the Banking and Manufacturing Sectors of the Economy.

Year	*Democratic Party*	*Republican Party*
1928	41.4	52.16
1932	34.7	46.8
1936	18.9	44.3
1940	10.5	47.7
1944	13.3	40.9

Source: Louise Overacker, *Presidential Campaign Funds* (1946), p. 15.

The pattern continued during the 1928 presidential campaign. At the national level, the GOP spent $4 million; the Democrats, $3 million. Add state and local money: $9 million dollars for the GOP and $7 million for the Democrats. (Louise Overacker suggested that these amounts were the results of intensive print, radio, and movie advertising.)

Both individuals and interests contributed money. Large amounts dominated the fund pools of both political parties. Overacker wrote on that banks and manufacturers were significant contributors to the Republican Party, and, in general, the better-off class dominated campaign contributions to both political parties.

Back then, it was public knowledge that money controlled the political process; that contemporary campaign spending was excessive. Some said politics was a rich man's game.

Overacker also pointed out, writing from a 1930s perspective, that as campaign costs increased, financial support from political party members was inadequate. Moneyed interests in the private sector filled the gaps, eventually supplanting the citizen contribution as the main source of supply.

They became the prime movers in the process. As indicated in previous chapters, the private sector, led by the big business corporation, created and sustained modernity, establishing a new contemporary political culture in which the political process functioned.

The relative sophistication of the new times, then (mass production, mass media, bigness, etc.), affected the entire electoral process. Using modern/contemporary technology and methods, such as radio and film, and advertising and public relations methods of persuasion, all cost more. Consequently, the traditional nineteenth-century methods of seeking public office and paying the campaign costs, could not keep up. This financial shortfall wound up being picked up by big business.

The trend soon became permanent. The modern political process followed modernity through the 1920s. As the American society modernized technologically and financially, so too did the core elements of its political process. It was swept along in the tide caused by the growing sophistication of contemporary life and its concomitant increases in costs.

Thus, running for office became part of this escalating process, and both political parties attempted to keep pace.

TABLE 6.2
Total Costs of Presidential Elections, Selected Years, in Dollars.

Year	Democratic Party	Republican Party
1876	900,000	950,000
1880	335,000	1,100,000
1892	2,350,00	1,700,000
1900	425,000	3,000,000
1904	700,000	2,096,000
1912	1,134,848	1,071,549
1920	1,470,371	5,417,501
1928	5,342,350	6,256,111
1932	2,245,975	2,900,052
1936	5,194,741	8,892,972

Source: Herbert E. Alexander, *Financing Politics* (1992), p. 80. Note, the numbers here are to show the long-term trend, even though sums varied by election cycle.

Consider the subtle participatory context. Overacker pointed out in *Money in Elections* that only a very small part of the electorate contributed to presidential campaigns during the first two decades of the twentieth century. At the same time, large contributions from a small number of individuals dominated the donor list.

If this pattern persisted, then the power and influence of these moneyed votes would logically outweigh a commoner's (like me). Hence, the electoral process skews toward those who pay the bills. Here's where the moneyed classes, and especially corporate citizens, have more clout regarding federal policy once an administration and the U.S. Congress begins governing This trend continued then and now, even through depression and war, to the present.

The friendly alliance between big business and the Republican Party continued unabated during the Depression Decade. In 1932, fewer manufacturers contributed to the Democrats than in 1928; large contributors too, such as J.P Morgan & Co., the Corn Exchange Bank, Bankers Trust, National City Bank, Kuhn, Loeb, Crocker National Bank, Mellon, Harris Trust and Savings, and Boatman's. Top-shelf contributors to the GOP during the 1936 general election included: Du Pont, the Pews—(Sun Oil), Rockefeller, Frick, Republic Steel, Bethlehem Steel, Jones & Laughlin, Monsanto, USS, and American Cyanamid, besides a number who also were with the Republicans in 1932. Most industry sectors were well represented on their donor lists. Overacker reported on the 1936 election, in 1937: "The Republicans became more definitely than in the past few campaigns the party of big business."[15] Money flowed into the Republican Party coffers, especially from those opposing the New Deal.

Thus, during these early twentieth-century decades, what would become a permanent pattern, emerged. The GOP welded itself to the business classes while becoming, in time, an effective countervailing force to the Roosevelt Coalition, until 1968, when they cracked it, and in 1980, when they finally defeated it, so they say. With that, corporate dominance of the political economy was soon to be.

In contrast, the Democratic Party, struggled to compete with the corporate and well-to-do largesse flowing to the GOP, this despite Franklin D. Roosevelt's successes at the polls. The Democrats received much less from those on the top shelf. Manufacturers and large-amount contributors gave less in 1932 than in 1928, and that occurred again in 1936.

Notable among contributors was Joseph P. Kennedy, albeit secretly, and William R. Hearst. Circumventing corporate campaign contribution prohibitions, via taking ads in the 1936 Democratic Party convention book were: Phillip Morris, Remington Rand, Dun & Bradstreet, Elizabeth Arden, Thomas Cook & Sons, F. W. Woolworth, William Wrigley, among others. Additional contributors to the Democratic Party included: R. J. Reynolds, International Harvester, Zenith Radio, Edison, Coca-Cola, and Ivory. Some like Armour and Firestone contributed to both political parties.

Also, that year, 1936, two precedents were set. The Democrats did their first 100-dollar-a-plate dinner to raise funds, and organized labor, led by the United Mine Workers Union, contributed significantly to the Democratic Party.

One year later, Louise Overacker observed that the GOP was becoming the party of the haves, while the Democrats, the party of the have-nots. In hindsight, her observations in 1937 were prophetic.

While the money flowed in, the participants attempted to control campaign finance throughout, albeit unsuccessfully or half-heartedly. The year 1867 was the beginning of campaign finance regulation when the U.S. Congress prohibited government officials from fundraising to shipyard employees. An 1876 law prohibited federal civil service employees from fundraising among themselves. The Pendleton Act of 1883, banned federal employees from contributing to campaigns, de facto, an assault on the prevailing political party assessment system. In 1907, the Tillman Act banned corporations from directly contributing to political parties and candidates in federal election campaigns, a reaction to the success of Mark Hanna's campaign-finance methods. In 1925, the Federal Corrupt Practices Act put limits on congressional campaign spending and required candidates to disclose contributions and spending. The 1940 Hatch Act placed limits on individual contribution amounts. In 1943, the Smith-Connally Act temporarily banned labor union campaign contributions, as a wartime exigency. The 1947 Taft-Hartley Act permanently banned labor union direct contributions. In 1971, the Federal Elections Campaign Act attempted to comprehensively regulate the federal election process.

In between these larger efforts, the U.S. Congress amended existing laws. All these were similar in their lax enforcement (or none), and loopholes. It could've been that these laws were at times, laws in name only, or on the books and not consistently enforced or improved. The time gaps between these early efforts and more recent attempts attest to this. Many of these laws spawned methods to maneuver around them; "cheatin'," or, as it was later referred to in stock car racing: They were just trying to get an edge.

In the political arena, this meant, among others, reimbursing employees for their individual contributions and creating shell organizations to launder money before it went to the political party. Wealthy families could divvy up a large contribution among family members when limits were imposed in 1940. A corporation might be prohibited from contributing, but not annual-report-level executives. Where, and how, they got the cash to donate can easily be left to conjecture. When unions were prohibited from directly contributing, the Congress of Industrial Organizations figured out a way around the prohibition by creating a political action committee, the first of its kind.

Essentially, these laws were either not enforced, or sort of—window dressing—laws on paper only. If money is the lifeblood of political careers, even back then, why would a politician attempt to control or eliminate campaign finance? (For example, there were no prosecutions under the Corrupt Practices Act from 1925 to 1971.) Thus, the precedent to evade regulation and hide behind loopholed window dressing was established early on, and then remained in place for the rest of the century. Elizabeth Drew observed this during the early 1980s. In *Politics and Money*, she wrote:

> The political practitioners who have learned their way around both the Presidential and the congressional campaign-finance laws—and all the skilled one have—view them with amusement. . . . The result of all this is that the basis on which our system of representative government was supposed to work is slipping away, if it is not already gone. The role of the public representative has been changing dramatically in recent years. The processes by which Congress is supposed to function have been distorted, if not overwhelmed, by the role of money. The ability of even the best legislators to focus on broad questions, to act

> independently, or to lead has been seriously impaired The race for money on Capitol Hill has turned into what one House member has described as 'a fever' that has taken over the institution. . . . The Washington lobbyists and political consultants understand what is going on and so do the politicians.[16]

Perhaps it is a universal within the political arena: Where there is a will to get over on the system, they will find a way.

George Thayer, in *The Money Tree*, had a different take on campaign finance which was quite blunt. He argued that corruption became more subtle when the Prosperity Decade ended. After the Great Depression, the evasion of campaign finance laws became more hidden. Enforcement of existing laws disappeared, and Thayer contended that subsequent laws were inadequate to the task. More important, he did not avoid the fundamental problem with campaign finance. He screeded thusly:

> Perhaps the most obvious change since the twenties has been the growing hypocrisy with which we have come to treat the subject. It has been most manifest in our speech. For example, while we previously called a bribe what it was—a payoff, a fix, or money for favors—we are now using euphemisms such as "speaker's fees," "convention book advertising," "testimonial dinners," and, on occasion, even, "campaign contributions" itself. . . . By the time the Great Depression was upon us, the blunt language of a frontier society appears to have given a way to the indirect idiom of a consumer-oriented middle-class society. Through the use of words we have come to sanitize the unsavory practice of bribery, the same way we have subsequently sanitized sewage by calling it "waste water." But the point should not be lost: these words may sound better to the ear, but it is still bribery and is no less corrupt.[17]

The system Thayer slammed persisted through World War II, and then abutted against postwar modernity. By 1950, the nexus of money and influence was a well known connection. It was also coupled to the lobbying and interest-group process, including its discreet, unspoken corrupt practices, and legal campaign financing. The persistent practice of underhandedness; of buying votes or legislators, or contributing to campaign coffers for past cooperation and for future favors probably still persisted from its heyday in the nineteenth century. The means were just more subtle while the substance remained similar.

Also, corporate personnel contributed money throughout the decade. They gave over $1 million in the 1952 election, mostly to Republicans; about $1.8 million in 1956; again, most of their money went to the GOP. Note, in the 1952 national election, campaigning included TV, airplane use, polling, consultants, computers, and the resulting large costs, for which the wealthy contributed to pay the bills.

During the 1956 election, some statistics reveal where the Republicans obtained their campaign financing from big business. Corporate officials of different-sized firms donated as follows. From the 225 largest corporations, 94 percent of total contributions went to the GOP; 96 percent from the largest oil companies to the Republican Party; 97 percent from the largest broadcasters; 81 percent from airline companies; 100 percent from thirty-seven advertising companies. Corporate concern over public policy and politics translated into money exchanging hands. I wonder why? If I'm running for office and you support my campaign, then what do I owe you?

During the 1960 election, the private sector participated in nonpartisan voter registration drives, complementing similar efforts by the League of Women Voters and the Heritage Foundation. Many corporations also promoted voter registration to their employees. Some firms also raised money, but Herbert G. Alexander in *Financing the 1960 Election* suggested that their efforts weren't significant. (Examples: Ford, Whirlpool, AT&T, Thiokol, Chase Manhattan, Kimberly-Clark.) Also of note: The United Republican Finance Committee of New York solicited presidents and board chairman of approximately 100 large corporations, asking them for $150–$500 from each individual. The program drew bad press, so it was stopped in progress. Overall, the Kennedy campaign conceded that general business support in the election to the Republican Party. This included contributions from fat-cat families such as Field, du Pont, Ford, Harriman, Mellon, Olin, Pew, and Rockefeller, among others.

Both business and labor continued their efforts during the 1964 election cycle. Overall, the Republicans, despite not being incumbents, raised more money than the Democrats. However, of immediate note was a switch in some business and fat-cat contributions away from the GOP to the Democrats. There was also a change in the type. This cycle, the Democrats received significant amounts from large contributors, while the Republicans received much of theirs from smaller amounts, in addition to their usual large-contributor base.

Although Goldwater drew almost exclusive financial support from the ideological right, the Republican business base was not as loyal. Of particular note was the switch by several members of the Business Council (BC), to the Democrats. During the other cycles, BC members mostly contributed to the GOP in 1956, 1960, 1968, and 1972. A similar pattern occurred among some members of the American Petroleum Institute, the American Iron and Steel Institute, and the Association of American Railroads, plus a host of others. (Note, consistent as always, directors of the NAM and USCOC increased their support for the Republican Party.)

Perhaps indicative of the future, there was, as usual, labor PAC support for the Democrats and the debut of the American Political Action Committee, the Business-Industry Political Action Committee (BIPAC), and the Council for a Livable World; all fundraised. Even more prophetic was the increase in campaign contributions from the West and South, concomitantly, with a decrease from the eastern and northern sections. (See Kevin Phillips, *The Emerging Republican Majority.*)

During the 1968 election, the private sector returned to supporting the Republican Party. This included a high level of support from corporate chief executives and the BIPAC and members of the BC. The Democrats continued to receive large contributions, but less than in 1964, and enjoyed a small increase in small amounts.

The Federal Elections Campaign Act of 1971, replacing the Corrupt Practices Act, changed the rules for campaign finance. Generally, campaign funds had to be reported in detail, quarterly, and in between primaries and runoffs; an immediate report (five days), of contributions exceeding $5,000; mandatory convention expenses reporting; limits on money spent on media; new limits on individual campaign contributions; government contractors were prohibited from contributing; unions and corporations could only contribute through independent political associations—PACs; PACs had to submit details on total contributions exceeding $1,000 per year.

Despite the new law, high-level corruption, including illegal corporate contributions and embodied in the Watergate scandal, marked the 1972 general election. Although the Watergate money laundering drew lots of negative attention to those culpable, it cannot be proven that this was typical of the corporate sector, in general. Just how ubiquitous this might have been is tantalizing, but unproven.

Afterward, these revelations led to well-meaning reform. Despite the notoriety, the Nixon campaign benefited from significant crossover support from unions, Jews, and disgruntled longtime Democratic Party supporters, while maintaining their now-traditional base of support from the business sector (e.g., the BC, NAM, USCOC, energy groups, defense contractors, business executives such as Howard Hughes and W. Clement Stone, and the upper crust, both old money and new, and PACs)

The fallout from the scandals affected the next election cycle. A FECA 1974 amendment provided for public funding and the U.S. Supreme Court's *Buckey v. Valeo* decision opened the door for PACs to enter the political arena in earnest.

The 1976 election was marked by the availability of public funds and more limits on private campaign contributions. Presidential candidates who took public money couldn't accept private contributions. This did not apply to congressional candidates, so consequently, PACs could contribute up to $5,000 per candidate. Herbert Alexander suggested this encouraged more PAC participation in congressional elections and set precedents for future involvement. Essentially, a political group could now contribute, more so than people. Notable and significant during this election was the active pursuit of PAC money by both political parties. Alexander also stated that the Republican Party sought increased contacts with PACs for future considerations.

However, corporations were slow to react to these new factors, and their PACs' participation in this election was insignificant. This changed, and in subsequent years, PAC influence grew noticeably. Trade and professional PACs were already established and ideological groups actively contributed.

By 1978, business PACs contributed twice the amount of money as labor PACs to congressional elections. This trend continued; by 1986, to three times as much. At the same time, candidates increased accepting PAC contributions. From 1974–1986, U.S. House members, who took one-third of their campaign funds from PACs, increased from 28 percent to 80 percent. During these years, more and more congressional election contestants increased their use of PAC money.

In hindsight, the 1980 general election might have been the foundational, defining event that ushered in what became the age of political action committees. That year, corporate PACs contributed 35 percent of total PAC money, of which 64 percent went to the Republican Party, while 36 percent went to the Democrats.[18] Generally, PACs-supported candidates won, and many of them leaned to the political right.

Kathryn Ashford, suggested that PAC money was instrumental in GOP congressional successes that year, when they won the White House and control of the U.S. Senate and garnered 33 seats in the U.S House.[19] (Also of note: Stern stated that 88 percent of PAC money went to incumbents.)

In the 1980 general election, the Republican Party outspent the Democrats, and for the first time, corporate PACs outspent labor political action committees. By the end of 1980, there were about 2,551 registered PACs; 1,204 were corporate and 294 labor; 2,146 contributed to candidates. PACs gave congressional candidates $20 million more than in 1978. Business and ideological groups contributed the most. Corporate contributions surged. The PAC money went chiefly to incumbents; more Democrats in the U.S. Congress than Republicans. Incumbency was more important to contributors than political party; wonder why? However, the gap between money going to Democrats more so than Republicans narrowed like it did in 1978, compared to 1976.

The Republican Party rising continued in 1984 with Reagan's reelection and congressional gains. PAC contributions played a larger role in financing these campaigns, in an upward trend since 1974. In this election cycle, 4,347 PACs, of all kinds, contributed $106.8 million to federal campaigns, a 29 percent increase from 1982, and 105 percent from 1980. Of these, corporate PACs contributed $36.2 million; labor PACs $25.1 million, and issues/ideological PACs $14.7 million. Continuing the pattern, incumbents received most from this largesse. Corporate PACs contributed $128 million to them, 77 percent of their total contributions. The Republican Party received $27.2 million of the total PAC contributions.

The 1988 election campaigns for all levels cost $2.9 billion, a 50 percent increase from 1984. Remarkably, the Democratic Party received 55 percent of business PAC contributions; incumbency prevailed over ideology regarding both parties.

Indeed, Philip Stern in *The Best Congress Money Can Buy*, pointed out that PACs contributed 88 percent of their funds to incumbents in the 1986 election; corporate PACs sent 96 percent of their contributions to incumbents. PAC contributions were an upward trend, especially increasing from 1982 to 1986: 71.8 percent of aggregate PAC money to incumbents for 1978; 78.9 percent for 1982; and 87.9 percent for 1988.

Also, of note was the use of so-called soft money. Sanctioned by the 1979 amendments to the Federal Election Campaign Act, soft money was unregulated campaign contributions. This type played a significant role in the 1980 and 1984 campaigns. Such money, contributed at the state and local levels, and indirectly applied to presidential campaigns, kept private money in the mix. This allowed contributors to give large amounts of money to organizations related to the candidates.

There were 4,729 PACs registered with the Federal Elections Commission for the 1992 election. Of those, 1,930 were corporate PACs; 372 labor, and the category unconnected, which are mostly ideological or issues-oriented PACs, equaled 1,377. Corporate PACs contributed $68.4 million, leading all categories, and 77 percent of these funds went to incumbents. Even though corporate PACs could be expected to support the GOP, in this election, both political parties almost received equal amounts.

In the 1996 campaign finance analysis *Financing the 1996 Election*, John C. Green noted the resurgence of large contributions by people and organizations; interest group contributions in undisclosed and even unlimited amounts, and large-scale circumvention of campaign finance law. Adding to the recipe were two recent ingredients: soft money donations, raised, usually at the state and local level, and issues-interest groups contributed money, indirectly, to federal candidates as an end run around campaign finance law. The 1996 election was the most expensive to that time: $4.2 billion, of which $765.3 million was spent on congressional elections. Once again, organizations prevailed, and so did the use of soft money.

There were more than 4,500 registered PACs in 1996. They contributed $200.7 million to congressional campaigns. Business PACs' contributions exceeded 64 percent of all PACs, while ideological PACs equaled 28 percent and labor PACs, 8 percent. A small number of PACs dominated the process: 10 percent of PACs contributed 76 percent of total contributions. Business PACs led the way, contributing 64 percent of the total (36 percent contributed by corporate PACs and 28 percent by trade associations). Interest group PACs followed. Incumbents, now lots of Republicans, received the largesse of PAC money. Business PACs channeled 70 percent of their total funds to the Republican Party, and overall, total PAC money went more to the Republicans than the Democrats. The trend continued into the new century.

This decades-long trend in campaign finance, was interpreted from a different angle, in 1971, by Morton Mintz and Jerry Cohen, in their *America, Inc.*:

> It costs money, more all the time, to seek elective public office. The money is obtained from where it's at, which is primarily large corporations and financial institutions. Their campaign contributions are really not that at all; they are investments in licenses to govern the government, or, if you prefer, to translate economic power into political power. Being prudent, the investors take out insurance by, for example, investing in both political parties at once.[20]

If so, such investment could wind up with favorable action for those lobbying and/or, contributing. Here's some examples, circa, 1966–1967, what business' investment in their politicians garnered: controlling or curtailing the perceived power of labor unions; exempting some businesses from the minimum wage; tax reductions; influencing interest rates; setting up government contracts guaranteed profit minimums; promoting brand-name drugs in federally funded programs such as Medicaid and welfare; gutting enforcement of industry regulations; tariffs and import quotas; federal subsidies for sugar or copper, among other commodities.

That the private sector expects to get what it pays for, how does it pay for services rendered by our legislative representatives? As of 1968, here are some ways of funding campaign contributions: bonuses paid to employees, part of the amount was to be kicked back as a contribution to a specified candidate; portions of salaries were designated as contributions to certain candidates; employees were paid by their employers while working on political campaigns; portions of attorney fees were to be contributed to selected candidates; donating short-term billboard space to certain candidates.

This is once again a triumph of the institution, in this case, big business, over ordinary citizens. As indicated earlier, the economic power of any given corporation, and all of the *Fortune* 500, necessarily begets institutional and political power within the framework of a corporate capitalist political economy.

This power is used to not only promote and sustain profitability. It also becomes the ways and means to fortify and sustain the corporate corpus, which by the 1960s already attained a level of self-sustaining and self-conscious perception. Thus, sustaining the entity became a good and a necessity in of itself. As a result, entering the arena to compete with other interests, reformers, and other entities and businesses, became necessary to sustain the life of the corporation.

This drive for institutional sustenance, an organic act, attempting to preserve the health of the firm, similar to the human self, became a driving force for corporations during the latter half of the twentieth century.

Like a real person, this institutional drive was fueled similar to human drives: personal survival, survival of the fittest, competing with, and dominating others, self-interest, and acquisitiveness.

These human attributes, when applied at the institutional level, played out, almost organically, and inevitably, in the political arena as the dance of the titans. With that metaphor, interest-group politics, lobbying for one's own institutional self-interest, and using whatever means necessary, whether legal or not, and cheatin' to get an edge, are organically, normal and natural to what the corporate titan became by the dawn of the 1960s.

As can be seen for our recent history, the corporate monolith, aided and abetted by a co-opted executive and legislative branches of the federal government, achieved baroque citizenship status by the end of the twentieth century.

As indicated, the political process in D.C., is now more complicated than ever because of the links among lobbying, interest-group politics, and campaign finance. Into this political cauldron of the 1960s (1963–1975), we can now add a new, powerful catalyst, political action committees.

Their appearance, later in force, was an accident. Past attempts to control campaign finance failed for the lack of enforcement mechanisms, or of almost built-in loopholes. In 1971, the U.S. Congress passed the Federal Election Campaign Act (FECA), another attempt to control campaign finance. This law mandated disclosing campaign contributions and expenditures. It also allowed corporations to set up a separate political fund, a.k.a., a political action committee, which could accept from shareholders and management and dispense campaign money. Subsequent amendments in 1974 limited the amounts a contributor could donate, placed spending caps on federal campaigns, and established public-funding option for the presidential election. This law also established the Federal Election Commission as enforcer.

A lawsuit resulted, and in *Buckley v Valeo* (1976), the U.S. Supreme Court declared that campaign spending limits on private contributions were an unconstitutional violation of free speech. This meant that private donations of money were protected, and so too were the candidates spending it.

This decision, also unintentionally created an unprecedented new method of lobbying and campaign finance: the legal sanctioning of political action committees, which are groups that raise and distribute campaign money. Now for the first time in several decades, corporations could legally raise money and de facto, contribute to federal election campaigns through these supposedly separate and independent committees.

The method might have been recent, but the means was not. Political action committees were not spontaneously generated as a result of *Buckley.* PACs originated during the New Deal from unlikely circumstances. The Hatch Act of 1940 was another attempt to address campaign finance. This law limited contributions and the amounts of money that national political-party committees could spend. There were also limits on purchasing products, such as the 1936 Democratic Party conventions ad-book. The law prohibited such fundraising devices, thus eliminating an effective way for corporations to donate.

Louise Overacker asserted that the law altered financing methods, but not patterns. During the 1940 campaign, trade unions, political workers, and small-time contributors were the main sources of Democratic Party money, while the GOP continued to draw sustenance from their corporate-based friends.

Because of the limits on money going to the two national political party committees, "independent non-party organizations" significantly participated in the 1944 elections. Some examples: the CIO Political Action Committee, Democrats for Dewey, the National Association of Pro-America, and the Peoples' Committee to Defend Life Insurance and Savings.

Enter the political action committee into the political arena. Inadvertently, the Hatch Act promoted decentralized and harder-to-monitor methods of campaign finance. Overacker stated that anonymous donations were accepted and door-to-door soliciting done. Money was thus distributed and limits exceeded. Overall, both political parties participated. In fact, using several local committees, large-amount donors effectively thwarted the Hatch Act's intent.

Unintended, no doubt, the Hatch Act restrictions might have helped to usher in a new era of campaign financing by paving the way for the eventual rise of political action committees.

The first of these might have been the Congress of Industrial Organizations political action committee, established in July 1943. The CIO-PAC was an umbrella organization that coordinated local committees, and worked with similar groups such as the National Citizens Political Action Committee. This first political action committee was staffed by 135 workers, established local branches, created campaign literature, registered voters, and propagandized (including voter guides), the electorate, promoting their cause and candidates.

In 1944, the CIO-PACs supported the Democratic Party despite the restrictions place on unions campaign financing by the Smith-Connally Act of 1943. Later, in 1947, the Taft-Hartley Act further restricted both organized labor and corporate campaign contributions.

It was so effective, its opposition candidates and corporations, eventually copied the CIO-PACs success, ushering in a new age of campaigning by political action committees, whereby those groups interested in the political process and governing, formed their own political action committees.

Although formally organized business PACs began with the AMA's, American Medical Political Action Committee (AMPAC), in 1962–1963, PAC influence in the electoral process began small in 1972 and 1974, then increased in the 1976 matchup. (Sabato cited 11 registered business PACs in 1964; 33 by 1968; 200 by 1972)

Throughout the decade, corporate PAC involvement remained insignificant. This changed when the NAM's Business-Industry Political Action Committee (BIPAC), and the USCOC's, National Chamber Alliance for Politics began to coordinate funds disbursement. Besides providing campaign contributions, BIPAC started identifying close election contests and then endorsing candidates or incumbents who were on the program. Both BIPAC and AMPAC spent money in both the 1964 and 1968 elections and continued to be influential during the ensuing years. BIPAC quickly gained access when the GOP controlled the federal government. The Republicans were more than receptive to BIPACs conservative agenda. Eventually, corporate PACs flocked to these two clearinghouse organizations sponsored by the NAM and the USCOC.

During the 1970s, corporate PACs took on their own characteristics and increased their influence in elections as an unintended consequence of election-reform efforts. The 1971 FECA allowed corporations to pay PAC expenses. Soon after, about two hundred private-sector and professional committees registered. Subsequent FECA amendments regulated such participation. In 1974, overall, there were about six hundred registered PACs; ten years later, approximately four thousand. A new age of politicking was about to begin.

In 1975, the Federal Elections Commission ruled in the Sun Oil decision, allowing corporations to form PACs that then could raise money from their own employees or stockholders. After that ruling, in November 1975, corporate PAC' registrations increased from 139, to over 400; by 1983, 3,500. PACs subsequently, and rapidly grew in number from 1978 to 1984, then leveled off. There were 608 PACs in 1974 and 4,009 in 1984; 4,172 in 1990. and more than 4,500 in 1996.

Despite PAC potential, corporations were slow to make the connection between PACs and political influence, to the chagrin of their lobbyists. Some corporate boards still believed their companies should keep a polite distance from campaign finance.

This changed quickly. In 1975, there were 89 corporate PACs. By the end of 1978 there were 812. By the fall of 1978, 196 of the *Fortune* 500 had PACs; 7 of the top 25; 16 of the top 30, and 29 of the top 100 companies. In 1976, 10 percent of all PACs were corporate; by 1980, 50 percent. By 1982, there were 1,467 registered corporate PACs. They rapidly grew from 1978 to 1984 and then leveled off. In 1978, corporate PACs campaign contributing was almost equal to labor PACs; by 1980, the former exceeded the latter.

Enabling corporate PACs couldn't occur at a more opportune time. As previously mentioned, business had been on the political defensive, but was now resurgent in 1978. Organized labor realized corporate PAC potential, fearing too, a combined effort by the private sector could dominate campaign financing, thus tipping elections toward anti-labor, anti-regulatory, ideologically conservative candidates.

At the same time, 1978, corporate PACs began to get legislators' attention, to the detriment of organized labor PACs. By 1980, Vogel argued, the availability of corporate PAC money (about one-half of the *Fortune* 500 companies had PACs), made even many Democrats less beholden to organized labor and more amenable to business interests. (The final death knell of the Roosevelt Coalition.)

How so? Once again, those that pay the bills, call the shots, or more formally, influence policy, or, euphemistically, gain access. For the recipient of campaign money, political survival is often a function of money. To govern, election campaigns must be paid for, and PAC money eventually became a significant addition to other fundraising.

But as usual, money typically doesn't arrive for nothing. (Donors like to call this an investment.) There's strings attached, often unsaid, but everyone involved knows it. Those that provide expect something in return, naturally. Barry Goldwater once said:

> It is not 'we, the people,' but political action committees and moneyed interests who are setting the nation's political agenda and are influencing the position of candidates on the important issues of the day.[21]

And Bob Dole:

> When these political action committees give money, they expect something in return other than good government.[22]

And Barney Frank:

> We are the only human beings in the world who are expected to take thousands of dollars from perfect strangers on important matters and not be affected by it.[23]

Thus, the politicians are beholden to their benefactors, and the more institutionally powerful the latter, the louder their money talks. For after all, who's more important, those that fork over the dough, or one's own constituents? The wishes and policy prerogatives of the corporate sector are top-shelf concerns of politicians; more so than of do-gooders and competing constituent interests.

Now, instead of congressional representation of local and home state citizens, PACs promote national interest-group citizenship, by channeling money from out of a representative's district or state. Over the years, de facto, interest-group citizenship is more important than individual citizenship, when it comes to influencing national policy-making.

The end result, again, is Griederesque. Governing becomes a function of satisfying those with institutional power, now translated in checkbook economics. The final fall in the clash of titans goes to the corporate sector.

Go through the literature on this and note the anecdotes and examples. (*Who Runs Congress* and *End Legalized Bribery*, *Selling Out*, are just a few examples) Because campaign finance is, de facto, bribery, it is often left unsaid. However, this dirty little secret is not so secret among the players. To them it's understood; not enough of it has been publicized. Most of them don't want exposure or investigations that could lead to indictments, or, almost as bad, in some minds, reform and more regulations. They believe that it is better off unsaid, don't rock the boat; keep the rest of us protected. Besides, who cares now about the truth? I got mine and got away with it. Indeed. This is human nature, take it for what it is. This is why the system works for them so effectively and why they're reluctant to change it.

Money talks, especially with senior politicians, when persisting in office is at stake. They would be more inclined to return the favor with voting the right way, "if you know what I mean, and I'm sure you do." (Right, Joe Bob Briggs?)

This relationship also trickles down to junior legislators. Here it's simply economic and too, a matter of political survival. It's better to vote the right way; to go along with the program. At that level in the U.S. Congress, they know their place and realize it's better to play by these established ways of doing things.

Thus, the system persists because most of those involved go along, for whatever reasons. The few that don't and vocalize the situation are often seen by the mainstream media as crying wolf. For after all, in our fairy-tale-based political economy, things are as they're supposed to be, on the up-and-up, more so than not. Don't you see, scandals occur only so often. They're aberrations and not typical of the whole process. Oh so it goes, doesn't it? Imagine if the omniscient observer tattled; he'd tell it differently. Imagine if he could testify.

Do-gooder organizations such as Congress Watch, Public Citizen, Common Cause, the Center for Public Integrity, and Citizens for Tax Justice, trace and analyze this relationship and can attest to the statistical relationship between money sources and politicians' voting records in the U.S. Congress. But what do they know? They're pinkos and un-American, and against God, or at least that's often what their opposition portrays them to be. As a result, the watchdogs get little credit or accolades for their efforts, let alone publicity. Consequently, in contemporary American politics, the truth might not ever be known. It is not in the politicians' interests for the public to know that both the political and policy-making process are controlled by big business through campaign finance and lobbying.

Thus, this is what a PAC is designed to do, and here's how they do it. A political action committee varies by type and in time. Although their purposes are usually similar, their structure, methods, and participatory level can vary.

Here's a composite. A corporate PAC is created at the management level, typically by top management, and administered by support staff. The committee is usually managed by a board of directors or executive committee. They also decide what political issue to address, policies, and what candidates to support. Lawyers, accountants, government affairs personnel, and other middle-management staff do the administrative work.

Each corporate PAC often has an office in D.C., where the direct action in the process of government occurs. Their work varies by PAC. It can include advising the home office of candidate cooperation; recommendations for support, and policy analysis. They also politick in earnest: candidate get-acquainted sessions, fundraising, lobbying, public relations campaigns, off-the-record and out-of-sight buttonholing and dealmaking. These committees are also information providers: hosting seminars, publishing newsletters, and propagandizing their causes.

I add to this. It is here too, in Washington, where the serious work occurs, especially where the money source, the PAC, combines with their lobbyists, the latter being the corporate bagmen and influence peddlers whose task it is to grease the legislative, policy-making, and regulatory process for their own advantage, and in combination with interest groups. They call this getting access; NASCAR drivers call it gettin' the edge; I call it cheatin.'

Contrary to pluralist political theory, corporate PACs often cooperate among themselves, especially by affiliating with larger umbrella organizations such as BIPAC, the NAM, the USCOC, the National Chamber Alliance for Politics, and the National Association of Business Political Action Committee, to name a few. These organizations vary in their provider services. Generally, they promote forming PACs; provide research and candidate recommendations and endorsements, form positions, and advise on political issues. Some also contribute money to candidates, while many do not.

The corporate sector, over the last few decades successfully created an effective and powerful new political institution, that now, in the twenty-first century, plays in the political arena as a big hitter, a newly formed estate, a fifth estate, and perhaps one of the most powerful and influential.

This newly effective alliance between organizational power, especially corporate power, and its money resources, ascended from its corporate wellsprings to become the controlling stream in the flow of money-fueled influence. This confluence of forces flowed together during the last twenty years of the twentieth century, aided and abetted by the ongoing, century-long alliance between big business and the GOP. It persisted even during the years when the Republican Party was the minority and then through their ascendancy to the throne in 1980, back and forth in the 1990s, and into the stratosphere of the baroque, recently. This final ascent began and proceeded, in fits and starts, after the 1980 presidential election.

Getting what they paid for, big business no doubt gleefully watched as the Reagan Regime gutted federal regulations, and de facto, attempted to roll back the reform efforts of the previous decades. The mixed successes they had were gains made through the already strong partnership between lobbying and interest groups, and later fortified by a new tandem of campaign finance and political action committees. As a result, this new form of the dance of the titans took a twirl that's hardly stopped since.

Regardless of the successes and failures of the Regime, a new age of allied PACs and interest groups began. This new method became the standard for how politics and policy-making was to be for the rest of the century. It has persisted and will probably be a permanent part of our body politic.

As a result, the business of lobbying so prospered during the 1980s, it proliferated, occupying office space throughout Washington, and eventually spilling over into the suburbs. Some observers believed there are tens of thousands in D.C. involved in the lobbying industry, all told. From 1961 to 1982, Washington-based, corporate lobbying offices grew ten times. From 1970 to 1980, trade associations moving into D.C. doubled. In 1971, 175 firms had lobbying offices in Washington; in 1982, 2,444. From 1973 to 1983, the number of registered lobbyists tripled. In 1995, there were 10,000 registered lobbyists; by 2000, approximately 15,000; as of June 2005, 36, 135. Citizen Baroque, indeed.

If not already part of the Washington establishment by 1994, the GOP election successes opened the door wider than it had been during the previous few decades. The now-Republican-controlled Congress attempted to do their benefactors' bidding by making a good effort to further shrink the regulatory state. Corporate lobbyists wrote this legislation and money flowed into Republican Party coffers in return. Here the influence-peddling was direct; things were understood among those involved with the K-Street Project and the Contract for America.

The latter also represents what interest group lobbying is recently. When the Democrats controlled the U.S. Congress, the petitioners had to deal on their terms. The idea is to function in a greased groove, adjusting to whoever holds political power. The entrenched system was uprooted from its foundation after the GOP triumph in 1994.

Soon after, changes began, and the mechanisms were adjusted via the K-Street Project. This was the Republican Party's attempt to stop lobbyists and campaign contributors from playing both sides of the political aisle. In 1995–1996, the GOP targeted the 400 largest corporate PACs suggesting they stop contributing to Democrats. At the same time they sought out about one thousand of the top lobbyists, suggesting they disconnect from the Democrats so to enhance their ability to do business effectively with the new Republican majority. This also meant replacing Democrat-friendly personnel with Republicans.

The stakes were high because by now, Continetti suggested interest-group lobbying was so significant a force that it was approaching the level of a fifth estate, a fifth branch of government. He added that, now, interest groups determined what policy issues rose to the top for consideration and those that got discarded. The nightmare scenario of the Greider school is now reality.

The typical congressman is no longer beholden solely to his constituents because they no longer pay the bulk of his campaign bills. During the past several decades, senators and representatives have been beholden to their new constituents—lobbyists and especially corporate lobbyists who have set the tone of doing business in the capital, and are armed with a bagful of campaign contributions. This new formula for getting things done was formidable even two decades ago. It would become beyond that, to baroque, daunting in its power to influence.

Thus, during the previous thirty-five years, interest groups became the standard mechanism to gain access within the halls of the federal government. Most of them use lobbyists as artificial constituents. Many have political action committees to strengthen their cause or issue. At the forefront of all of these groups, still, is the business lobby.

As a result of their success, everyone now seems to lobby. In such an organizational society, those with a cause must form an interest group and fortify themselves with a PAC to effectively lobby their governments (from federal to local), and financially support the candidacy of those that will do their business, once in office. (This includes one-issue or ideologically based PACs) This is a nationwide trend that affects all levels of government. Overall, the method enables a level of citizenship that few individuals have.

The trend began during the late 1960s early 1970s, when public interest and grassroots, single-issue associations jumped into the political arena. They too, quickly adopted interest-group lobbying techniques. Consider this form of lobbying a forerunner to forming a PAC a bit later.

From this overall context, above, the contemporary system evolved. Today's lobbyists and interest groups, in general, have to compete with each other, as they've done for a few decades, regarding federal government policy-making, law, and regulations. Usually, their overall goals are similar to influence the process favorable to their cause or issue.

This can be a tinkering process where pieces of law, as riders and amendments, are changed, added, or dropped. This includes hindering the efforts of other lobbyists. Probably in an ideal sense, lobbyists attempt to write the text of the bill, which they often do. If not, then they want access to legislators, and in other cases, the writers of regulations, and to those who are responsible for policy-making decisions. This also spills over to the regulatory process, where they try to influence how laws are enforced through subsequent regulations. (The GOP loves to gut these agencies by putting managers from the industry to be regulated, or better, anti-regulation ideologues who through inaction negate the intent of the law/regulation, and the power of the agency to enforce in charge.) In all cases, they must persuade or dissuade decision-makers to be favorable to their specific policy agenda.

Birnbaum suggested that the leaders of the pack are corporate lobbyists (and I would argue, too, their interest groups and trade associations). He portrays the 1980s lobbying system as:

> Over time, the sheer pervasiveness of corporate lobbyists has had a major impact on government policy, beyond just the lucrative margin of legislation. The fact that lobbyists are everywhere, all the time, has led official Washington to become increasingly sympathetic to the corporate cause. This is true among Democrats as well as among Republicans.
>
> Lawmakers workdays are filled with meetings with lobbyists, many of whom represent giant corporations. And their weekends are stocked with similar encounters. When lawmakers travel to give speeches, they rarely address groups of poor people. The big-money lobbies often pick up the tab, and their representatives fill the audiences, ask the questions, and occupy the luncheon tables and throng the cocktail parties that accompany such events.[24]

The process above often operates on different levels. Officially, the lobbyists swarm Capitol Hill during the typical workday, armed with information, argument, and text. This is their official capacity as information-providing persuaders.

Lobbying organizations use a variety of methods, and their employees follow different routines. Here's an amalgamation of their workday:

Reading is an important part of the job—the *Washington Post*, *Wall Street Journal*, *New York Times*, trade journals, and the current copy of the *Congressional Record*.

Time spent at the capitol often includes attending hearings, direct lobbying of U.S. House and Senate representatives, or their staff. Face time might also include meeting regulatory officials, and sometimes White House staff. They also use indirect methods, especially advocacy and public relations campaigns designed to manipulate the electorate and adjunct stakeholders that could be affected by the policy issue. Contacting and networking with other players and attending meetings rounds out the routine.

Office work includes meeting with support staff and adjuncts to the whole process such as P.R. and advertising people, pollsters, accountants, lawyers, economists, and other experts, consultants, and specialists, depending on the policy issue.

The process often extends past the 9–5 workday to include formal and informal social functions such as dinners, fundraisers, get-acquainted socials, country-clubbing, sporting events, etc. Essentially, normative off-hours leisure time, for lobbyists and politicians, become work-time and part of the whole process. Interest groups and lobbyists also work on an informal level. The legendary martini lunch, social events, junkets, the club circuit.

At this level it can be quite personal, but ubiquitous. Call it institutionalized back-scratching and glad-handing, where favors are done out of mutual obligation. Throughout this process, corporate lobbyists, interest groups, and PACs set the tone; leading at the front of the line, or escorted to the front, while everyone else waits their turn.

Combine personal business relationships, social familiarity, and money, within an ethos of interest group culture, and the result is an effective method for getting some. If so, then corporate culture fits nicely with interest-group culture. It should, because one helped create the other.

This cozy relationship has a place for the already well-established in-and-out method between the public and private sectors. A revolving-door relationship between government service and lobbying is a lucrative benefit of this system. It also serves to feed the system by providing an almost unlimited and perhaps incestuous labor pool of government policy makers cum lobbyists. Both of them know how the system works and are more than willing to participate.

Anecdotally, people work within government and then are actively recruited by the private sector because of their work experience and its expected institutional and social connections. Having worked in a congressional office, for example, or agency, especially if creating law or policy, makes an individual an attractive catch to the lobbying trade. Experience in writing the text of law or regulations, and/or the skills in interacting to create policy, is believed to be a highly desirable and transferable skill to lobbyists. Thus, if you did this for them, come over to us and do the same thing and make more money to boot.

The method of a revolving door, and/or an open gate between business and government mentioned in chapter 5, thus also exists here. It's similar to bureaucrats and businessmen working in both the private and public sectors. In the latter, they manage government; the former, they influence government. Thus, when they switch jobs from one to the other, they take with them their connections and knowledge of how each sector works.

This, then, connects the legislator and political appointee with the petitioner—the lobbyist as go-between for their corporate client and the government. This translates into obligations fulfilled as the result of campaign finance, acquiescing to PAC and interest group pressure, and the one-on-one interaction of lobbyists pitching their cause or issue.

Providing reliable and accurate information on a particular policy issue enables an interest group to influence its development. The lobbyist, as an information provider, becomes part of the process and method, while injecting its interests into the construction of the bill or regulation.

Keep in mind this whole process is a tandem relationship. The lobbyist uses their own intellectual and social skills and reputation to persuade. At the same time, the organization they represent supports their efforts. Underlying this dual relationship is the fundamental influence the particular interest group has on the government official through campaign finance. Note too, this method can influence the creation and enforcement of regulations. At times, the political party in power actively applies or coerces its governmental philosophy on the agency's career bureaucrats.

Lobbying, interest groups, and campaign finance are powerful components of the contemporary political process, more so than in previous decades. The individuals who do this, who make the system go, are parts of work groups that often include professionals, who together are more than the caricature of handshaking, backslapping, and cigar-chomping bagmen.

In 1992, Jeffrey Birnbaum assessed the position of lobbyists at the federal level. He wrote:

> Washington has become a club in which the line between those inside and those outside the government is not clearly drawn. Corporate lobbyists have

> so suffused the culture of the city that at times they seem to be part of the government itself. One result is that corporate America, once a perennial sacrificial lamb when it came to government crackdowns, has become something of a sacred cow. Not only are lawmakers and policy-makers reluctant to make changes that would hurt businesses, they even have a tendency to try to help them, as long as budgetary pressures do not interfere.[25]

Indeed, perhaps through lobbying, combined with campaign finance, big business finally triumphed in its century-long dance of the titans. By the end of the Carter administration, big business was on the verge of attaining elite citizenship status. During the next twenty years, corporations transcended their rise and reach for the stratospheric heights of power, influence, and grandeur. By the end of the twentieth century, big business would top out, exceeding achieved levels during the Gilded Age, reaching the unprecedented levels of baroque.

During the Reagan-Bush Regime, and certainly during the Cheney-Rove Junta, the federal government became a de facto corporate-managed institution where its principal role has been to make life easier for its most important constituents—its corporate citizens. As William Greider wrote:

> Instead of popular will, the government now responds more often to narrow webs of power—the interests of major economic organizations and concentrated wealth and the influential elites surrounding them. These organizations and individuals manage to shape the largest outcomes to the extent anyone does, while they neutralize or deflect what ordinary people think and believe.[26]

As a result, big business' status in the political economy can be called corporate baroque. This means that as an institution playing in the top arena among other institutions, big business is triumphant in directing the political economy and American society as an add-on. Their first-class citizenship becomes "Citizen Baroque."

The lobbyist/interest groups sector has a potent, subtle, weapon in its operational arsenal—campaign finance. It could be called their after-dark or dinner-plate component. Attending fundraisers and dispensing election campaign funds are all-important parts of the lobbying process because contributing to a politician's election campaign war chest all but guarantees some level of access to legislators. This relationship is understood by both the dispenser of funds and the recipient. Money buys access and hopefully, influence.

Expressed euphemistically, campaign contributions gains (read: buys), access to harried, busy, politicians. In effect, lobbyists become citizen constituents. At the same time, however, behind closed doors, it is usually an unspoken rule, but clearly understood among the givers and takers: If you take campaign contributions, then you are expected to do their bidding, to take care of them. PAC money buys influence. That's its purpose. Why else would PACs give money to shoo-ins; to both candidates in an election; to politicians they don't agree with; later, to the eventual election winner, even if they didn't originally support? (Two plus two has always been four on my side of the working-class tracks.)

In other words, as a politician, you do not bite the hand that feeds you. It's government's dirty little secret. Money was, is, and always will be, power. Money for nothing is, at best, a myth; at worst, a lie. To get what you pay for is reality. To believe that campaign contributions don't necessarily get results is fairy tales. Money *does* buy influence and campaign finance when stripped of its spin, and dodge and weave, is de facto, grease, bribery, payment for future considerations.[27] Both the givers and the takers know this, and both sides believe in it regardless of any sense of distaste. William Grieder is right.

Now immersed in the era of interest-group politicians and its PAC money, it is commonly understood by seasoned politicians and then taught to budding politicians, that to get elected to the U.S. Congress, one must enter the PAC money system. This is standard operating procedure among the Washington community operatives: politicians, bureaucrats, lobbyists, PAC managers, consultants, etc.

Once money is taken, a business relationship results, and the contributor expects cooperation from the politician and political party for money tendered. This means a politician is expected to legislate in a friendly manner. Is it, de facto, bribery and influence peddling? Of course it is. Hooded behind the veneer of popular democracy, it is essentially a reversion to the corruption ethos of the nineteenth-century political machine. It just has a new face, but it still nods and winks, just like it did a century ago. It's more subtle, but it's understood by most politicians that campaign contributions usually have strings attached. Now, and over the last few decades, to get ahead in D.C. costs money, specifically campaign financing. This is the way it is in an organizational political economy of rabidly competing interests.

"You get what you pay for," is, at least usually, true, in politics. Of course campaign finance contributions in large amounts are, de facto, bribery; a close adjunct to, and part of, what lobbying really is—influence peddling. Those in power, especially those managing large corporations or unions, or special-interest/advocacy groups, know that they want something for their money. Thus, "If this guy from ______________ won't do business with us, we'll go around him and work through someone else." This is partially innate and incipient behavior. Defenders of the system would call it natural behavior and an accepted way of doing business. As presented, this system began over one hundred years ago and will persist since those who seek office will not poison the blood that sustains them. It is self-preservation.

Campaign finance has a life of its own and it too, is now at the baroque level, despite McCain-Feingold and its predecessors. The major participants—

politicians, lobbyists, PACs and their contributors—all know how the system they created together operates. Their system is successful for all of those involved and because it works well enough to get what they want, they have little impetus to change it, despite their critics.

The politician wants a job and the power and prestige that goes along with this occupation. To get this, he has to finance a campaign, and he knows well what is necessary to get from declared candidate to elected official. Despite public rhetoric and private recrimination and mea culpa's, most of them quickly get on the program and hustle for the money. Thus, they will not make much of a concerted effort to change the system that enables them to achieve what they want. Why would a politician attempt to change a system that benefits all those involved, despite public rhetoric to the contrary? Lament all the while, it seems normal to go along with the status quo; go with the flow; don't make waves; get on the program. If you want a career in politics, you must play the game of networking; doing grassroots work as an apprentice, and then rising through the ranks of either or both the private-sector job, and/or the political party, and then ultimately positioning yourself to seek office and fund it. Once these preliminaries are accomplished, these hoops jumped through, the process ascends ethereally where manna, campaign finance, is the air, food and blood of the political animal. There, the political universe is set; the rules are established. In order to survive, one must get along and go along with the way it is. Consequently, in this context, why would the politician want it to change? Even those that oppose the system as it is are outnumbered, and also realize that the system is greater than the sum of its participants. They don't want to make waves, and they certainly fear and maybe even loathe those who promote and perpetuate the system as it is. Thus, it persists.

This combination of political action committee with interest-group politics formed the final planks in the new structure of organization taking control of our political process. It was the final and perhaps the most important triumph of the organizational revolution.

Through the potent combination of campaign finance and lobbying, big business strongly influences, if not controls, the electoral process and the subsequent ideology and method of policy-making and management of the federal government. Even though it took over one hundred years to accomplish, the concept of corporation, as originally created by the captains of industry during the Gilded Age, now directs the American political economy, similar to what they accomplished in the private sector.

In this century-long process, they supplanted the nineteenth-century paradigm with a new organizational revolution. The Wiebian paradigm can now be replaced with Greider's, where the citizen baroque now turns the wheel that steers society.

Notes

1. George Draffan, *The Elite Consensus*, 5.
2. Thayer, *Money Tree*, 35, 30–31.
3. Thomas C. Cochran and William Miller, *The Age of Enterprise*, 154–155.
4. Gregory Kolko, *The Triumph of Conservatism*, 161–162. (Original cite: *Bankers' Magazine*, Volume 62, 1901, pp. 497–499.)
5. Schriftgiesser, *The Lobbyists*, 35.
6. Woodrow Wilson and William B. Hale, *The New Freedom*, 23–24, 32, 97.
7. Thomas C. Cochran and William Miller, *The Age of Enterprise*, 343–344.
8. Schriftgiesser, *The Lobbyists*, 48.
9. *Annals*, September 1929, 34.
10. Stuart Chase, *Democracy under Pressure*, 23.
11. Deakin, *The Lobbyists*, 8–9.
12. David J. Saari, *Global Corporations and Sovereign Nations* 94.
13. Vogel, *Kindred*, 277.
14. Marchand, *Corporate Soul*, 2.
15. Louise Overacker, "Campaign Funds in the Presidential Election of 1936," *American Political Science Review*, 31 (June 1937), 497.
16. Elizabeth Drew, *Politics and Money* 2–3.
17. Thayer, *Money Tree*, 66–67.
18. Dan Clawson, et al., "The Logic of Business Unity: Corporate Contributions to the 1980 Congressional Elections," *American Sociological Review*, 51 (December 1986), 803, 806.
19. Kathryn L. Ashford, "The Role of Corporations in the 1980 Congressional Elections," *Sociological Inquiry*, 56 (Fall, 1986), 409–410, 415, 420–426; Vogel, *Fluctuating*, 240–242.
20. Mintz and Cohen, *America, Inc.*, 151.
21. Quoted in, Stern, *Best*, 194.
22. Stern, *Best*, 77.
23. Berry, *Interest*, 117.
24. Birnbaum, *Lobbyists*, 4.
25. Birnbaum, *Lobbyists*, 3.
26. Greider, *People*, 12.
27. Here is an acute example: In 1987, Charlie Keating's Lincoln Savings & Loan failed. Allegations surfaced that he received favorable treatment from the U.S. Senate from some politicians who had received loopholed campaign contributions. Later, when questioned about this, Keating replied: "whether my financial support in any way influenced several political figures to take up my cause, I want to say in the most forceful way, I can certainly hope so." (Green, *Selling Out*, pp. 66–67; Sorauf, *Inside Campaign Finance*, p. 171; Birnbaum, *The Money Men*, p. 46.)

7

Sovereign Baroque

Multinational Enterprise and Globalization

IN MARCH 1972, during spring break, I went to Torremolinos in Spain.[1] While there, I had my first experience with globalization. There, I had at least one meal in Wimpy's. I don't remember what I ate; however, I do recall that the coffee was served with a beaker of cream. I said, then, after adding the cream you could easily cut it with a knife. It was that strong.

We were lodged in luxury, what today we call a timeshare, fully furnished, almost a palatial condo (a bidet was an object of mystery), kitchen and dining room included, with a seaside view. We bought Campbell's Soup so we could see what it tasted like even though we couldn't read the label. Then, I noticed, but since forgotten, other American-made food products for sale, far away from the soup factory nearby my home in Chicago.

While hobnobbing along the Mediterranean, we took a side trip, renting a car, and paying about $2.50 for gas, I think? Our destination through early morning fog and rain was the town of Ronda and the nine-hundred-foot gorge that ran through it. We arrived at dawn. The site was magnificent. The town looked medieval, with narrow, cobblestoned streets barely wide enough for two small European-made cars. That Sunday morning, all in black, walked women to church, no doubt. It was like a subtitled movie scene, except that amid the postcard-quality antiquity were small, bright yellow and red signs of contemporary reality—Kodak. Indeed, an American presence even there, in this very old place, and the year was 1972.

That presence was nothing new to Europeans. By then, an American corporate presence was a common occurrence. Some had been there for decades, and a few others, for almost a century.

During its emergence and subsequent development, American corporations expanded their markets overseas, thus becoming multinational corporations.[2] Usually a firm started out small and simple. This could be setting up sales offices or retail stores; buying into an existing foreign company, there; opening up purchasing offices, etc.

These efforts often served as seeds to grow within foreign economies, where American corporations could replicate there what they did here. During this stage, vertical integration could occur: plantations, refineries, and factories; mines and smelters purchased; exporting within the host-country's regional market. Eventually, some of these firms began to resemble their parent company in structure, function, and method.

For this chapter, an American multinational company is a large corporation created, chartered, and based in the United States. This firm has either production, assembly, offices, sales or service facilities, in foreign countries.

International trade has been part of the human condition for much of time. Over this millennium, worldwide trade grew and expanded as societies progressed. From these deep roots, multinational enterprise (MNE), emerged, and grew to dominate international trade and finance. American corporations have been part of this process from our colonial beginnings. By the end of the twentieth century, this ascent can be called globalization. It is also a principal foundation of corporate baroque.

The rise of American business interests to these celestial heights of baroque had simple beginnings. Our first internationally focused businesses were our colonial merchants, who engaged in commodities trade and shipping. These operations typically were family-sized firms, usually self-financed, and operating on a small scale. Of note, these were the first companies to either send agents abroad or have someone represent them overseas.

They operated in a political economy strictly defined by British mercantilism, which limited what could be done by a subject colony. In this economic world, the colonial agents operated as part of a greater system, with a government that set policies, terms, and controls that usually favored the metropolitan mother country over its colonial subjects.

Despite its protection, colonial merchants diligently defied its restrictions, pursuing their own interests. They did operate within the British colonial system, like loyal subjects were expected to. However, when the opportunity arose to give the colonial merchants an edge, they violated the system's operating conditions. This contentiousness was not resolved. Instead, the colonies separated, winning their independence.

As colonies grew to become a new country, American merchant traders had to enter the world trade arena alone and as a new, undersized participant. Then, we were truly an underdeveloped country. Nevertheless,

American merchant traders, expanded their efforts abroad and increased their global trade.

These efforts lagged behind those of the Europeans, but prior to the American Civil War, American firms were setting up merchant-trader outposts far away in Canton, China, the Philippines, Russia, Hawaii, Madagascar, Zanzibar, Bombay, Chile, Argentina, and nearby in Canada, Mexico, and Cuba, and also in London and Liverpool.

Like their colonial predecessors, these merchant firms were typically small and many were short-lived. Nevertheless, the seeds of the future American multinational enterprise (AMNE), were planted there and then. (W. R. Grace, an original, dates back to 1854, for example.) These disparately scattered seeds, germinated slowly, if at all, surrounded and dominated by old-growth European-based competitors. However, it was the start of a business culture that over the subsequent 200 years, did grow and expand to eventually dominate a global economy.

That road to dominance was long and winding, and, at times, seldom traveled during much of the nineteenth century. This new country, the United States of America, as the rest of the Western Hemisphere, lagged behind the Old World in production, trade, and commerce. For much of that century, American economic participation abroad was limited to trading and shipping; railroad and telegraph building; some banking; selling or exporting what few American homemade products there were at the time. Of the latter, Samuel Colt built a pistol manufacturing plant in England, in 1852. That company, the first American foreign factory, failed, and was sold in 1859.

However, this first-time effort was not a predictor of the future. To the contrary, American enterprise began to emerge after the Civil War, and in its wake, AMNE eventually followed.

Mira Wilkins wrote two seminal books on AMNE. In the first, *The Emergence of Multinational Enterprise*, she stated that the lack of a transoceanic connection was a fundamental reason impeding American direct foreign investment (DFI). Adding to this, I offer a lack of interest by American businessmen. Instead of looking out to sea, America looked to the West and the conquest of their continent. At the same time, American industry was not developed enough. These companies (except for Standard Oil), were, at best, slightly larger than mid-sized and not capable of exporting capital or even expanding their markets. This wouldn't occur until after 1890. Then, interest in overseas markets emerged, perhaps as an adjunct to the burgeoning American industrial revolution and the subsequent rise of American corporate capitalism.

When American enterprise started to look out to sea, the first were seeking export sales; a few wanted to manufacture overseas (others developing railroads, mining, and agriculture in Canada and Latin America), and as a response to worldwide protectionism. This was the general pattern of American DFI from 1863 to 1897. Overall, it was a gradual process, less noticeable than significant. Instead, during those decades, Manifest Destiny prevailed.

During that era, there was one, significant, pioneering exception. Mira Wilkins wrote that our first international company was Singer Sewing Machine. Standard Oil, General Electric, NCR and International Harvester, followed.

Isaac M. Singer created the Singer Sewing Machine Company, then called I. M. Singer & Company. He tinkered and improved what was on the market in 1850 and patented his version, in 1851, here and abroad. (Of note, back then, using a contraption to sew, was something new. Demand had to be created. Also, this included credit plans and technical support to both business and home customers.)

In 1855, he sold his French patent to a merchant over there. Singer also provided technical assistance at that start-up. Despite good intentions, this first effort wasn't very successful because the French licensee didn't fulfill its agreements. Consequently, in 1863, Singer focused his strategy on direct sales in its American market. Here, the machines began selling to consumers on installment. They were successful. In 1855, Singer sold 883 machines; in 1859, more than 10,000.

From this success, Singer sent sales agents to Glasgow and London, by 1861. Britain became a base for marketing sewing machines to Belgium and then Spain, and into Germany, by 1865. In 1868, Singer began assembling machines in Glasgow. By 1874, approximately half of Singer's sewing machine sales were abroad. (Of note, its main European competitor, Wheeler & Wilson Company, began direct sales in Europe in 1878. They couldn't compete with Singer.) By the end of the decade, Singer was number one, with twenty-six sales offices in Britain and others in Paris, Madrid, Brussels, Milan, Basil, Cape Town, Bombay, and Auckland. There, Singer sold wholesale and retail. From such regional outposts, Singer marketed throughout Europe, Africa, China, Australia, the Philippines, Brazil, Peru, and Chile. Before 1900, Singer had manufacturing or assembly plants in Switzerland, Canada, and a foundry in Austria. By then it was the largest sewing machine company.

Between 1870 and 1899, other American companies followed Singer's lead. Some followed its example of licensing sales, then assembly and manufacturing: Baldwin Locomotives, NCR, International Harvester, Remington, and Otis Elevator, were some of the first. Others also expanded abroad: Western Union, Bell Telephone, Edison Electric, Western Electric, GE, Westinghouse, Parke-Davis, Eastman (Kodak), Standard Oil, Equitable, New York Life, Mutual, American Express. Thus, by the turn of the century, American interests abroad included: sewing machines, typewriters, electrical appliances, printing presses, cameras and film, drugs, elevators, boilers, reapers, insurance, mining and agricultural plantations. Mira Wilkins suggested that early on, our nascent corporate sector created products that became the first symbols of America abroad: McCormick reapers, Kodak and Standard Oil; later, in the twentieth century—Coke, Ford, IBM, Boeing, and Helena Rubenstein followed the trail laid out by these corporate pathfinders.

After the turn of the century, American corporations built on their predecessors' initial efforts abroad. Consequently, American corporate internationalization was both an adjunct to and a significant factor in the twentieth-century phase of our industrial revolution. Several types of American corporations looked abroad: Alcoa, Bethlehem Steel, DuPont, American Tobacco, the future IBM, Ford, GM, USS, SO-NY, SO-NJ, and United Fruit.

According to Mira Wilkins, by 1900, Standard Oil was a major multinational (MNC) or (MN's). SO's foreign investment was horizontally and vertically integrated: sales, marketing, distribution, purchasing, refining, extraction and shipping. Their foreign interests were in the Far East, Europe, and Canada. Evan after the breakup of the Standard Oil Trust, in 1911, the various companies maintained and expanded their foreign investments. These twentieth-century corporations followed similar paths overseas, in the footsteps of their nineteenth-century pathfinders. Thus the spread of AMNE progressed.

Prior to World War I, American corporations invested worldwide. How much and to what degree varied. Europe received the most, then Canada. For example, in 1901, England's largest plant was our Westinghouse Corporation. The largest oil company operating in Europe was Standard Oil. Shortly after Henry Ford went into business, Canadians and Brits proposed arrangements.

There was less interest elsewhere. Since Latin America was typically rural and undeveloped, almost all U.S. entrepreneurial activity there focused on natural resources: mining, oil extraction, and agriculture. Copper mines in Chile attracted most American DFI. Some sales offices, oil exploration, plantation agriculture, and building public utilities and railroad systems drew U.S. entrepreneurial interest. Mexico received the most. Thus, the American corporate investment horizon stretched across the Atlantic toward our metropolitan forefathers, and south to our neighbors. There was little interest in Africa or Asia.

The foundations for the future AMNE were in place on the eve of the guns of August 1914. Within a few years, this foundation became a launchpad, advancing American corporate presence throughout the world economy. This presence survived World War I, accelerated during the 1920s, and stagnated during World War II. After that, AMNE began a fifty-year rise into the stratosphere, toward sovereign baroque by the end of the millennium.

Back before World War I, AMNE continued the previously established patterns: Canada, South America, and Western Europe. During the war in Europe, some U.S. MNs attempted to fill trade vacuums. The war did not deter American efforts to expand in noncombatant areas. Generally, this occurred in lesser-developed countries (LDCs), and nearby, in Canada; less frequently in Asia. In these regions, American corporations usually invested in agriculture, produce growing and processing, mining and ore processing, oil exploration and production, indigenous transportation systems, and some manufacturing and distillation. Their markets of opportunity included: Canada, Mexico, Indonesia, and Japan. For example, in Sumatra, the U.S. Rubber Company bought 80,000 acres of plantation land in 1910 and expanded their holdings; Goodyear did similarly, in 1917. Both Firestone and Goodyear also had purchasing offices in Singapore. Other American corporations made similar investments in other markets: Cuban sugar; meat packing plant expansions and start-ups in South America by Swift, Armour, Wilson, and Morris. General Electric Co. began manufacturing light bulbs in Brazil and increased direct investment in Japan. Throughout, it was typical to selectively invest; buying piecemeal, on a small scale, became the pattern.

By war's end, AMNE improved their overall international standing, as the result of a second wave of DFI. They were not yet sector leaders, just improving their market positions. In Europe, nation-rebuilding hindered American corporate efforts to vigorously expand immediately after the armistice. Complicating matters was a worldwide, postwar recession, 1920–1921. Instead, AMNE looked to England, Canada, and in the Western Hemisphere, to increase their presence, or to initiate new ventures. Such economic doldrums persisted until about mid-decade. By then, the American economy righted itself (circa, 1923), prosperity and boom times followed after 1925. MNE, too, was part of this revival. For example, American food products moved overseas in various forms. Some companies sold their products only, while others also produced them there; joint ventures and licensing too. Thus, brand-name products by Borden, Swift, Carnation, and Pet could be found on store shelves in Canada and Europe.

There was no set pattern for this expansion abroad. It varied by industry type and country, with big business leading the way. American big business corporations marketed their products almost globally, using a variety of methods. Some licensed their products through existing native companies. Other companies built their own plants on foreign soil. The degree to which that corporations set up overseas varied by company, industry group, locale, foreign circumstances, and institutional status. During that decade, several American big business corporations had interests overseas, but in degrees and types: Westinghouse, DuPont, GE, Jantzen, Montgomery Ward, Woolworth's, A&P, Safeway, and Piggly-Wiggly, among others.

Consider General Electric, which by 1919 was an international company, operating in Latin America, Europe, and Asia with sales offices in Australia and South Africa. In contrast, competing Westinghouse had only licensing arrangements abroad.

In the automobile industry, with Ford leading GM and Chrysler, they manufactured or assembled cars abroad during the 1920s. Ford had sites in Canada, Latin America, Turkey, and Spain. GM expanded abroad similarly.

By decade's end, Goodyear, Firestone, Kodak, SO-NJ, Texaco, Cities Service, Sun Oil, Union Oil, Quaker State, Anaconda, Hoover, Remington Rand, Proctor & Gamble, and others could be called international.

By 1929, there were 1,057 AMNE manufacturing sites overseas. An American presence, to some degree, extended globally, and despite another war, and a cold war, their presence was on the way to becoming permanent and eventually baroque.

The worldwide depression during the 1930s altered the makeup of AMNE abroad. Economic and political turmoil overseas often negatively affected American corporate ventures. In some countries, political revolutions occurred. In politically stable places, changing economic conditions and resulting policy adjustments, currency devaluations, restrictions on money leaving the country, fluctuating foreign exchange rates, tariffs, import restrictions, tax increases, and expropriation, all could affect the American transnationals. Across world economies such factors as these remained in place until the world went to total war at decades's end.

Altogether, host country conditions diminished American corporate interests from sustaining a significant level of foreign investment, or expanding what assets they already had abroad. In some places, shutdowns occurred. Other firms sold their interests, and in an odd irony, tariff restrictions forced some American corporations to expand their foreign holdings so that they could remain operating in those lands.

Overall, in most of these cases, the host's situations deteriorated as the world depression deepened, resulting in plant closures anyway. In other instances, where host country conditions discouraged direct investment, American corporations sought alternatives elsewhere. When this did occur, it was usually in new markets such as in Latin America, Asia, or Australia. Such actions, which varied by country and industry sector, were noble efforts, and exceptions. The global economy in worldwide depression offered few sustainable opportunities for DFI.

There was at least one significant exception to this pattern; an effort that would reverberate globally, for the rest of the century. In 1933, Standard Oil-California (SOCAL), contracted with King ibn Saud to explore for oil. In 1939, SOCAL increased the exploration area, and later added more American firms: Texas Company/later, Texaco, Standard Oil of New Jersey/later Exxon, and

Socony-Vacuum Oil Company/later Mobil. In 1944, this consortium became the Arabian American Oil Company (ARAMCO).

They essentially went into a desert wasteland and extracted revolutionary wealth for the Saudis. In the process, the Americans also altered traditional Saudi society from top to bottom, bringing a millennial prosperity, based on modern big business methods, institutional power, and capital assets. AMNE planted these seeds in the desert during the dead season of world depression. The resulting oasis persisted, altering the world in the process. What they accomplished there became the institutional foundation and eventual catalyst for economic expansion, culminating with what we recently call globalization.

But this did not occur elsewhere during the 1930s. Contemporary economic theory did not offer solutions to these problems.[3] Mobilizing for war, did, and once hostilities began, the world economy changed. Domestic industries all turned toward their war effort, and American holdings abroad, if in Axis countries, were expropriated for that effort.

World war caused market destruction at worst, and at best, disruption. After the war ended, AMNE attempted, in fits and starts, to rekindle the spark. How they proceeded depended on market sector, host economic and internal political conditions, and company strategy, among others.

Most of Europe and Asia were war torn; much of once-occupied Europe, Germany, Japan, and Russia, destroyed. Consequently, diplomatic factors and military situations, the lack of reconstruction funds and viable native currencies, destroyed economies and infrastructure, all combined to stifle AMNE investment abroad.[4]

Eventually, postwar global reconstruction presented opportunity for the spread of AMNE. At first, it was a difficult task because a shattered global economy didn't offer immediate marketable opportunities. Consequently, most American firms marketed domestically. Exporting, was a typical, albeit temporary, method for trading abroad. War-damaged societies had to be rebuilt first, and then opportunity followed.

This took about ten years, to the mid-1950s, when European economies righted themselves enough to create a significant demand for American products. A rapid overseas expansion occurred, and American corporations moved abroad in force. Robert Gilpin suggested that *Pax Americana* was an important enabler for the spread of AMNE then. Professor John Fayerweather wrote that the MNC became "a central institution in the tremendous postwar expansion of international business."[5]

Thus, over a twelve-year period, AMNE ascended, initiating the modern era of MNE at this time, circa 1955. By 1957, 2,800 U.S. firms invested in about 10,000 endeavors overseas. Ten years later, there were over 4,500 firms. Their global reach extended throughout what was then called the Free World:

North and South America, Canada, Northern and Western Europe, Australia; parts of Africa, Asia Minor, and Asia. To where, and what degree, again, varied according to a variety of conditions. Generally, AMNE principally set up in Western Europe, perhaps in response to the competitive threat posed by the start-up of the European Common Market, in 1958. By 1960, Europeans could buy a variety of American products: frozen pies, instant coffee, ready-to-wear clothing, hair dye, roll-on deodorants, and shaving cream, among others. (Many of these came with advertising jingles selling them, created by American advertising companies such as: J. Walter Thompson, McCann-Erickson, BBDO, Young & Rubicam, Foote, Cone & Belding.) They could also patronize supermarkets, discount stores, and roadside motels, all American brands.

The term "multinational corporation" appeared in the 1960s. By 1963, American investors held ownership in thousands of European situations, with most of them in Great Britain. Others of note were in Switzerland and West Germany.

In total, 386 of the 500 largest U.S. corporations, and a host of smaller-sized firms, had international holdings. Most of these efforts were in Western Europe: Union Carbide, Corn Products, IBM, Celanese Corporation, American Express, SO-NJ, and Monsanto, for example, all made major investments prior to 1973. Some others were: Heinz, Raytheon, Pet Foods, Colgate. Some of the American products in Europe were: Corcidin, Coke, cigarettes, Aunt Jemina, Uncle Ben's, Minute Maid, Heinz Ketchup, Del Monte, Maxwell House, Sea & Ski, Remington razors, Gillette Blue Blades, Camay, Palmolive, and for me, in Spain, Campbell's Soup.

As a result, by mid-decade, AMNE generated a significant part of their production, through exports. Some were also manufacturing in more than one country. For example, IBM, Ford, and International Harvester did not build complete products in any single nation. Ford built transmissions in Belgium, engines in England, and the Capri automobile in England and West Germany. They built the Escort there similarly. Harvester built tractors, combining components from France and West Germany. IBM combined their 360 model mainframes from components made in Britain, France, West Germany, and Italy.

Consider the method, above, and the salutations, below, to be foreshadowing globalization years before it occurred. Perhaps, its seeds were here?

Already in 1963, *Business Week* crowed that AMNE was ubiquitous worldwide. Also, during these times, GM chairman Frederic Donner touted: "the emergence of the modern industrial corporation as an institution that is transcending national boundaries."[6]

Christopher Tugendhat, in Europe, observed the budding phenomenon of international corporations. He wrote, in 1971, that since 1945, there had been incredible growth in DFI, and that the international company with subsidiaries in many countries is no longer a rarity; it is well on the way to becoming the characteristic industrial organization of the age.

The Americans are mainly responsible for the change.[7]

Thus, awareness of TNCs as a budding force during the 1960s. By 1967, 364 of the 500 top world corporations were American. In total, American corporations invested $54.6 billion, in 1966; compared to $25.2 billion, in 1957, and $7.2 billion in 1946. Nasrollah Fatemi charted American TNC growth as: 7,417 foreign affiliates in 1950; 10,272, in 1957; 23,282, in 1966.

By 1970, more than 3,000 American firms had foreign holdings of various size and type. In 1950, U.S. overseas investment equaled $32 billion; 1968, $146 billion. When ranked by national product, a 1970 list of countries included GM at 24th; Standard Oil, at 27th; Ford, 29th.; GE, 43rd; and Mobil, Chrysler, and Unilever, 47th to 49th. When AMNE abroad, are added together, as a single economy, it ranked third, in 1970, behind the United States, and the USSR. Then, most TNCs were American. They led the way. By 1977, there were 2,286 American TNCs; Great Britain, 1,706; Germany, 1,450.

This trend slackened during the 1970s due to political factors and economic conditions worldwide. Noticeable sell-offs of foreign holdings occurred between 1971 and 1975. Profits decrease was the cause.

This pattern was temporary; MNE surged during the next decade. Recall that large institutions, corporations in this case, usually have the ability to weather most of the potential problems within any marketplace or political economy. This was true, then. TNCs weathered the economic doldrums of the 1970s, and continued to progress.

By the 1980s, AMNE extended far across the horizons, doing business almost worldwide. This economic sector was strongly poised for what came next—globalization, a topic that later concludes this chapter.

Perhaps the process overseas was similar to the corporate sector's domestic triumphs. The expansion of the product or service and its producer or provider creates increments of economic, then political and social power. This occurred in the U.S. throughout the twentieth century. Eventually, a similar process repeated itself when an American corporate institution went overseas: Singer, Coca-Cola, Standard Oil, Ford, etc.

Over time, this pattern introduced a new institutional cultural factor that was the next step above the baroque citizenship defined in chapter 6. Now, individual corporations, through their presence and influence within host countries, have experienced and acquired some of the trappings of nation-state sovereignty: influencing policy making and governing within their host countries; affecting the course of the host economy by its presence and market power; carrying out semblances of foreign policy either competing with, or independent of, or with the U.S. government. In extreme cases, a corporation forces or lobbies our federal government to make certain policy decisions, or act at the diplomatic level. Thus, AMNE goes beyond its original role as a participant in any given economy. It becomes a political and social force, both home and abroad.

Big American corporations had rights of citizenship in the United States. Abroad, big business became quasi-institutional citizens adhering to their host country's laws and regulations, operating in and influencing their host's political economy, and, in some instances, that of the surrounding region. Over time, these interactions varied by firm, by host country, and in some instances, by decade.

As foreigners, American corporations faced a variety of situations overseas: host country laws, social and cultural customs, political philosophies, diplomacy and foreign relations, domestic policies and politics, and economic systems, to name a few. These conditions often varied by country and region.

On a higher plane, AMNE sometimes had to maneuver among conflicting foreign policies at home and abroad. World war and the Cold War were the larger situations. Beneath these were lesser factors such as multinational or bilateral trade agreements (i.e., the Common Market, later GATT and NAFTA), foreign country diplomatic policies and global competition with other countries' multinational enterprise.

Within this complex latticework, AMNE grew and expanded successfully after World War II. Along the way, these corporations fostered the growth of globalization, becoming a prime mover worldwide, similar to what they did at home. Hence, sovereign baroque.

This institutional growth was the direct result of corporate economic power. Being a source of finance capital, top-notch technology, managerial expertise, and makers of good stuff, combine to enable a big corporation to commiserate with those in the hall of nation-states. This arrangement and rise to this level was a century-long process that trailed and then paralleled America's domestic corporate growth. An institutional journey that began as an economic manifest destiny, piloted by the late nineteenth-century captains of industry, eventually became a global triumph.

Similar to the dance of the titans within the American domestic political economy, AMNE had to do another dance within the nation-states where they wanted to do business. This interaction ranged from the plenipotentiary level to functioning correctly within new locales, in faraway places.

The contest abroad went similarly as it did at home. The corporation wanted to satisfy its own goals, strategies, and outcomes, and so did their host governments. In turn, a corporation's way of doing things had to fit into where they were setting up. This also included negotiations and renegotiations between company and host country, making contracts that reflected what each negotiator wanted for themselves. These clashes of corporate institutional cultures and foreign political economies marked the twentieth-century history of AMNE abroad.

Overseas, this dance of the titans is over 100 years old. Back then, this included fitting into, or competing with the legal European cartel system; being required to manufacture products where they were sold; tariffs, customs laws, import restrictions; favoritism of domestic producers, and inducement subsidies.

Here's some examples of this. Mexico invited foreign investment, beginning in 1877. Then, they sought railroad-building financing. During the 1890s, Mexican mining laws also encouraged foreign investment. Soon after, copper mining boomed, and silver and lead mining also prospered. All this occurred within the Mexican political economy that included internal taxes, export taxes, labor unrest, and government purchases of railroad stock.

After 1911, turmoil in Mexico changed the relations between the government and foreign businesses. Afterward, Mexican newspapers emphasized how American corporations controlled, and thus, exploited domestic resources, and the labor force. Contrasts between American wealth and Mexican poverty, drew resentment. American corporate company towns drew similar scorn. Festering nationalism and lingering resentment of the war in 1848, added to this antipathy. Rumors also spread regarding American corporate interference in the 1911 government overthrow. While civil war raged, American businessmen faced labor shortages, and in some places, rebels expropriated American supplies and property. This caused some American firms to divest their holdings. Those that remained (i.e., oil companies), had to function under the rules set up by whatever political or military group was in power, at a given time or place. Complicating the situation there, the U.S. government intervened in 1914, landing troops at Vera Cruz.

Similarly, political events also affected American DFI in the Caribbean Basin: the Spanish-American War of 1898, the Panama Canal, and internal dissention in Venezuela. Prior to 1898, there was little American DFI in this region. Railroads, mining, public utilities and more so, agriculture, drew American interest. The grand total was small.

The five-month-long Spanish-American War changed the circumstances in the Caribbean. American entrepreneurs invested within Cuba, especially in sugar plantations. One year later, in 1899, the United Fruit Company (UF), began operations there. Later, it became a major AMN throughout Latin America. Other American interests included tobacco and banana plantation start-ups. The American Tobacco Company began making cigars and cigarettes in Puerto Rico in 1899 and invested in Cuba in 1902. Soon to follow were Pabst Blue Ribbon and Coca-Cola. American entrepreneurial interests, of various sizes and endeavors, ranging from agriculture to banking, then spread further into the region, to Panama and Nicaragua. Building the Panama Canal boomed that area somewhat.

For example, the United Fruit Company emerged as a dominant American presence, one that persisted, in Latin America, for decades. When first formed, United Fruit had holdings in Jamaica, Santo Domingo, Cuba, Costa Rica, Columbia, Nicaragua, and Honduras. This original product base included orange trees, coconut, rubber, cacao, sugar, and cattle production.

To operate in the region, UF and others had to negotiate their status with each host government. This could include taxation, land-grant use; building or operating railroads; setting up public utility systems, and building company towns.

American entrepreneurs did not have unfettered access to these countries. Colombia blocked entry. Venezuela didn't encourage an American presence for a time. Mexico nationalized railroads, imposed more taxes and coerced loans. Others canceled concessions contracts summarily. Where there were times of trouble, the host government often couldn't control civil unrest or suppress revolutions or counterrevolutions.

During these early times of North American business expansion into Latin America, their corporate presence in any given country varied with who was governing a country, and for how long. Sometimes, host governments welcomed foreign interests, placing a positive value on such entrepreneurial presence. Others didn't want a North American presence. This could change depending on who governed and how they persisted. Such instability marked the Latin American political economies that our corporations functioned in, for the first decades of the twentieth century. Indeed, before World War II, the general attitude of Latin American nation-states toward the presence of Anglo-European MN's was more negative than positive. The prevailing attitude, usually created by indigenous elites, viewed foreign corporate presence as dangerously exploitative. This was especially the case regarding extractive industries, such as plantation agriculture, and mining. The presence of United Fruit is a case in point, representing both the good and bad relationship between foreign corporations and host country.

Of all the American entrepreneurial activity in the Caribbean Basin, United Fruit Company emerged a giant. It grew to dominate some of the economies where it operated, and its presence in the region, lasted through most of the twentieth century.

Usually, the corporate monolith abroad, similar to at home, triumphed in the long run. Their successes sustained their institutional persistence, with most AMNE surviving whatever trepidations they encountered, with the huge exception of their corporate deaths, succumbing to communism. Even the Ugly Americans usually succeeded more so than failing.

Although American DFI in Latin America lagged compared to other regions, it was one component of a larger expansive movement abroad by American entrepreneurs prior to August 1914. During these nascent times, American DFI was an adjunct to, and roughly paralleled the burgeoning mass-production industrial revolution developing at home. As American enterprise emerged and started up the path to splendor, its overseas little brothers followed their leader's pathway to institutional greatness and power. This process was still in its beginnings. It was, nevertheless, a trend that would strengthen and persist despite obstacles of all size and scale, subsequently encountered over the decades of the rest of the century. The first of these impediments was the result of smoldering nation-state power politics, a long fuse that finally ignited, in 1914, in the Balkans. The Great War was about to begin.

Wartime affected DFI first and foremost. During World War I, the Central Powers seized control of all foreign-owned enterprises. Germany had foreign investments in the U.S., and as a result, according to Mira Wilkins, Germany was not harsh in policies toward American interests there.

This was not the case in newly revolutionized Russia. There, Singer Sewing Machines, New York Life Insurance, International Harvester, GE, Westinghouse, and Parke-Davis all took heavy losses. In contrast, American corporations in Great Britain and in unoccupied France flourished (GE, Ford, Singer, for examples), operating as part of their host's war production effort.

After the war, the 1920s might have roared in the United States. Such exuberance and progress did not spill over abroad. The prosperity decade resounded only on our side of the Atlantic. Worldwide, doors closed as nation-states politically, economically, and diplomatically retrenched. Doldrums in Europe resulted in storm clouds, again, gathering on the horizon.

Conditions also weren't favorable in the Western Hemisphere, south of our border. Postwar Latin America presented an unstable economic environment. Most of these recently independent nations operated similarly to their colonial past. Despite model governments on paper, dictators controlled. Coupled with nascent anti-foreign nationalism, host countries could be unstable environments for foreign holdings. Where once countries welcomed the presence of DFI, now in several places, nation's attitudes became negative. Sometimes, host governments took direct action. In the decades after World War I, host regimes throughout Latin America, nationalized foreign-owned companies. This was the case for railroads and trolley companies and electric utility firms.

For example, in Mexico, political instability negatively affected AMNE prior to World War I; some of it carrying over into the war years. Afterward, Mexican economic nationalism flexed its muscles. Expropriations occurred in agriculture. In mining, AMNE contended with strict domestic policy and interference. Mining and smelting companies had to either hire or train Mexican citizens for professional-level positions such as engineers, lawyers, doctors, etc.

American oil companies had to deal with ongoing threats of nationalization and increasing taxation, labor unrest, and occasional cancellation of drilling permits. In response, some AMNE started putting money into ventures elsewhere. Venezuela, with very favorable foreign investment laws, especially drew American DFI. This occurred despite the country's past political instability.

During the 1930s, compounded by worldwide depression, AMNE had to function abroad at the mercy of host governments' attempts to address their own economic problems. At the extreme, perhaps, American oil and mining companies faced the threat of expropriation in Latin America, as did other firms in different industry sectors. AMNE had to compete with, often, state-sponsored domestic companies, with laws in force favoring the native companies. In most of these areas, AMNE did not produce or compete in unregulated or unfettered market situations. In all, their host governments almost always hovered in the background, strictly controlling their own political economies.

The disintegration of the postwar world, during that decade, further encumbered the growth of AMNE. Nation-state aggression added to the disequilibrium caused by worldwide economic depression. Flashpoints ignited in Manchuria, Spain, Ethiopia, and ultimately, Poland, where the world detonated into a fully involved conflagration.

Five years earlier, this resolution could not be clearly foreseen. Later, in 1939, the participants in the war to end all wars, the Great War, remobilized and went at it again. As a result, AMNE was swept up in a world holocaust of fury.

AMNE was consumed by these forces. In Axis-occupied countries, AMNE succumbed. American corporations sought alternatives in Allied-controlled areas. On both sides, existing industries participated in their war efforts, as the clash of civilizations dragged nation-states and their societies over the brink. For most of its participants, it was a descent into an all-consuming maelstrom, from which only the United States emerged triumphant, in 1945. From that debris, the U.S. rebuilt war-torn nation-states, providing the foundation for AMNE to flourish over the next fifty years.

Even as the blitzkrieg raged ("and the bodies stank"), AMNE kept operating despite restrictions and losses of personnel who answered their motherland's calls to arms. Some corporations sold their holdings to local management. (SO-NJ destroyed its refinery in Le Havre, France.) However, most firms overseas were put to work as part of the Axis war production effort.

AMNE experienced a similar fate in Japanese-controlled Asia. Most American corporations sold their holdings to affiliates on the Japanese home islands, prior to Pearl Harbor. After that, the Japanese military took control of American holdings throughout Asia: in Sumatra, Malaysia, and the Philippines, for example. Here, as in occupied Europe, AMNE became part of their war-production effort, perhaps the ultimate form of expropriation.

Similarly, in Allied-controlled regions, AMNE took part in their war-production, for example in England, Canada, Latin America, Australia, New Zealand, India, and Africa. In some of these regions, absent of fighting, AMNE operated as before, relatively unencumbered by wartime exigencies. In some of these, AMNE increased their holdings.

But for the most part, the war production effort necessitated an inward focus. When the sleeping giant awoke, its food was American corporate might. Armed to the teeth, the American giant wore down the once seemingly invincible Philistines in both Europe and Asia. Much of the world was laid waste in the process. By war's end, in 1945, at the top of the heap, stood the giant, triumphant, intact, war weary, but unsullied. It was poised for greatness, its power at its peak, the world seemingly at its feet. There was monumental rebuilding, much work to be done. The American Century was about to begin, in earnest.

Regional postwar conditions varied widely. Much of the world was war torn. Other parts were politically unstable, such as in Eastern Europe, China, and Korea. Nationalism contributed to instability in Latin America, Africa, and in the Middle East. American corporations seeking to fill the vacuum in these places had to function, often, within, conflicting and changing foreign political economies. In occupied Japan, AMNE faced bureaucratic delays when attempting to reacquire their prewar property rights. It took until 1950. Afterward, AMNE began to reestablish business relations, usually via joint ventures with Japanese interests. Nearby in China, despite efforts by AMNE to reestablish, or set up positions, the communist takeover nullified such efforts. On December 29, 1950, the communist government took over all American corporate holdings on the mainland.

It took a decade for Western Europe to rebuild to a semblance of normalcy. That improvement attracted more American DFI, beginning in 1956. The potential of the proposed European Common Market also increased that region's attractiveness. Domestic stability and market rationalization became positive inducements. Adding to this, these governments started promoting American corporate investment. In some countries, such programs lasted for a decade.

Western Europe remained fertile ground for the spread of AMNE, despite misgivings from some. Their economies were open and existing competitors weren't that strong and their host governments were usually inclined to be less restrictive. Most of these countries were more open than not to foreign corporate presence. Perhaps the potential AMNE offered economically was more attractive than the nationalism, nativism, and other misgivings this new American invasion portended. France, for example, did impose more restrictions than its neighbors. Great Britain, Belgium, West Germany, and the Netherlands took some measures to protect home industries.

Europe seemed to suddenly mobilize in response to AMNE's invasion, perhaps fueled by a book by political activist and publisher, Jean-Jacques Servan-Schreiber, who wrote *The American Challenge*, published in 1967. The author stated that Europe was in decline and since it had not effectively integrated via the Common Market, the resulting vacuum was being filled by American corporations. (Hence the presence of my Campbell's Soup and Wimpy's in Torremolinos, in 1972.) In turn, he viewed our corporate presence as representative of American power abroad.

Servan-Schreiber was not necessarily against the vibrancy of the American way of doing things. Rather, he asserted that Europe should consider adapting some of the American methods. In particular, he was impressed with American organization, methods, and how those have been applied to our version of capitalism. Within that culture, management and its subculture of administrative components were the key ingredients. These, when integrated in the sum total of American society, were the cause for its spectacular success. Europe, instead of fighting this, should follow American examples, selectively adapting its methods to their own national political economies. Regardless of this controversy, all together, Western Europe was less restrictive and more receptive to AMNE than other regions.

In contrast, Central and Eastern Europe were a world away, taking a different postwar path. After World War II ended, the Iron Curtain in Eastern Europe prevented AMNE investment in the eastern bloc, in effect, until 1967, when communist Yugoslavia allowed foreign investment. (Hertz and Avis were the pathfinders into Eastern Europe.)

Eventually, joint venture agreements provided limited access to these closed countries. The Western corporation provided the technology and business administration, while the host country set up the physical plant, and provided labor. Not until 1972 could AMNE get legally involved. Until then, it was unlawful to export high technology to the Soviet bloc. Once these restrictions ended, Occidental Petroleum was one of the first to do business in the Soviet Union.[8]

As an alternative to the markets shuttered behind the Iron and Bamboo curtains, AMNE looked anew to the Less Developed Countries (LDCs), during the 1960s. The so-called Third World included countries from all over the globe. They were in Latin America, Africa, Asia, and Oceania, and they had been avidly avoided by most American corporations, who preferred the safety of developed nations, where they could set up manufacturing or assembly plants. Mining and petroleum remained the mainstay of DFI in LDCs. Realistically, in such nations, their mineral wealth was their main exploitable asset. Whether or not to invest in a LDC varied from company to company, depending on risk analysis. Some did, most did not.

Perhaps, here, in LDCs, the most noticeable relationship occurred between AMNE and host governments. Here, American corporate presence significantly affected its hosts, both good and bad; in some cases, fine, and others, not so. AMNE presence varied widely with place, and over time. Their effects were often controversial and long-debated by observers, especially the long-term tendencies and results. In some cases, these observers gave more weight to the negatives.

Generally, the positive view of AMNE in LDCs was the minority. Corporations were praised for bringing scarce resources, sophisticated technology, and administrative know-how, jobs, income, products, services, and in some places, social services, to the hosts' local and national economies. The AMNE improved the lot of all those in contact with them. Druckerian advocates believe that over time, once the differences were worked out between business and government, the typical American multinational, or the whole sector, depending on place, brought more to indigenous people than problems. This assumes the premise that a consumption-spending ideology is a basic good; a noble and positive, supportive pleasure-invoking ethos. Thus, what corporate America created in our domestic economy, from 1900–1960, they vigorously attempted to transport overseas. Anecdotally, as the world economy rebuilt itself after World War II, and then proceeding to the end of the century's global economy, AMNE was successful; a triumph of Drucker's World Shopping Center model. As a result, intrinsically, and de facto, American corporations became a vital force abroad, similar, but to a lesser extent, to the way they were at home. Baroque indeed!

In contrast, to most observers, negative aspects of the presence of AMNE, far outweighed the good. Here's a sample of their gripes.

After World War II, many LDCs viewed American corporations as their new overlords, replacing colonial nation-states and perpetuating a similar dependency. This also involved extreme corporate control of some of the host economy, which was seen as doing more harm than good. Similarly, foreign MNE took more out of the host economy then what they put in. This was especially so where natural resources were extracted.

The presence of a foreign corporation did not necessarily guarantee improvement or economic progress for the host. In many cases, MNE was viewed as more a disruptive monopolizer, or dominator, than competitor. When foreign corporations bought domestic firms that gave the outsider the ability to influence the host's economy. Such foreign control was often perceived as a huge negative to host governments and their private sector.

Some critics also asserted that the presence of MNE caused more problems then benefits for the host country. The latter was the result of belief or hope, rather than reality. For example, MNE often caused more unemployment then opportunity; more disparities in income distribution than increases; higher product prices; minimal influence on export income for the host's balance of payments.

Foreign corporations were accused of using local capital, instead of their own or from the wealth of the U.S. Using host money diverted it from domestic investment. It also provided opportunity to control this sector. Subsequent profits were then sent to the home base rather than reinvested indigenously. Outflows of revenue generated by the MNE took away resources that could have been used to improve the host economy.

Early on, the presence of the foreign MNE drew the host into an international economy where the host occupied a diminished, substandard position. This meant exploitation of the host's resources. More is gained by the corporation and its metropolitan base, than by the places they operated in. This dependency theory, sharply contested, and vied for precedence, with the more positive Druckerian model.

Inevitably, in the political economy, the corporate sector promoted a consumption-spending ethos that was often both unsustainable and incompatible with the host's status quo. Critics saw this as stress on both the domestic economy and their social web. Some places, particularly in Latin America, resented the American presence, and especially their own dependence on outsiders. Concomitantly, an antipathy resulted toward the concept of MNE and the perception that corporations had the ability to subvert host nation-state sovereignty.

Couple the Ugly American reputation AMNE acquired during the formative days of our corporations first going overseas, with later interactions, and the sum of these factors created a persistent tension between host government and corporation. It was a relationship pervading thirty years of participation, 1950–1980, and included response and reaction by both institutions, that were more adversarial and risk aversive than cooperative.

Corporate impact seemed greater in Latin America than elsewhere. In many cases, AMNE was not a panacea for their hosts' economic problems. In some of these economies, AMNE's presence was deleterious.

Generally, throughout Latin America, antipathy developed toward American corporations for a variety of reasons: believed exploitation of the continent's natural resources for corporate good alone; a history of intervention by the U.S. government in local political affairs, including military action, sometimes on the behalf of American firms; challenges to national sovereignty; too much influence and control by American corporate elites on local economies, societies, and political economies; and domineering market positions of American imports, among others.

This could affect how host governments treated AMNE. Sometimes referred to as economic nationalism, this is an attitude and resulting policy that ranged from increased regulation and restrictions on the operations of foreign companies to nationalization. It played out variously across the continent, and in LDCs, generally. It persisted into the 1970s.

In the decades following World War II, Latin American governments began to demonize AMNE presence, singling out particularly, Anaconda Copper, Kennecott, Phelps Dodge, and American Smelting and Refining Company. Action often followed words. Existing American operations had to abide by more host government control. Manufacturers had to make their products there, where they were to be sold. Mining companies had to process the ore locally. Foreign corporations had to finance their operations from home country banks. Joint venture requirements could include: mandatory partnerships, including financing; managers had to be locals. Some places were unionized. Other restrictions included profit ceilings, price controls, and prohibitions on horizontal integration. Some host governments required occupational safety and fringe benefits. LDCs used these strategies worldwide. It became typical in the Third World. Even some developed countries used these tactics to obtain leverage over MNCs.

AMNE response, too, varied. Some corporations divested their holdings, or suspended expansion, such as W.R. Grace, Ford, Exxon, and Kodak. Others took their assets elsewhere, to places less threatening. It was a risk-aversive strategy.

A root concern of AMNE was political risk, an estimate of potential instability within a host country. It's often considered in worst-case scenarios or government collapse or expropriations of assets. From 1950 to 1970, the political economies of LDCs weren't ideal settings for MNE. A number of negatives complicated each country, ranging from political turmoil to critically deficient economies. AMNE were often reluctant to go into such varied and unstable environments. For example, by the end of the 1960s, AMNE, generally, viewed

DFI in Latin America negatively. The next decade, investing in Latin America seemed to be a lost cause because of nation-state political instability, with the threat and reality of expropriation driving it home.

Indeed, except for war, perhaps the only true source of fear for a monolithic institution the size of AMNE is the nationalization/expropriation or confiscation of one of their foreign assets by a host country. (I'm using nationalization and expropriation interchangeably, as synonyms, for host government takeover of foreign corporate assets.)

This occurred throughout the twentieth century, most notably when Russia, Eastern Europe, China, and Cuba turned to communist totalitarianism. Consequently, AMNE, in those areas, were lost, often without compensation. At times, nationalization became host-country policy, over the decades, especially in LDCs. Venezuela, Chile, Guyana, Mexico, Peru, Bolivia, Argentina, Jamaica, Trinidad and Tobago, Iraq, Kuwait, Saudi Arabia, Libya, Indonesia, all, at one time or another, took over foreign corporate assets. In *International Business*, Roback and Simmonds stated that from 1960 into 1974, there were 875 such incidents, dispersed over 62 nations. This trend continued during the 1970s and then faded away in the next decade.

Depending on place, circumstances changed a bit more favorably for AMNE during the latter part of the 1970s, and beyond. A number of host countries emerged from the crisis of negativity and politically improved during the next two decades. Some see the early years of globalization as a positive contributing factor.

Thus, business-government relations improved in Third World political economies. During the last two decades of the twentieth century, a greater sense of accommodation evolved between TNCs and their host governments. This involved a two-sided relationship, where corporate management sought more negotiated relationships with hosts, offering a greater sense of acquiescence to prevailing law, policies, and customs abroad. TNCs found it better to improve attempting to fit in, to institutionally assimilate where possible, and essentially to strive to get along to go along.

These successes varied by time and place. The overall trend was gradual improvement.

Host governments' willingness to accommodate went through decades-long change. The amount and degree, too, varied by place and over time. Some host economies matured, making integration of TNCs easier. In some places, local industries grew to compete with foreign firms. Changes in tariff (GATT), and trade treaties, such as NAFTA, improved overall relations between the private sector and the public, thus improving the prevailing ethos wherein negotiations and business-government relations operated.

From 1980 to 2000, more and more countries attempted to integrate MNCs into their political economies, and in several places, ameliorating their attitudes and policies regarding DFI. This even occurred within the Third World, but to a lesser degree. Generally, the trend toward accommodation emerged prior to globalization. Latin America began this process after 1980; the Eastern Bloc, after the Iron Curtain opened. In the latter case, the potential of progress through accommodation with MNE, and nascent globalization might have contributed to putting some cracks in the curtain, at the outset.

But the road to this accommodation wasn't smooth. Nation-state diplomacy also significantly affected TNC behavior and strategy. Changing political economies complicated AMNE operations worldwide. A new sense of nationalism and protectionism forced limits: increased taxation, foreign unionization, patent disputes; concerns about domestic business competitiveness; outward cash flow; stifling home businesses; unfavorable balance of payments. Such factors often prompted host governments to alter the rules of doing business regarding foreign companies.

Whenever possible, AMNE assessed risk and outcomes, and adjusted. Economic and practical considerations often determined the status of any given transnational, more so than ethical or moral considerations. If there was profit potential, more so, than political risk, then it was likely the MNC would go into that market regardless of whether the host country's political system or domestic policies agreed with ours.

At the same time, nation-state politics reared its head, resulting in AMNE often getting caught in the middle, even when they weren't instigating problems between home and host's governments. The 1973–1974 Arab oil embargo, during the Arab-Israeli, *Yom Kippur* war, was one such acute example.

Even before hostilities broke out between Israel and some of its neighbors, in October 1973, OPEC's Arab members attempted to intervene by cutting oil production and embargoing exports to countries friendly to Israel. This meant that MNCs operating within these countries had to comply, thus American oil companies were unable to ship oil home. (At the extreme end, in September 1973, Libya expropriated 51 percent of the oil fields worked by Exxon, Texaco, and SOCAl; in October 1973, Iraq nationalized Exxon and Mobil assets.)

This even affected the Arabian-American Oil Company (ARAMCO), operating in Saudi Arabia, which at the time, was the largest oil company. When the Saudi's threatened the company's production contracts, ARAMCO began lobbying the U.S. government regarding American foreign policy toward Israel. When war broke our, Saudi Arabia directed ARAMCO to move oil to those countries fighting Israel. Eventually, Saudi Arabia, too, joined the OPEC embargo, forcing ARAMCO to decrease exporting oil to the U.S. This nation-state intervention lasted five months and AMN oil producers had to go along with their hosts, for fear of losing all they had in Saudi Arabia.

Also, during the 1970s, other American and European TNCs got caught up in nation-state politics. The United Nations placed economic sanctions on Rhodesia. During the Carter administration, the federal government sustained the sanctions and in response it was alleged that Mobil Oil, and others, were shipping petroleum products illegally into Rhodesia, as a result of cutting deals with the Rhodesian government. Then, I recall reading an essay accusing one American oil company of actually smuggling the stuff into Rhodesia in unmarked containers.

Similar shenanigans occurred in nearby South Africa, where MNCs were maneuvering around another U.N. trade sanction, an arms embargo. In this case, Olin International got busted in the U.S. for essentially, smuggling small arms to South Africa with their government's complicity.

Rather than exceptions, I view these examples as, in the least, plausible actions by AMNE, and for many of them, discreetly or covertly probable. An institutional mindset is also indicated by these incidents. The point here is the MNC attitude of doing what's best for them despite their home governments. The fact that AMNE defied the federal government and international agreements to further their own interests are significant statements of asserting international power and influence.

On one level, each MNC made the decision to negotiate as an equal partner with foreign governments, to trade, do business, in defiance of home country law and policy, let alone international. This, in itself, was an act of bold self-assertion; a willingness to do what's institutionally good for them regardless of legal and public relations consequences, among others. It harkens back to the century-long dance of the titans played out in our domestic political economy; a contest that, in the long run, the corporate monolith won, largely the result of translating its economic power into sociopolitical power.

This same pattern evolved in the international arena, when the corporate institution could take on both their home governments, as they were used to, and sometimes, simultaneously, their host governments. Here to, corporate economic power fostered institutional power, enabling corporations to become quasi-sovereign, as mini-states, when encountering a foreign ship of state. In 1993, Paul J. Dosal argued in *Doing Business with the Dictators*:

> The domestic corporation is often superior to the power of the states in the U.S. federal system, and, in a world of states, the multinational corporation may act likewise pursuing its equivalent of policies of divide and rule, balance of power, and containment and expansion toward (sic) at least the majority of the 135 states in the world.[9]

Deferring to the persistent power of nation-states, I'd rather write that an organization, institution, or corporation has influence rather than overt power. Corporations influence power. This is not the same process as police or military power to coerce, or to injure, or kill with force. In this context, the state has power and corporations and associations have the economic or political wherewithal to influence. Nation-state power is, by nature, overt, while corporate, institutional, or associational power to influence, is covert, subtle.

Anecdotally, this top-shelf level of interaction occurred before 1990, when remarkably, globalization and its alleged transcending of the nation-state dominance, was only a theory among academics, and wishful thinking and hopes of corporate executives. That corporations could assert themselves at this level was the beginnings of its evolution to sovereign baroque. If so, then its nascence was mostly unnoticed; its nurturing largely unopposed, or minimally threatened. Writing in 1978, Lewis D. Solomon, in his, *Multinational Corporations and the Emerging World Order*, would now read almost as prophecy. He asserted, the rise of multinationals "as a global force . . . ranks as one of the key features of the second half of the twentieth century."[10]

Thus, the success of AMNE enhanced their political power at home, abroad, and even on the world diplomatic platform as well. This increased to a point where by the end of the century, AMNE had a say in how the world economy functioned. They dealt with other nations and with NGOs, such as the WTO and took positions influencing policy regarding GATT, NAFTA, and the Common Market. Often, AMNE participation approached quasi nation-state level, depending on the situation. Baroque, indeed.

As AMNE weaved its way across the globe, it might have been affecting places where it did not have a significant presence. Perhaps it was unintended, or not even considered beforehand, the postwar movement of AMNE abroad was simultaneously fostered by federal government foreign policy, and assisted, congruently, by corporate efforts to set up overseas on their own. If so, then American corporate capitalism was successfully exported via the corporate institutional form, transplanted overseas. Thus, in hindsight, the American corporation became an unintended weapon, successfully used during the Cold War era.

It might well turn out that the presence of AMNE influence abroad during the last fifty years was the underlying factor that put an end to the Cold War, and the final defeat of statist socialism. Also, AMNE might have been the main catalyst for the creation of the global economy and its trappings.

A key ingredient contributing to the fall of Soviet tyranny was America's secret war cold war weapon—the dollar bill and the American way of life it represented; once created and then proselytized by corporate capitalism, especially after World War II. Then, the cornucopia of good stuff flowing throughout the U.S., slowly, but eventually spilled across the globe, and ultimately, it undermined the economic, political, and social foundations that held the Eastern Bloc together, beneath the ever-present Soviet tanks that controlled its surface.

Whatever the causes that still are being debated, the disintegration of the Eastern Bloc opened the doors to true globalization for AMNE. However, the degree to, and kind of, westernization and market access varied by country. American corporate market penetration slowly occurred; western European MNCs also sought entry.

Since then, several kinds of AMNs set up within the Eastern Bloc, perhaps led by GM, in Hungary, Armand Hammer's Occidental Petroleum, in the Soviet Union, and Coke, Pepsi, and McDonalds, and Motorola.

Despite the enormous potential of an accessible Soviet market, AMNE was all but blocked during that era, and then afterward, moved in gradually. Soviet-style communism was called a centralized, command economy, whereby all such activity was state controlled. Thus, within this almost totally self-contained system, there was no place for foreigners. Hence, AMNE access to the Soviet state-controlled economy was limited. This changed during the 1980s, when the Soviet government allowed American corporations to negotiate joint ventures. Archer Daniels Midland, Combustion Engineering, and Pepsi were some of the first to do business. However, in the waning days of the Soviet Union, AMNE, generally, showed little enthusiasm for setting up shop there. Prior to 1990, there was little interest except for early efforts by Chevron, RJR Nabisco, and Kodak, among others. Even these were exploratory, beginning in 1988. A closed, state-controlled economy, perhaps, wasn't fertile enough to draw AMNE interest, for after all, capitalism and communism, both economic systems, were considered incompatible. This meant that East could not do business on West's terms, and vice versa. At least, that was the prevailing ethos until Gorbachev's efforts, prior to the dissolution of the Evil Empire, as it was then referred to. Only after the withering away of the Soviet state did a new era have the potential to begin. That tale is still in process, thirty years later.

Cracks, too, appeared in the Bamboo Curtain after Richard Nixon's visit to China. AMNE sought to follow his lead, and slowly, the Chinese reopened the door, after decades of it being slammed shut. They allowed joint ventures with home industry, and by the end of 1990s, some AMNE were there. Motorola was one of the first. The trend gradually expanded, despite China's communism, and the inherent risk of functioning in that kind of limited and controlled system.

As the twentieth century ebbed, the world seemed to flatten to AMNE, with Asia within range. For the most part, Western-aligned Asian nations controlled MNE in their economies. The degree varied by country. At century's end, corporate capitalism thrives in Malaysia and Indonesia, and is a-budding in Indochina. The latter, riven by despots and anti-Western angst, were resisting. Globalization fueled by TNCs is a contemporary force powerful enough to precipitate change, especially in places where traditional indigenous cultures have already been diluted by the presence of once-European colonialism. In the new century, globalization and its Friedmanesque model is still taking shape; its outcome and story yet to be determined.

If China and other closed societies flatten, then it would be another triumph for corporate capitalism, directed by MNE; significantly AMNE, in its titanic dance with nation-states. If triumphant in the ensuing decades, indeed, it would be another accolade (and predicted by some believers, during the 1980s), on the shelf in the great palaces of sovereign corporate baroque.

Since after World War II, AMNE functioned in an evolving and increasingly complicated world, interacting on multiple levels, with host and home governments; competing with other MNCs and with native businesses within host countries and regional economies; later global. Their presence, and ways of doing business, positively and negatively affected all these levels, from the plenipotentiary to the village crossroads.

On the highest plane where regions and nations lie, MNE has been accoladed for their overall contributions in rebuilding devastated nations after World War II. Similarly, TNCs made contributions in advancing LDCs. Corporations brought investment capital, institutional resources, and economic development, and jobs and products, thus affecting local and national economies. In several countries, MNE could dominate economies, while being integrated into them, by offering brand-name products, often at reasonable prices, that might be better than what's available from local competitors. Later in the century, MNCs created, organized, and managed globally.

On a different level, some MNCs brought science, technology, and innovations in production, distribution, and business administration. This infusion, of know-how often resulted in the transfer of skills in production planning and method; subsequent quality control; management and business administrative practices such as accounting, budgeting, purchasing, etc.

Throughout the twentieth century, American technology, know-how, and innovation, together, or in part, served as an incredibly attractive draw to foreign governments. Consequently, these institutional strengths often opened doors worldwide to American corporations.

Early in that century, mass production and distribution were magnets, soon followed by American management, business administration practices, and advertising methods.

As our scientific and technological successes developed, so to were they applied overseas: power generation, transportation, automated mass production, intercontinental telephone and later, satellite and mainframe computing. Together, all occurred before the recent information revolution.

All of this can be especially valuable when the host lacks these skills, abilities, and attributes. What a MNC brings to a region often diffuses, a sort of trickle-down, spill-over effect, or an injection of new ingredients into the prevailing mix. Or, in other words, when these vacuums are filled, the potential for progress often improves. This is especially lucrative in stagnant economic regions of developing nations, and more so, in LDCs. In the latter, the setup of an MNC or MNCs can serve as a short- or long-term catalyst for local and domestic economic improvement.

The presence of a large MNC can affect a host country and region at multiple levels. Most visible are business-government relations, finance, diplomacy, and politics; basically, a large, institutional type of interaction. This varies by country and region, with the kind and depth of presence of the foreign firm.

Any given MNC can subtly affect foreign countries through both its physical presence and marketing techniques. Advertising and selling products and services is the most visible; publicity and institutional behavior, less so, but nevertheless significant.

Less visible are the intrinsic effects: brand-name marketing, mass-media entertainment, retail outlets, etc. Over the decades, these, too, affected host country living habits, and in many cases, culture as well.

Recall my encounters with Kodak, in Spain, in 1972. Since those days of my youth, American products of all kinds are available, and by now, almost worldwide. Coca-Cola was one of our first instruments of American corporate halogenation, followed later by Levi jeans, and more recently, Nike.[11] The presence of American corporations and their products and services probably influenced indigenous cultures in most places. The advertising of brand names had similar effects worldwide, as it did for decades, in the U.S. This effect varied, over time, place and culture; so too, the degree of influence or American homogenization. By the end of the twentieth century, indeed, it might just be as Barnet and Cavanaugh declared in *Global Dreams*: "Marlboro Country is everywhere!"

The sum total of this, all corporate delivered, is the subtle spread of at least, the image of our American lifestyle and culture, via our products and services. Over time, since the so-called Cocacolaization of Europe during the mid-decades of the twentieth century, the social and cultural effects vary with the scale and depth of the product's availability; the level of absorption by locals of the thing into their lifestyles and society, and the amount of availability that host countries allow.

Anecdotally, when mass production and mass distribution combined with mass marketing and advertising, the cornucopia of American made good stuff became available worldwide. This availability might have been the main catalyst of what became globalization, by the end of the twentieth century. Indeed, Marlboro Country might be just about everywhere. Think of the cultural and psychological impact of what American corporations marketed overseas during the last few decades. It is as Robert Sobel once wrote: "the Americanization of the world would be accomplished as much by the force of business and investment as by any other medium."[12]

AMNE became a purveyor of things American, and in the process, an immediate symbol of it. Although this was probably unintended, American corporations had to add this factor to their methods. Again, the successes, and failures too, varied widely. Ultimately, in the long run, AMNE became a prime mover of a trend that became globalization.

Peter F. Drucker viewed AMNE's role positively. He argued that the American version of capitalism, a good in itself, eventually spread globally. Mass-consumption comforts, also positive, disseminated in variations to all social classes, similar to the pattern in the U.S. earlier in the twentieth century. Just like Americans, Drucker argued that people elsewhere wanted good stuff, modern comforts, and a better life. All this was possible through marketplace corporate capitalism and the modernity it fostered.[13]

Buying a bicycle or car or certain kinds of personal-care products is the obvious value of a market economy, and de facto, American corporate (later, global), capitalism. Indirectly, this means the dissemination of the sum total of the American Way, through advertising consumer products or services and the availability of movies and broadcast programs. All of these can operate as potentially significant disseminators of foreign culture, with a strong possibility of altering prevailing economic and social habits, and even ingraining itself in individual and collective psyches. (It is also a restatement of the power of advertising, now worldwide. The late, great John K. Galbraith would concur regarding the creation of consumer demand or the engineering of desire.)

From my viewpoint, AMNE has been very successful during the last forty years selling itself and our way of doing things, worldwide, even within the limitations imposed upon them within the frameworks of economic and cultural nationalism.

Capable of interacting on these levels, figuratively, a MNC dances in the nation-state plenipotentiary ballroom, simultaneously, it leads the street dance in the neighborhoods and villages. The potential power and influence MNE possesses throughout a host country's political economy and society, can pack a wallop.

As indicated, the international dance of the titans is inevitably complex, and now interlocked. The process was not necessarily stable and accommodating. A variety of negatives accompany the positives that MNCs bring to any given host country. They range from the contest between nation-state and business, over power, to MNCs effects on a local society. It was as John Fayerweather wrote during the 1970s:

> Thus, the protective spirit of nationalism is fundamentally at odds with this foreign entity which seeks to invade its territory for purposes of control and profit.[14]

Hence, at the plenipotentiary level, MNCs are believed to pose a threat to national sovereignty. Corporate presence, power, and influence can disrupt a host's own external and internal economic objectives, internal politics and governing methods, and its international relations. For decades, corporations got involved or caught up in international power politics and regional diplomacy, or drew in their home governments over conflict with the host. Consequently, some government participants and observers viewed MNCs as potentially uncontrollable, becoming equal to or more powerful than nation-states.

This contentious negativity seemed to accelerate from 1970–1990, prior to the globalization process. In this new universe, the corporate institution operates across borders, in a sense, becoming borderless and stateless, de facto, the dialectical antithesis of the national firm and home government where it originated. The result seems to have the corporate-vectored private sector operating on a plane, veering away to parallel the traditional nation-state system. During the first years of the twenty-first century, this interaction is ongoing.

The presence of a wealthy, powerful, and influential foreign sector causes a simultaneous sense of dependence and resentment because the foreigner becomes a source of investment capital, valuable economic assets, yet at the same time, a suspicious stranger. In some places, the threat a MNC represents overshadows its benefits. This relationship and its resentment can fester, undermining potential progress and ultimately destroying the relationship between foreign company and hosts.

To host countries, corporate sins varied widely, and in time, and place. Considered an unfair advantage, MNCs had access to large amounts of investment capital, and could move it in, out, and through a country. This could influence a host country's policies on exchange rates, balance of payments, credit, gross national product, tariff, and foreign corporate tax rates.

Once in, MNCs could dominate or control a host's domestic economy, upsetting prevailing market conditions, becoming the sector leader, or worse, monopolizing one or several market sectors. Such could potentially prevent the growth of domestic industry, or stifle existing expansion. At the same time, the arrival and especially the persistence of MNE could disrupt the host's national planning; negatively affect environmental quality and local infrastructure; alter prevailing wage rates and prices. Overall, MNCs often created and executed strategy from afar, with little or no consideration of subsequent effects within a host country.

The presence of these companies threatened native ways of doing things. Different legal systems caused problems. Business practices and ethics abroad often conflicted with the American way of doing business. Contentions also arose over corporate social responsibility, aggressive advertising and marketing tactics, attitudes toward unionization, corporate promotion policies, and functioning within the existing local class structure. The generalized aggressive reputation of American corporate culture, and unwillingness or reluctance to conform to the host's ways of doing things, often garnered AMNE the Ugly American image, or as the American behemoth, corporate bully. This was often seen as affronts to national pride and threats to political and cultural nationalism. Always in the background was the option for the transnational to pack up and go home, taking his baseball and bat with him, thus preventing others from playing. Literally, corporations could effectively threaten host governments with a quick exit, and subsequently removing the socioeconomic assets they brought with them. The significance of this potential threat varied over time and place. It probably affected nations with weaker economies or market niches, more so, than the stronger. Whether or not the threat would, or could, be carried out effectively did not diminish the significance of its strategic, value; its gamesmanship use.

The sum of all these institutional strengths can conjure a negative image of the foreign presence. National pride is hurt, or culture and tradition insulted, similar to an athletic event, where the MNC is the competitor, and also a denigrating force, capable of dispensing unwanted doses of national humility. Negativity also abounds in countries where people resent the infusion of American culture, or where they have religious opposition to the assault on their values that things foreign represent.

This can then trigger a nationalistic and defensive attitude that can leave the host nation's government and people (especially the latter), believing the MNC is unfriendly, threatening, or even an enemy.

In response to all this, host governments reacted in several ways. They aided their own industries while placing competitive restrictions on foreign companies. Hosts could restrict market access and subsequent operations, prohibit profits from leaving the country, or impose controls. Some governments attempted to indirectly or directly control how the foreign firm operated: restrict foreign ownership of native companies or require research and development be done locally. Some governments mandated that host-country law was in effect, trumping a corporation's home laws. This was specifically designed to counter the intervention of other nations in what a host country considered domestic policy and assertion of nation-state sovereignty.

Ultimately, a corporation will seek its home company's ends first and foremost, more so than acquiescing to the prerogatives or protocols of their host country. That is, they will push their host for whatever they can get away with while pursuing their own self-interest. Just like at home, loyalty to the corporation is more important than conforming to what the government wants. The fealty to the corporate institution is more important than to the state, any state. So too abroad.

Perhaps building these economic and institutional foundations, some observed that the process of becoming international increased the power and influence of a large corporation over time and place.

If so, then this evolutionary process followed a similar pattern internationally, as it did nationally. Thus, on both levels, the large corporate institution organically grows, taking on a life of its own, too, as it did in order to achieve the level necessary to expand globally, and sustain itself at that high level. It can grow and gather strength. Hence, institutionally, the economic power of a MNE becomes nation-like, which can result in garnering sociopolitical power similar, but not equal to that of a small nation-state. Again, this is institutional-level sovereignty and when a TNC attains it, it becomes like a ships of state—sovereign baroque. As a result, AMNE and their foreign competitors became prime movers in political economies worldwide. This development itself was a paramount event in U.S. and world history. Its occurrence will likely direct world development for the next one hundred years.

Although the contemporary use of the term globalization began before the 1990s, the real trend slowly developed during the four previous decades. Furthermore, I define globalization, as a system, including the expansion and de facto, integration of MNE, trade, commerce, production, distribution, marketing, and cultural dissemination, across borders. Also, this section does not contain discussion about the morality of globalization, or the place of MNCs. Rather, it accepts the reality of MNCs as international, quasi-nation-states, and globalization, as two things that are here to stay; just like governments. None of them will wither away, except as the result of human cataclysm.

Globalization

As a contemporary concept, globalization was fueled by, at first, AMNE, and then later, other TNCs. Together, they spawned, then nurtured globalism, and so far, have sustained it. The successes of DFI, in especially, developed countries, fostered more economic expansion, and more successes, that eventually led American corporate execs to start thinking about their firms as stateless, a-national entities, operating within worldwide, borderless markets.[15] This belief resembled the nineteenth-century laissez-faire ethos, but now they envisioned it across borders (a zipless market, perhaps?), begat action, beginning in the 1970s. This trend and ideology slowly evolved to what we commonly call globalization.

Technology advances in communications and transport fostered this preliminary advance, enabling global product movement, marketing, and finance. Similar to an expanding domestic market, a global equivalent evolved, fostered, then fueled by AMNE.

Thus, contemporary globalization was a product of several interrelated, technological and market factors. Scientific advances in technology, adopted and marketed by corporations, led the way: jet planes, satellite communications, media expansion, computers, and ultimately the World Wide Web; later, the digital world.

Big business had the institutional strength, assets, and financial means to harness and marshal these forces together into a prime-mover power. The results were the internationalization of corporate capitalism on a worldwide scale. By the end of the twentieth century, the term globalization, reflected this reality.

The original, centuries-long idea was unfettered world trade. It morphed into complete integration of communications; product assembly and movement; global marketing; transnational product distribution; worldwide dissemination of services; global movement of money, etc. This process can be seen as the expansion/internationalization of the concept of national economies. Many of the parts of a developed country's domestic economy are now globalized. What used to be done between and among national economies can now be executed worldwide and all at the same time.

Globalization as we know it did not suddenly appear like a new star on the horizon. Instead, the process was gradual, taking a few decades to develop. It was fueled by MNE, with AMNE leading the way during the 1960s, as corporations spread their market share worldwide. When this economic, institutional, and technological mix precipitated, the result, by the end of the century was the world of Thomas L. Friedman and his school of thought—the borderless economy, the Druckerian world shopping center, and the homogenization of everyday life and popular culture. (Or so it seemed.)

This early hint of what became globalization was to be ushered in by preferably, stateless TNCs, with AMNE leading the way. This process started with the spread of MNE, through DFI, spurred by American corporations, and then by others. At first, it was simply expanding one's corporate presence abroad, and at the same time, its markets and supporting infrastructure. The results were an expansion of regional production and distribution, and the spread of goods and services to more places. (In some cases, mergers of TNCs from different home countries occurred.) It was largely economic and financial, affecting markets and national economies.

In *Global Reach*, Barnet and Muller defined the trend as increasing control and dispersion of production, finance and marketing. This means that specific economies no longer dominate where a product comes from. For example, cars don't have to be made in Detroit and then exported; the same for IBM computers, etc. Even then, these products weren't being produced in one place. They could be assembled from components made elsewhere, then shipped, finished, and delivered. This later became so-called global webs or networked corporations, a common trait of globalization by century's end.

This trend accelerated during the 1980s and 1990s, opening up and then integrating domestic economies globally. Led by TNCs, some of these are now diluting the decades-long power and influence of AMNE. Regardless of home chartering, these corporations view themselves increasingly as global members rather than national. Now, more than ever, their focus is on the worldwide market, viewing borders as nuisances; national origins and subsequent loyalties are inoperative and out-of-date variables. Richard Barnett observed that "global corporations chartered in Delaware and flying the American flag now see themselves, even advertise themselves as 'stateless.' Corporate executives disavow any special relationship to the United States or its people."[16] To many corporate managers the nation-state plays or should play a diminished role within the global economic arena. The MNC has, in the globalist view, transcended the old nation-state parameters of economic policy making and interventionist action. By decade's end, MNCs saw themselves as truly transnational, with their focus global; their loyalties were only to themselves and not from where they came.

Once again, the dance of the titans repeats itself, but this time the arenas are multiple and the contestants numerous. Whether the TNC sector is superseding governments as the dominant force in economic policy making is still debated.

Some of them view the TNC as a monolith, extending its economic power and sociopolitical influence across borders, based on a viewpoint that transcends the traditional boundaries of statism, its principles of sovereignty, and its power to act in the typical political economy. Adherents believed that unfettered, free market globalization would eventually foster worldwide prosperity, democracy, and improved international relations. Some even believed that globalization could evolve to a global society.

The result is a new dialectical synthesis; a new world that is Druckerian and Friedmanesque—flat. If so, American-style corporate capitalism created the method and nurtured it enough so it could be adapted by other capitalistic systems during the last thirty-five years or so.

However, globalization, while a powerful factor, will not dominate the world economy as many fear. It has to function in too many different economies and social climates. The internal conditions in regions and countries are still formidable obstacles. Globalization is not powerful enough to flatten them.

Any given nation-state is the sum total of its political, social, and cultural past. (We are our past, both individually and collectively, so Professor Koch often said when I attended Harvard-in-the-Cornfields, circa 1974–1975) These are the attributes of factors that in time can be, in the long run, genetically imprinted, or, in the short run, inculcated. Thus, heritage becomes ingrained in both the national and individual psyches.

Such attributes are fundamental supports of societies, and cannot be effectively eliminated in the short run. Influenced, yes; drastically altered, no. Thus, drinking Coke at an American fast-food outlet is culturally changed behavior. Raising a family, or practicing religion, or governing, are behavior, less affected by modernity's trends. These are fundamental attributes and they are grounded in deeply rooted social, religious, and cultural foundations.

This ingrained instinct and social learning also has a strong influence, when coupled with religion. There, eating fast food and drinking soda, while wearing Levi's and Nike T-shirts and listening to pop music, does not for most, dilute their religious beliefs, and especially, the cultural trappings that are part of their national heritage. This is especially prevalent in places were secularism is either incipiently, or mandated secondary to religious tenets. Thus, cultural nationalism is an especially significant countervailing force, and it prevails through much of the world, even in the new century.

Besides such religious strengths, cultural nationalism has a strong ally—nation-state loyalty, patriotism. Again, imbibing in Globalization's good stuff can homogenize only so much. Despite an addiction to Coca-Cola or Marlboro, or to Nike, one can still be a loyal, country-loving patriotic Frenchman, Canadian, etc. Thus, despite what the Globalists and World Managers hope and plan for, their efforts, over the long run, will never transcend nationalism. This cultural force, now imprinted into most cultures, and systematically reinforced through native socialization, and generationally, via cultural transmission, will always blunt or dilute the shaping power of globalization. True, globalization will remain a powerful economic and significant social force wherever it interacts with native populations. That interaction, despite what the globalists extol, will not unhinge what every country-loving citizen holds or cherishes about his home turf. It might be neon-lit and pock-marked with billboards, but despite the constant bombardment, globalization's influence will always be secondary to the power and grip the nation-state and its societies have on their citizens.

Despite corporate global power, the prerogatives, especially the power to coerce, regulate, make and enforce domestic law and societal sanctions—all traditional nation-state powers—continue to serve as institutional bulwarks, countervailing against the perceived power of the state-less multinational corporation.

Typically, nation-states, too, are entrenched institutions, consisting of political, military, economic, social, religious, and cultural assets. Many countries are all but monolithical in their scale and scope, which means they will not be supplanted by economic behemoths or trends and processes such as globalization. Instead, the state will not wither away, rather, it will continue its dance at all levels, including holding its own in the globalized arena. Thus, the nation-state counters globalization. The ship of state persists as a powerful institution, fortified by its own military and police power; its laws and customs, culture, religion, and the deeply inbred sense of identity and loyalty of its citizens.

These attributes of any given nation all add up to a powerful, countervailing force to whatever perceived threat globalization presents. At the same time, keep in mind that even MNCs still, and must, function within a larger universe of nation-state domestic law and international agreements. These are broad, more distant constraints or limiters on the conduct of any particular MNC. Thus, regardless of the economic, social, and political power of TNCs (the components that both hold globalization together and serve as is fuel), the nation-state is not a toothless lion. It will persist too, sustained by fuel of equal potency to that of the TNCs. Hence, the dance of the titans continues; now, with new participants and old, and both perhaps with more powerful assets than their predecessors.

Thus, it's impossible to be flatly globalized as it proponents declare. There are too many factors and peculiarities among nation-states, and their economies, to eliminate or dilute. What's typical of countries, their societies, and regions, is too deeply entrenched to be tempered by the Global Shopping Center. Instead, the flat earth of a global market economy will coexist with traditional nation-state political economies. The two will continue to interact in a system of attractions and repulsions, remaining separate and distinct, no matter how close they dance, spar, or spin with each other.

Regardless of the power, or the goods and bads of globalization, its generator and fuel had been big business, at first here, in the U.S., and then later, in other countries. Corporate capitalism is once again a prime mover, but now in the global arena.

Thus, the monolith evolved, creating a nurturing environment to sustain and advance its own institutional life within the next level; the global level, where it reigns similarly to the nation-state.

American multinational enterprises are the foundations, anchors, rudders, and fuel for the global economy. (During the 1990s, the U.N. estimated there were 60,000 MNCs, of all sizes, with 800,000 affiliates.)[17]

That a large corporation can interact with a nation-state government, participating in and influencing policy at the plenipotentiary level, and significantly affecting the host country's economy and culture, makes AMNE, de facto, mini-institutional-level states, and hence, sovereign baroque.

At the end of the nineteenth century, the U.S. continental frontier line disappeared. One hundred years or so, later, the corporate frontier line is still moving; its new range is global.

Years ago, when I researched and then wrote the paper (chapter 1), that spawned this book, I stated the corporate future will be an amalgamation of *Brave New World*, *Player Piano*, *A Clockwork Orange*, *Blade Runner*, and *Max Headroom*. I suspect this triumph of corporation over life and society will occur and then create its own destructive dialectic. This, now-in-process, final assertion of corporate culture and power, an act of ultimate hubris, will result in the eventual destruction of the planet, perhaps one hundred years hence. The monolith will then die out for lack of fuel and sustenance, but so will everything else as the final result of this prime mover. The aftermath will be more like *A Canticle for Leibowitz* or *Ringworld*.

Notes

1. See James Michener, *The Drifters*. At the time I was ferociously in love and in the process of losing that love. So while I was in Spain, I was only interested in sightseeing. We did go to one club, but it was a flamingo program. We were up early to tour, traveling to Nerja, Granada, Ronda, Algeciras, and Tangier, so nightlife was not a high priority or practical. On the one night we decided to go clubbing, we all fell asleep and slept through to the next morning.

When I returned to Eastern Illinois University for the spring quarter, one of my peers asked about the action. I was shocked to learn that I had been visiting what was then the Ft. Lauderdale of Europe. No wonder I never saw anyone my age out during the day. They were probably sleeping it off. I was handed a copy of Michener's book and instructed to read the first page: "If you can't get laid in Torremolinos, you should quit the human race." That adage has reared its truthful but ugly head a number of times during the subsequent decades.

2. I will be using the different labels interchangeably: American multinational enterprise, multinationals, transnationals, multinational enterprise, etc., with abbreviations.

3. General list of American corporations operating overseas: Alcoa, Allied Chemical, American Cyanamid, American Tobacco, Anaconda, Armour, Bethlehem Steel, Bordens, Cities Service; Crown, Cork & Seal, Coca-Cola, Diamond Match, DuPont,

Firestone, Ford; General Foods, Goodyear, Gulf Oil, GE, Gillette, International Harvester; Heinz; Kennecott, Kodak; Liggett & Myers; New York Life Insurance, NCR, Norton, Otis Elevator, PPG, Phelps Dodge, Parke-Davis, Quaker; Singer, Sinclair Oil, Sun Oil, Swift, SO-NJ, SOCAL, SO-Indiana, SO-NY, Sherwin-Williams, Texaco, Union Carbide, Union Oil, United Fruit, US Rubber, USS; Western Electric, Westinghouse, among others.

Source: Compiled from books above, and Wilkins, *Maturing*, 143–145.

4. Wilkins, *Maturing*, 299–301; Robert Gilpin, *U.S. Power and the Multinational Corporation: The Political Economy of Foreign Direct Investment* (New York: Basic Books, Inc., 1975), 6–7.

Of note: At the beginning of the German occupation of Paris, a Singer sewing machine employee watched the Wermacht parading in triumph. Suddenly, a tank wheeled up to the store and stopped. A soldier jumped off the tank, walked in, and introduced himself as a former Singer employee in Germany. He spent a few minutes talking sales, left, hopped back unto the tank and rejoined the parade. (Source: Probably Wilkins . . .?)

5. John Fayerweather, "The Internationalization of Business," *Annals of the America Academy of Political and Social Science* 403 (September 1972), 1.

6. *Business Week* (April 20, 1963), 63, 68.

7. Tugendhat, *Multinationals*, 45.

8. Note: Armand Hammer first went to the Soviet Union during the 1920s, where he struck a deal to ship grain. In the process, he became his own ambassador to Lenin. In 1922, his company, the Allied American Company, became the official representative of U.S. companies trading with the USSR. This personal diplomacy ceased from 1930–1961, but resumed, in the latter, when Hammer returned. From then, Hammer began and sustained a long progression of unofficial, personal contacts with Soviet leaders through Gorbachev. In 1972, Hammer won preliminary trade agreements for oil and gas and chemical ventures and construction of a fertilizer plant and hotels. (Source: Steve Weinberg, *Armand Hammer: The Untold Story*, 1989, 43–48, 52,139,141, 218, 225.)

Armand Hammer might have been more like an original captain of industry than the modern man in the gray flannel suit. He was a capitalist cum diplomat, more so than a MNC corporate executive. Perhaps one-of-a-kind, who came of age during the 1920s corporate capitalist nascency; living long and building his company into the 1980s.

9. Dosal, *Doing*, 285–286.

10. Solomon, *Multinational*, 3.

11. For an early example of this, see "The Sun Never Sets on Cacoola," in *Time*, May 15, 1950, pp. 28–32. The essay claimed that Coca-Cola was ubiquitous worldwide: "People almost everywhere are buying it as if it were the biggest glass of ambrosia in the world for a nickel. . . . Coke's peaceful conquest of the world is one of the remarkable phenomena of the age" (p. 28).

12. Robert Sobel, *The Age of Giant Corporations: A Microeconomic History of American Business, 1914–1970* (Westport, Connecticut: Greenwood Press, Inc., 1972) 234.

13. Peter F. Drucker, *The Age of Discontinuity: Guidelines to Our Changing Society* (New York: Harper & Row, Publishers, 1968), 78–81.

14. John Fayerweather, *Annals* (September 1972), 5.

15. On page 10, of the November 11, 2003 issue of *U.S. News & World Report*, a cartoon illustrates an important objective of a state-less corporation.

Visualize a meeting of either a corporate board of directors, or top management, gathered around a conference table, in private.

The chairman pontificates: "Now gentlemen, as you know we have thought about moving production to China, which would result in much greater profits. But I have decided to keep production here in the United States. After all, we are Americans and we owe it to our fellow Americans."

The speaker then bursts out loudly: "Just kidding!!" (in large bold-faced letters) to laughter all around the table. One of which leans over to his neighbor and says: "Our fellow Americans! Ha!"

16. Richard J. Barnett, "Stateless Corporations: Lords of the Global Economy," in Kevin Danaher, *Corporations are Gonna Get Your Mama: Globalization* (Monroe, Maine: Common Cause Press, 1996), 35.

17. Legrain, *Open*, 136.

Note: As of 1999, the twenty largest U.S. MNCs were: GM, Wal-Mart, Exxon, Ford, GE, IBM, Citigroup, U.S. Postal Service, AT&T, Philip Morris, Boeing, Bank of America, SBC Communications, Hewlett-Packard, Kroger, State Farm Insurance, Sears, AIG, Enron, TIAA-CREF. In Europe, their largest 20: Daimler-Chrysler, Royal Dutch-Shell, AXA, BP, Volkswagen, Siemins, Ailans, ING Group, Deutsche Bank, Assicurazioni Generali, E.On, Fiat, Nestlé, Credit Suisse, Metro, Total Fina Elf, Vivendi, Unilever, Fortis, Prudential Insurance. (Source: Rugman, *The End of Globalization*, pp. 157–158.) See also *Fortune*, April 18, 2005, for its lists of top world corporations, etc.

Bibliography

Adams, Michael C. C. *The Best War Ever: America and World War II*. Baltimore: The Johns Hopkins University Press, 1994.

Adams, Samuel H. "The New World of Trade: The Art of Advertising" part 1. *Colliers*, 43 (May 22, 1909), 13–15.

Alexander, Herbert E. *Financing Politics: Money, Elections, and Political Reform*. Washington, DC: Congressional Quarterly Press, 1992.

Alexander, Herbert E. *Financing the 1960 Election*. Princeton, New Jersey: Citizens' Research Foundation, 1960.

Alexander, Herbert E. *Financing the 1964 Election*. Princeton, New Jersey: Citizens' Research Foundation, 1966.

Alexander, Herbert E. *Financing the 1968 Election*. Lexington, MA: Heath Lexington Books, 1971.

Alexander, Herbert E. *Financing the 1972 Election*. Lexington, MA: Lexington Books, 1976.

Alexander, Herbert E. *Financing the 1976 Election*. Washington, DC: Congressional Quarterly Press, 1979.

Alexander, Herbert E. *Financing the 1980 Election*. Lexington, MA: Lexington Books, 1983.

Alexander, Herbert E., and Brian A. Haggerty. *Financing the 1984 Election*. Lexington, MA: Lexington Books, 1987.

Alexander, Herbert E., and Monica Bauer. *Financing the 1988 Election*. Boulder, Colorado: Westview Press, 1991.

Alexander, Herbert E., and Anthony Corrado. *Financing the 1992 Election*. Armonk, NY: M.S. Sharpe, 1995.

Allen, Frederick L. *The Great Pierpont Morgan*. New York: Harper & Brothers, Publishers, 1949.

Allen, Frederick L. *The Lords of Creation.* New York: Harper & Brothers, 1935.

Allen, Frederick L. "The Big Change in Suburbia," Part I *Harper's Magazine* 208 (June 1954), 21–28.

Anderson, H. Dewey, and Percy E. Davidson. *Occupational Trends in the United States.* Stanford: Stanford University Press, 1940.

Anderson, H. Dewey, and Percy E. Davidson. *Recent Occupational Trends in American Labor.* Stanford: Stanford University Press, 1945.

Annals of the American Academy of Political and Social Science Special Issue: "Pressure Groups and Propaganda" 179 (May 1935).

Annals of the American Academy of Political and Social Science Special Issue: "The Multinational Corporation" 403 (September 1972)

Architectural Forum, July 1948.

Argyris, Chris. *Personality and Organization: The Conflict Between System and the Individual.* New York: Harper & Row, Publishers, 1957.

Argyris, Chris. "The Individual and Organization: Some Problems of Mutual Adjustment," *Administrative Science Quarterly* 2 (June 1957), 1–24.

Ashford, Kathryn L. "The Role of Corporations in the 1980 Congressional Elections," *Sociological Inquiry* 56 (Fall 1986), 409–431.

Badger, Anthony. *The New Deal: The Depression Years, 1933–1940.* Chicago: Ivan R. Dee, paperback edition, 2002 (1989).

Barber, Benjamin. *Jihad vs. McWorld.* New York: Times Books, 1995.

Barnett, Richard J., and Ronald E. Muller. *Global Reach: The Power of the Multinational Corporation.* New York: Simon & Schuster, 1974.

Barnett, Richard J., and John Cavanagh. *Global Dreams: Imperial Corporations and the New World Order.* New York: Simon & Schuster, 1994.

Barnouw, Erik. *Tube of Plenty: The Evolution of American Television.* New York: Oxford University Press (1975), reprint edition, 1977.

Barovik, Richard L. "Report from Washington—Congress Looks at the Multinational Corporation," *Columbia Journal of World Business* 5 (May–June 1970), 75–79.

Baruch, Bernard, and (editor) Richard H. Hippelheuser, Richard H. *American Industry in the War: A Report of the War Industries Board.* New York: Prentice-Hall, Inc., 1941.

Bellush, Bernard. *The Failure of the NRA.* New York: W. W. Norton & Company, Inc., 1975.

Beney, Ada. *Wages in the United States, 1914–1929.* New York: National Industrial Conference Board, Inc., 1930.

Beney, M. Ada. *Wages, Hours, and Employment in the United States, 1914–1936.* New York: National Industrial Conference Board, Inc., 1936

Bensman, Joseph, and Arthur J. Vidich. *The New American Society: The Revolution of the Middle Class.* Chicago: Quadrangle Books, 1971.

Benson, Susan P. *Counter Cultures: Saleswomen, Managers, and Customers in American Department Stores, 1890–1940.* Urbana: University of Illinois Press, 1986

Berkhofer, Robert F. Jr. "The Organizational Interpretation of American History," *Prospects* 4 (1979), 611–629.

Berle, Adolf A., and Gardiner C. Means. *The Modern Corporation and Private Property.* New York: Harcourt, Brace & World, Inc. (1932) revised edition, 1968.

Bernays, Edward L. *Public Relations*. Norman, Oklahoma: University of Oklahoma Press, 1972.

Bernays, Edward L., editor. *The Engineering of Consent*. Norman: University of Oklahoma Press, 1955.

Berry, Jeffrey M. *The Interest Group Society*. Boston: Little, Brown and Company, 1984.

Birnbaum, Jeffrey H. *The Lobbyists: How Influence Peddlers Get Their Way in Washington*. New York: Random House, 1992.

Birnbaum, Jeffrey H. *The Moneymen: The Real Story of Fund-Raising's Influence on Political Power in America*. New York: Crown Publishers, 2000.

Blackford, Mansel G., and K. Austin Kerr. *Business Enterprise in American History*. Boston: Houghton Mifflin Company, 1986.

Bogart, Leo. *The Age of Television: A Study of Viewing Habits and the Impact of Television on American Life*. New York: Frederick Unger Publishing Co., 1957.

Boorstin, Daniel J. *The Americans: The Democratic Experience*. New York: Random House, 1973.

Boulding, Kenneth E. *The Organizational Revolution: A Study in the Ethics of Economic Organization*. Chicago: Quadrangle Books (1953), 1968.

Bowen, Catherine D. *The Most Dangerous Man in America: Scenes from the Life of Benjamin Franklin*. Boston: Little, Brown and Company, 1974.

Brody, David. *Workers in Industrial America: Essays on the Twentieth Century Struggle*. New York: Oxford University Press, 1980.

Burns, James M., and Susan Dunn. *The Three Roosevelts: Patrician Leaders Who Transformed America*. New York: Atlantic Monthly Press, 2001.

Business Week, "The Stateless Corporation" (May 14, 1990), 98–105.

Business Week, "Television: The New Cyclops" (March 19, 1956), 76–104.

Business Week, "Special Report—Multinational Companies: Why and How They've Grown in Today's Global Market" (April 20, 1963), 62–86

Calder, Lendol. *Financing the American Dream: A Cultural History of Consumer Credit*. Princeton, NJ: Princeton University Press, 1999.

Catton, Bruce. *The Warlords of Washington*. New York: Harcourt, Brace and Company, 1948.

Chandler, Alfred D. Jr. *The Railroads: The Nation's First Big Business*. New York: Harcourt, Brace, & World, Inc., 1965.

Chandler, Alfred D. Jr. *Scale and Scope: The Dynamics of Industrial Capitalism*. Cambridge, MA: Belknap Press, 1990.

Chandler, Alfred D. Jr. *Strategy and Structure: Chapters in the History of Industrial Enterprise*. Garden City, New Jersey: Doubleday & Company, Inc. (1962). Anchor Books edition, 1966.

Chandler, Alfred D. Jr. *The Visible Hand: The Managerial Revolution in American Business*. Cambridge, MA: The Belknap Press, 1977.

Chandler, Alfred D. Jr., and Bruce Mazlish. *Leviathans: Multinational Corporations and the New Global History*. Cambridge, UK: Cambridge University Press, 2005.

Chandler, Alfred D. Jr. "The Railroads: Pioneers in Modern Corporate Management," *Business History Review* 39 (Spring 1965), 16–40.

Chase, Stuart. *Democracy under Pressure: Special Interests vs. the Public* Welfare. New York: The Twentieth Century Fund, 1945.

Clarkson, Grosvenor B. *Industrial America in the World War: The Strategy Behind the Line, 1917–1918.* Boston: Houghton Mifflin Company, 1923.

Clawson, Dan et al. "The Logic of Business Unity: Corporate Contributions to the 1980 Congressional Elections," *American Sociological Review* 51 (December 1986), 797–811.

Cleveland, Alfred S. "NAM: Spokesman for Industry," *Harvard Business Review* 26 (May 1948), 353–369

Cochran, Thomas C. "The Organization Man in Historical Perspective." *Pennsylvania History* 24 (January 1957), 9–24.

Cochran, Thomas C., and William Miller. *The Age of Enterprise: A Social History of Industrial America.* New York: Harper Torchbooks, revised edition, 1961.

Cohen, Lizabeth. *Making a New Deal: Industrial Workers in Chicago, 1919–1939.* New York: Cambridge University Press, 1990.

Cohen, Lizabeth. *A Consumers'Republic: The Politics of Mass Consumption in Postwar America.* New York: Knopf, 2003.

Collier's, February 14, 1948.

Continetti, Matthew. *The K Street Gang: The Rise and Fall of the Republican Machine.* New York: Doubleday, 2006.

Cook, Fred J. *Lobbying in American Politics.* New York: Franklin Watts, 1976.

Cooling, Benjamin F. *Gray Steel and Blue Water Navy: The Formative Years of America's Military-Industrial Complex, 1881–1917* Hambden, CT: Archon Books, 1979.

Cooling, Benjamin F., editor. *War, Business, and American Society: Historical Perspectives on the Military-Industrial Complex.* Port Washington, NY: Kennikat Press Corp., 1977.

Cooper, John M. *The Warrior and the Priest: Woodrow Wilson and Theodore Roosevelt.* Cambridge, MA: Belknap Press, 1983.

Crawford, Kenneth G. *The Pressure Boys: The Inside Story of Lobbying in America* New York: Julian Messner, Inc., 1939.

Croly, Herbert. *The Promise of American Life* New York: Macmillan Co., 1909

Croly, Herbert. *Marcus Alonzo Hanna: His Life and Work* New York: The MacMillan Company, 1912.

Cross, Gary. *An All-Consuming Century: Why Commercialism Won in Modern America.* New York: Columbia University Press, 2000.

Cuff, Robert D. *The War Industries Board: Business-Government Relations During World War I* Baltimore: The Johns Hopkins University Press, 1971.

Cyphers, Christopher. *The National Civic Federation and the Making of a New Liberalism, 1900–1915.* Westport, Conneticut: Praeger, 2002.

Daedalus Special Issue: "What Future for the State?" 124 (Spring 1995).

Danaher, Kevin. *Corporations are Gonna Get Your Mama: Globalization.* Monroe, ME: Common Courage Press, 1996.

Deakin, James. *The Lobbyists.* Washington, DC: Public Affairs Press, 1966.

Dean, John W. *Conservatives Without Conscience.* New York: Viking, 2006.

Diamond, Edwin. "Young Wives," *Newsweek* 55 (March 7, 1960), 57–60.

Dichter, Ernest. *Motivating Human Behavior.* New York: McGraw-Hill Book Company, 1971.

Dichter, Ernest. *The Strategy of Desire.* New York: Doubleday & Company, Inc., 1960.

Domhoff, G. William. *The Bohemian Grove and Other Retreats: A Study in Ruling-Class Cohesiveness.* New York: Harper & Row, Publishers, 1974.

Domhoff, G. William. *The Higher Circles: The Governing Class in America.* New York: Random House, 1970.

Domhoff, G. William. *Who Rules America: Power and Politics*, Fourth Edition. Boston: McGraw-Hill, 2002.

Domhoff, G. William. *The Powers that Be: Processes of Ruling-Class Domination in America.* New York: Vintage Books, 1979.

Dosal, Paul J. *Doing Business with the Dictators: A Political History of United Fruit in Guatemala, 1899–1944.* Wilmington, Delaware: SR Books, 1993.

Douglas, Paul H. *Real Wages in the United States, 1890–1926.* Boston: Houghton Mifflin Company, 1930.

Draffan, George. *The Elite Consensus: When Corporations Wield the Constitution.* New York: Apex Press, 2003.

Drew, Elizabeth. *The Corruption of American Politics: What Went Wrong and Why.* New York: The Overlook Press, 2000 (1999).

Drew, Elizabeth. *Politics and Money: The New Road to Corruption.* New York: Macmillan Publishing Company, 1983.

Drucker, Peter. *The Age of Discontinuity: Guidelines to Our Changing Society.* New York: Harper & Row, Publishers, 1968.

Drucker, Peter F. *Concept of the Corporation.* New York: The John Day Company, revised edition, 1972 (1946).

Drucker, Peter F. *The New Society: The Anatomy of the Industrial Order.* Westport, Connecticut: Greenwood Press, reprint, 1982 (1949).

Drucker, Peter F. "Multinationals and Developing Countries: Myths and Realities," *Foreign Affairs* 53 (October 1974), 121–134.

Eiler, Keith E. *Mobilizing America: Robert P. Patterson and the War Effort, 1940–1945.* Ithaca: Cornell University Press, 1997.

Eisendrath, Craig, et al. *The Phantom Defense: America's Pursuit of the Star Wars Illusion* Westport, Connecticut: Praeger, 2001.

Emmet, Boris and Jeuck, John E. *Catalogs and Counters: A History of Sears, Roebuck & Company.* Chicago: The University of Chicago Press, 1950.

Ewen, Stuart. *All Consuming Images: The Politics of Style in Contemporary Culture.* New York: Basic Books, Inc., Publishers, 1988.

Ewen, Stuart, and Elizabeth Ewen. *Channels of Desire: Mass Images and the Shaping of American Consciousness.* Minneapolis: University of Minnesota Press, 1992.

Fayerweather, John. "The Internationalization of Business," *Annals of the American Academy of Political and Social Science* 403 (September 1972) Special Issue, "The Multinational Corporation," 1–11.

Filene, Edward A. *The Way Out: A Forecast of Coming Changes in American Business and Industry.* New York: Doubleday, Page & Company, 1925.

Fitzpatrick, F. Stuart. *A Study of Buseiness Men's Associations.* Olean, New York: Olean Times Publishing Company Press, 1925.

Fortune. "The Lush New Suburban Market," 48 (November 1953), 128–131, 230–37.

Foth, Joseph H. *Trade Associations: Their Services to Industry.* New York: The Ronald Press Company, 1930.

Fox, Stephen P. *The Mirror Makers: A History of American Advertising and its Creators.* New York: Vintage Books, 1985.

Frank, Thomas. *The Conquest of Cool: Business Culture, Counterculture, and the Rise of Consumerism.* Chicago: The University of Chicago Press, 1997.

Frank, Thomas. "High Corporate Baroque" *The Nation* 12/30/1996

Frederick, Christine. "New Wealth, New Standards of Living and Changed Family Budgets," *Annals of the American Academy of Political and Social Science* 115 (September 1924), 74–82.

Friedan, Betty. *The Feminine Mystique.* New York: W. W. Norton & Company, Inc., 1963.

Fromm, Eric. *The Sane Society.* New York: Henry Holt and Company, 1955.

Fromm, Erich. "The Present Human Condition," *The American Scholar* 25 (Winter 1955–1956), 29–46.

Fussell, Paul. *Thank God for the Atom Bomb and Other Essays.* New York: Summit Books, 1988

Galambos, Louis. *America at Middle Age: A New History of the United States in the Twentieth Century.* New York: McGraw-Hill Book Company, 1983.

Galambos, Louis. *Competition and Cooperation: The Emergence of a National Trade Association* Baltimore: The Johns Hopkins University Press, 1966.

Galambos, Louis, and Joseph Pratt. *The Rise of the Corporate Commonwealth: U.S. Business and Public Policy in the Twentieth Century.* New York: Basic Books, Inc., Publishers, 1988.

Galambos, Louis. "The Emerging Organizational Synthesis in Modern American History," *Business History Review* 44 (Autumn 1970), 279–90.

Galambos, Louis. "Technology, Political Economy, and Professionalization: Central Themes of the Organizational Synthesis," *Business History Review* 57 (Winter, 1983), 471–92.

Galbraith, John K. *American Capitalism: The Concept of Countervailing Power.* Revised Edition. Boston: Houghton Mifflin Company, 1956 (1952).

Gans, Herbert J. *The Levittowners: Way of Life and Politics in a New Suburban Community.* New York: Pantheon Books, 1967.

Garraty, John A. *The Great Depression.* New York: Anchor Books, 1987.

Garvey, Ellen G. *The Adman in the Parlor: Magazines and the Gendering of Consumer Culture, 1880s to 1910s.* New York: Oxford University Press, 1996.

Gilbreth, Frank B. *Primer of Scientific Management.* New York: D. van Nostrand Company, 1914.

Gilpin Robert. *Global Political Economy: Understanding the International Economic Order.* Princeton: Princeton University Press, 2001.

Gilpin, Robert. *U.S. Power and the Multinational Corporation: The Political Economy of Foreign Direct Investment.* New York: Basic Books, Inc.,1975.

Gilpin, Robert, and Jean M. Gilpin. *The Challenge of Global Capitalism: The World Economy in the 21st Century.* Princeton: Princeton University Press, 2000.

Going, Charles B. *Principles of Industrial Engineering.* New York: McGraw-Hill Book Company, 1911.

Gold, Herbert. "The Age of Happy Problems," *The Atlantic Monthly* 199 (March 1957), 58–61.

Goldsmith, Selma et al. "Size Distribution of Income since the Mid-Thirties," *The Review of Economics and Statistics* 36 (February 1954), 1–32.

Gordon, Colin. *New Deals: Business, Labor, and Politics in America, 1920–1935.* Cambridge University Press, 1994.

Gossett, William T. *Corporate Citizenship.* Lexington, Virginia: Washington and Lee University, 1957.

Gourevitch, Peter A. "Breaking with Orthodoxy: The Politics of Economic Policy Responses to the Depression of the 1930s," *International Organization* 38 (Winter 1984), 95–129.

Green, Mark. *Selling Out: How Big Corporate Money Buys Elections, Rams Through Legislation and Betrays Our Democracy.* New York: Regan Books, 2002.

Green, Mark J., and Michael Waldman, et al. *Who Runs Congress?* New York: Dell Publishing Co., 1984 (4th Edition)

Greenberg, Edward S. *Serving the Few: Corporate Capitalism and the Bias of Government Policy.* New York: John Wiley & Sons, Inc., 1974.

Greider, William R. *Who Will Tell the People?: The Betrayal of American Democracy.* New York: Simon & Schuster, 1992.

Gulick, Luther. *Administrative Reflections from World War II.* University, Alabama: University of Alabama Press, 1948.

Halberstram, David. *The Fifties.* New York: Villard Books, 1993.

Hawley, Ellis W. *The New Deal and the Problem of Monopoly.* Princeton: Princeton University Press, 1966.

Hawley, Ellis W. "Herbert Hoover, the Commerce Secretariat, and the Vision of an 'Associative State,' 1921–1928," *Journal of American History* 61 (June 1974), 116–140.

Heard, Alexander. *The Costs of Democracy.* Chapel Hill: The University of North Carolina Press, 1960.

Hearn, Charles R. *The American Dream in the Great Depression.* Westport, CT: Greenwood Press, 1977.

Henderson, Henry. "The Mass Produced Suburbs—Part I, How People Live," *Harper's Magazine* 207 (November 1953), 25–32.

Henderson, Henry. "Rugged American Collectivism—The Mass Produced Suburbs, Part II." *Harper's Magazine* 207 (December 1953), 80–88.

Hendrickson, Robert. *The Grand Emporiums: The Illustrated History of America's Great Department Stores.* New York: Stein and Day, 1979.

Hettinger, Herman S. *A Decade of Radio Advertising.* Chicago: The University of Chicago Press, 1933.

Hickman, Bert G. *Growth and Stability of the Postwar Economy.* Washington, DC: The Brookings Institution, 1960.

Hicks, John D. *Republican Ascendancy 1921–1933*. New York: Harper & Brothers, Publishers, 1960.

Himmelberg, Robert F. *The Origins of the National Recovery Administration: Business, Government, and the Trade Association Issue, 1921–1933*. New York: Fordham University Press, 1976.

Hine, Thomas. *Populuxe*. New York: Alfred A. Knopf, 1986.

Hogan, Michael J. *A Cross of Iron: Harry S. Truman and the Origins of the National Security State, 1945–1954*. Cambridge University Press, 1998.

Horowitz, Daniel. *The Morality of Spending: Attitudes Toward the Consumer Society in America, 1875–1940*. Chicago: Ivan R. Dee Publisher (1985) Elephant Paperbacks, 1992.

Horowitz, Daniel *Vance Packard and American Social Criticism* Chapel Hill: The University of North Carolina Press, 1994.

Horowitz, David, editor. *Corporations and the Cold War*. New York: Monthly Review Press, 1969.

Hounshell, David A. *From the American System to Mass Production, 1800–1932: The Development of Manufacturing Technology in the United States*. Baltimore: Johns Hopkins University Press, 1984.

Hower, Ralph M. *The History of an American Advertising Agency: N.W. Ayer & Son at Work, 1869–1949* Cambridge: Harvard University Press, Revised Edition, 1949.

Israel, Jerry, editor. *Building the Organizational Society*. New York: The Free Press, 1972.

Jackson, Kenneth T. *Crabgrass Frontier: The Suburbanization of the United States*. New York: Oxford University Press, 1985.

Jacoby, Neil H. *Corporate Power and Social Responsibility: A Blueprint for the Future*. New York: Macmillan Publishing Co., Inc., 1973.

Janeway, Eliot. *The Struggle for Survival: A Chronicle of Economic Mobilization in World War II*. New Haven: Yale University Press, 1951.

Johnson, Haynes. *Sleepwalking Through History: America in the Reagan Years*. New York: W. W. Norton, 1991.

Johnson, Hugh J. *The Blue Eagle from Egg to Earth*. Garden City, New York: Doubleday, Doran, & Company, Inc., 1935.

Josephson, Matthew. *The Politicos, 1865–1896*. New York: Harcourt, Brace & World, Inc., 1938.

Josephson, Matthew. *The Robber Barons, the Great American Capitalists, 1861–1901*. New York: Harcourt, Brace Jovanovich, Publishers, 1934.

Josephson, Matthew. *The Money Lenders: The Great Finance Capitalists, 1925–1950*. New York: Weybright and Talley, 1972

Josephson, Matthew. *The President Makers: The Culture of Politics and Leadership in an Age of Enlightenment, 1896–1919. New York*: Frederick Ungar Publishing Co., 1964 (1940).

Kammen, Michael G. *The Rope of Sand: The Colonial Agents, British Politics, and the American Revolution* Ithaca: Cornell University Press, 1968.

Kanigel, Robert. *The One Best Way: Frederick Winslow Taylor and the Enigma of Efficiency*. New York: Penguin Books, 1999 (1997).

Kapoor, Ashok, and Phillip D. Grub. *The Multinational Enterprise in Transition: Readings and Essays* Princeton, NJ: The Darvin Press, 1972.

Kaysen, Carl. *The American Corporation Today*. New York: Oxford University Press, 1996.

Kaysen Carl. "The Social Significance of the Modern Corporation," *American Economic Review* 4 (July 5, 1957), 311–319.

Keats, John. *The Crack in the Picture Window*. Boston: Houghton Mifflin Company, 1956.

Key, Vladimir O. Jr. *Politics, Parties & Pressure Groups*. New York: Thomas Y. Crowell Company, 1964 (Fifth Edition) (1942).

Kindleberger, Charles P. *American Business Abroad*. New Haven, Connecticut: Yale University Press, 1969.

Klein, Maury. *The Flowering of the Third America: The Making of an Organizational Society, 1850–1920*. Chicago: Ivan R. Dee, 1993.

Klein, Maury. *The End of the Rainbow: The Crash of 1929*. New York: Oxford University Press, 2001.

Koistinen, Paul A. C. *The Military Industrial Complex: A Historical Perspective*. New York: Praeger, 1980.

Koistinen, Paul A. C. "The Industrial-Military Complex in Historical Perspective," in Pursell, Carroll W. *The Military-Industrial Complex*. New York: Harper & Row, 1972.

Koistinen, Paul A. C. "The 'Industrial-Military Complex' in Historical Perspective: World War I," *Business History Review* 41 (Winter 1967), 378–403.

Kolko, Gabriel. *The Triumph of Conservatism: A Reinterpretation of American History, 1900–1916*. New York: The Free Press, 1963.

Korten, David C. *The Post-Corporate World: Life After Capitalism*. West Hartford, Connecticut: Kumarian Press and San Francisco: Berrett-Koehler Publishers, 1999.

Kroos, Herman E. *Executive Opinion: What Business Leaders Said and Thought on Economic Issues, 1920s–1960s*. Garden City, New Jersey: Doubleday & Company, Inc., 1970.

Landsberger, Henry A. *Hawthorne Revisited: Management and the Worker, Its Critics and Developments in Human Relations Industry*. Ithaca, NY: Cornell University, State School of Industrial Relations, 1953.

Leach, William. *Land of Desire: Merchants, Power, and the Rise of a New American Culture*. New York: Pantheon Books, 1993.

Lebergott, Stanley. *Pursuing Happiness: American Consumers in the Twentieth Century*. Princeton: Princeton University Press, 1993.

Lebhar, Godfrey M. *Chain Stores in America, 1859–1962*. New York: Chain Store Publishing Corporation, 1963 Third Edition.

Legrain, Phillippe. *Open World: The Truth about Globalization*. London, England: Abacus, 2002.

Leuchtenberg, William E. *Franklin D. Roosevelt and the New Deal, 1932–1940*. New York: Harper Torchbooks, 1963.

Leuchtenberg, William E. *The Perils of Prosperity, 1914–1932*. Chicago: The University of Chicago Press, 1958.

Lingeman, Richard R. *Don't You Know There's a War on? The American Home Front, 1941–1945*. New York: G. P. Putnam's Sons, Capricorn Books, 1976 (1970).

Link, Arthur. *Woodrow Wilson and the Progressive Era, 1900–1917*. New York: Harper & Brothers, Publishers, 1954.

Lipset, Seymour M., and Reihard Bendix. *Social Mobility in Industrial Society.* Berkeley: University of California Press, 1964 (1959)

Luce, Henry R. "The American Century," *Life* 10 (February 17, 1941), 61–65

Lynd, Robert, and Helen M. Lynd. *Middletown: A Study in American Culture*. New York: Harcourt, Brace & World Inc. (1929), 1956.

Lynd, Robert, and Helen M. Lynd. *Middletown in Transition: A Study in Cultural Conflicts*. New York: Harcourt, Brace, & World, Inc. (1937), 1965.

Lynd, Robert, and Alice C. Hanson. "The People as Consumers," in *Recent Social Trends in the United States: Report of the President's Research Committee on Social Trends*, Volume II, New York: McGraw-Hill Book Company, Inc., 1933.

Lynes, Russell. *A Surfeit of Honey*. New York: Harper & Brothers Publishers, 1953.

Lyon, Leverett S. et al. *The National Recovery Administration: An Analysis and Appraisal.* Washington, DC: The Brookings Institution, 1935.

MacDonald, J. Fred. *One Nation Under Television: The Rise and Decline of Network TV*. New York: Pantheon Books, 1990.

Magdoff, Harry. *The Age of Imperialism: The Economics of U.S. Foreign Policy*. New York: Modern Reader Paperbacks, 1969.

Magleby, David B. *Financing the 2000 Election.* Washington, DC: Brookings Institution Press, 2002.

Magleby, David B. *Outside Money: Soft Money and Issue Advocacy in the 1998 Congressional Elections.* Lanham, Maryland: Rowman & Littlefield Publisher, 2000.

Marchand, Roland. *Advertising the American Dream: Making Way for Modernity, 1920–1940.* Berkeley: University of California Press, 1985.

Marchand, Roland. *Creating the Corporate Soul: The Rise of Public Relations and Corporate Imagery in American Business.* Berkeley: University of California Press, 1998.

Marling, Karal A. *As Seen on TV: The Visual Culture of Everyday Life in the 1950s.* Cambridge: Harvard University Press, 1994.

Matthews, Donald. *The Social Background of Political Decision Makers.* Garden City, New York: Doubleday, 1954.

May, Stacy, and Galo Plaza. *The United Fruit Company in Latin America*. New York: Arno Press, 1976 (1958) original edition used?

McClure's September 1910, p. 250.

McCreary, Edward A. *The Americanization of Europe: The Impact of Americans and American Business on the Uncommon Market.* Garden City, New York: Doubleday & Company, Inc., 1964.

McMahon, A. Michael. "An American Courtship: Psychologists and Advertising Theory in the Progressive Era," *American Studies* 13 (Fall 1972), 5–18.

McQuaid, Kim. *Big Business and Presidential Power from FDR to Reagan*. New York: William Morrow and Company, Inc., 1982.

McQuaid, Kim. *Uneasy Partners: Big Business in American Politics, 1945–1990.* Baltimore: The Johns Hopkins University Press, 1994.

McQuaid, Kim. "Corporate Liberalism in the American Business Community, 1920–1940," *Business History Review* [ ] (Autumn 1978), 342–368.

Meade, Emily F. "The Place of Advertising in Modern Business," *Journal of Political Economy* 9 (March 1901), 218–242.

Merkle, Judith A. *Management and Ideology: The Legacy of the International Scientific Management Movement*. Berkeley: University of California Press, 1980.

Meyer, Stephen III. *The Five Dollar Day: Labor Management and Social Control in the Ford Motor Company, 1908–1921*. Albany: State University of New York Press, 1981.

Mills, C. Wright. *The Power Elite*. New York: Oxford University Press, 1956.

Mills, C. Wright. *White Collar: The American Middle Class*. New York: Oxford University Press, 1956 (1951).

Mintz, Morton, and Jerry S. Cohen. *America, Inc.,: Who Owns and Operates the United States*. New York: The Dial Press, 1971.

Montagu, Ashley. *The American Way of Life*. New York: G. P. Putnam's Sons, 1967 (1952).

Morris, Edmund. *Theodore Rex*. New York: Random House, 2001.

Mowry, George. *The Era of Theodore Roosevelt, 1900–1912*. New York: Harper Torchbooks, 1958.

Nash, Gerald D. *The Crucial Era: The Great Depression and World War II, 1929–1945* (Second Edition). New York: St. Martin's Press, 1992.

Nelson, Donald M. *Arsenal of Democracy: The Story of American War Production*. New York: Harcourt, Brace and Company, 1946.

Ohmann, Richard. *Selling Culture: Magazines, Markets, and Class at the Turn of the Century*. New York: Verso, 1996.

Olney, Martha L. *Buy Now, Pay Later: Advertising, Credit, and Consumer Durables in the 1920s*. Chapel Hill: University of North Carolina Press, 1991.

O'Neill, William L. *American High: The Years of Confidence, 1945–1960*. New York: The Free Press, 1986.

O'Neill, William L. *A Democracy at War: America's Fight at Home and Abroad in World War II*. New York: The Free Press, 1993.

Overacker, Louise. *Money in Elections*. New York: Arno Press, 1974 (1932).

Overacker, Louise. *Presidential Campaign Funds*. Boston: Boston University Press, 1946.

Overacker, Louise. "Campaign Funds in the Presidential Election of 1936," *American Political Science Review* 31 (June 1937), 473–498.

Packard, Vance. *The Hidden Persuaders*. New York: Pocket Books, 1957.

Packard, Vance. *The Naked Society*. New York: David McKay Company, Inc., 1964.

Packard, Vance. *The People Shapers*. Boston: Little, Brown and Company, 1977.

Packard, Vance. *The Pyramid Climbers*. New York: McGraw-Hill Book Company, Inc., 1962.

Patten, Simon N. *The Consumption of Wealth*. Publications of the University of Pennsylvania, 1901.

Patten, Simon N. *The New Basis of Civilization*. Cambridge: Belknap Press, Reprint edition, 1968 (1907).

Pells, Richard H. *Radical Visions and American Dreams: Culture and Social Thought in the Depression Years*. New York: Harper & Row, Publishers, 1973.

Pendergast, Tom. *Creating the Modern Man: American Magazines and Consumer Culture, 1900–1950*. New York: Columbia University Press, 2000.

Phillips, David G. *The Treason of the Senate*. New York: The Monthly Review Press (reprint), 1953.

Phillips, Joseph D. "Economic Effects of the Cold War," in David Horowitz, *Corporations and the Cold War*. New York: Monthly Review Press, 1969.

Phillips, Kevin. *Arrogant Capital: Washington, Wall Street, and the Frustration of American Politics* (paperback). Boston, MA: Back Bay Books, Little, Brown and Company, 1995 (1994).

Polenberg, Richard. *War and Society: The United States, 1941–1945*. New York: J.B. Lippincott Company, 1972.

Postman, Neil. *Amusing Ourselves to Death: Public Discourse in the Age of Show Business*. New York: Penguin Books, 1986.

Potter, David M. *People of Plenty: Economic Abundance and the American Character*. Chicago: University of Chicago Press, 1954.

Presthus, Robert. *The Organizational Society*. New York: St. Martin's Press, Revised edition, 1978 (1962).

Prewitt, Kenneth, and Alan Stone. *The Ruling Elites: Elite Theory, Power and American Democracy*. New York: Harper & Row, Publishers, 1973.

Public Papers of the Presidents of the United States, Dwight D. Eisenhower "Farewell Radio and Television Address to the American People, January 17, 1961," pp. 1035–40. Washington, DC, 1960–61.

The Railroad Gazette. December 18, 1882, December 22, 1882, December 29, 1882.

Randall, Gregory C. *America's Original GI Town, Park Forest, Illinois*. Baltimore: Johns Hopkins University Press, 2000.

Recent Social Trends in the United States: Report of the President's Research Committee on Social Trends, Vol. II. New York: McGraw-Hill Book Company, Inc., 1933.

Rees, Albert. *Real Wages in Manufacturing, 1890–1914*. Princeton: Princeton University Press, 1961.

Richberg, Donald. *The Rainbow*. Garden City, New York: Doubleday, Doran & Company, Inc., 1936.

Riddle, Donald H. *The Truman Committee: A Study in Congressional Responsibility*. New Brunswick: Rutgers University Press, 1964.

Riesman, David. *Abundance for What?* New Brunswick, New Jersey: Transaction Publishers, 1993.

Riesman, David, et al. *The Lonely Crowd: A Study of the Changing American Character*. Garden City, NY: Doubleday, 1953.

Riesman, David. "The Suburban Dislocation," *The Annals of the American Academy of Political and Social Science*, 314 (November 1957), 123–46.

Riesman, David. "Abundance for What?" *Bulletin of the Atomic Scientists* 14 (April 1958), 135–139.

Robock, Stefan H. and Simmonds, Kenneth. *International Business and Multinational Enterprises*. Richard D. Irwin, Inc., 1983 (Third Edition).

Rolfe, Sidney E., and Walter Dunn. *The Multinational Corporation in the World Economy: Direct Investment in Perspective*. New York: Praeger, 1970.
Rosen, Steven, editor. *Testing the Theory of the Military-Industrial Complex*. Lexington, MA: Lexington Books, 1973.
Rosenberg, Emily J. *Spreading the American Dream: American Economic and Cultural Expansion, 1890–1945*. New York: Hill & Wang, 1982.
Rothman, David. *Politics and Power: The United States Senate, 1869–1901*. Cambridge, MA: Harvard University Press, 1966.
Roy, William G. *Socializing Capital: The Rise of the Large Industrial Corporation in America*. Princeton: Princeton University Press, 1997.
Rugman, Alan. *The End of Globalization: Why Global Strategy Is a Myth & How to Profit from the Realities of Regional Markets*. New York: AMACOM, 2000.
Saari, David J. *Global Corporations and Sovereign Nations: Collision or Cooperation*. Westport, Connecticut: Quorum Books, 1999.
Sabato, Larry. *PAC Power: Inside the World of Political Action Committees*. New York: W. W. Norton & Company, 1984.
Sabato, Larry, and Glenn R. Simpson. *Dirty Little Secrets: The Persistence of Corruption in American Politics*. New York: Times Books, 1996.
Sampson, Anthony. *The Arms Bazaar, From Lebanon to Lockheed*. New York: The Viking Press, 1977.
Sampson, Anthony. *Company Man: The Rise and Fall of Corporate Life*. New York: Random House, 1995.
Sayre, Robert A. *Consumer Prices, 1914–1948*. New York: National Industrial Conference Board, Inc., 1948.
Scanlon, Jennifer. *Inarticulate Longings: The Ladies Home Journal, Gender, and the Promise of Consumer Culture*. New York: Routledge, 1995.
Schattschneider, E. E. *The Semisovereign People: A Realist's View of Democracy in America*. New York: Holt, Rinehart and Winston, 1960.
Schattschneider, E. E. "Pressure Groups Versus Political Parties," *Annals of the American Academy of Political and Social Science* 259 (September 1948), 17–23.
Schlesinger, Arthur Jr. *The Cycles of American History*. Boston: Houghton Mifflin Company, 1986.
Schlesinger, Stephen, and Stephen Kinzer. *Bitter Fruit: The Untold Story of the American Coup in Guatemala*. Garden City, NJ: Anchor Press/Doubleday, 1982.
Schneirov, Matthew. *The Dream of a New Social Order: Popular Magazines in America, 1893–1914*. New York: Columbia University Press, 1994.
Schriftgiesser, Karl. *Business Comes of Age: The Story of the Committee for Economic Development and its Impact upon the Economic Policies of the United States, 1942–1960*. New York: Harper & Brothers, 1960.
Schriftgiesser, Karl. *Business and Public Policy: The Role of the Committee for Economic Development, 1942–1967*. Englewood Cliffs, NJ: Prentice-Hall, Inc., 1967.
Schriftgiesser, Karl. *The Lobbysists: The Art and Business of Influencing Lawmakers*. Boston: Little, Brown and Company, 1951.
Scott, Walter D. *The Theory of Advertising*. New York: Garland Publishing, Inc., Reprint edition, 1985 (1903).

Sennett, Richard. *The Uses of Disorder: Personal Identity & City Life*. New York: Vintage Books, 1970.

Servan-Schreiber, J. J. *The American Challenge*. New York: Atheneum, 1968 (1967).

Silk, Leonard, and Mark Silk. *The American Establishment*. New York: Basic Books, Inc., 1978.

Sivulka, Juliann. *Soap, Sex, and Cigarettes: A Cultural History of Advertising*. Belmont, California: Wausworth Publishing Company, 1997.

Skocpol, Theda, and Kenneth Finegold. "State Capacity and Economic Intervention in the Early New Deal," *Political Science Quarterly* 97 (Summer 1982), 255–78.

Skowronek, Stephen. *Building a New American State: The Expansion of National Administrative Capacities, 1877–1920*. New York: Cambridge University Press, 1982.

Smith, George H. *Motivation Research in Advertising and Marketing*. New York: McGraw-Hill Book Company, Inc., 1954.

Smith, Neil. *The Endgame of Globalization*. New York: Routledge, 2005.

Smuylan, Susan. *Selling Radio: The Commercialization of American Broadcasting, 1920–1934*. Washington: Smithsonian Institution Press, 1994.

Sobel, Robert. *The Age of Giant Corporations: A Microeonomic History of American Business, 1914–1970*. Westport, Connecticut: Greenwood Press, Inc., 1972.

Solomon, Lewis D. *Multinationals and the Emerging World Order*. Port Washington, N.Y.: Kennikat Press, 1978.

Sorauf, Frank J. *Inside Campaign Finance: Myths and Realities*. New Haven: Yale University Press, 1992.

Sorauf, Frank J. *Money in American Elections*. Glenview, Illinois: Scott, Foresman and Company, 1988.

Spears, Timothy B. *100 Years on the Road: The Traveling Salesman in American Culture*. New Haven: Yale University Press, 1995.

Stead, William T. *The Americanization of the World The Trend of the Twentieth Century*. New York: Garland Publishing, Inc., 1972 (1902)

Steigerwalt, Albert K. *The National Association of Manufacturers,1895–1914: A Study in Business Leadership*. Ann Arbor: University of Michigan, Bureau of Business Research, 1964.

Steiner, George A. *Government's Role in Economic Life*. New York: McGraw-Hill Book Company, Inc., 1953.

Stern, Philip M. *The Best Congress Money Can Buy*. New York: Pantheon Books, 1988.

Stone, Isidore F. *The War Years: A Nonconformist History of Our Times, 1939–1945*. Boston: Little, Brown and Company, 1988.

Stover, John F. *History of the Baltimore and Ohio Railroad*. West Lafayette, Indiana: Purdue University Press, 1987.

Strasser, Susan. *Satisfaction Guaranteed: The Making of the American Mass Market*. Pantheon Books, 1989.

Struber, John, and Sheldon Rampton. *Toxic Sludge is Good for You: Lies, Damn Lies, and the Public Relations Industry*. Monroe, ME: Common Courage Press, 1995.

Tasogawa, Hiroshi. *All The Emperor's Men: Kurosawa's Pearl Harbor*. Milwaukee: The Rowman & Littlefield Publishing Group, Inc., 2012. Google Books.

Tawney, R. H. *Religion and the Rise of Capitalism: A Historical Study*. New York: Harcourt, Brace and Company, 1926.

Tedlow, Richard S. *New and Improved: The Story of Mass Marketing in America*. Boston: Harvard Business School Press, 1996 (1990).

Thayer, George. *Who Shakes the Money Tree: American Campaign Financing Practices from 1789 to the Present*. New York: Simon & Schuster, 1973.

Theobald, Robert. *The Challenge of Abundance*. New York: Clarkson N. Potter, Inc. Publisher, 1961.

Thompson, Margaret S. *The "Spider Web." Congress and Lobbying in the Age of Grant*. Ithaca, NY: Cornell University Press, 1985.

Thurow, Lester C. *The Future of Capitalism: How Today's Economic Forces Shape Tomorrow's World*. New York: William Morrow and Company, Inc., 1996.

Tichi, Cecilia. *Electronic Hearth: Creating an American Television Culture*. New York: Oxford University Press, 1991.

Time. May 24, 1945

Time. "The Sun Never Sets on Cacoola," May 5, 1950, pp. 28–32.

Time. "Running with the Pacs" October 25, 1982. 19–26.

Time. "The Sun Never Sets on Cacoola," May 5, 1950, pp. 28–32.

Time. "Running with the Pacs" October 25, 1982. 19–26.

Tobin, Harold J., and Percy W. Bidwell. *Mobilizing Civilian America*. New York: Council on Foreign Relations, 1940.

Tolson, Jay. "Hamilton's Moment," *U.S. News & World Report* (September 20, 2004), 66–67.

Trachtenberg, Alan. *The Incorporation of America: Culture and Society in the Gilded Age*. New York: Hill & Wang, 1982.

Twitchell, James B. *Lead Us Into Temptation: The Triumph of American Materialism*. New York: Columbia University Press, 1999.

Tugendhat, Christopher. *The Multinationals*. Harmondsworth, England: Penguin Books (1971), 1973.

Turner, Frederick J. *The Frontier in American History*. Tucson: The University of Arizona Press, 1986. (1920)

Turner, Frederick J. "Social Forces in American History," *The American Historical Review* 16 (January 1911), 217–33.

Turner, Louis. *Multinational Companies and the Third World*. New York: Hill & Wang, 1973.

Turner, Louis. *Multinational Companies and the Modern World*. New York: Harcourt Brace Jovanovich, Inc., 1970

U.S. News & World Report, 11/11/2003.

van der Zee, John. *The Greatest Men's Party on Earth: Inside the Bohemian Grove*. New York: Harcourt Brace Jovanovich, Inc., 1974.

Vatter, Harold C. *The U.S. Economy in the 1950s: An Economic History*. Chicago: The University of Chicago Press, paperback edition, 1985 (1963).

Vernon, Raymond F. *In the Hurricane's Eye: The Troubled Prospects of Multinational Enterprises*. Cambridge, MA: Harvard University Press, 1998.

Vernon, Raymond F. *Storm Over the Multinationals: The Real Issues* Cambridge, MA: Harvard University Press, 1977.

Vidich, Arthur J., and Joseph Bensman. *Small Town in Mass Society: Class, Power, and Religion in a Rural American Community.* Princeton: Princeton University Press, 1968, [1958]

Vogel, David. *Fluctuating Fortunes: The Political Power of Business in America.* New York: Basic Books, 1989.

Vogel, David. *Kindred Strangers: The Uneasy Relationship Between Politics and Business in America.* Princeton: Princeton University Press, 1996.

Waddell, Brian. *The War against the New Deal: World War II and American Democracy.* DeKalb: Northern Illinois University Press, 2001.

Watson, John B. *Behaviorism*. New York: W. W. Norton & Company, Reprint Edition, 1970 (1930).

Weber, Max. *The Protestant Ethic and the Spirit of Capitalism*. New York: Scribner, 1958.

Weinberg, Steve. *Armand Hammer: The Untold Story*. New York: Little, Brown, and Company, 1989.

Weinstein, James. *The Corporate Ideal in the Liberal State, 1900–1918.* Boston: Beacon Press, 1968.

Wendt, Lloyd, and Herman Kogan. *Give the Lady What She Wants: The Story of Marshall Field & Company.* South Bend, Indiana: and books/the distributors, reprint edition, 1985 (1952).

Whitney, Simon N. *Trade Associations and Industrial Control: A Critique of the N.R.A.* New York: Central Book Company, 1934.

Whyte, William H. "The Corporation and the Wife," *Fortune*, 44 (November 1951). 109–11, 150–58.

Whyte, William H. "How the New Suburbia Socializes," 48 (August 1953), 120–22, 186–90.

Whyte, William H. "The Outgoing Life," *Fortune*, 48 (July 1953), 84–89, 156–60.

Whyte, William H. "The Transients," *Fortune*, 47 (May 1953), 112–17, 221–26.

Whyte, William H. "The Wife Problem," *Life* 32 (January 7, 1952), 32–48.

Whyte, William H. Jr. *The Organization Man*. New York: Simon & Schuster, 1956.

Wiebe, Robert H. *Businessmen and Reform: A Study of the Progressive Movement.* Cambridge: Harvard University Press, 1962.

Wiebe, Robert H. *The Search for Order, 1877–1920.* New York: Hill & Wang, 1967.

Wiebe, Robert H. *The Segmented Society: An Introduction to the Meaning of America.* New York: Oxford University Press, 1975.

Wiebe, Robert H. "The House of Morgan and the Executive, 1905–1913," *American Historical Review* 65 (October 1959), 49–60.

Wilkins, Mira. *The Emergence of Multinationals Enterprise: American Business Abroad from the Colonial Era to 1914.* Cambridge: Harvard University Press, 1970.

Wilkins, Mira. *The Maturing of Multinational Enterprise: American Business Abroad from 1914–1977.* Cambridge: Harvard University Press, 1970, and the 1974 edition looked at in 2005.

Wilson, Sloan. *The Man in the Gray Flannel Suit.* New York: Simon & Schuster, 1955.

Wilson, Woodrow, with William B. Hale, editors. *The New Freedom.* London: J. M. Dent & Sons, Ltd. (1916).

Winkler, Allan M. *Home Front U.S.A.: America During World War II.* Wheeling, IL: Harlan Davidson, Inc., 1986.

Wood, Robert C. *Suburbia: Its People & Their Politics.* Boston: Houghton Mifflin Company, 1958.

Wycoff, D. Daryl. *Railroad Management.* Lexington, MA: Lexington Books, DC Heath and Company, 1976.

Yearley, Clifton K. *The Money Machines: The Breakdown and Reform of Governmental and Party Finance in the North, 1860–1920.* Albany: State University of New York Press, 1970.

Zunz, Olivier. *Making America Corporate, 1870–1920.* Chicago: The University of Chicago Press, 1990.

Zunz, Olivier. *Why the American Century?* Chicago: The University of Chicago Press, 1998.

Index

About the Author

Thomas J. Dorich, from the Bridgeport neighborhood on Chicago's near southwest side, is the son of a truck driver and clerk typist. He received his basic education from Immaculate Conception Grammar School and De La Salle High School. He has a BS in secondary education (1973) and a MA in history (1975) from his beloved alma mater, Eastern Illinois University. He received a PhD in American history from Arizona State University, where he specialized in the American West, urban and community history, the Progressive Era, public history, and quantitative history. He has journal articles published on Jerome, Arizona, and its United Verde Copper company, Chicago history, and the Pella Window Corp.

His working life included doing clerical work in two Fortune 500 corporations, one medium company and at the Dallas Public Library, Arizona State Law Library, and the U.S. Census Bureau. Later in life he worked seasonally for the Educational Testing Service AP Program, the National Park Service, and the U.S Forest Service.

His liberal arts gypsy career includes living in eighteen places since 1982. As a senior citizen and unrepentant Baby Boomer, Professor Tom spends his time reading books and magazines and observes modern life in great third places such as libraries and coffeehouses, at public events, and during happy hour. He also plays fantasy sports year-round.

www.ingramcontent.com/pod-product-compliance
Lightning Source LLC
LaVergne TN
LVHW091533200926
848483LV00002B/382
* 9 7 8 1 4 9 8 5 9 5 9 7 1 *